Child Development in Social Context 1

Becoming a Person

Child Development in Social Context

Other volumes in the series:

If you would like to study this course, please write to The Central Enquiries Office, The Open University, Walton Hall, Milton Keynes MK7 6AA for a prospectus and application form. For more specific information write to The Higher Degrees Office at the same address.

Child Development in Social Context 1

Becoming a Person

A Reader edited by
Martin Woodhead, Ronnie Carr
and Paul Light
at The Open University

London and New York
In association with The Open University

First published 1991
by Routledge
11 New Fetter Lane, London EC4P 4EE

Simultaneously published in the USA and Canada
by Routledge
a division of Routledge, Chapman and Hall, Inc.
29 West 35th Street, New York, NY 10001

Typeset by Witwell Ltd, Southport
Printed and bound in Great Britain by Mackays of Chatham PLC, Kent

British Library Cataloguing in Publication Data
Woodhead, Martin
  Becoming a Person – (Child Development in Social Context,
  v. 1)
  1. Children. Development
  I. Title II. Carr, Ronnie III. Light. Paul IV. Series
  155.4

  ISBN 0–415–05828–7
  ISBN 0–415–05829–5 pbk

Library of Congress Cataloging in Publication Data
Child Development in Social Context.
  p. cm.
  Readings compiled for the Open University's MA in Education. course
  E820
  Includes bibliographical references and index
  Contents: v. 1. Becoming a Person/Edited by Martin Woodhead.
  Ronnie Carr, and Paul Light
  ISBN 0–415–05828–7 (Hb:v. 1): L35.00–ISBN 0–415–05829–5
  (Pb: v. 1): L8.99
  1. Child development I. Woodhead, Martin II. Light, Paul IV. Open University
  1940–   III. Light, Paul IV. Open University
  HQ767.9C4448 1990
305.23'1–dc20   90–8834
                                                        CIP

Contents

Figures

Tables

Preface

Child Development in Social Context is a module of the Open University's taught MA in Education. This is the first of three volumes of readings specially selected to serve as students' major source material. They should provide suitable reading for all psychology students, as well as teachers and others concerned with child development and education. These readings cover a range of topics from infancy through to the primary school years. They illustrate the increasing attention now being paid by developmental psychologists to social context and social relationships as fundamental in shaping the course of development, the processes of learning and thinking, and the construction of personal identity and educational achievement.

The emphasis on social context in developmental psychology is evident at various levels. In terms of methodology, there is growing dissatisfaction with artificial experimental procedures. Bronfenbrenner (1977) was prompted to remark, 'much of contemporary developmental psychology is the science of the strange behaviour of children in strange situations with strange adults for the briefest possible periods of time'. Whereas in the past developmental psychologists tended to model their work on the physical sciences, referring at conferences to 'research going on in my lab', many are now spending time squatting in the corners of sitting-rooms and classrooms making naturalistic observations of everyday life in families and schools. Of course there is still a place for controlled experiments, and modern research technologies have greatly amplified the power of the researcher's observations. This is especially true in the field of infancy, where frame-by-frame analysis of fleeting everyday encounters between young children and their parents has greatly enriched our understanding of interrelationships between the responsiveness of caregivers and the emerging competencies of children. This line of work is well illustrated by many of the articles in this first volume of the series, *Becoming a Person.*

Taking account of context is not only about adopting sensitive research methods. As Richards and Light put it, 'social context is . . . intrinsic to the developmental process itself'. It isn't just 'the icing on the cake, it is as much a part of its structure as the flour or eggs' (1986: 1). This is nowhere more clearly illustrated than in changing perspectives on cognitive development during the past decade. Piaget's theory has informed a popular image of the child as a solitary thinker struggling to construct a personal understanding of the mathematical and logical properties of the physical world. But this image is now giving way to a view of the child being initiated into shared cultural understandings through close relationships with parents and teachers, as well as siblings and peers. Viewing children's learning and thinking as embedded in social relationships owes much to the insights of Vygotsky. It is the major theme of the second volume of the series, *Learning to Think.*

The co-existence of these very different paradigms of child development is a reminder of psychology's ambivalent position as a science. While the psychologist may rightly keep one foot firmly in the exactitude of the laboratory, the other foot is entangled in more ephemeral cultural ideas about the nature and needs of children. Major psychological accounts of the child have not originated independently of social and educational practices, nor arguably should they. The problems arise when scientific statements become ethical imperatives, or when descriptive accounts become normative (Kessen 1979). This tendency is well illustrated by the role of psychological theory in reinforcing social attitudes to child care in and out of the family. This issue, along with studies of development in that more recent cultural invention, the school, is amongst the topics of the third volume in the series, *Growing up in a Changing Society.*

The underlying theme of all these volumes is that the study of the individual child, once taken to be the solid bedrock on which to build psychological knowledge, turns out to be a shifting sand. Children are physically distinct and separated off, but psychologically they are embedded in a particular society and culture. Clearly, in adopting this perspective, there are dangers of substituting for an untenable universalistic model of human development an extreme culturally relativistic model which, as Campbell has acknowledged, carries the risk of 'ontological nihilism' (cited in Edelstein 1983). In defence, there is no dispute that children inherit a distinctive human nature.

However, the expression of that nature depends on another distinctive inheritance, human society and culture.

In one sense the new emphasis on context in child development represents a long-overdue *rapprochement* between the individualism of psychology, the social structural concerns of sociology and the cultural descriptions of anthropology. The idea that individuals are shaped by the social order is of course the 'bread and butter' of introductory sociology courses. But just as psychology has remained myopic about the significance of social influences, so sociology has failed to look seriously beyond such favourite general concepts as 'socialization' and 'social reproduction', in search of a more thorough understanding of the process of interpenetration between the social and the individual. The problem has been characterized by Super and Harkness (1981) by analogy with the well-known perceptual conflict between figure and ground popularized by 'gestalt' psychologists. Hopefully the current shift towards a more context-sensitive psychology will restructure the gestalt sufficiently that we shall before long be able to hold figure and ground, individual and social context, simultaneously in perspective.

REFERENCES

Bronfenbrenner, U. (1977) 'Toward an experimental ecology of human development', *American Psychologist* 32: 513–31.

Edelstein, W. (1983) 'Cultural constraints on development and the vicissitudes of progress', in F. S. Kessel and A. W. Siegel (eds) *The Child and Other Cultural Inventions*, New York: Praeger.

Kessen, W. (1979) 'The American child and other cultural inventions', *American Psychologist* 34: 815–20.

Richards, M. and Light, P. (1986) *Children of Social Worlds*, Cambridge: Polity Press.

Super, C. M. and Harkness, S. (1981) 'Figure, ground and gestalt: the cultural context of the active individual', in R. M. Lerner and N. A. Busch-Nagel (eds) *Individuals as Producers of Their Own Development*, New York: Academic Press.

Part one
First relationships

Introduction

> The baby . . . is . . . 'adapted' to speak paradoxically, to being
> unadapted, 'adapted' to a complete dependence on an adult human
> being. He is made to be cared for . . . .
>
> (Macmurray 1961: 48)

Few would argue with the general point that children's welfare and
development depends on their relationships with others. The controversy starts once more detailed questions are asked. How many
relationships can the child sustain? Does deprivation inevitably
damage development? Deprivation of what kinds? The articles in this
section illustrate a range of perspectives on these issues. (For other
perspectives see Volume 3 of this series.)

Schaffer (Chapter 1) offers a succinct but comprehensive overview
of some of the main themes of recent research, including his own
detailed analyses of mother–infant interaction. The picture that
emerges is of a dynamic, changing pattern of developmental priorities,
driven by maturational processes in combination with the sensitive
responsiveness of the caregiver.

'Sensitive responsiveness' is the key concept underlying Ainsworth's
research into crying and obedience in infancy. Following John
Bowlby's theory of attachment, she argues (Chapter 2) that proximity-
seeking behaviours in infants and nurturant behaviours in adults are
part of our biological inheritance, species-specific characteristics
adapted to the environmental pressures in which humanity evolved.
The implication is that there are strict limits to the range of cultural
practices that is consistent with 'healthy' social development.

Cultural variation is the starting point for the chapter by Super and
Harkness (Chapter 3). They offer evidence of remarkable cross-
cultural consistency in the emergence of smiling around four months,
and separation–distress towards the end of the first year. Accepting

that this does point to a universal sub-stratum of human emotional development, they introduce the concept of 'niche' to characterize the way universal qualities are differentially patterned according to the structural arrangements for care and the beliefs and practices of caregivers. Super and Harkness's field work in a Kenyan society, where older siblings traditionally have major child-care responsibilities, draws attention to the insularity of much psychological theorizing, especially about the exclusivity of the mother–child relationship.

This theme is explored in the chapter by White and Woollett (Chapter 4). Research into the role of fathers has been something of a growth industry in recent decades, perhaps reflecting changing roles within the family and workplace. Much emphasis has been placed on fathers being present at the birth, but research is inconclusive about whether they are subsequently more involved in their babies' development. One thing is clear. There are significant differences in the way fathers relate to boy versus girl babies, highlighting the cultural processes through which gender identity is constructed (see Part four).

REFERENCE

Macmurray, J. (1961) *Persons in Relation*, London: Faber & Faber.

1 Early social development

Rudolph Schaffer

Source: Slater, A. and Bremner, G. (eds) (1989)
Infant Development, Hillsdale, N.J.: Earlbaum, pp. 189–210.

INTRODUCTION

Research on early social development has a short history, confined to just the last 30 years or so. Yet even in this brief period there have been marked changes in the way the subject has been thought about, in the methods adopted to investigate it, and especially in the questions being asked in order to further our knowledge. These changes involve a progressive widening of the focus of interest which one can best represent in terms of three stages, concerned respectively with the *individual*, the *dyad*, and the *polyad* as the unit of study.

Initially social behaviour was seen as a class of *individual* behaviour. Thus questions were asked about the first appearance of particular social patterns in children (the first smile, the onset of attachments, the beginnings of cooperative play, etc.), or about the incidence of certain forms of behaviour (e.g. the amount of fear of strangers under various conditions, the amount of aggressive behaviour in boys as opposed to girls, the amount of social play at different ages, etc.). In all these cases behaviour was thought of as describing the characteristics of individuals; their activity may have been observed in the presence of other people, but the behaviour of these others was not taken into account.

In the early 1970s this changed; the focus became increasingly fixed on the *dyad* as the unit of study. The to-and-fro between child and social partner was now of primary interest. Interactions, rather than individuals interacting, became the main topic of research. The questions asked concerned such problems as how interactions are established at different ages, how they are maintained and developed over time, and in what ways the roles played respectively by child and adult interlock (see Schaffer 1977 for some illustrative studies). We have learned a lot from this dyadic approach: for instance, about the abilities children of different ages bring to social interaction and how they use them, about the techniques adults adopt to support these abilities, and about the nature of interpersonal synchronisation and how that is accomplished.

However, very recently a new approach has emerged, which I shall refer to as the *polyadic* approach (a fuller treatment is provided in Schaffer 1984). It is based on the recognition that children live in a multi-person world; dyadic interactions occur but do so in the context of other interactions and relationships that the individual has with persons outside the dyad. What is more, how the child interacts with the group may well require different skills compared with those used in interacting with one other individual. Indeed it could be that a set of quite different concepts is needed to explain polyadic interaction compared with those in use for dyadic interactions.

We thus have three different levels at which social development has been studied. It should be emphasised that any one is not necessarily 'better' than any other; each is valid in its own right, each useful for answering certain questions distinctive from those found at the other levels. However, in so far as most of the recent work on early social development has been carried out with the dyad as the basic unit of study I shall confine myself primarily to the body of knowledge generated at that level.

SOME CONCEPTUAL GUIDELINES

Let us first consider the nature of psychological development in general. It has become increasingly apparent that such development is best conceived of in terms of sequential reorganisation rather than steady quantitative accretion. The child's mental life, that is, will periodically and relatively suddenly show transitions to new psychological levels that, in certain respects at least, are *qualitatively* different from preceding levels. As Piaget above all has shown, new sets of capacities emerge from time to time which drastically alter the child's mode of adaptation to the environment and which thus reveal major changes in psychological organisation. Whether these take the across-the-board form which Piaget described or whether they apply to much more specific functions as Fischer (1980) argued remains to be settled. In the early years in particular, however, it is apparent that major transition points can be located when such realignments are evident, and various attempts have recently been made to list these (e.g. by Emde *et al.* 1976; McCall *et al.* 1977; Fischer 1980). In each case, development is conceived of as a step-like course, where progression to qualitatively different modes of behaviour occurs from time to time, bringing about new modes of adaptation on the part of the child. Each break represents a period of instability when, conceivably, the child is particularly vulnerable; each new phase requires the consolidation of whatever achievements were ushered in at the point of transition.

The following has been put forward (Schaffer 1984) as a developmental scheme that is particularly useful in considering infants' social behaviour and the progressive changes that take place therein during the first 2 years:

1 *The immediate post-birth period.* At that time the most urgent developmental task for the parent–child couple is to regularise the infant's basic biological processes such as feeding and waking–sleeping states and to harmonise these with environmental requirements.

2 *From 2 months on.* At the age of 2 months a marked increase in attentiveness to the external world takes place, with particular reference to other people. As a result the regulation of responsiveness in face-to-face interactions then becomes a central theme for infant and care-taker.

3 *From 5 months on.* Largely as a result of newly emerging manipulative abilities a shift of attention from people to objects is found at this transition point. Increasingly, encounters with social partners occur around objects. How to incorporate objects in such encounters and thus ensure topic sharing becomes the new developmental task confronting infant and partner.

4 *From 8 months on.* A number of profound changes take place at this age, in particular the emergence of the ability to interrelate diverse environmental features and to produce coordinated activity to more than one aspect at a time. As a result the infant's behaviour becomes much more flexible; reciprocity and intentionality come to characterise social exchanges, and the relationship with the care-taker thus becomes a more symmetrical one.

5 *From the middle of the second year.* At this point the capacity for symbolic representation gradually emerges. Social interactions increasingly incorporate verbal aspects and growing self-awareness leads the infant to reflect more on its and on other people's behaviour and to guide its actions accordingly.

Social development in infancy may thus be thought of as constituting a sequence of changes, heralded by various perceptual, motor, and cognitive events taking place in species-typical fashion. But whatever powerful inherent push may be responsible in the first place for the emergence of new capabilities and new levels of functioning, a propensity cannot become reality unless the infant's caretaker supports, maintains, completes, and furthers the child's efforts. All psychological functions develop in a social context; the younger the child the more important it is to regard it as part of a unit which inevitably includes the care-taker as a vital complement to the child's state of immaturity. The intimate dependence of human development on the rearing environment must be acknowledged; each stage brings with it particular developmental tasks that can only be tackled by child and care-taker jointly. Thus changes in the child's psychological organisation have implications not just for the child alone but also for its relationship with others and for the role that these others need to adopt. After every transition point the parent must be prepared to help the child deal with new tasks and offer new forms of support; only if this is done successfully can the child progress to the next level. Appropriate input from social partners must therefore be added to the list of perceptual, motor and cognitive factors that enable children to pass through the various developmental phases.

Thus, two conceptual guidelines should be borne in mind when examining the course of early social behaviour:

1 Development occurs through a series of sequential reorganisations.
2 Development is a joint enterprise involving the efforts of both child and adult care-taker.

Our account of some of the themes which arise from an examination of social behaviour in infancy will be based on these two general guidelines.

SOCIAL PRE-ADAPTATION

The new-born is not a formless blob of clay, devoid of all psychological organisation. On the contrary, it comes into the world with certain predispositions – certain tendencies, that is, selectively to attend to particular kinds of stimuli and to structure its responses in particular ways. What is especially striking is the way in which both perceptual and response tendencies are pre-adapted to mediate the infant's interaction with the social environment.

Perceptual organisation

It has become apparent that from the early days of life on, infants have surprisingly good perceptual capacities. But it has also become apparent that these capacities are selective in nature, and that the types of stimuli to which they are particularly attuned are those generally associated with other people, such as their faces and voices.

The topic of face perception has attracted a great deal of attention (see Sherrod 1981 for a detailed review). Most studies on this subject use one of two methodologies: the *visual preference technique*, whereby the amount of attention paid by an infant to each of a pair of stimuli is ascertained, and the *operant sucking technique*, which examines the amount of effort exerted by an infant to produce a particular stimulus (such as the picture of a human face) by sucking for it. It is now generally agreed that initially it is not 'faceness' as such that attracts infants' attention but rather a set of more primitive qualities that are inherent in human faces such as contour density, complexity, three-dimensionality, and mobility. Each of these characteristics alone is attention-worthy; when combined (as they are in 'real' faces) they ensure that the social partner is a highly salient source of stimulation. This is particularly so as the optimal visual fixation point is initially confined to a distance of about 8 inches – a distance at which mothers quite naturally place their faces when interacting with a young infant. On the basis of this initial attraction infants can then in due course begin to pay attention to other features of the social partner, in particular those distinguishing one person from another, and thus become capable of differentiating familiar and unfamiliar people.

A *matching* process is thus evident between, on the one hand, the visual capacities of infants that are available to them from birth and, on the other hand, the stimulus qualities of those aspects of the environment that are biologically of greatest importance to them, i.e. other people. The same applies to auditory responsiveness: here too there is evidence (Hutt *et al.* 1968; Molfese and Molfese 1980) that human speech-like noises have a particular potency for young infants not possessed by other auditory stimuli. Thus the structure of the auditory apparatus at birth is such as to ensure that the voice of other people is a particularly attention-worthy stimulus. Taken in conjunction with demonstrations that infants appear to have a pre-adapted capacity to make meaningful phonemic distinctions within speech long before they themselves begin to speak (Eimas 1975), it appears that on the auditory as on the visual side infants arrive in the world especially attuned to the kind of stimulation provided by other people.

Response organisation

As well as such perceptual sensitivities infants demonstrate a number of behaviour patterns specifically designed to bring them into contact with people. Of these, smiling, crying, rooting and sucking are the best known and most closely studied. Their survival value during the initial period of helplessness is evident; each is linked to a set of highly specific stimulus conditions and operates at first along somewhat stereotyped lines before assuming more complex, flexible and intentional form towards the end of the first year (Bowlby 1969).

One particular attribute of early response organisation to which we must draw attention is its temporal structure, for in this respect too there are implications for social interaction. They may best be illustrated by reference to the feeding situation – one of the earliest contexts in which an infant encounters another person. The infant's sucking response has been shown (e.g. by Wolff 1968) to be a high-frequency micro-rhythm that is organised as a burst–pause pattern – i.e. bursts of sucks are followed by pauses, the length of each component varying somewhat according to a number of conditions. As Kaye (1977) has shown, this temporal patterning is highly suited for incorporating feeding into a more general social interaction sequence, for mothers tend to interact with their infants in precise synchrony with the burst–pause pattern. Thus during bursts they are generally quiet and inactive; during pauses, on the other hand, they jiggle, stroke and talk to the baby. The mother, that is, fits in with the baby's natural sucking rhythm, responds to its signals such as ceasing to suck, accepts the opportunity to intervene offered by pauses, and in this way sets up a turn-taking pattern which, as we shall see, is typical of many other forms of early interaction. The infant's behaviour is thus structured in such a way as to facilitate coordination with the partner's behaviour; the to-and-fro which characterises most dyadic exchanges among human beings is therefore evident from the beginning, and in this respect too we may consequently conclude that social pre-adaptation determines the nature of the infant's initial encounters with other people.

THE CHANGING NATURE OF SOCIAL INTERACTION

A suitable way of viewing infants' development of social competence is to adopt a *modular model*, similar to that proposed for the acquisition of sensory–motor skills (e.g. by Bruner 1973). According to this model individual units of action (so-called subroutines) are learned first, each being practised to the point where it can occur with minimal conscious attention, leaving the child free to attend to those action units not yet mastered. The various components can then be combined into organised wholes, thus forming new, more complex, higher-order patterns which are constituted by the totality of the individual modules but in which the separate existence of the modules is no longer acknowledged. The acquisition of social interactive skills in infancy goes through such a process. Initially (during the period 2–5 months approximately) infants are absorbed in the task of learning about their care-takers: Direct face-to-face encounters are the principal contexts for social interaction and enable infants to become acquainted with the physical characteristics of the adults and perfect the art of fitting their own behavioural flow to theirs. Around the age of 5 months, coinciding with the onset of manipulative competence, infants turn abruptly away from a preoccupation with faces to a similarly intense preoccupation with the world of things: attention is now taken up by the newly acquired ability to act upon objects and during the next few months priority is given to becoming competent in this sphere. Eventually, some time around the age of 8 months, there are indications that infants become capable of putting together these separate accomplishments: instead of attending to only one thing at a time (person *or* object) the infant can now integrate these diverse features and interact with other people via objects and other such external topics. Let us consider the various phases of this developmental timetable.

Face-to-face interaction

The most urgent requirement during the first few weeks is to regulate the infant's basic biological processes of feeding, sleeping and arousal, i.e. to stabilise these and to establish a timetable that not only conforms with the infant's requirements but also with those of its care-takers. Mutual adjustment thus takes place round the infant's endogenous functions. From about 2 months, however, infants turn increasingly to their outer environment – in large part, no doubt, due to a sharp increase in visual efficiency (Bronson 1974). As a result their behaviour towards other people changes: direct eye contact is made with the partner, periods of prolonged gaze ensue, and the first externally elicited smiles appear. Social interactions thus occur primarily in the context of face-to-face encounters, and the main developmental theme for adult and child becomes the regulation of mutual attention and responsiveness.

Such regulation takes various forms. Take the way in which mother and infant establish mutual gazing. Among adult dyads such gazing is mostly symmetrical in nature: the on–off looking patterns of the two individuals tend to have the same characteristics and the initiation and termination of mutual gaze episodes are determined by both to a similar extent. Not so in mother–infant pairs, where asymmetry of looking patterns is much more typical. The mother, that is, looks at the infant for extremely long periods, constantly ready to respond to any sign of attention on the infant's part and to adjust her behaviour to the child's. She thus provides a 'frame' (as Fogel 1977 has described it) within which the infant's gazing may cycle to and fro. These gazes are much briefer than the mother's; they are originally constrained by biologically determined limits which regulate the alternation of gazing-at and gazing-away periods (Stern 1974) and show none of the flexibility and intentionality that characterise looking patterns in older individuals. Responsibility for initiation and termination is thus also unequally distributed: it is far more likely that the mother will be the first to look and the infant the first to look away. The mother, that is, appears to be almost constantly ready for interaction, but it is up to the infant as to whether that interaction in fact takes place. It may well be that prolonged gazing at the mother would be too arousing an experience in the early months, and looking away by the infant therefore serves to modulate the level of its arousal. Certainly mothers can be observed continually to adjust the timing, nature and intensity of the stimulation they provide during such episodes, using the infant's gaze at their face as a cue to begin stimulation and the gaze away as a cue to cease stimulation, thereby helping the infant to maintain optimal arousal.

A similar picture of early interaction is provided when we turn to another feature of social encounters, namely vocal interchange. In adult conversations mutual adjustment is essential: if both members of a dyad were to talk simultaneously the communication of information would be virtually impossible. A turn-taking pattern is therefore required, involving the sequential integration of the two participants' individual contributions as well as knowledge of the rules whereby speaker and listener exchange roles. Such knowledge can hardly be attributed to young infants, yet vocal interactions with mothers are already marked by a turn-taking pattern. Just how prevalent that pattern is (as opposed to 'coaction', i.e. a pattern marked by simultaneous vocalisation) has been subject to some debate (see Schaffer 1984 for a more detailed review); suffice it to say that precise turn-taking can occur already during the early months and certainly long before the onset of formal speech. Let us stress, however, that turn-taking is a dyadic phenomenon and that it tells us nothing about the 'abilities' of infants to take turns. It seems in fact more likely that it is brought about by the mother's action in skilfully inserting her contributions in the pauses between bursts of vocalisations produced by the infant. As we have already seen, mothers are highly attentive to their infants in face-to-face encounters and can therefore time their vocal interventions in such a way as not to interrupt the baby. The mother, that is, allows herself to be paced by the infant and thereby takes the responsibility for converting the encounter into a dialogue that, in certain formal respects, has all the hallmarks of a conversation. The difference when compared with adult dialogues is, however, that only one of the partners knows the rules; from that point of view the exchange is more accurately labelled a 'pseudo-dialogue'. Nevertheless we can speculate that by involving infants in such mature interaction formats from an early age on mothers facilitate children's acquisition of the necessary skills to participate eventually in social exchanges as 'full' partners.

Mutual gazing and vocal interchange are two examples of early face-to-face interactions. They point to some common features, but above all to the fact that there is already a 'smoothness' in the dyadic encounters of infant with adult that suggest a mutually satisfying meshing of the two sets of individual contributions.

Topic sharing

With the onset of manipulative abilities around the age of 5 months infants turn increasingly to the world of things. Not that they are any less responsive to people when directly confronted by another person; it is rather that they have now discovered a new sphere of interest, i.e. objects on which they can directly act and produce effects upon. Attentional capacity is as yet limited; being unable to incorporate two different environmental features into their activity infants will attend to an object *or* a person but not to both. The exclusive fascination with faces typifying the earlier months is replaced by the new function pleasure derived from the mastery of toys and other objects to handle. No wonder that Kaye and Fogel (1980), in a longitudinal study of face-to-face interactions, found a drop in visual attention to the mother from 70 per cent of total session time at 6 weeks of age to 33 per cent at 26 weeks; the mothers, moreover, reported that they no longer felt the direct face-to-face situation to be appropriate at the older age and that instead their task was now to share with the child reactions to external events.

Every social interaction has a topic to which the participants address themselves, but whereas during the face-to-face encounters in the early months the topic arose from within the dyad itself it now refers to some external focus that comes to be incorporated in the interaction. At this stage, however, given the infant's attentional limitations, it is entirely due to the adult's initiative that such incorporation takes place. The mother, that is, uses a variety of procedures to share with the infant the objects that interest it and so converts an *infant–object* situation into an *infant–object–mother* situation.

Take the phenomenon of 'visual coorientation' – a term used to indicate the joint attention of two or more people to some common focus in the environment. In a study of mothers and infants who were confronted by a display of toys along the wall of a playroom (Collis and Schaffer 1975), several things became apparent from an analysis of videorecordings obtained of their behaviour. In the first place, there was a strong tendency for both mother and infant to be attending to the same toy at the same time – the phenomenon of visual coorientation. In the second place, when examining how this was brought about it emerged that almost invariably it was the infant that took the lead by spontaneously looking from one toy to another while the mother, closely monitoring the baby's gaze direction, immediately followed and looked at the same toy. Mutual reference to an external topic was thus brought about, thanks to the powerful effect which the infant's direction of gaze appeared to exert on the mother. And in the third place, such topic sharing was rarely an end in its own right; more often, having established joint attention, the mother used that topic in order to further the course of the interaction with the infant, e.g. she would elaborate on it by pointing to the toy, labelling it, commenting on it, and taking other steps to incorporate it in the exchange with the infant.

There are indications that infants do not become capable of following another person's gaze until 8 months or so (Collis 1977). Even then they can do so only under certain situational conditions, such as the need for the target to be located within the periphery of the infant's visual field (Butterworth and Cochrane 1980). It does appear, however, that by the end of the first year another person's gaze direction has become a meaningful signal to the infant, and that the onus for topic sharing therefore no longer rests exclusively with the mother.

Somewhat similar conclusions arise from studies of another means of achieving topic sharing, namely by gestures such as pointing. As

Murphy and Messer (1977) have shown, infants aged less than 9 months are mostly unable to follow the direction of a pointing finger: they look at the finger itself rather than at the object indicated. Thereafter they follow correctly, but only under 'easy' conditions as defined by the spatial relationships of infant, finger and target (in particular, when the latter two are in the same sector of the visual field). Infants' own use of pointing does not emerge until the very end of the first year; when it does, however, it appears first in the form of 'pointing-for-self', i.e. the infant points to the object but without checking whether the other person is following the gesture. This, according to Werner and Kaplan (1963), shows pointing initially to be an attentional mechanism which merely indicates that the infant is now able to distinguish self from object. 'Pointing-for-others', as a communicative phenomenon indicative of the infant's desire to share the object with another person, emerges later.

The third principal means of topic sharing, one which comes to assume great importance in the post-infancy period, is referential speech. People share topics, that is, by verbally referring to them and thus one of the child's tasks is to acquire labels which can be used in communicative situations. Yet curiously, long before children become verbally competent, adults use speech when interacting with them – indeed from the neonatal period on (Rheingold and Adams 1980) language appears to be a natural means of relating to an infant, despite the fact that the infant may still be many months away from comprehending what is said. But the nature and timing of the speech used is far from arbitrary – on the contrary, it is carefully geared to infants' attentional capacities (being high-pitched in delivery, repetitive, chunked in brief phrases, and plentifully accompanied by facial distortions and hand gestures, Snow 1977). It is also precisely synchronised with the infant's ongoing behaviour at the time, as illustrated in a study by Messer (1978) based on observations of mother-infant couples during a joint play session. The great majority of the mothers' verbal references to particular toys turned out to co-occur with either the infant's or the mother's manipulation of that toy. The mothers, that is, showed the watchfulness so typical of many of their interactions with young children and thus were able closely to synchronise their speech with ongoing manipulative activities. Labels were therefore supplied to the infant at a point where its attention was focused on the relevant object; language, that is, was closely tied to the non-verbal context as defined by the child's own behaviour.

Person–object integration

At about 8 months a new developmental achievement becomes apparent in infants' behaviour. It is marked by the onset of relational abilities, i.e. infants now become capable of interrelating diverse events and combining them into one coordinated activity. Whereas previously an infant would play with the mother *or* with a ball it is now able to play ball *with* the mother; similarly it can request an object from another person or point out an interesting toy to someone else. In short, the infant now starts to coordinate multiple activities that could previously be performed only separately and thus to combine person-directed actions with object-directed actions.

It has been suggested that the coordination achieved at that time is *specific* to integrating objects with people and that there is an earlier stage where acts can be combined within the two realms of objects and people respectively but not across them (Sugarman-Bell 1978). This is not so (see Schaffer 1984 and 1986 for further details); there is considerable evidence that the growth of coordination applies to *any* set of actions directed at multiple stimuli and that it can just as well be observed *within* the social and *within* the object sphere. Take the 'social referencing' phenomenon (Feinman 1982): up to the third quarter of the first year infants tend to relate to one individual at a time, e.g. to the mother *or* to a stranger; from then on, however, infants can regulate their reaction to a stranger by affective signals from the mother, thus relating the characteristics of one person to those of another. Or take studies of play (Fenson *et al.* 1976): up to 8 months or so infants typically play with one object at a time; thus, if offered a toy while holding another they are likely to drop the latter before taking the former. Simple relational actions like banging one object with another or manipulating two objects simultaneously emerge only subsequently.

One implication of the new-found ability is that social interactions become more reciprocal and less one-sided. This is particularly well illustrated by some of the games which are such a marked feature of the daily lives of infants and parents. Take Bruner's (1977) description of the development of give-and-take games. Up to 8 months the infant's participation is limited to 'take': the mother offers the toy, the infant takes it, and the sequence ends with the child dropping the toy. After that age the game ceases to be so one-sided: infant begins to initiate the sequence by showing or offering the toy to the mother; it may also now hand it to her at her request. The exchanges are still hesitant, with the infant constantly checking between object and mother as though not sure of the procedure; by the end of the first year, however, the game has definitely become established as a set of routines, the infant having learned the basic rule, i.e. that the roles of giver and taker are reciprocal and also exchangeable.

Of all the developmental transitions to be found in the early years of life that taking place around 8 months of age is probably the most far reaching (Schaffer 1986). The consequences for behaviour are considerable and the list of new achievements a lengthy one (Trevarthen and Hubley 1978), but they add up to the fact that behaviour becomes vastly more flexible, more coordinated and more integrative, that the infant is less reactive and more proactive, and that it can now begin to monitor its own activity and adjust its reactions according to the perceived effects on the environment. The consequences for social behaviour are considerable: instead of being tied to separate, here-and-now events involving other people the infant becomes increasingly capable of welding together interactive sequences out of series of individual responses; more and more these sequences assume an intentional character in that infants begin to anticipate future goals and to plan their behaviour accordingly; and other people come to be represented as individuals in their own right, with a permanent existence independent of the infant's own existence.

ATTACHMENT

Many of the issues outlined above have been investigated under the rubric of attachment development. The ability to form focused, permanent and emotionally meaningful relationships with specific others is one of the most important acquisitions of the infancy period; how this is achieved, the timing of the various steps involved, the choice of attachment objects, the influence of such extraneous factors on the relationship as maternal employment and day-care and the implications of that first bond with another person for relationships formed in future years – these have been the main issues to which research has addressed itself ever since the topic first surfaced in the 1950s. The relevant literature is thus considerable; here we can only touch briefly on some of the main conclusions.

There is general agreement regarding the developmental course of attachment formation. Once again the third quarter of the first year is pinpointed as the crucial period for drastic change; it is then that the first indications are given that the infant has focused its attachment behaviour on specific individuals. Up to that point infants are by and large indiscriminate; care-takers are interchangeable and are not missed in their absence. This does not mean that familiar people cannot be recognized and distinguished from strangers; this accomplishment is achieved quite early, certainly by 3 months of age (Schaffer 1971). However, such perceptual distinction is only a necessary but not a sufficient condition for the development of permanent attachment bonds; the infant, that is, may recognise a person as unfamiliar and yet accept care from her as readily as from the mother. It is only from 7 or 8 months on that there is, as it were, a parting of the ways: on the one hand the infant now seeks the proximity of just certain individuals and becomes distressed by being separated from them (Schaffer and Emerson 1964), and on the other hand proximity avoidance is shown to other, unfamiliar people and fear of strangers first emerges (Schaffer 1966). Thus the developmental course of attachment formation takes place over a quite prolonged period, though the actual onset of discriminative relationships (as given by such indices as separation upset and stranger fear) is usually quite rapid, occurring suddenly in a step-wise fashion.

Bowlby's theory

The most comprehensive theoretical account of attachment formation has been provided by John Bowlby (1969). It is heavily influenced both by psychoanalysis and by ethology and has become the most widely used conceptual framework within which research on attachments has been conducted in recent years.

According to Bowlby, attachment is based on a number of species-specific action patterns (such as sucking, crying and smiling) that have emerged in the course of evolution because they afforded survival advantage in the 'environment of evolutionary adaptedness'. Each of these initially functions like a fixed action pattern, i.e. it is activated by certain quite specific stimulus conditions and then runs its course in a more or less mechanical fashion until terminated by further specific stimulus conditions. The function of these patterns is to promote proximity to and interaction with the care-taker; the fact that they share this function entitles one to classify them together as 'attachment responses' and to regard them as constituting a behavioural system.

In the course of development several changes occur in this system. Two are particularly notable. The first refers to the progressive narrowing down that occurs in the range of eliciting and terminating stimuli. For instance, smiling is initially elicited by nothing more than two dots – a primitive sign-stimulus that triggers the smile in the same way that the red dot on the herring gull's beak triggers the pecking response of the young bird. In time the dots must become more and more eye-like in shape to have that effect; subsequently they must be accompanied by more and more facial features until the face as a whole is required as the sufficient stimulus, and finally it is no longer *any* face that has that effect but only that of certain familiar individuals (Sherrod 1981). This means that the fixed action patterns are no longer independent of each other but have now become integrated by being focused on one individual, usually the mother. The second noteworthy development is that the attachment system becomes an organised whole which increasingly functions in a 'goal-corrected' manner. Thus the young baby does not vary its cry according to whether the mother is far or near or whether she is coming or going; the older infant, on the other hand, is capable of continually adjusting its behaviour in the light of prevailing circumstances, taking note of the discrepancy between stimulus conditions and thus making use of feedback information to control its own behaviour. Its actions thus become flexible and purposive, organised in accordance with 'plans'.

The attachment system is, of course, not the only behavioural system in the infant; it is antithetically related to such other systems as exploration and stimulus seeking, and a child's behaviour at any one time is the outcome of the interplay of these various systems. In so far as the set-goal of attachment is the maintenance of proximity it will be activated by any conditions that interfere with the goal: separation, insecurity, fear, and so forth. The knowledge that the attachment figure is available provides the child with security: she constitutes a safe haven and a base from which the child can explore. Any conditions that activate attachment behaviour will result in cessation of exploration; the appearance of a stranger, for instance, may well stop the child in its tracks and cause it to scuttle back to the mother for reassurance and security.

There are certain features of Bowlby's account that have attracted criticism. One example is his concept of 'monotropism', i.e. the notion that infants are initially unable to form attachments with more than one person, and that all other attachments are only formed subsequently and will be of minor significance compared with the basic one. This has not been borne out (Schaffer and Emerson 1964): infants are capable of forming multiple (yet still discriminative) relationships and individuals such as fathers, siblings and day-care personnel may thus also assume importance in the child's emotional life. And another point which has not found universal acceptance is Bowlby's suggestion that the biological function of attachment is protection against predators, i.e. that such behaviour evolved in order to ensure that helpless infants remain with protective care-takers and are not prey to hostile attacks from others. This is, of course, speculative and quite impossible to verify; it does seem worthwhile, however, to point out that attachment serves so many useful functions that to single this one out as the biological basis seems somewhat far-fetched. Nevertheless, the theory as a whole is a most imaginative one; it is a great advance on previous accounts derived from psychoanalysis and learning theory (Gewirtz 1972), and in particular so because it does justice to the planned, purposive, and intentional nature of behaviour which emerges later in infancy. Thus the infant is seen not just as an organism driven by inner needs or outer stimuli in some blind and mechanical fashion; it is described instead as quickly evolving its own intentions and plans and so becoming capable of steering its own course.

The 'strange situation'

In order to highlight individual differences in infants' attachment (Ainsworth evolved a procedure (known as the 'strange situation') that, when applied around the end of the first year, is said reliably to elicit behaviour indicative of such differences (Ainsworth *et al.* 1978). It consists of a series of standardised episodes that take place in an unfamiliar laboratory playroom and that include being confronted by a strange adult, being left by the mother with the stranger, and being left entirely alone. According to Ainsworth three main groups of children can be distinguished on the basis of their behaviour in the 'strange situation', with particular emphasis laid on their response to the mother on reunion following two brief separation episodes:

1 *Group A infants* are conspicuous by their avoidance of the mother after reunion; they are judged to be insecurely attached.
2 *Group B infants* actively seek contact with the mother after the separation episode and show little or no avoidant behaviour; they are thus said to be securely attached.
3 *Group C infants* are ambivalent, in that they seek contact with the mother on reunion but mingle this with resistant behaviour towards her; they too are regarded as insecurely attached.

According to most studies of American children, approximately one-quarter to one-third fall into groups A and C, these being the groups that are generally evaluated negatively from the point of view of social adjustment and mental health. The classification is said to be stable over time: A child allocated to Group A at age 12 months is likely still to be assessed as a Group A child at age 18 months, though the avoidant behaviour which was the main criterion for such a judgement may well take quite different forms at the two ages due to motor and other developmental changes (Waters 1978). However, such consistency is only found when the environment remains stable: Vaughn *et al.* (1979) tested 100 economically disadvantaged infants at both 12 and 18 months and found that changes in classification were related to changes in family circumstances. One further claim relates to the predictive power of the tripartite classification with respect to other spheres of behaviour: thus securely attached infants are said to develop greater competence in play, less fear of strangers, and more positive and confident peer relationships than insecure infants (Ainsworth *et al.* 1978).

Most of the attachment research conducted in recent years has been carried out within the 'strange situation' paradigm, examining individual differences rather than the nomothetic trends outlined by Bowlby. The great advantage of this paradigm has been to highlight the fact that these differences need to be expressed in terms of *patterns* rather than by means of single responses; the latter generally change in the course of development but the former are organisational properties which are more likely to endure. However, the technique does bring with it considerable methodological problems (Lamb *et al.* 1984), and of these special mention must be made of the highly artificial nature of the assessment situation, the failure to take into account the effects of the mothers' behaviour in the 'strange situation', and the extraordinarily narrow data base (i.e. the two reunion episodes, each lasting no more than a few seconds) on which assessment depends. Additional techniques for evaluating infants' social competence are clearly required.

Cognitive processes

The interrelationship of social and cognitive development is a complex one – far more so than past accounts have led us to believe. These have generally considered cognitive changes as 'causing' changes in social behaviour: a unidirectional conception that does little justice to the difficulties involved in disentangling the two sets of processes. Take the onset of focused attachments, which has been explained as emerging because around the same age (of 8 months) infants first become capable of object permanence (Schaffer and Emerson 1964). Just as a child can now search for a missing object and thereby show that it no longer functions on the basis of 'out of sight, out of mind', so now the appearance of separation upset indicates that it is capable of remaining oriented towards a missing mother and that permanent social bonds can now be formed. The assumption is that a basic cognitive restructuring occurs which then has implications, *inter alia*, for social behaviour. Such a conception is to a large extent due to Piaget's almost wholly a-social account of early development – an account which disregards the social context in which children are reared and which thus tends to explain developmental change entirely in terms of processes *within* the child. In so far as phenomena such as separation upset and fear of strangers make their first appearance at virtually the same age across a wide range of cultures and child-rearing practices (Konner 1982) there may well be a temptation to consider this as evidence (as Kagan 1984 has put it) 'that these talents follow orderly changes in the central nervous system', i.e. that the transition is solely dependent on a biologically determined timetable. There are indications, however (further explained in Schaffer 1986), that the social context does matter and that the child's experience with other people may have a crucial influence, jointly with inherent forces, on developmental transitions. Piaget's description of object permanence concentrated entirely on the infant–object relationship, yet let us consider as one example the hiding games that mothers play with young infants – how they teasingly cover the toy again and again for a second or two at a time, how they make it disappear very slowly to ensure the child's attention is properly focused on the hiding place, or how they leave it half exposed to tempt it to recover it. Similarly with peek-a-boo games that mothers play with their infants (Bruner and Sherwood 1976), in which hiding is again carried out in a manner carefully adapted to the child's present capacities yet at the same time challenging it to further achievements. Thus in the period preceding object permanence the child is involved in a series of many exper- iences, set up and flexibly managed by other people, that would appear to be highly relevant to the acquisition process. Taken in conjunction with the fact that under conditions of severe social deprivation, separation upset and fear of strangers fail to emerge (Schaffer 1986), it is apparent that interpersonal experiences are intimately involved in bringing about psychological reorganisation which will then in turn have implications for both cognitive and social functioning.

The later course of attachments draws attention to one very important cognitive development, namely the role of central represen- tations. As Bowlby (1969) pointed out, children come to construct internal working models of their attachment figures; these evolve out of experienced relationships but are no passive reflections of such events in that the child actively construes its experience and acts on the basis of the meaning attached to that experience. Most past research on attachments has concerned itself with infants' overt behaviour, and the adoption of techniques such as the 'strange situation' was therefore appropriate. As attachment work comes to be carried forward beyond the infancy period, and in particular from the middle of the second year on when representative abilities emerge in more marked form, it becomes increasingly important to find new methods that do justice to the child's cognitively more sophisticated status and that can adequately describe the nature of the increasingly complex working models formed of other people (see Bretherton and Waters 1985 for some examples). How children come to construe attachment figures, how these representations relate to representations of the self, and how they influence overt behaviour are problems to which research must turn if the development of social behaviour from late infancy onward is to be understood.

THE RESPECTIVE ROLES OF INFANT AND PARENT

It is characteristic of human development that the child's functioning needs to be supplemented by the parent. This is particularly evident early on in life; the precise form which this supplement takes, however, varies from one stage to another. Parent and child may be regarded as a mutually accommodative interactive system, but how that accommodation is achieved at any one stage varies according to the particular circumstances prevailing at that time, with special reference to the child's current competencies. Thus each of the transition points found during early development heralds a new *interactive issue*, i.e. the task confronting parent and child to which they must jointly address themselves changes with the mastery of previous developmental challenges and the advent of new ones. At each phase the parent is required to play a complementary role that in certain respects is different from that played at earlier phases.

Interaction with peers

The respective roles of parent and infant are highlighted by comparing parent–child with peer–child interactions. In the latter we can observe participants of equal psychological status; unlike the former, the two partners are not likely to fill in for each other and the ways in which care-takers make up for their children's deficiencies and foster their development thus become apparent.

According to Sylva *et al.* (1980) the creativity of pre-school children's play tends to be lowest when the child is on its own, rather greater when with other children and greatest when in the company of an interested adult. The effectiveness of adult intervention can already be observed in the play of babies as young as 6 months, according to a report by Bakeman and Adamson (1984): when babies played together with their mothers they were capable of operating at a higher cognitive level in certain respects than when another baby of the same age was present. It seems that joint involvement episodes of adult and child provide a setting in which one can obtain optimal performance from a child and where one can assume that learning and the acquisition of skills are fostered to an extent that does not happen when the child is either alone or in the company of a child of similar developmental status.

Precisely what it is that the adult contributes needs to be specified. Vygotsky (1978) long ago drew attention to the fact that development occurs in social contexts and that it proceeds from an interpersonal to an intrapersonal level; his concept of the 'zone of proximal development' stresses that children's performance varies according to the type of support given by a sympathetic adult. Similarly Bruner (1982) used the notion of 'scaffolding' in order to emphasise the supportive role which the adult plays in compensating for the child's deficiencies, and Kaye's (1982) concept of 'apprenticeship' also stresses the need for the young child to acquire skills and knowledge with the help of a sensitive adult. Let us note, however, that terms such as zone of proximal development, scaffolding, and apprenticeship by themselves have no explanatory value. They serve to draw our attention to the fact that much of early learning is essentially of a social nature; we need to go one step further, however, and specify precisely what it is that an adult provides which enables the young child to perform competently. As yet our knowledge in this respect is very limited.

Parental sensitivity

What is apparent is that if the adult is to have any effect on the child it is essential that she must be closely attuned to that child – she must, that is, be highly sensitive to the child's interests, abilities and skills as they unfold themselves from one moment to the next in the course of the interaction and thus be able constantly to use feedback information from the child in order to judge what kinds of support are appropriate at any given point.

Sensitive responsiveness has recently emerged as a dimension of particular interest to those attempting to understand parental behaviour and the implications of that behaviour for children's psychological functioning (see Schaffer and Collis 1986). Essentially, the term refers to adults' awareness of children as individuals in their own right. It is a continuum: at one end are the optimally sensitive adults who are able to see things from the child's point of view, are alert to the child's signals and communications, can interpret these correctly, and then respond promptly and appropriately. At the other end are the adults who cannot see the child at all as a separate individual, who distort the child's communications in the light of their own needs, and who interact with the child on the basis of their own wishes rather than the child's. Whether these characteristics refer to a unitary dimension or whether the term is merely an umbrella for a lot of different aspects has not yet been established; it is possible, for instance, that there are at least three distinct components, namely responding promptly, responding consistently and responding appropriately.

However this may be, variations in this set of parental qualities are believed to be associated with variations in children's psychological functioning. Two aspects in particular have been mentioned: the infant's attachment security and its developmental progress. As to the first, it has been suggested (Ainsworth *et al.* 1978) that the security of an infant's attachment to the mother depends on the sensitivity with which the mother has treated the child in the past. When a mother answers the child promptly and predictably the child will build up a set of expectations about her from which it derives security; by learning that it can affect the environment by its behaviour the child will in due course develop a sense of personal effectiveness and confidence. This does not occur with an insensitive mother who conveys that she is not interested in the child's needs and an anxious, insecure personality will thus be fostered.

The second effect, that concerned with the child's developmental progress, has been investigated mainly in relation to language acquisition. It is now well established that it is not so much the quantity of talk directed to children that fosters the beginnings of language development but rather the meaningfulness of that talk. Thus what the adult says should be related to the child's interests, attentional focus and actions at that moment. The mother therefore needs to be attuned to the child and tie in her own comments with the child's concerns as well as with its abilities to process what she says. There are indications

(Nelson 1973; Moerk 1975; Cross 1978) that under such circumstances language development proceeds more quickly than when the adult imposes her own ideas on the child and talks about these; similarly when she takes little note of the child's current processing skills she is likely to provide an input that is too meaningless for the child to profit from it.

It must be emphasised that there are no grounds as yet for making cause-and-effect statements involving parental practices and child outcomes. We cannot be certain that the parents' speech is directly responsible for the nature of the child's language progress, any more than we know for sure that a mother's sensitive treatment is a determinant of the child's security. It is at least plausible that the cause-and-effect sequence goes in the opposite direction, from child to adult; it is even more plausible that parent and child exert a *mutual* set of influences on each other that in practice is far from easy to unravel. In general, our knowledge of early social development is soundest on the descriptive side, i.e. *how* infants and their care-takers behave toward each other at different ages and stages. When it comes to stipulating the *mechanisms* of that development, and in particular the part played by adults in bringing about change in the child, we are still extraordinarily ignorant. Much of what happens during the first 2 years or so can be considered in terms of a gradual progression from being largely *other-controlled* to becoming increasingly *self-controlled*; how this is brought about is one of the major challenges for future research.

REFERENCES

Ainsworth, M. D. S., Blehar, M. C., Waters, E. and Wall, S. (1978) *Patterns of Attachment*, Hillsdale, N.J.: Erlbaum.

Bakeman, R. and Adamson, L. R. (1984) 'Coordinating attention to people and objects in mother–infant and peer–infant interaction', *Child Development* 22: 1278–89.

Bowlby, J. (1969) *Attachment and Loss*: vol. 1 *Attachment*, London: Hogarth Press.

Bretherton, I. and Waters, E. (eds) (1985) 'Growing points of attachment theory and research', *Monographs of the Society for Research in Child Development* 50: 1–2 (Serial No. 209).

Bronson, G. (1974) 'The postnatal growth of visual capacity', *Child Development* 45: 873–90.

Bruner, J. S. (1973) 'Organization of early skilled action', *Child Development* 44: 1–11.

Bruner, J. S. (1977) 'Early social interaction and language acquisition', in H. R. Schaffer (ed.) *Studies in Mother–Infant Interaction*, London: Academic Press.

Bruner, J. S. (1982) 'The organization of action and the nature of adult–infant transaction', in M. von Cranach and R. Harre (eds) *The Analysis of Action*, Cambridge: Cambridge University Press.

Bruner, J. S. and Sherwood, V. (1976) 'Early rule structure: The case of "peekaboo" ', in R. Harre (ed.) *Life Sentences*, London: Wiley.

Butterworth, G. E. and Cochran, E. (1980) 'Towards a mechanism of joint visual attention in human infancy', *International Journal of Behavioural Development* 4: 253–72.

Collis, G. M. (1977) 'Visual coorientation and maternal speech', in H. R. Schaffer (ed.) *Studies in Mother–Infant Interraction*, London: Academic Press.

Collis, G. M. and Schaffer, H. R. (1975) 'Synchronization of visual attention in mother–infant pairs', *Journal of Child Psychology and Psychiatry* 16: 315–20.

Cross, T. (1978) 'Mothers' speech and its association with rate of linguistic development in young children', in N. Waterson and C. Snow (eds) *The Development of Communication*, Chichester: Wiley.

Eimas, P. D. (1975) 'Speech perception in early infancy', in L. B. Cohen and P. Salapatek (eds) *Infant Perception: from Sensation to Cognition*: vol. 2, New York: Academic Press.

Emde, R. N. Gaensbauer, T. J. and Harmon, R. J. (1976) 'Emotional expression in infancy: a behavioural study' *Psychological Issues* 10 (1): 37.

Feinman, S. (1982) 'Social referencing in infancy', *Merrill–Palmer Quarterly* 28: 445–70.

Fenson L., Kagan, J., Kearsley, R. B. and Zelazo, P. R. (1976) 'The developmental progression of manipulative play in the first two years', *Child Development* 47: 232–6.

Fischer, K. W. (1980) 'A theory of cognitive development: the control and construction of hierarchies of skills', *Psychological Review* 87: 477–531.

Fogel, A. (1977) 'Temporal organization in mother–infant face-to-face interaction', in H.R. Schaffer (ed.) *Studies in Mother–Infant Interaction*, London: Academic Press.

Gewirtz, J. L. (ed.) (1972) *Attachment and Dependency* New York: Wiley.

Hutt, S. J., Hutt, C., Lenard, H. G., Bernuth, H. V. and Muntjewerll, W. J. (1986) 'Auditory responsivity in the human neonate', *Nature* 218: 880–90.

Kagan, J. (1984) *The Nature of the Child*, New York: Basic Books.

Kaye, K. (1977) 'Toward the origin of dialogue', in H. R. Schaffer (ed.) *Studies in Mother–Infant Interaction*, London: Academic Press.

Kaye, K. (1982) *The Mental and Social Life of Babies*, London: Methuen.

Kaye, K. and Fogel, A. (1980) 'The temporal structure of face-to-face communication between mothers and infants', *Developmental Psychology* 16: 454–64.

Konner, M. (1982) 'Biological aspects of the mother–infant bond', in R. N. Emde and R. J. Harmon (eds) *The Development of Attachment and Affiliative Systems*, New York: Plenum Press.

Lamb, M. E., Thompson, R. M., Gardner, W., Charnov, E.L. and

Estes, D. (1984) 'Security of infantile attachment as assessed in the "Strange Situation": its study and biological interpretation', *Behavioural and Brain Sciences* 7: 127–71.

McCall, R. B., Eichorn, D. H. and Hogarty, P. S. (1977) 'Transitions in early development', *Monographs of the Society for Research in Child Development* 42 (3): 171.

Messer, D. J. (1978) 'The integration of mother's referential speech with joint play', *Child Development* 49: 781–7.

Moerk, E. (1975) 'Verbal interaction between children and their mothers during the preschool years', *Developmental Psychology* 11: 788–94.

Molfese, D. L. and Molfese, V. J. (1980) 'Cortical responses of preterm infants to phonetic and nonphonetic speech stimuli', *Developmental Psychology* 16: 547–81.

Murphy, C. M. and Messer, D. J. (1977) 'Mothers, infants and pointing: a study of a gesture', in H. R. Schaffer (ed.) *Studies in Mother–Infant Interaction*, London: Academic Press.

Nelson, K. (1973) 'Structure and strategy in learning to talk', *Monographs of the Society for Research in Child Development*, 38 (149).

Rheingold, H. L. and Adams, J. L. (1980) 'The significance of speech to newborns', *Developmental Psychology* 16: 397–403.

Schaffer, H. R. (1966), 'The onset of fear of strangers and the incongruity hypothesis', *Journal of Child Psychology and Psychiatry* 7: 95–106.

Schaffer, H. R. (1971) *The Growth of Sociability*, Harmondsworth: Penguin.

Schaffer, H. R. (ed.) (1977) *Studies in Mother–Infant Interaction*, London: Academic Press.

Schaffer, H. R. (1984) *The Child's Entry into a Social World*, London: Academic Press.

Schaffer, H. R. (1986) 'Psychobiological development in a social context', in H. Rauh and H. C. Steinhausen (eds), *Psychobiology and Early Development*, Amsterdam: North Holland/Elsevier.

Schaffer, H. R. and Collis, G. M. (1986) 'Parental responsiveness and child behaviour', in W. Sluckin and M. Herbert (eds) *Parental Behaviour in Animals and Humans*, Oxford: Blackwell.

Schaffer, H. R. and Emerson, P. E. (1964) 'The development of social attachments in infancy', *Monographs of the Society for Research in Child Development*, 29 (3): 94.

Sherrod, L. R. (1981) 'Issues in cognitive–perceptual development: the special case of social stimuli', in M. E. Lamb and L. R. Sherrod (eds) *Infant Social Cognition: Empirical and Theoretical Considerations*, Hillsdale, N.J.: Lawrence Erlbaum Associates Inc.

Snow, C. E. (1977) 'The development of conversation between mothers and babies', *Journal of Child Language* 4: 1–22.

Stern, D. N. (1974) 'Mother and infant at play: the dyadic interaction involving facial, vocal and gaze behavior', in M. Lewis and L. A. Rosenblum (eds) *The Effect of the Infant on Its Caregiver*, New York: Wiley.

Sugarman-Bell, S. (1978) 'Some organizational aspects of pre-verbal communication', in I. Markova (ed.) *The Social Context of Lanugage*, Chichester: Wiley.

Sylva, K., Roy, C. and Painter, M. (1980) *Childwatching at Playgroup and Nursery School*, London: Grant McIntyre.

Trevarthen, C and Hubley, P. (1978) 'Secondary intersubjectivity: confidence, confiding and acts of meaning in the first year', in A. Lock (ed.) *Action, Gesture and Symbol*, London: Academic Press.

Vaughn, B., Engeland, B., Sroufe, A. L. and Waters, E. (1979) 'Individual differences in infant–mother attachment at twelve and eighteen months: stability and change in families under stress, *Child Development* 50: 971–5.

Vygotsky, L. S. (1978) *Mind in Society*, Cambridge, Mass.: MIT Press.

Waters, E. (1978) 'The reliability and stability of individual differences in infant–mother attachment', *Child Development* 49: 483–94.

Werner, H. and Kaplan, B. (1963) *Symbolic Formation: An Organismic-Developmental Approach to Language and the Expression of Thought*, New York: Wiley Hillsdale, N.J.: Lawrence Erlbaum Associates Inc.

Wolff, P. H. (1968) 'The serial organization of sucking in the young infant', *Pediatrics* 42: 943–56.

2 Infant–mother attachment and social development: 'socialisation' as a product of reciprocal responsiveness to signals

Mary D. Salter Ainsworth, Silvia M. Bell and Donelda J. Stayton

Source: Richards, M.P.M. (ed.) (1974) *The Integration of a Child into a Social World*, Cambridge: Cambridge University Press, pp. 99–135.

The term 'socialisation' is applied to the process through which a child is *made social*. It refers to what must be done so that a child learns rules, proscriptions, values, and modes of behaviour which fit him to his appropriate role in a social group and which make him acceptable to others. It implies that a child is not social at the beginning, but only gradually becomes social. Learning theory holds that a child learns these responses because they have been reinforced; psychoanalytic tradition implies that he takes over the behaviour of those with whom he identifies. Although dissimilar in many respects these views share the basic assumption that an infant's initial repertoire of responses is ill-suited for living in a social world and that profound alterations must be effected before he is fit for society.

It is our view that infants are genetically biased towards interaction with other people from the beginning. Their sensory equipment is responsive to stimuli most likely to stem from people, and many of their behavioural systems are most readily activated (or terminated) by such stimuli. A child is pre-adapted to a social world, and in this sense is social from the beginning. To be sure, the social role of an infant differs from that of adults, but [. . .] an infant is predisposed to become adult. If an infant is reared in a social environment not too dissimilar from that in which the species evolved – an environment in which adults are responsive to the signals implicit in his behaviour – it seems likely to us that he will gradually acquire an acceptable repertoire of more 'mature' social behaviours without heroic efforts on the part of his parents specifically to train him to adopt the rules, proscriptions and values that they wish him to absorb. Because of these considerations we find the concept of 'socialisation' essentially alien to our approach.

For some years we have been concerned with research into the development of the attachment relationship between an infant and his mother in the first year of life. In the course of this research findings have emerged that seem relevant to issues that are commonly conceived to pertain to 'socialisation'. Two of these issues are considered in some detail in this chapter. Under what conditions does an infant learn to cry less than he did in the beginning and thus become less demanding and less of a nuisance? Under what conditions does an infant come to comply readily with his mother's commands and prohibitions?

Before presenting research findings pertinent to these issues, it is first desirable to discuss the theoretical context of the research itself. This theoretical background has been substantially influenced by ethological principles and findings. It owes much to Bowlby's (1958, 1969) formulations, although it has also been considerably influenced by our own empirical work. The next section gives a condensed account of our attachment theory – a theory that has been presented in more detail elsewhere (e.g. Ainsworth 1969, 1972, 1973; Ainsworth and Bell 1970).

BACKGROUND OF ATTACHMENT THEORY AND RESEARCH

Definitions

> *An attachment* may be defined as an affectional tie that one person or animal forms between himself and another specific one – a tie that binds them together in space and endures over time. The behavioral hallmark of attachment is seeking to gain and to maintain a certain degree of proximity to the object of attachment, which ranges from close physical contact under some circumstances to interaction or communication across some distance under other circumstances. *Attachment behaviors* are behaviors which promote proximity or contact. In the human infant these include active proximity – and contact-seeking behaviors such as approaching, following, and clinging, and signaling behaviors such as smiling, crying and calling.
>
> (Ainsworth and Bell 1970: 50)

Some highlights of attachment theory

Although active proximity and contact-seeking behaviours are not in evidence until locomotion and reaching have developed, even a newborn human infant has a repertoire of reflex-like behaviours which promote the maintenance of physical contact once it has been achieved – behaviours such as rooting, sucking, grasping, and postural adjustment when held. For increasing proximity or gaining physical contact with his mother, however, a very young infant must rely on his mother's approach in response to signalling behaviours, such as crying and smiling. It is hypothesised that these behaviours are genetically programmed – both those effective at birth or very soon afterwards, and those that develop later but are nevertheless species-characteristic. It is further postulated that adults generally – despite a massive overlay of learned behaviours – are biased to respond to the species-characteristic signals of an infant in ways that are also species-characteristic. To be sure, there are individual differences in maternal responsiveness, presumably much affected by individual experiences and personality development. Thus, for example, some mothers, perhaps because they are depressed or compulsively occupied with other matters, are relatively impervious even to urgent infant signals. Other mothers are so sensitively perceptive of an infant's behaviour that his entire behavioural repertoire has to them a signalling function. Evolutionary theory suggests that a species-characteristic behaviour is adapted to some significant aspect of the environment in which the species evolved, and that social behaviours are adapted to reciprocal behaviours of conspecifics – or of particular classes of conspecifics. Thus, for example, male mating behaviours are adapted to the behaviours of females, and maternal behaviours are adapted to the behaviours of offspring. In this vein, it is reasonable to hypothesise that infant attachment behaviours are adapted to reciprocal maternal behaviours, that a mother responsive to infant signals is a salient feature of the environment of evolutionary adaptedness, and that unresponsive mothers may be viewed as the product of developmental anomalies and likely themselves to foster anomalous development in their infants.

Evolutionary theory suggests further that any species-characteristic behaviour becomes pre-adapted because it fulfills a significant function that forwards survival of individual, population, or species. Although in mammals, one of the common (predictable) outcomes of infant–mother contact is that the infant will be fed, Bowlby (1969) argues that the essential biological function of attachment behaviour and of reciprocal maternal behaviour is protection of the infant, perhaps especially protection from predators. In espousing this view he was influenced both by the phenomenon of imprinting in precocial birds (in which an infant–mother bond is formed rapidly despite the fact that the infant is not dependent on his mother for food), and by

Harlow's experimental studies (e.g. 1958, 1961, 1963) in the rearing of rhesus monkeys in which the infant's attachment behaviours – featuring clasping and clinging in this species – lead him to seek proximity and contact more often with an inanimate surrogate mother figure which is soft and claspable than with another which yields milk. Furthermore, Harlow demonstrated that once an attachment has been made to such a figure, the infant is able to use it as a secure base from which he can explore even a strange and otherwise alarming situation, and as a haven of safety when faced with a fear-arousing stimulus.

Whatever role feeding and other aspects of nurturance may play in the development of attachment, it seems to us likely that Bowlby is correct in identifying protection as the essential biological function of attachment behaviour. Although danger from predators seems insignificant in present-day Western environments, Bowlby argues that this was a major danger in the 'environment of evolutionary adaptedness' – presumably the savannah environment in which the human species is believed to have first evolved. In any event, even in present-day Western environments, there are still dangers from which children must be protected, and it is reasonable to view attachment behaviours and reciprocal maternal behaviours as continuing to have a significant protective function. Furthermore, it is clear that conditions of alarm dependably activate attachment behaviour at a high level of intensity.

Development of attachment

Although an infant may be viewed as genetically biased to behave in ways that promote proximity and/or contact with adult figures, it is clear that learning is implicated in the development of attachment. An infant is not attached to anyone at first, but if he is reared in a social environment that approximates the environment of evolutionary adaptedness – an environment in which at least one or more adults are consistently accessible to him – he becomes attached to one or a few specific figures about the middle of the first year of life. There is some evidence that he becomes attached to the figure or figures with whom he has had most interaction.

The learning component of attachment is first conspicuous in an infant's acquisition of discrimination of his mother figure from others. As this discrimination is learnt his attachment behaviour becomes increasingly differential, and specifically directed towards her and/or other attachment figures who have become discriminated concomitantly. Furthermore, as he develops he becomes increasingly effective in seeking proximity and contact to his preferred figures on his own account, for example, through approaching, following, and clinging. He also becomes increasingly able to maintain interaction across a distance through a varied repertoire of signals and communications.

During the second half of the first year of life an infant's attachment behaviour becomes increasingly 'goal-corrected' (Bowlby 1969). This implies that in any given situation, in accordance with environmental and intraorganismic conditions, a child will have a certain 'set-goal' of proximity to his attachment figure, and his attachment behaviour will be activated if that distance is exceeded. But, by this time, his systems of attachment behaviour, originally distinctively activated and terminated, become somewhat interchangeable and capable of being organised into new patterns of behaviour which are flexibly adjustable and continuously being corrected in order to maintain the set-goal. Or, in Piaget's (1936) terminology, attachment behaviours may be viewed as 'schemata' which have become 'mobile' as a child has become capable of distinguishing between means and ends. Furthermore, as Piaget (1937) demonstrates, an infant at this time begins to be able to search for hidden objects, and thus shows the first substantial beginning of the concept of an object as having permanence despite its absence from his perceptual field. The acquisition of 'object permanence' marks a momentous shift in the nature of infant–mother relations. It is not until a child is cognitively capable of conceiving of an attachment figure as existing while not actually present perceptually that his behaviour can have the time- and space-bridging qualities that distinguish attachments from other transactions with the environment.

Attachment distinguished from attachment behaviour

Elsewhere (e.g. Ainsworth and Bell 1970; Ainsworth 1972) we have discussed the implications for the concept of attachment of a child's response to a definitive separation from his attachment figures and his subsequent reunion with them. Although attachment behaviour may be greatly heightened in some phases of a child's response to such a separation and may be entirely absent in other phases, the attachment as a relationship to a specific figure tends to survive undiminished. These and other considerations (some of which will be discussed shortly) have led us to distinguish between an 'attachment', as a stable propensity intermittently to seek proximity or contact with a specific figure, and 'attachment behaviours', through which proximity is promoted or sought.

[. . .]

Whereas, according to this view, the 'attachment' is stable and enduring, attachment behaviours are variable, intermittent, and situationally determined in regard to both activation and intensity. In particular, it is necessary to view attachment behaviours as interacting with other behavioural systems which may also be activated in a given situation and which may either be compatible or incompatible with them. Of these other systems, exploratory behaviour deserves special notice.

Attachment and exploratory behaviours

In the familiar environment of his own home it is common for a child freely to leave his mother's side to explore and to play, perhaps for extended periods, before returning to her. Under these circumstances attachment behaviour may be described as having a low level of activation, while exploratory and/or play behaviour are more intensely activated. The proximity set-goal may be described as having a wide setting. If mother moves away to another room, the child's attachment behaviour is likely to be activated, however, although perhaps at relatively low intensity, by the fact that set-goal distance is exceeded, and the child will tend to gravitate after his mother, following her into closer proximity before moving off again to play. If, however, she seems about to depart from the house, or if something alarming happens, or indeed if intraorganismic conditions change, the set-goal will shift to one of closer proximity, attachment behaviour will be activated at a high level of intensity, and balance between the attachment and exploratory systems will be tipped away from exploration and towards proximity-seeking.

The dynamic balance between exploratory and attachment behaviour may be seen to have significance from an evolutionary point of view. Whereas attachment behaviours and reciprocal maternal behaviours serve a protective function during the long, helpless infancy of a species such as the human which can adapt to a wide range of environmental variations, exploratory behaviours reflect a genetic bias for an infant to be interested in the novel features of his environment, to approach them, to manipulate them, to explore, to play, and to learn about the nature of his environment and the properties of the objects in it. It is an advantageous arrangement for an infant to be activated to explore without straying too far from an adult who can protect him if he encounters danger, for him to be programmed to maintain a reasonable degree of proximity on his own account without requiring that the adult be always alert to do so, and for him to be activated to seek quickly a closer proximity or contact should he become alarmed.

The advantageous arrangement described above is not unique to the human species. Studies of ground-living non-human primates (e.g. Southwick, Beg and Siddiqi 1965; DeVore 1963; van Lawick-Goodall 1968; Hinde, Rowell and Spencer-Booth 1964; Hinde and Spencer-Booth 1967; Harlow and Harlow 1965) have provided ample evidence that whereas at first mother and infant are in almost continuous contact, soon the infant ventures forth increasingly to investigate his surroundings and to play with other infants, and spends increasingly more time 'off' his mother. His mother, in turn, becomes increasingly less restrictive and retrieves him less frequently. Alarm, or threat of separation, however, tip the balance towards intense activation of attachment behaviour (and maternal retrieving behaviour) and bring mother and infant quickly together again.

Experimental studies of human infants have shown that an infant will explore even an unfamiliar environment freely while his mother is present, although exploration is weak or absent and attachment behaviour conspicuous should she be absent (Arsenian 1943; Cox and Campbell 1968; Rheingold 1969). Nevertheless, an infant will freely leave his mother on his own initiative to enter another unfamiliar room to explore it (Rheingold and Eckerman 1970). If mild alarm is introduced by the entrance of a stranger, exploration tends sharply to diminish, and if the mother herself departs exploration halts and attachment behaviour is strongly activated (Ainsworth and Witting 1969; Ainsworth and Bell 1970). It appears that whether a strange environment is perceived as novel and elicits exploration or as alarming and elicits attachment behaviour depends in large measure upon the presence of an attachment figure.

Individual differences and previous studies thereof

Our discussion of attachment has thus far described common behavioural trends. There are individual differences even in species-characteristic behaviours, and these common trends must be viewed merely as 'normative' (both in the sense of biologically normal and of statistically average) and by no means as invariable in all members of the species. Our first study of individual differences, directed to the balance between attachment relationship with the mother *and exploratory behaviour*, showed a smooth balance and vironment during the last quarter of the first year of life and in a strange situation at the end of the first year (Ainsworth, Bell and Stayton 1971). The most frequent pattern in our sample of twenty-six infants followed the normative trend that might be expected from our theoretical generalisations. These infants, who may be described as having a secure attachment relationship with the mother, showed a smooth balance and integration between attachment and exploratory behaviours. They did indeed use the mother as a secure base from which to explore; they moved freely away from her, active in locomotion and manipulation; they kept track of mother's whereabouts with an occasional glance and moved back to her to make brief contact from time to time; if picked up they responded positively, but they did not want to be held for more than a few moments; when put down they moved happily off to play again. In a strange situation, without exception, their behaviour followed the normative trends described earlier.

Half the sample, however, showed patterns of behaviour reflecting a disturbed balance between attachment and exploratory behaviour, and these same infants similarly showed departures from the norm in the strange situation. A systematic account of these several patterns of disturbance is given elsewhere (Ainsworth, Bell and Stayton 1971). Here it must suffice to say that they included the following features in various constellations: ambivalence in attachment behaviour, especially in behaviour relating to physical contact; heightened separation anxiety so that very minor everyday separations or threats thereof unduly disrupted exploratory behaviour; passivity, whether intermittent or consistent, that damped down both exploratory behaviour and active attachment behaviour; and proximity-avoiding behaviour that effectively blocked the appropriate activation of attachment behaviour and resulted in a degree of independence that seemed both premature and inappropriate. Findings such as these, together with findings to be reported later in this chapter, strengthened our conviction that there are striking and stable individual differences, even in the first year of life, in the way in which attachment behaviour is organised around and directed towards the mother figure. There seems no doubt that all of these infants had become attached to their mothers. The quality of attachment relationship differed, however, from one individual to another, and affected both attachment behaviour and exploration even when (as in the strange situation) the environmental conditions remained essentially the same.

Whatever may be the role of constitutional differences between infants in influencing the quality of the infant-mother attachment relationship, there is strong evidence that it is influenced substantially by the kind of interaction with his mother the infant has experienced throughout his first year, and whatever contribution the infant himself may have made to this interaction, his mother's contribution is significant. Later reference will be made to detailed codings of maternal behaviour. Here we shall draw attention to four dimensions of maternal behaviour which were found to be related significantly to quality of infant-mother attachment as reflected in the balance of attachment and exploratory behaviour both in the strange situation and at home (Ainsworth, Bell and Stayton 1971). These dimensions are labelled as follows: sensitivity-insensitivity, acceptance-rejection, co-operation-interference, and accessibility-ignoring. They were measured by nine-point rating scales, each of which has five anchor points with detailed behavioural specifications.

The first scale[1] dealt with the degree of sensitivity the mother showed in perceiving and responding promptly and appropriately to the infant's signals and communications. It turned out to be a key variable, in the sense that mothers who rated high in sensitivity also, without exception, rated high in acceptance, co-operation and accessibility, whereas mothers who rated low in any one of the other three scales also rated low in sensitivity. Thus, for example, a rejecting mother was insensitive even though she might not also be especially interfering or inaccessible. Without exception, the infants whose mothers rated high in sensitivity displayed the normative behaviour described earlier in the strange situation, and a smooth balance between attachment and exploratory behaviour at home. Without exception the infants whose mothers rated low in sensitivity displayed one or another of the behaviour patterns (to which reference was made in the preceding paragraph) which reflected a disturbed attachment-exploration balance both at home and in the strange situation. Furthermore, different patterns of infant disturbance were related to specific patterns of maternal behaviour. Thus, for example, the infants showing one pattern tended to have rejecting-interfering mothers; those showing another had rejecting-ignoring mothers; others had another ignoring but non-rejecting, and non-interfering mothers, and so on.

The mothers whose behaviour facilitated harmonious interaction with their infants and thus attachment relationships of secure quality showed a remarkable lack of emphasis on procedures intended to socialise their babies. Such a mother tended to work with the grain of her baby's social repertoire rather than against it. Although she did not deliberately attempt to train her baby, her transactions with him nevertheless facilitated his acquisition of socially desirable modes of behaviour.

Not all of those mothers whose behaviour was so insensitive as to make for disharmonies interaction and disturbed infant-mother attachments were intent on socialisation, however. Some of them were themselves too disturbed or impervious to act sensitively, but some of them were deliberately insensitive and ignoring, rejecting or interfering in an attempt to train the infant to cry less, to demand less, to adapt to household schedules, to fit into an adult-centred social group, and in general to do what adults wished when they wished it and to learn not to expect to 'get their own way'. Their efforts were largely unsuccessful, and their babies were slower to acquire socially desirable modes of behaviour than were those whose mothers were sensitively responsive.

In the next two sections we shall deal in more detail with the relationship between maternal practices and two aspects of infant development: first, the changes that take place in one specific attachment behaviour – crying – in the course of the first year of life, and second, the development of infant obedience to maternal commands, a development that emerges as closely related both to infant–mother attachment and to exploration.

INFANT CRYING

A review of US Children's Bureau *Infant Care* pamphlets between 1920 and 1940 attests to the fact that the fear of 'spoiling' a baby by responding to his cries has been a recurrent theme guiding pronouncements on infant care. A baby should not be picked up in between feedings, mothers are admonished, lest he learn 'that crying will get him what he wants, sufficient to make a spoiled, fussy baby, and a household tyrant whose continual demands make a slave of the mother' (US Children's Bureau 1926: 44). Although more recent advice of the Bureau encourages mothers to follow their natural impulse to respond to crying, the notion that this may result in increased crying persists, perhaps supported by untested and presumably naïve extrapolations from learning theory that assume that to respond to a cry will strengthen crying behaviour.

Crying is classed as an attachment behaviour because it serves to bring mother and baby into proximity with each other. When viewed in the context of attachment theory, both crying and maternal responsiveness to it are seen as behaviours crucial to the survival of the young infant. Crying can be regarded as the earliest communicative signal at the disposal of the child – a signal which is relatively undifferentiated at first, but comes in time to be integrated into a wide range of complex modes of communication. Despite the fact that mothers tend, of necessity, to respond to a large percentage of an infant's cries, crying decreases with age, as more effective modes of communication become operative. The older child, in fact, tends to resort to crying primarily when frustrated and distressed after these other modes have failed. The question before us is to determine which characteristics of maternal care tend to promote this typical outcome.

Bell and Ainsworth (1972) conducted a study of the development of crying in the first year of life. One of the purposes of the study was to explore specifically the relation between maternal responsiveness to crying and changes in the frequency and duration of crying throughout the year.

Twenty-six white, middle-class mother–infant pairs were observed in the home for four-hour periods, at three-week intervals throughout the first year of life. Thus, babies were seen, on the average, four times in each quarter of the first year, for a total of sixteen hours per quarter. All instances of crying, fussing and unhappy vocalisations were recorded, and their duration assessed. In addition, the presence or absence of a maternal response to the cry was noted, as well as the duration of the delay between the onset of the cry and the mother's response.

Two measures of crying were obtained for each baby in each observation period: 'frequency of crying episodes' and 'duration of crying'. The measures of maternal responsiveness obtained were: the number of cries the mother ignored, the length of time that a baby cried without obtaining a response from her – i.e. the duration of maternal unresponsiveness – the types of intervention produced by the mother, and, finally, the conditions which successfully terminated the cry. The information obtained was averaged over the four visits of each quarter, in order to obtain a stable measure of the maternal and infant behaviours characteristic of each three-month period.

Wide individual differences were found both in infant crying and maternal responsiveness. Whereas a mother's tendency to ignore or respond to the cry tended to be stable throughout the year, individual differences in infant crying did not become stable until the second half of the first year of life. The findings indicated that infants achieved a characteristic pattern of frequency and duration of crying as a result of interaction with the mother, and thus that maternal responsiveness was the main factor to account for individual differences in crying.

Table 2.1 shows the relation between episodes of crying ignored by the mother and frequency of infant crying. There are three parts of the table upon which to focus. The diagonal, which gives the correlation of maternal and infant behaviours in the same quarter, shows that the relation between episodes ignored and frequency of crying is not significant either within the first nor within the second quarters, but

Table 2.1 Episodes of crying ignored by the mother and frequency of crying

| | | Episodes ignored by the mother | | | |
		First quarter	Second quarter	Third quarter	Fourth quarter
Frequency of crying	First quarter	−0.04	0.34	0.48*	0.21
	Second quarter	0.56†	0.35	0.32	0.29
	Third quarter	0.21	0.39*	0.42*	0.40*
	Fourth quarter	0.20	0.36	0.52†	0.45*

*$p < 0.05$. †$p < 0.01$.
Note: The figures in italics have been corrected to avoid confounding.

becomes significant in the second half of the year. The lower portion of the matrix shows that maternal ignoring in each quarter correlated significantly with infant crying in the following quarter. Thus, tiny babies do not respond immediately by crying more frequently, but from the third month of life on, they tend to be more insistent in their crying as a result of the past history of mother's ignoring tactics. Finally, the correlations reported in the upper right cells of the table indicate that the effects of infant crying on maternal behaviour are not marked, nor statistically significant, until the fourth quarter. Thus, when inspected longitudinally over the whole first year of life, it seems that maternal ignoring increases the likelihood that a baby will cry frequently from the third month of life on, whereas the frequency of crying has no consistent influence on the number of episodes the mother will be likely to ignore.

Table 2.2 shows the results of a comparable analysis of the relation between duration of maternal unresponsiveness and duration of crying. The findings are analogous to those obtained in the previous analysis and suggest that crying in each quarter is highly correlated with maternal unresponsiveness in the previous quarter. In addition, this table shows that, by the second half of the first year, an infant's persistence in crying affects the mother, tending to make her more reluctant to respond promptly. This indicates that by the end of the first year a vicious spiral has been established. Babies whose cries have been ignored tend to cry more frequently and persistently, which further discourages prompt responsiveness.

Table 2.2 Duration of mother's unresponsiveness to crying and duration of crying

| | | Mother's unresponsiveness | | | |
		First quarter	Second quarter	Third quarter	Fourth quarter
Duration of crying	First quarter	*0.19*	0.37	0.12	0.41*
	Second quarter	0.45*	*0.67†*	0.51†	0.69†
	Third quarter	0.40*	0.42*	*0.39***	0.52*
	Fourth quarter	0.32	0.65†	0.51†	*0.61†*

*$p < 0.05$.   †$p < 0.01$.
Note: The figures in italics have been corrected to avoid confounding.

In the first three months of life, approximately three-quarters of the crying episodes were produced when the baby was not in proximity or contact with the mother. Analysis of the types of intervention mothers produced in response to the cry revealed that more than 90 per cent of maternal responses involve mother bridging the distance, if not actively decreasing the distance, between her and the baby. Contact was the most effective response throughout the first year, terminating a cry in almost 90 per cent of the instances in which it was instituted. Even behaviours involving distance interchanges between mother and baby were effective more than 40 per cent of the time in the first quarter, and became increasingly effective towards the end of the first year. Although some maternal responses were more effective than others in terminating a cry, no relationship was obtained between maternal tendency to respond with one or another type of intervention and frequency of crying. Thus, the findings point to the conclusion that the single most important factor associated with a decrease in infant crying, at least in the first year, is the promptness with which the caretaker responds.

Changes in crying were also examined in the context of the general quality of the mother–infant relationship. Four maternal care rating scales were selected for comparison with the infant crying measures. Two of these, mother's 'sensitivity–insensitivity' and 'acceptance–rejection', have been described in an earlier section of this chapter and assess maternal care in the fourth quarter of the first year. Two

Table 2.3 Rank-order correlations between infant crying and maternal-care ratings

Crying measures	First quarter		Fourth quarter	
	Appropriateness of interaction	Amount of physical contact	Sensitivity	Acceptance
Frequency of crying	−0.20	−0.32	−0.61*	−0.68*
Duration of crying	−0.51*	−0.64*	−0.72*	−0.71*

*$p < 0.01$.

additional scales, 'appropriateness of mother's social interaction with the baby' and 'amount of physical contact', were used to assess maternal care in the first three months of life. High ratings on these scales suggest that maternal care is appropriate, and that there is a high degree of harmony in the interaction between mother and baby.

The result of the comparison, shown in Table 2.3, indicates that in the first three months of life the quality of maternal care tends to affect the duration of crying, but is not associated with frequency of crying episodes. By the fourth quarter of the first year, however, both crying measures are highly correlated with maternal sensitivity and acceptance. A more complex statistical analysis[1] showed that maternal sensitivity was associated with a steady decrease in both crying measures from the first to the fourth quarter of the first year. These findings support the hypothesis that promptness of maternal responsiveness to crying, in the context of a generally accepting and sensitive relationship between mother and baby, is associated with a decrease in crying during the first year of life.

Since those babies whose mothers had been responsive cried less frequently in the last quarter, it was of interest to determine whether other modes of communication had developed to replace crying. All the babies were classified into three groups on the basis of the subtlety, clarity and variety of their communicative signals – a relatively uncommunicative group, a moderately communicative and a communicative group of babies characterised by the ability to produce a varied range of clear, subtle signals through facial expression, gesture and vocalisation. The assessment was based on signals observed and described by the observer, whether these were directed towards the mother or another; the assessment did not depend upon how the recipient of the signal responded to it. Table 2.4 shows that infant communication is negatively correlated to crying, and to mother's

Table 2.4 Infant communication in the fourth quarter, crying and maternal responsiveness

	Fourth Quarter Infant Communication
Duration of crying	-0.71*
Frequency of crying	-0.65*
Mother's unresponsiveness	-0.63*
Episodes ignored by mother	-0.54*

*$p < 0.01$.

unresponsiveness to crying. Thus, babies who, by the end of the first year, had developed the most adequate channels of communication were the same who cried little, and whose cries had been promptly heeded.

These findings suggest that crying is the earliest of a system of signalling behaviours through which proximity and contact with the mother are maintained. Maternal responsiveness tends to terminate an episode of crying and to result in the decrease of crying behaviour while it fosters the development of other communicative signals. Although our analysis did not deal directly with maternal responsiveness to these non-crying communications, it seems likely that the more sensitive mothers would tend to be responsive to them as well as to crying signals. Thus, it appears that responsiveness to infant signals of all kinds, including crying, facilitates the development of varied modes of communication while weakening the tendency to signal through crying.

Although a more thorough discussion of the theoretical relevance of these findings is left to the concluding section of the chapter, it is relevant to note here that they support a theory of early social development such as the one described in the earlier sections of this chapter, which ascribes survival function to the child's inherent predispositions to produce signals which elicit a response from certain key members of his surroundings. In order that the mother's protective function be fulfilled, it seems essential (*a*) that a mother should respond to the crying infant and (*b*) that undifferentiated forms of communication, such as crying, become differentiated and used selectively in conjunction with more specific, clearer communicative signals. Our findings indicate that these two essentials are causally linked so that the most appropriate maternal behaviour – i.e.

responsiveness – fosters infant development in the most adaptive direction.

The present study, however, was limited to maternal and infant behaviours in the first year of life, as observed in the context of the average middle-class home. It seems plausible that in older children some forms of fussing might be strengthened by over-solicitousness, and it is a fact that under the extremely depriving conditions characteristic of institutions, crying, as well as most forms of infant initiative, can be lessened to a point of near extinction. Within the range of interaction characteristic of mother–infant pairs in the first year, however, maternal responsiveness seems to set the tone for mutual co-operation – the more attentive the mother, the less demanding and impatient the baby learns to be.

INFANT OBEDIENCE

Although crying, as a particularly changeworthy behaviour, has been a conspicuous target of socialisation practices, the inculcation of obedience is perhaps their major objective. Compliance to commands and prohibitions is generally considered to precede and to be at the core of internalised standards and values that mediate moral behaviour. Until a child – or an adult, for that matter – demonstrates a willingness to comply with the rules, values and proscriptions of his parents – or society in general – he is considered to be asocial and a liability to society, if not indeed antisocial and a menace.

Traditional theories of socialisation assume that the social environment modifies a child's asocial tendencies by supplying not only the *standards for behaviour* but also the *motivation* necessary for adopting these standards. A child's motives are generally believed to be hedonistic. Therefore, it is held that he must acquire social behaviour through reward and punishment or through such processes as identification and modelling. In either case, it is generally believed that firm and consistent training and discipline are required if obedience is to develop.

We do not believe that obedience in an infant or very young child should be conceived as the outcome of learning of specific acts and avoidances. Rather, we propose that infant obedience may be best understood as an instance of pre-adaptation, and that it should be viewed within the context of the attachment theory summarised in the introductory section.

Infant obedience, when first observed, consists of compliance to adult signals and communications such as 'No! no!', 'Come here!',

'Don't touch!', and 'Give it to me!'. Later, infants may display a self-imposed compliance to commands previously given but this is relatively rare in the first year of life. A baby shows such 'internalised' control when he arrests himself in the act of approaching a previously prohibited area or reaching for a forbidden object.

To an infant, an adult's commands and prohibitions are probably not at first semantically meaningful; rather he is likely to respond not so much to the verbal content of a command as to the tone of voice with which it is issued, and to accompanying facial expression, gesture and posture. These, in the context of the baby's activity in progress and the situation as a whole, yield the crudely specific 'meaning' of the command. Often enough, however, compliance is achieved if he stops what he is doing or approaches the adult or both. It is our hypothesis that an infant is biased to respond to some signal properties of commands and prohibitions, and that he is predisposed to comply with these signals under most circumstances.

Obedience in the human infant is usually first observed about the time that his locomotion becomes effective and he is first capable of moving away from his mother or from where she has placed him. As his interest in his physical environment increases and he begins to venture away on his own initiative, his actions in an environment which may be filled with hazards unsuspected by him must, if he is to survive, be modifiable by signals given across some distance by his mother or other protective figure. Obedience to signals may thus be perceived to supplement attachment behaviour in fulfilling the biological function of protection, and may be viewed as particularly useful in the context of infant exploration.

There are both situational and individual differences which affect the likelihood of occurrence of obedient behaviour. Perhaps of first importance is the degree of alarm and threat present in the situation. A mother who signals her infant in a very alarmed and excited (and therefore alarming) manner is more likely to arrest infant exploration and to activate proximity-seeking behaviour than is a placid mother who sends non-alarming signals. Particularly when an infant is preoccupied with exploration, the signal must be intense and urgent if it is to turn his attention back to his attachment figure. This expectation is consistent with the notion that an infant's behavioural systems operate in a dynamic equilibrium and sometimes compete with one another.

The matter of individual differences bears more directly upon attachment theory and the quality of the infant–mother relationship. It is our thesis that a disposition to be obedient, like other social dispositions, is an essential manifestation of the normal infant–mother attachment relationship. As the quality of a mother's care deviates from the degree of responsiveness to which an infant's attachment behaviours are pre-adapted, however, his attachment relationship will deviate from the norm, and anomalies may occur in his social development – including deviations from the norm of obedience.

Stayton, Hogan and Ainsworth (1971) undertook an analysis of the relationship between infant obedience and the quality of maternal care. This analysis was prompted by the impression that infants in our sample who had developed a secure attachment relationship, and who had therefore experienced harmonious relations with their mothers, tended to be compliant to maternal commands and prohibitions without specific training directed towards the learning of obedience. Framed as hypotheses, the expectations were that an infant whose mother is accepting, co-operative and sensitive to signals will tend to obey her verbal commands and prohibitions more consistently than will an infant whose mother is rejecting, interfering and insensitive, and that this tendency to comply is independent of the mother's specific socialisation tactics or disciplinary procedures.

The sample for this investigation was the same as that described in the crying study. The observations were also the naturalistic accounts of the home behaviour of the mother–infant pairs, which were made at three-week intervals for four hours throughout the first year of life. For the purposes of the obedience analysis, observations covering the period from age nine to twelve months were used.

The narrative reports were analysed for two infant behaviours: compliance to commands and internalised controls. *Compliance to commands* was defined by the percentage of instances in which a baby heeded his mother's verbal commands. *Internalised controls* refers to self-inhibiting, self-controlling behaviour. Three groups were distinguished according to whether self-inhibition was clearly demonstrated, ambiguous, or never observed. Infant sex and I.Q. (Griffiths Scale of Mental Development) were also recorded.

Three maternal variables were coded from the narrative accounts to assess the extent to which the mother tried to train, discipline and/or control the baby's behaviour: the frequency of verbal commands, the frequency of physical intervention and floor freedom. The *frequency of verbal commands* refers to the mean number of commands and prohibitions issued by the mother per visit. The *frequency of physical intervention* refers to the mean number of discipline-oriented physical interventions by the mother per visit. This included instances of slapping the baby, dragging and jerking him away from things and the like. *Floor freedom* refers to the degree to which a baby was permitted to be free on the floor or in a walker during his waking hours.

The quality of the mother's care was assessed by three scales: sensitivity–insensitivity, acceptance–rejection and co-operation–interference. These scales were mentioned earlier in this chapter.

The findings suggest that in the first year of life, an infant is more likely than not to obey his mother's commands. The group mean indicates that the infants in our sample complied 67 per cent of the time to their mother's commands. When mothers were divided into two groups depending on whether they were above or below the median in sensitivity, it was found that the infants of the more sensitive mothers obeyed 86 per cent of the time and infants of the less sensitive mothers obeyed 49 per cent of the time.

[. . .] The findings of most relevance here are that neither of the two disciplinary practices, the frequency of the mother's commands nor her physical interventions, were positively related to the measures of infant obedience. The three measures which assess the quality of the mother's care – sensitivity, acceptance, and co-operation – however, were positively related to compliance to commands and internalised controls.

[. . .]

> The findings suggest that a disposition toward obedience emerges in a responsive accommodating social environment without extensive training, discipline, or other massive attempts to shape the infant's course of development. These findings cannot be predicted from models of socialization which assume that special intervention is necessary to modify the otherwise asocial tendencies of children. Clearly, these findings require a theory that assumes that an infant is initially inclined to be social and (somewhat later) ready to obey those persons who are most significant in his social environment
>
> (Stayton *et al.* 1971: 1065–6)

The conclusions drawn from this study gain considerable support from the field studies of other species. Very early compliance to the mother's signals has been described in a wide variety of animals. There is no report of maternal efforts to train obedience; rather, naturalistic observations suggest that infants are predisposed to respond to many signals characteristic of their species. McCann (1956), for example, observed wild mountain sheep and reports that when the mother gives a warning snort, the lamb drops immediately to the ground and remains motionless. Altmann (1963) described mother–infant alarm patterns in the moose and elk. When a dam moose freezes with angry bristling, her calf also freezes, ready to follow when she gives intention movements. In the case of the elk, the mother's warning bark causes the calf to drop back and hide.

Primates have more complex communication signals which usually consist of a constellation of vocalisation, gesture and facial expression. For example, DeVore (1963) noted that a mother baboon may indicate that she is ready to walk away by a swift glance over the shoulder at the infant, by a slight lowering of her hindquarters, by a quick step directly away, or by some combination of these. On several occasions an infant was called down from a tree by his mother who thrust her face towards him, staring intently and lip-smacking loudly. Van Lawick-Goodall (1968) observed that a chimpanzee mother, wishing to move on, may gesture the infant to cling by touching him or gesturing with one or both arms. An alarmed mother may also signal with a 'hoo' whimper. Occasionally, an infant chimpanzee fails to respond when his mother gestures him to cling or to follow, but infants do not refuse to cling when their mothers are in a hurry or alarmed.

Thus, naturalistic studies of subhuman species suggest that the attachment bond between mother and infant disposes the infant to comply with his mother's signals. These studies have not yet focused on individual differences with regard to obedience. It is our thesis, however, that socialisation results from reciprocal mother–infant responsiveness. When the mother is less sensitive and less responsive to her infant than is expected in the social environment of evolutionary adaptedness, the infant more than likely will be less responsive and hence less compliant to the signals of his mother and other social companions. Subhuman infants, as well as human, are affected by the quality of maternal care. However, since deviations in maternal behaviours and reciprocal infant behaviours may endanger a mother–infant pair in the wild, it is not surprising that individual differences are difficult to detect.

Our assumption that obedience is a behavioural predisposition does not exclude the importance of learning. Certainly, learning may facilitate or may even be required for some communications and commands to acquire signal value. Learning is probably a more important factor for humans than other species if only because humans possess such a complex communication system. Our position is that it is the *willingness to be obedient* rather than the understanding of the contents of the communication that is fostered by the attachment bond.

The relationship between obedience in infancy and later obedient acts has not been explored. The typical 'negativism' of the toddler suggests that a child will not always conform to demands of his parents no matter how loving and understanding they may continue to be. Factors such as intellectual competence, peer group and cultural values begin to play more significant roles. None the less, a willingness to comply with the rules and values of others seems to mediate most social standards of conduct. It is our belief, then, that early attachment relationships must be considered for understanding the development and maintenance of mature moral behaviour.

DISCUSSION

Both our attachment theory and our empirical findings portray an infant as social from the beginning. He does not need to be taught to be social. During his first three months of life he is more likely to cry when he is alone than when he is near his mother, and least likely to cry when he is actually being held by her. When he does cry, the most effective way to soothe him is to give him physical contact. He seems to be programmed to 'want' proximity and contact to judge by the fact that he is well equipped with signalling systems that promote these outcomes. It is in this sense that even the neonate may be described as social; he does not need to learn to signal for someone to come to him. These signalling systems, however, achieve their 'predictable' outcome only because they serve to activate approach and other appropriate behaviours in the adult. To the extent that there is reciprocity between a newborn's attachment behaviours and the behaviour of adult figures who have assumed the responsibility for his care, he may be described as integrated into a social world from the beginning, at least in a prototypical way appropriate to this early stage of development.

The success of this early 'integration' seems to depend very largely upon the extent to which his mother figure and/or other figures close to him are programmed (whether through genetic underpinnings or experience or a combination of both) to respond to his repertoire of behavioural signals. To be sure, it must be acknowledged that neonates differ from the beginning in their behavioural repertoire, so that some perhaps signal more effectively than others. But in our sample of normal, healthy infants we found some evidence (as illustrated in our report of infant crying) that differences in infant behaviour seem to be more influenced by maternal responsiveness than does maternal behaviour seem to be influenced by infant characteristics.

Although an implicit assumption of many theoretical explanations of socialisation is that the child is basically asocial, the main thrust of the concept of 'socialisation' is that natural behavioural dispositions of a child must be altered – whether curbed, redirected, or eradicated – if he is to be integrated eventually as a desirable participant in an adult social world. There is no question that the prototypical integration of the newborn into a loving and protective family must give way gradually to integration into a widening social world at progressively more mature levels. The question is how this 'socialisation' process may best be achieved. According to the most widely held views, it is to be achieved either through consistent efforts by caretakers to train him or to condition him (thus bringing his behaviour under effective environmental control) or through his own efforts to do what is expected of him for fear of losing parental affection. (There are other sophisticated views –such as socialisation through identification – that are not covered by this simple generalization, but they have had relatively less influence upon childrearing procedures in Western society than have the 'training' and 'loss of love' views.)

A major implication of our findings is contrary to these widely held views, at least in so far as the first year of life is concerned. We have shown that specific efforts to train an infant, or otherwise consciously to push him into the desirable behavioural mould, tend to prolong behaviour deemed to be changeworthy, whereas to accept him as he is, to respect his natural behavioural patterns as valid, to be accessible to him and to respond sensitively to his signals tend to facilitate the development of the kinds of behaviours commonly believed to be desirable in infancy. Specifically, we have reported that maternal responsiveness to infant crying tends significantly to reduce the frequency and duration of crying throughout the first year, and that maternal acceptance, co-operation, and sensitivity to signals are strongly related both to infant compliance with maternal commands and with the beginnings of 'internalisation' of prohibitions.

[. . .]

Both the normative trends and the individual differences in our sample are congruent with the evolutionary implications of our attachment-theory model. An essential focus of this model is the protective function of attachment behaviours and reciprocal maternal behaviours, and equally essential corollaries are the advantage of an interlocking balance between these behaviours and infant exploratory behaviour and the close relationship between them and fear behaviours. It is of survival advantage for an infant to emit signals that draw adults to him and activate their protective and other caretaking behaviours. It is advantageous also that he rapidly develop various active models of seeking proximity and contact on his own account, to supplement his repertoire of signals. It is not only of immediate survival advantage but also in the interests of his integration into a wider social group that he expand his repertoire beyond simple signals such as crying and smiling to include other modes of communication, such as varied facial expressions, gestures and non-crying vocalisations, also including intentional communications eventually embracing language. It is a finding of very considerable interest that maternal responsiveness to the more primitive signals including crying promotes the development of a wider repertoire of communication.

The survival advantage for an infant of both crying and other later forms of communication is illuminated by an attempt to picture an infant in the original environment in which man is believed to have evolved, in which relatively much time may be presumed to have been spent away from shelters and relatively much on the open ground where predators and other dangers were not unlikely. In such an environment it would be advantageous for an infant to emit clear signals – and soon more varied communications – whenever alone, alarmed, or in general distressed, and for a mother to respond to these by coming to him promptly. It would be advantageous for an infant to redouble his crying should his mother ignore him at first. On the other hand, a crying infant might attract the attention of predators, so it would be even more advantageous for his mother quickly to come to quiet him. Finally, it seems adaptive for an infant to come to reserve crying for the more alarming of the situations he encounters, and to use less urgent modes of communication otherwise – as elucidated in the folktale of the boy who cried 'Wolf!' too often.

[. . .]

We have found that an infant becomes well-socialised if he has enjoyed a harmonious attachment relationship with his mother figure. The picture is one of mutual co-operation – or reciprocal responsiveness to signals. The mother has accepted the baby and responsibility for his care, despite the fact that he interferes with her other activities. She respects his autonomy as a separate individual and indeed enjoys noticing his individuality and the ways in which he asserts his wishes. She remains consistently accessible to him – or is careful to provide adequate substitute care when she feels she cannot be there. She is sensitively aware of his signals, and responds to them promptly. Infants naturally respond to such mothers co-operatively, and become increasingly responsive to the signal qualities of maternal behaviour. Rather than becoming 'spoiled' or overdependent, these infants can best be characterised as secure. They tend to cry little, to be affectionate and unambivalent towards the mother, to explore and play eagerly on their own, and to obey her commands. In short, they come to exhibit a desirable balance between independent competence and harmonious interaction with others.

Clearly, the fear of 'spoiling' a child by responding to his signals is not borne out by our data. An infant who might be labelled 'spoiled' is fussy, demanding, unco-operative and generally difficult to handle. This label is more appropriate for infants in our sample whose mothers have been insensitive to signals, unduly interfering with infant activity, rejecting, punitive and/or inaccessible. Closely connected with the fear of spoiling is a fear of fostering overdependence in a child, and also a fear that a child whose signals are heeded may gain tyrannical control over his mother. Associated with this fear also is the apprehension that babies who have been responded to may become children who are unable to understand and to respect the point of view of others.

Since our investigations have focused on the first year of life, we cannot with assurance state that secure attachment relationships in the first year guarantee a continuance of co-operative and 'socialised' interaction – but we hypothesise that they are likely to do so provided that maternal co-operation does not undergo an abrupt change. Certainly in the first year independence seems fostered rather than hampered by a secure and harmonious attachment relationship, whereas 'overdependence' seems a product of insensitive mothering. Also in the first year sensitive mothering seems to make an infant progressively less demanding rather than more so. Finally, much of the basis of the security of a one-year-old seems to be that he can trust his mother – that he can anticipate her actions, her absences and her returns, and her response to his communications – whereas much of the insecurity of the fussy, ambivalent and demanding one-year-old seems due to the fact that his mother is unpredictable. It seems reasonable to suppose that trust in the predictability of an attachment figure is the first step towards understanding the motivations and set-goals of that figure – a clear step away from 'egocentricity' and towards empathy and understanding and respecting of another's point of view. On the other hand, a figure who is unpredictable is impossible to understand.

Perhaps the long-standing uncertainty about the causes of spoiling and continuation of egocentricity has been based upon a widespread failure to perceive the biological function of infant behaviours that constitute an inconvenience to the adult caretaker. Crying, demands for contact, intolerance of separation, and other such phenomena have been widely viewed as changeworthy behaviours. Although it has been acknowledged that a young infant is helpless and defenceless, he has also been viewed as infinitely malleable. To be sure, one great asset of the human species is the environmental lability of his behaviours, but this lability is not unlimited. It is when we set aside our admiration of human flexibility, and our concern with moulding and changing behaviour, and begin to study a child's development in his naturalistic setting, that we come to appreciate both the fact that changeworthy behaviours have a significant function and that development proceeds optimally when an infant's caretakers provide an environment for his development which does not depart in important respects from the environment to which the behavioural equipment of the infant of the species is adapted. Of course, only research can identify the limits of variation in the infant-care environment that hamper social development or, in the extreme, produce developmental anomalies that are difficult to reverse.

[. . .]

NOTE

1 By means of a non-parametric analysis-of-variance techniques.

REFERENCES

Ainsworth, M. D. S. (1969) 'Object relations, dependency and attachment: a theoretical review of the infant–mother relationship', *Child Development* 40: 969–1025.

Ainsworth, M. D. S. (1972) 'Attachment and dependency: a comparison', in J. L. Gewitz (ed.) *Attachment and Dependency*, Washington, D.C.: V. H. Winston & Son (distributed by Wiley, New York).

Ainsworth, M. D. S. (1973) 'The development of infant–mother attachment', in B. M. Caldwell and H. N. Ricciuti (eds) *Review of Child Development Research*, vol. 3, Chicago: Univ. Chicago Press.

Ainsworth, M. D. S. and Bell, S. M. (1970) 'Attachment, exploration and separation: illustrated by the behaviour of one-year-olds in a strange situation', *Child Development* 41: 49–67.

Ainsworth, M. D. S. and Witting, B. A. (1969) 'Attachment and exploratory behavior of one-year-olds in a strange situation', in B. M. Foss (ed.) *Determinants of Infant Behaviour*, vol. 4, London: Methuen.

Ainsworth, M. D. S., Bell, S. M. and Stayton, D. J. (1971) 'Individual differences in strange situation behavior of one-year-olds', in H. R. Schaffer (ed.) *The Origins of Human Social Relations*, London: Academic Press.

Altmann, M. (1963) 'Naturalistic studies of maternal care in moose and elk', in H. L. Rheingold (ed.) *Maternal Behavior in Mammals*, New York: Wiley.

Arsenian, J. M. (1943) 'Young children in an insecure situation', *J. Abnorm. Soc. Psychol.* 38: 225–49.

Bell, S. M. and Ainsworth, M. D. S. (1972) 'Infant crying and maternal responsiveness', *Child Development* 43: 1171–90.

Bowlby, J. (1958) 'The nature of the child's tie to his mother', *Int. J. Psychoanal.* 39: 350–73.

Bowlby, J. (1969) *Attachment and Loss*, vol. 1, *Attachment*, London: Hogarth Press.

Cox, F. N. and Campbell, D. (1968) 'Young children in a new situation with and without their mothers', *Child Development* 39: 123–31.

DeVore, I. (1963) 'Mother–infant relations in free-ranging baboons', in H. L. Rheingold (ed.) *Maternal Behavior in Mammals*, New York: Wiley.

Harlow, H. F. (1958) 'The nature of love', *Amer. Psychol.* 13: 673–83.

Harlow, H. F. (1961) 'The development of affectional patterns in infant monkeys', in B. M. Foss (ed.) *Determinants of Infant Behaviour*, vol. 2, London: Methuen.

Harlow, H. F. (1963) 'The maternal affectional system', in B. M. Foss (ed.) *Determinants of Infant Behaviour*, vol. 2, London: Methuen.

Harlow, H. F. and Harlow, M. K. (1965) 'The affectional systems', in A. M. Schrier, H. F. Harlow and F. Stollnitz (eds) *Behavior of Nonhuman Primates*, vol. 2, New York: Academic Press.

Hinde, R. A. and Spencer-Booth, Y. (1967) 'The behaviour of socially-living rhesus monkeys in their first two and a half years', *Anim. Behav.* 15: 169–96.

Hinde, R. A., Rowell, T. E. and Spencer-Booth, Y. (1964) 'Behavior of socially-living rhesus monkeys in their first six months', *Proc. Zool. Soc. Lond.* 143: 609–49.

Lawick-Goodall, J. van (1968) 'The behaviour of free-living chimpanzees in the Gombe Stream Reserve', *Anim. Behav. Monog.* 1, part 3.

McCann, L. J. (1956) 'Ecology of the mountain sheep', *Am. Midl. Nat.* 56: 297–324.

Piaget, J. (1936) *The Origins of Intelligence in Children* (2nd ed. 1952), New York: Internat. Univ. Press.

Piaget, J. (1937) *The Construction of Reality in the Child* (2nd ed. 1954), New York: Basic Books.

Rheingold, H. L. (1969) 'The effect of a strange environment on the behavior of infants', in B. M. Foss (ed.) *Determinants of Infant Behaviour*, vol. 4, London: Methuen.

Rheingold, H. L. and Eckerman, C. O. (1970) 'The infant separates himself from his mother', *Science* 168: 78–83.

Southwick, C. H., Beg, M. A. and Siddiqi, M. R. (1965) 'Rhesus monkeys in North India', in I. DeVore (ed.) *Primate Behavior: Field Studies of Monkeys and Apes*, New York: Holt, Rinehart & Winston.

Stayton, D. J., Hogan, R. T. and Ainsworth, M. D. S. (1971) 'Infant obedience and maternal behavior: the origins of socialization reconsidered', *Child Development* 42: 1057–69.

US Children's Bureau Publications (1926) *Infant Care*, Washington, D.C.: US Government Publications.

3 The development of affect in infancy and early childhood

Charles M. Super and Sara Harkness

Source: Wagner, D. and Stevenson, H. (eds) (1982) *Cultural Perspectives on Child Development*, W. H. Freeman.

I had occasion twice in one week to meet passengers from ships at the ocean terminal in Sydney. One ship was the *Southern Cross*, from Southampton, and the other was the *Galileo Galilei* from Milan. In the one case the dockside was crowded with a throng of people, babies and grandparents, laughing, weeping, shouting. Men embraced and kissed; women shrieked and rushed into passionate greetings. There was tumultuous confusion. From the other ship the passengers passed sedately down the gangplank, in orderly groups; there were waves of hands and smiles, polite handshakes, and impassive greetings such as 'How nice to see you again.'

(Nash 1970: 428)

Group differences in publicly visible emotional behavior have been a source of amazement, amusement, and trouble since time immemorial, for they have a particularly personal aspect. Language differences do not share this personal quality, for they are experienced subjectively as a rupture in the medium of communication. Behind the odd sounds lie thoughts which, once translated, we assume we would understand. Emotional displays, however, seem to be the content of a communication, not its medium. Laughter, tears, and silence appear universal in meaning; we need no translator. But why are other people so cold or so boisterous? Have they no heart or no decency? Seeing the African laugh at a blind man's confusion, or the European tenderly waste scarce food on a dog, we 'know' what the other is doing; we only ask how it is possible that a person could do such a thing.

CULTURE AND PERSONALITY

Emotional states and expressions are among the behaviors related to culture. Partly regulated themselves by values and beliefs about reality, emotions work to support (or sometimes to subvert) social institutions such as marriage, warfare, charity, cooperative labor groups, and legal mechanisms for settlement of disputes. How is it that people from different cultures come to display different emotional behaviors in apparently similar circumstances? For several decades, it was thought that the study of infancy and early childhood in other cultures would provide an answer. People in other cultures behave differently, the theory said, partly because they have different personalities. They have different personalities because they were reared in a way very different from the way we were reared.

The relationship between personality and larger cultural dimensions is a recurring focus of theory and research in the social sciences. The field of 'culture and personality' emerged within anthropology as Margaret Mead, Ruth Benedict, John Whiting, and other pioneers in the field recognized that anthropology could not fulfill the task of understanding culture without accounting for how culture operates through the individual. The anthropologist never sees a culture – only the things and behaviors produced by the members of a culture. The knowledge and skills, beliefs, and values of the culture are held by individuals who acquired them in the past and will pass them on to the next generation. An important aspect of understanding how cultures work, therefore, is understanding how individuals learn to use their cultures.

In pursuing this inquiry, social scientists of the culture-and-personality are (roughly the 1930s to the 1950s) naturally looked to psychological theories of the time to help them understand child development. In many ways the interdisciplinary fit was a good one, for a prominent school of thought in psychology at the time was the new and promising field of psychoanalysis. Freud and those influenced by his ideas focused their attention on the role of childhood experiences in shaping adult personality. The psychologists' work coincided with the theoretical needs of the anthropologists.

In the 1950s and 1960s, by and large, both anthropology and psychology become more diverse in their theoretical focus, and the driving unity behind 'culture and personality' weakened. There are many reasons for this, some of them related to the natural history of scientific fields as they explore paradigms of inquiry. More immediately, however, there were three problems with the culture-and-personality school of investigation that continued to frustrate a sense of resolution despite considerable effort and progress. One was the challenge of more positivist kinds of investigation: the dissection, measurement, and quantitative analysis that were revolutionizing psychology, sociology, and other fields. Qualitative methods of cultural analysis, like those of psychoanalysis, too often seemed inferior but were at the same time difficult to supplement when dealing with such large and complex subjects as culture. Second, the approach depended on concepts such as 'national character' or 'modal personality' for each culture, resulting from the 'typical' methods of child rearing. Many anthropologists came to think that more allowance was needed for diversity within a culture. Finally, the stature of psychoanalysis and learning theory, the grand schemes of psychology that were used in the culture-and-personality approach, began to crumble within the field of psychology as they seemed to require more and more detail to explain less and less.

The momentum of creative and exciting research on culture and personality stalled, in effect, somewhere in the 1950s, just as the experimental approach to studying American children's behavior started to grow in both success and size. Cultural perspectives on infancy and early childhood have not figured large in recent research and teaching in child development, in part because of weaknesses in the ethnographic and cross-cultural work, in part because of the enormous outpouring of experimental research, and in part because of ethnocentricity, an insensitivity to cultural variation, by psychologists and the field of psychology in general (see Harkness and Super 1980; LeVine 1980).

THE NEW 'INTERDISCIPLINE'

Today there is a new interest in revitalizing the interdisciplinary endeavor, for psychological anthropology (heir to culture and personality) and comparative child development are emerging with new vigor in their own fields, incorporating recent theoretical advances with traditional strengths and reaching at the same time for the complementary powers of the sister disciplines. Cycles of progress, like cycles of fashion, have a way of building on the conceptual lines of a full generation before, restating the useful questions and concepts, abandoning hypotheses and viewpoints that proved disappointing, and trying out new ideas for theory and research.

Social and affective development appears to be a particularly promising domain for the new synthesis. The older culture-and-personality effort suffered from too broad and shallow a sweep, while traditional developmental approaches to this topic have been too insular. In our view, a satisfactory theory of social and affective development must eventually incorporate three elements: (1) a statement of the thrust of growth universal to our species, (2) a recognition of the expressive behavioral patterns encouraged by culturally regulated socialization for particular situations, and (3) an appreciation of the sequences of developmental events as they occur in the context of the full span of life.

In this essay we consider aspects of these three points from a comparative perspective. First, we present evidence of the universal emergence of some basic emotional displays, namely happy social play with caretakers and distress at their departure. Second, we illustrate the shaping of these universals into patterns of particular cultural significance. Third, we discuss the importance of the sequences of emotional learning within a culture in understanding the consequences of early affective socialization. Our examples are drawn from a variety of sources and locales, but in the second and third sections we describe in more detail the affective development of children in Kokwet, a Kipsigis community in rural Kenya.

THE EMERGENCE OF EMOTIONAL DISPLAYS

The display of any behavior, or integrated complex of behaviors, rests on neuromotor competence. Mature, appropriate displays of emotional behavior involve not only the overt acts (such as smiling), but also associated internal feeling states and the cognitively influenced connections among a particular environmental circumstance (such as a greeting from a friend), a feeling state, and a behavioral display. While the socialization of affect is a psychological and cultural process, it occurs only in coordination with a biological substrate that is unique to, and generalized across, our species. In short, there are neurological and hormonal universals in the way humans work; these universals contribute to the mechanisms of emotional socialization and also limit the possible range of variation. Since infants do not enter the world with these or any other biological mechanisms fully mature, observations on the maturationally guided emergence of particular kinds of behavior provide a useful technique for understanding possible universals. Knowing some of the universal elements, the process of tracing environmental influences is much easier.

One of the most dramatic early changes in emotional behavior occurs when a baby is 3 or 4 months old. To the American parent, the baby begins to seem more 'like a real person'. The third month, it is occasionally said, makes the first two worthwhile. The baby becomes not only less incessantly demanding – often sleeping through the night, for example, and fussing less – but also more reliably rewarding. Many American parents find a qualitative change in the baby's social responsiveness and expressiveness that brings real joy. A similar reaction by Kipsigis mothers in rural Kenya may be reflected in the fact that they begin to refer to their babies as 'children' at this time, and no longer as 'monkeys'.

There is a parallel change at this point in the mothers' behavior in the two cultures: they are more likely to be found holding their babies than they were in the previous month, even though the general trend over the first year is to decrease physical contact (Super 1980). The kinds of mutual, flowing social play that are salient at this time look very similar in the two groups. Observational recording in the home indicates that Kipsigis mothers and their 4-month-old infants smile and look at each other with about the same frequency as do upper-middle-class mother–infant pairs in Boston, Massachusetts.

Exactly what the behavioral changes in the baby are, and how they become encouraged by the mother's reactions, have yet to be fully documented. Smiling, however, is certainly a central feature of the changes in the baby's behavior. The frequency of smiling in normal infants rises dramatically during the third and fourth months in infants from many different cultures around the world. Figure 3.1 illustrates this for four groups of babies in Israel: those from lower- and middle-class urban families, from a kibbutz settlement with cooperative child care arrangements, and from a group of semi-nomadic Bedouin families in the Negev desert (Landau 1977). The frequency of smiling by these babies, as observed in the course of a normal day, rises in a similar manner despite substantial differences in the social context of care.

The similarity in the emergence of smiling in Israeli samples, and in other even more diverse groups, suggests an underlying maturational cause—not a complete and sufficient cause, for maturation can proceed only through interaction with an environment, but still a necessary and driving force. The co-occurrence of this behavior change with a number of other developments at the same age supports the hypothesis of a broad underlying maturational factor. Important transitions at 3 to 4 months have been noted in other areas of emotion as well as cognition, motor skills, and sleep (for example, McGraw 1946; Piaget 1952; Spitz *et al.* 1970). There is evidence for changes in brain structure, most notably rapid myelinization in the cerebral cortex and limbic (emotional) areas of the brain (Yakovlev and Lecours 1967). Further support is available from studies of blind infants, who show an early growth in smiling that is slightly delayed

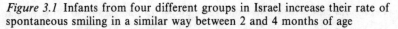

Figure 3.1 Infants from four different groups in Israel increase their rate of spontaneous smiling in a similar way between 2 and 4 months of age

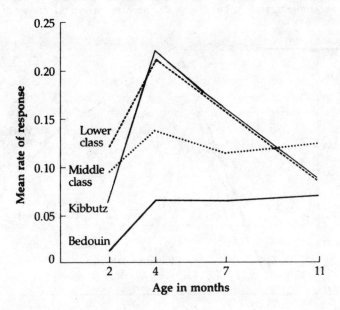

Source: Data from Landau 1977: 389–400.

but otherwise quite similar to development in normal infants (for example, Freedman 1964; Parmalee 1955).

Infant distress in response to being left by the mother also appears at a very similar rate in a number of diverse settings. In experiments conducted in urban America, rural Guatemala, the Kalahari desert of Botswana, and Israeli kibbutzim, infants generally do not cry when the mother leaves until about 7 or 8 months of age, after which point distress becomes more and more frequent until a peak sometime after the first birthday (see Figure 3.2 adapted from Kagan 1976). The similarity here, it is argued, is not so much in the development of a particular behavior, but rather in a cognitive ability to detect and evaluate (and therefore sometimes fear) unusual and unpredictable events (Kagan *et al.* 1978). Regardless of whether the change is viewed as 'primarily' cognitive, emotional, or biological, or as an inseparable blend, the data again point to a remarkably ordered emergence of emotional displays in early life.

Figure 3.2 Infants from five different groups around the world show similar increases during the first year in the likelihood of crying at maternal departure in an experimental setting, but diverge during later years in the decline of this response

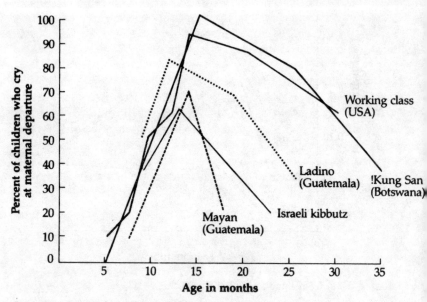

Source: Adapted from Kagan 1976: 186–96.

THE SOCIALIZATION OF EMOTIONAL DISPLAYS

As the ability to display particular affective behaviors emerges, and especially as the ability becomes more stable and highly organized, the cultural system engages the infant's responses in particular ways. While the psychological mechanisms that lead to smiling are fundamentally universal, the opportunities and contexts for smiling in different cultures diverge. There appear to be two major pathways of cultural divergence in the emotional training of infants and young children: (1) the direct expression of parental values or beliefs, and (2) the less intentional structuring of the child's developmental niche by the physical and social resources for caretaking.

Parental values and beliefs

The most interesting aspect of parental values as they influence early socialization is that their expression is not usually a direct effort to achieve some later effect. Their expression is, rather, a more immediate reflection of adult psychological functioning. That is, values influence behavior more in the sense of 'This is the way I feel like acting with my baby' or 'This is the way I would like to see my baby act', rather than 'I want to train my baby in this skill in order to facilitate social and economic advancement in later life'. Socialization values at this age are expressive goals in their own right, not only means to some later goal. Nevertheless, the effect of such socialization is usually to provide the infant or young child with practice in culturally appropriate social and emotional behavior.

Examples of concordance between parents' expressive interaction with infants and larger cultural values can be found from all parts of the world. In Uganda, adults and siblings talk and smile to infants more than is true in many other cultures, trying to coax a happy smile in return. It seems the natural way to play with babies. The social skills both expressed and trained in such interaction, however, are talents needed for personal advancement in the relatively mobile Baganda social order. Today, as has traditionally been the case in this group, personal skills are powerful means to gaining status and material resources. Unlike the situation in many traditional African groups, social standing can be individually earned, rather than being ascribed primarily on the basis of sex, age, or lineage (Kilbride and Kilbride 1974; Kilbride and Kilbride 1975).

Japanese mothers, compared to American mothers, spend large amounts of time soothing and lulling their infants, rather than stimulating them with active 'chatting'. The kinds of social intercourse that result are consonant with the patterns of interaction at later ages and with the larger patterns of social organisation in the two societies. American mothers, partly to fulfill their own expectations of appropriate affective behavior, encourage open, expressive, assertive, self-directed behavior, while the Japanese mothers seek quiet, contented babies (Caudill and Frost 1973; Caudill and Weinstein 1969).

In some cases adult beliefs about the nature of infants or about the world in general shape the emotional lives of infants. The Kwoma of New Guinea and Zinacantecans of Mexico, for example, have beliefs about supernatural threats and the vulnerability of infants that lead to keeping their babies close, quiet, and calm (Brazelton *et al.* 1969; Whiting 1971). The cumulative effect on the infants' level of excitement may be substantial, even though the parents' motivations focus primarily on other matters. In contrast, many American parents in the mid-twentieth century were concerned with the possibility of lasting psychological damage that could result from excessive inhibition of 'natural' feelings such as jealousy. This belief about the nature of personality development influenced their reaction to some kinds of emotional displays in their young children, for they thought it important to allow emotional conflicts to be expressed and played out where they could be discussed and managed (for example, Spock 1968: 12).

Structural features of care

The expression and regulation of emotional behavior are also mediated by structural features of infant care that are not so obviously related to adult values or beliefs. Many aspects of a young child's environment are influenced by the way families are organized for other purposes. The use of child caretakers to supplement maternal care is an important example. In many societies around the world, the moment-to-moment care of a baby is given to an older sibling or other relative, typically a 7- or 8-year-old sister (Weisner and Gallimore 1977). While attitudes within any group concerning the desirability of single versus multiple caretakers are probably consistent with the dominant pattern in that group, it would appear that aspects of social organisation, such as means of economic production, family size, and mothers' work load, are more effectively related to use of child caretakers than are the values themselves. Certainly in American society over the past decades, it can be argued that maternal employment has been the driving force behind increased group care for young children, while attitudes consistently lagged behind.

In illustrating structural environmental influences on early affective development, and in the remainder of this essay, we describe in some detail the early social life of Kipsigis children in western Kenya. It is difficult, however, to understand the integrating function of a culture's environment for children without some knowledge of the larger cultural system. Before describing structural features of the early environment in Kokwet, therefore, we will briefly present some background ethnographic information.

The Kipsigis of Kokwet

The Kipsigis of western Kenya are a Highland Nilotic people (Sutton 1968) numbering about half a million. Traditionally they lived by herding cattle and raising simple crops; their life was seminomadic as they shifted pasture and field in response to the land and to sporadic fighting with neighbouring groups. More permanent residence and land tenure became common in the early part of this century, encouraged by increasing contact with the British settlers and colonial administrators, especially the force of their economics and occasionally their force of arms (Manners, 1967). As in most of East Africa, the period following World War II initiated especially rapid change.

Kokwet, the Kipsigis community where we lived for 3 years in carrying out our investigation, consists of 54 homesteads spread out along 3 miles of a ridge of land formed by 2 streams that drain the Mau forest of the western highlands. To the north and east lie fine, rolling farmland and, a few hours away by dirt road, the tea estates of Kericho. To the south and west, the land dries and slopes down to the savannahs of the Mara, home of zebra and lion and of the Masai people.

The people of Kokwet have adapted successfully as farmers to the national economy. All the families are self-supporting in basic foodstuffs, maize (corn) and milk being major components of the daily diet. Milk, maize, and pyrethrum (a daisy-like flower with insecticidal properties) are grown for cash marketing as well. Each family has about 18 acres of useful land, an unusual situation created by the initial terms of the settlement scheme set up by the Kenyan government at the time of national independence (1963). The land was purchased from a departing white settler and distributed to indigenous citizens. Neighbouring lands had never been alienated for European use, and the people of Kokwet moved in from the surrounding areas. The relative abundance of fertile land in Kokwet has permitted, for the present, a continuation of the agricultural adaptation to modern life without disruptive pressures to leave the farm and seek wages in towns or plantations.

While there is no 'village center' to Kokwet, households often cluster near the borders of their land to form small groups within the community. The typical round houses, with mud walls and straw roofs, overlook the family's pastures and fields most of the year, sometimes hidden by the tall maize as harvest approaches.

Despite fundamental changes in Kipsigis life, many traditional features persist in Kokwet. Social organisation of the community continues to operate at the face-to-face level, with conflicts and disputes confronted and resolved in this context (Harkness *et al.* 1981). Communal efforts among households are important for ceremonies, large projects, and some major activities, such as harvesting and weeding groups. Most adults have little or no formal education, and many families consist of one man, his two wives, and their children. While there are major divisions of role by age and sex, all members of a family participate in its maintenance through household chores, agricultural labor, and tending cattle. Most children now attend at least a few years of school, but more traditional forms of preparation for adult life continue in the home and in the larger community, for example adolescent initiation and circumcision rites for both boys and girls. Christian missions have been active in the general area for half a century, but most men and women are, in their own words, 'not yet' converted.

The infant's niche in Kokwet

The infant in Kokwet is born into a physical and social setting that is different from the one familiar to Americans. Until the baby is 3 or 4 months old, the mother is almost always with the child. Most of the time, in fact, mother and baby are actually touching; the baby might be sitting propped up in the mother's lap while she prepares food, riding on her back (secured and covered with cloth) as she goes to the river for water, cradled in her arms for nursing, or straddling her hip as she moves around the yard doing chores. By the time the baby is 4 months old, a child caretaker has taken over a large share of the daytime care, holding and carrying the baby and providing entertainment, but often within sight of the mother. A little later the mother may go to the garden, perhaps 10 minutes away, or visit a neighbour while leaving the baby with the child caretaker.

The baby's emotional life is influenced in a number of ways by this organisation of care, or niche. Of particular interest here are the embededdness of infant life in the continuing social and economic functioning of the family, and the adaptations to and by the several caretakers. A useful example is the regulation of sleep–wake behaviour. Unlike many American families, Kipsigis households do not make major modifications in their living quarters or family routines to facilitate infant sleep. There is no baby's room and no nap schedule. One reason this is possible is that care of an awake infant is more compatible with the mother's daily chores and pleasures. The Kipsigis mother can carry, hold, or entertain the baby reasonably well while sweeping the house, relaxing after the midday meal, fetching firewood, or preparing food. This is less true for the American mother who does not have the same customary repertoire of carrying and holding practices, and whose activities include PTA meetings, balancing the checkbook, driving to the supermarket, working in an office, and watching television.

A second circumstance that contributes to the divergence in sleep–wake scheduling is the availability of other caretakers. When the

Kipsigis mother needs to be free of the baby for some kinds of garden work or for her peace of mind, there is almost always a sibling caretaker, a co-wife, or another relative to take the child. She does not need to rely on the baby's sleeping for a chance to disengage from continuous care.

As one consequence of these differences in the infant's niche, Kipsigis babies do not sleep quite as much as American infants, and they do not develop long periods of sustained sleep so soon. At 4 months of age, the average Kipsigis baby sleeps just over 12 hours each day, compared to about 15 in America. The longest episode of sleep is about 4.5 hours, compared to 8 (Super and Harkness 1977).

The pattern of adaptation in sleep is related to adaptations in feeding, elimination, and even social interaction. In each domain the Kipsigis infant is likely to have briefer and less regular cycles of activity and rest, while the American baby is likely to have fewer, longer periods of sleeping, feeding, and playful interaction. The circadian flow of behavior has different patterns of tension and resolution in the two niches. The Kipsigis and American babies, in sum, are learning the emotional structure of their cultural niche.

The particular adaptations and embeddedness in each group are only part of the emotional structure of the niche. Of critical importance are the ways the niche can and cannot adapt to the individual characteristics of the infant, for the areas of rigidity and flexibility determine the kinds of behavior that will create upset and difficulty. For the American baby, scheduling activity by the clock may be of considerable importance to the mother because of her value system or because of her own needs. For the baby in Kokwet, adaptation to the different styles of care provided by several caretakers is essential for happy functioning of the family. Within any group, babies vary in their behavioral dispositions (Thomas and Chess 1977). Regularity and adaptability are dimensions of variation among infants in both cultures, but their significance depends on the typical niche and its points of flexibility. In both groups, a mismatch between the needs and adaptability of the baby and those of the caretaking niche results in a situation that is stressful for all concerned. The early socialization of emotional life includes learning the sensitivities of one's niche.

Long-term adaptations to the niche play another role in emotional life, namely the building of expectations concerning what constitutes normal life and what is bizarre. While infants in Kokwet, as in other communities, are often upset when their mothers leave them for short periods, this response does not last long. They become accustomed to care by several people, and so maternal absence by itself does not occasion distress. As Figure 3.2 shows, after the universal emergence of distress at separation from mother, at about 1 year of age, there is considerable diversity among cultures in its decline in the second and third years of life. For the American and !Kung San children, for example, who are cared for almost exclusively by the mother, the distress reaction remains frequent for a relatively long time. In the other groups, however, where siblings or other persons play an important role in the day-to-day care of infants and toddlers, there is a more rapid decline in the amount of distress.

Distress at maternal departure ('separation anxiety') is often linked in developmental theory to distress at the approach of a stranger ('fear of strangers'). While the common thread of cognitive competence is important in the emergence of these two responses (Kagan *et al.* 1978), the regulation of the reactions by features of daily life can lead to different patterns in later months. Many American children have a single caretaker but are exposed to a large number of strangers when they visit the doctor's office, the supermarket, and their older sibling's school. In Kokwet, the cast of characters for daily life remains stable and relatively small, despite the fact that two or three individuals are routinely involved in care. Informal observations suggest that fear of strangers is more intense and sustained for Kipsigis children than it is for Americans, even though distress at maternal departure is less so. In each case, the children are making equally successful adaptations to their social niche, minimizing distress in the long run and sensitizing the toddler to unusual situations. The important point for emotional development, however, is that the universal reactions are becoming differentially patterned into the structure of daily life, and that adaptation in the two settings leads to contrasting responses to the identical situation.

Summary

In summary, parental beliefs and values and the structure of infant care together provide a niche in which the baby develops an emotional life. Various features of the physical and social niche are integrated, in most cases, in a way that both reflects and reinforces larger aspects of the surrounding culture. In the infants' adaptations to the niche can be seen the early, culturally directed organisation of emotional behavior and the socialization of emotional displays.

DEVELOPMENTAL SEQUENCES AND CONSEQUENCES

There is a long history of speculation and inquiry in psychology concerning long-term consequences of early emotional development. Much of this work has focused on possible pathological sequelae of traumatic events or instances of extreme deprivation (Clarke and Clarke 1976); it does not address several important issues in the continuities of normal development. In the normal case there is not only a continuity of the mind but also some continuity of the environment. It becomes difficult, therefore, to disentangle psychological consequences of early experience from later environmental sequences.

The learning of emotional behaviors does not stop at 3 or 13 or 30, nor does the role of culture in patterning that learning. As the child grows older, he or she encounters a larger variety of social settings. Each setting has a typical cast of characters and scenario, each has a particular meaning and prescription for proper behavior; one way a culture socializes is in the settings it provides (Whiting 1980). The emotional differentiation of settings in early childhood is part of the culturally regulated sequence of development. Intimately related to the differentiation of settings is the way superficially similar developmental transitions can yield divergent psychological meanings depending on the preceding and surrounding experience. Very few childhood experiences are absolute in their emotional message. The emergent patterning of emotional expression across settings, and the sequence of settings across time, are probably more important for the normal socialization of affect than learning in any one situation. In this patterning and sequencing are intertwined the values, beliefs, customary practices, and ecological forces that are integrated by the culture and that are the cultural context of development (Harkess 1980).

Cultural divergence in the verbal expression of inner thoughts and feelings illustrates the importance of developmental sequences in socialization. Social interaction during infancy, as indicated earlier, is similar in Kokwet and American settings in the frequency of smiling and mutual regard (face-to-face interaction). The rate of vocalization in Kokwet, however, is only half the American rate; both the mothers and babies in Kokwet 'speak' to each other less often than those in an American sample. While the interaction appears equally warm and affectionate in the two settings, it is quieter in Kokwet.

As the children grow through the familiar sequence of crawling, walking, talking, and other milestones of development, there is a variety of skills parents can choose to encourage. Mothers in Kokwet encourage some activities that are relatively neglected by American parents (Super 1976), but they do not see themselves as having a major role in 'teaching' a child to talk. That function, it is believed, is filled by the child's siblings. Mothers' verbal interaction with 2- and 3-year-olds is not as frequent as that found in American homes and has a relatively high frequency of commands. Increasingly as the child moves into early childhood, the mother's verbal communication becomes directing, comforting, and scolding rather than eliciting of verbal reply (Harkness and Super 1977).

A particular focus of this maternal interaction is the child's initial steps toward becoming a responsible and productive member of the large household. Small tasks start early through a blend of assignment and imitation – watching that the goats or calves do not approach drying produce, carrying small cans of water, helping shell maize cobs. The father, who has had relatively little interaction with his child up to this point, joins in the affectionate responsibility for leading the child toward a maturing role in the family. It is as though the parents' traditional attitude is that children will learn to talk soon enough on their own, but they must be taught to understand requests and instructions and to obey them. The parents' goal for young children is verbal comprehension, not production.

Near the beginning of the transition from toddlerhood to early childhood, generally in the second year of life, the Kipsigis child has been weaned from the mother's breast for feeding, from her back for carrying and comforting, and from her bed for sleeping. Usually a younger sibling has appeared on the scene to take up those places. Interaction with adults actually decreases in the following few years, while siblings, half-siblings, and neighbor children become the main partners in social interaction. Children in the new social group range over several years in age, and while relations are ordered to some extent by the hierarchy of age and sex, a strong camaraderie develops. In this context the children appear as active and vocal as children anywhere, playing games, tussling on the ground, chasing a stray chicken, and swinging from the beams of a maize storehouse. While verbal aggression and precocity may not play the role in such children's groups that they do in some other cultures, there is certainly not the stricture of silence and respect found in the presence of adults.

There are two points to be made from the brief description of the social life of young children in Kokwet. First, the patterning of emotional expression in various settings is as important to affective development as is the character of expression in any one setting. Children are socialized not only into *how* they should behave, but also into how they should behave *where*.

Second, the meaning of how children should behave in different settings depends to some degree on the larger developmental sequences. The transition to early childhood in America shares some characteristics with the Kipsigis case – the pattern of interaction becomes more demanding of obedience, for example. The Kipsigis toddler, however, is already accustomed to having several important social partners to whom can be transferred some kinds of verbally expressive interaction. The meaning of the transition is affected as well by events to follow. Fewer than half of the American children witness a similar process in a younger sibling, while in Kokwet more than 80 per cent see in their own family that this process is part of everyone's life.

There is a continuing sequence of niches in childhood and maturity, and each culture has its own pattern of continuities and disconti-nuities. In some cases the thematic parallels are striking. The Amer-ican baby who is scheduled to bottle and bed is later scheduled to school bell, and still later to time card or deadline. The Kipsigis baby whose state was more personally mediated by several people must as an adult accept community mediation of disputes rather than imper-sonal and externally imposed judgments (Harkness *et al.* 1981). Nevertheless, each life stage has a variety of affective settings, and an individual draws upon the variety of past experiences to know how to feel and how to express the feeling.

CONCLUSION

The mosaic of emotional behavior expressed by people of different cultures reflects in part their past experience. It is too simple, however, to see that residue of experience only in the shape of personality as traditionally drawn by Western psychology. Any particular expression builds on the motives and the understanding of the world acquired in a long history of culturally constituted experience. The elements of expression are universally human, but they are organised, practiced, and regulated by culture. The values and settings that started the socialization process are at least thematically related to aspects of later functioning, but the patterning and shading of feeling and expression reflect the continuing process of adaptation and growth. So it is with grief, fear, excitement, and pride; so it is with walking in the dark, arguing in a bar, mourning a lost child, chasing in the hunt, and disembarking from the ocean liner in Sydney. We may not need a translator to know how the people are doing it, but we need to know where they have come from to see what they are really doing.

REFERENCES

Brazelton, T. B., Robey, J. S. and Collier, G. A. (1969) 'Infant development in the Zinacanteco Indians of southern Mexico', *Pediatrics* 44: 274–90.

Caudill, W. and Frost, L. A. (1973) 'A comparison of maternal care and infant behavior in Japanese-American, American, and Japanese families', in W. Lebra (ed.) *Mental Health Research in Asia and the Pacific*, vol. 3: *Youth, Socialization, and Mental Health*, Honolulu: University Press of Hawaii.

Caudill, W. and Weinstein, H. (1969) 'Maternal care and infant behavior in Japan and America', *Psychiatry* 32: 12–43.

Clarke, A. M. and Clarke, A. D. B. (1976) *Early Experience: Myth and Evidence*, New York: Free Press.

Freedman, D. G. (1964) 'Smiling in blind infants and the issue of innate vs. acquired', *Journal of Psychology and Psychiatry* 5: 17–184.

Harkness, S. (1980) 'The cultural context of child development', in C. M. Super and S. Harkness (eds) 'Anthropological perspectives on child development', *New Directions for Child Development* 8: 7–13.

Harkness, S. and Super, C. M. (1977) 'Why African children are so hard to test', in L. L. Adler (ed.) 'Issues in crosscultural research' *Annals of the New York Academy of Sciences* 285: 326–31; reprinted in L. L. Adler (ed.) *Issues in Cross-Cultural Research*, New York: Academic Press.

Harkness, S. and Super C. M. (1980) 'Child Development theory in anthropological perspective', in C. M. Super and S. Harkness (eds) 'Anthropological perspectives on child development', *New Directions for Child Development* 8: 1–5.

Harkness, S., Edwards, C. P. and Super, C. M. (1981) 'Social roles and moral reasoning: a case study in rural Africa', *Developmental Psychology*.

Kagan, J. (1976) 'Emergent themes in human development', *American Scientist* 64: 186–96.

Kagan, J., Kearsley, R. B. and Zelazo P. R. (1978) *Infancy: Its Place in Human Development*, Cambridge, Mass.: Harvard University Press.

Kilbride, J. E. and Kilbride, P. L. (1975) 'Sitting and smiling behavior of Baganda infants: the influence of culturally constituted experience', *Journal of Cross-Cultural Psychology* 6: 88–107.

Kilbride, P. L. and Kilbride, J. E. (1974) 'Sociocultural factors and the early manifestation of sociability behavior among Baganda infants', *Ethos* 2: 296–314.

Landau, R. (1977) 'Spontaneous and elicited smiles and vocalizations of infants in four Israeli environments', *Developmental Psychology* 13: 389–400.

LeVine, R. A. (1980) 'Anthropology and child development', in C. M. Super and S. Harkness (eds) 'Anthropological perspectives on child development', *New Directions for Child Development* 8: 71-86.

Manners, R. A. (1969) 'The Kipsigis of Kenya: culture change in a "model" East African tribe', in J. H. Steward (ed.) *Three African Tribes in Transition*, Urbana, Ill.: University of Illinois Press.

McGraw, M. B. (1946) 'Maturation of behavior', in L. Carmichael (ed.) *Manual of Child Psychology*, New York: Wiley.

Nash, J. (1970) *Developmental Psychology: A Psychobiological Approach*, Englewood Cliffs, N.J.: Prentice-Hall.

Parmalee, A. H., Jr. (1955) 'The developmental evaluation of the blind premature infant', *Journal of Diseases of Children* 90: 135-40.

Piaget, J. (1952) *The Origins of Intelligence in Children*, New York: International University Press.

Spitz, R. A., Emde, R. N. and Metcalf, D. R. (1970) 'Further prototypes of ego formation: a working paper from a research project on early development', *Psychoanalytic Study of the Child* 25: 417-41.

Spock, B. (1968) *Baby and Child Care*, New York: Pocket Books.

Super, C. M. (1976) 'Environmental influences on motor development: the case of "African infant precocity" ', *Developmental Medicine and Child Neurology* 18: 561-7.

Super, C. M. (1981) 'Behavioral development in infancy', in R. L. Munroe, R. H. Munroe, and B. B. Whiting (eds) *Handbook of Cross-Cultural Human Development*, New York: Garland Press.

Super, C. M. and Harkness, S., (1977) 'The infant's niche in rural Kenya and metropolitan America', in L. L. Adler (ed.) *Issues in Cross-Cultural Research*, New York: Academic Press.

Sutton, J. E. G. (1968) 'The settlement of East Africa', in B. A. Ogot (ed.) *Zamarii: A survey of East African History*, Nairobi, Kenya: East African Publishing House & Longman Group.

Thomas, A. and Chess, S. (1977) *Temperament and Development*, New York: Brunner Mazel.

Weisner, T. S. and Gallimore, R. (1977) 'My brother's keeper: child and sibling caretaking', *Current Anthropology* 18: 169-80.

Whiting, B. B. (1980) 'Culture and social behavior: a model for the development of social behavior', *Ethos* 8: 95-116.

Whiting, B. B. and Whiting, J. W. M. (1975) *Children of Six Cultures: A Psycho-Cultural Analysis*, Cambridge, Mass.: Harvard University Press.

Whiting, J. W. M. (1971) 'Causes and consequences of the amount of body contact between mother and infant', paper presented at meeting of the American Anthropological Association, New York, 18 November.

Yakovlev, P. I. and Lecours, A. (1967) 'The myelogenetic cycles of regional maturation of the brain', in A. Minkowski (ed.) *Regional Development of the Brain in Early Life*, Oxford: Blackwell.

4 The father's role in the neonatal period

David G. White and E. Anne Woollett

Source: Harvey, D. (1987) *Parent–Infant Relations*, New York: Wiley, pp. 33–56.

Until recently the role of fathers in the development of preschool children has been largely ignored. This is now changing and fathers are thought to be more involved in child rearing and to make an important contribution to their development. There are three areas of research that have been instrumental in focusing attention on fathers and on their role. One such area has been the psychological investigation of the impact of fathers in the development of their children. This work arose largely from investigations of attachment relations of infants to their parents, but particularly to their mothers. The investigation of fathers as attachment figures started slowly with the work of Schaffer and Emerson (1964), but built up momentum in the 1970s (Lamb 1982). With the recognition that fathers had an important role to play in the infant's social and emotional development, interest spread to the investigation of other potential paternal roles. These included fathers' role in the development of their offsprings' curiosity, exploratory behaviour, intellectual skills, social skills, emotional stability, sex-related behaviors and language development (Lamb 1981; Parke 1981).

A second area of research that has helped to focus attention on the role of fathers has been investigations of the transitions to parenthood. This research area considers the adjustment that men and women have to make as they become parents and spans the boundary between psychology and sociology. Thus it looks at the stresses, attitude changes and role changes associated with pregnancy, birth and the early weeks of parenthood for both women and men (Beail 1982; Entwisle and Doering 1981; Parke 1981). From these investigations it is clear that there are wide variations in the nature and extent of men's participation in child development and these are determined in part by their preparation for parenthood, their experiences during pregnancy and at birth, and on the balance they make between themselves and the mothers.

A third research area to focus attention on fathers is that of bonding, which owes much to the work of paediatricians especially Klaus and Kennell (see, for example, Kennell *et al.* 1979). Bonding was viewed initially as a rapid process, occurring within a sensitive period shortly after birth, during which mothers become attached and committed to their infants. More recently a similar process has been postulated for fathers (McDonald 1978; Sasmor 1979). An underlying assumption of the notion of bonding is that parental involvement is fragile and unless optimal conditions are encountered parenting behaviours will be undermined. We discuss these assumptions later.

The work that has arisen from these three areas of research has focused attention on fathers and on their roles. It has also pointed out differences between fathers in their involvement and in the roles they fill. As a result attempts have been made to identify the factors associated with these variations in paternal involvement and in their child-directed behavior. The transition to fatherhood studies and the bonding studies focus attention on one set of factors – the potential importance of early father–child encounters as a determinant of fathers' involvement and behavior. In this chapter we examine this area and consider the role of fathers in the neonatal period, and how they typically interact with their newborn babies in the early hours, days and weeks of life. We consider the implications of these interactions for the development of the infant. Some variables that modify fathers' infant-directed behavior are discussed. Finally, we examine some of the theoretical assumptions that underlie this work.

WHAT FATHERS DO WITH THEIR INFANTS IN THE FIRST WEEKS

Information about what fathers do with their children in the first weeks comes from two sources. One source of information is questionnaires and interviews of parents about their experiences of childbirth and rearing, with these often looking at historical changes. The second source is direct observations of fathers with their newborn babies, both in the maternity hospital and at home. The technique of direct observation is most frequently employed to investigate fathers of children aged 3 months and above; it has been used less for younger infants because of the problems of recruiting fathers.

It is clear from the questionnaire and interview data that ideas about fathers' roles are changing. Compared to a decade ago mothers, fathers and others today have greater expectations of fathers' involvement with their young children (Beail and McGuire 1982). But what is the extent of such involvement? In a survey reported by Woollett *et al.* (1982) of child-rearing practices in the period 1940 to 1980 it was found that mothers perceived fathers as being relatively unavailable in the 1940s, but as being more available from the 1950s, with only relatively small increases in the 1960s and 1970s. Thus they find evidence of only a slight increase over the last 40 years in the time fathers spent with their children. However, the same survey shows that, over the 40-year period, mothers report that fathers were taking an increasingly active part in their children's care. This heightened involvement shows itself in fathers' increased willingness to look after their children, to play with them, to bath them, to change them and to put them to bed.

Even though fathers are more willing to get involved with their young children, studies comparing mothers and fathers indicate quite clearly that the extent of father involvement is limited and small compared with mothers. So, for instance, Fein (1976) interviewed 32 first-time fathers 6 weeks after the birth. At that time only 59 per cent reported that they regularly took responsibility for infant care and only one father claimed to do as much as the mother. Mothers still retain primary responsibility for child care and what fathers do is considered by them, and by mothers, as help (La Rossa and La Rossa 1981; Oakley 1979). Moreover, when fathers engage in caretaking activities they chose to do the clean, easy jobs (e.g. fetching drinks and putting to bed) and avoid the dirty jobs, especially feeding and nappy changing (Oakley 1979; Richards *et al.* 1977; Robinson 1977). These are not only clean, easy jobs, but are activities that in contrast to mother's child-directed activities demand little attention, occupy little time and can be fitted in with other activities (Robinson 1977).

Because most of the information about how fathers behave with their young children comes from interviews and diaries it inevitably focuses on relatively major child-directed activities, e.g. playing, feeding, washing, changing, putting to bed and going on outings – i.e. on clearly definable events. The assumption is then made that these episodes are the most important episodes for defining paternal role in child development. However, this assumption could well be wrong, for while these episodes are important for both the young child and their parents and allow for rich interactional exchanges to occur, very large numbers of equally important interactional exchanges occur outside these settings. These other interactive exchanges can go undetected by using interviews, but are detected more readily by direct observations of fathers' behavior with their infants. The behavior that these observational studies have chosen to measure most frequently are holding, touching and vocalizing.

Studies of parental holding suggest that most fathers engage in it from the earliest opportunity. Thus Packer and Rosenblatt (1979) observed many deliveries in one British hospital and noted that 50 per cent of fathers held their newborns in the delivery room, while Woollett *et al.* (1982) observed a 66 per cent holding rate in a different British hospital. Interestingly, these high levels of holding are not only found for straightforward deliveries but also for more complicated births. Thus in a continuing British study of parents of twins, mothers have reported that 56 per cent of fathers held their babies in the hour after birth (Clegg 1982). Clegg interviewed mothers 2 or 3 days after birth. Many of these births involved a lot of medical attention and most of the babies were small.

In an American study of fathers, Parke and O'Leary (1976) report that during hospital visits in the first 3 days, fathers held for an average of 56 per cent of the observation periods when mothers were present and 65 per cent of the periods when they were on their own. Bowen and Miller (1980) reported 52 per cent holding from 12 to 72 hours after birth. In another study, again of British fathers, Richards *et al.* (1977) report that fathers hold a great deal in the first ten days of life, but they give no further details. Studies using questionnaires and interviews find similar holding rates to those reported on the basis of observational studies (Entwisle and Doering 1981; Jones 1981).

There is evidence, therefore, from both types of studies that when they are with their babies fathers hold them a great deal and for similar periods of time as mothers (Parke and O'Leary 1976; White and Woollett 1981).

It has often been argued that holding is an important parenting behavior and is directly associated with the development of a number of skills in the child (Ainsworth *et al.* 1974; Yarrow *et al.* 1975). Thus, babies who are held form stronger attachments than those who are not. It has also been claimed that babies who are held develop cognitive and social-skills more rapidly. However, holding is also important because if provides the opportunity for the occurrence of other parental behavior which are themselves important for the babies' development. Lamb (1977) claimed that parents hold their babies for a number of reasons; he observed five different things that parents did when they held their babies. They held their babies: to engage in various caretaking activities including feeding; to soothe and comfort them when they were distressed; as an overt sign of affection, by cuddling them close; as part of a play routine, normally vigorous play; to control them or discipline them when they got out of hand. Clearly, these are all important behavior. White *et al.* (1982) have also pointed out that holding may be important because of the ways in which both parents and babies behave during holding periods. They suggest that the position in which a baby is held determines the sorts of interactions that then occur. Thus, when babies are held in positions that allow for face-to-face contact between themselves and the holding parent this helps social exchanges between the two and consequently is important for social development and language. This particular hold position has been discussed by de Château and Wiberg (1977), Kennell *et al.* (1979) and Rodhölm (1981). Because it does allow for rich interactional exchange they all write about the hold as an index of parental involvement and attachment. Another of the hold positions discussed by White *et al.* (1982) allows both the baby and parent to watch whatever is happening around them. During this, parents tend to label objects that have caught the baby's eye (Collis and Schaffer 1975) and to talk about them. This is an important process for the development of language and for the development of the child's curiosity. This hold is also used when there are other people present, so the parent is often labelling the social world. White *et al.* suggest that this hold is important for the development of triadic interactions and for broadening the range of the baby's social interactions.

Turning now to touching, there are a number of studies that report that from their first contact with their infants, fathers engage in a great deal of touching. In one such study, conducted by McDonald (1978), seven fathers who had assisted at the birth of their infants were observed interacting with them for the first nine minutes. Parents were on their own with the newborns and mothers held the newborns for all of the time. There was an initial burst of activity from the father with a great deal of intense behavior particularly touching the newborn, which occurred for 33 per cent of the observation period. All fathers went through a similar sequence of touching; at first hands and feet were touched with the fingertips and then later with the whole hand. Only later did the touching extend to the body and finally to the face.

In another study of fathers, conducted in Sweden, Rodhölm and Larsson (1979) observed 15 initial father–newborn interactions with infants delivered by Caesarian section. The infants were brought to their fathers when they were 15 minutes old, placed on a table and then the fathers were left alone with their own newborns for 10 minutes. Their behavior was recorded by a remote-control camera. All the fathers touched their newborn during the 10-minute observation period. They spent over 70 per cent of the time touching. Again the sequence of touching was highly predictable, starting with the extremities and proceeding to the trunk, the head and finally the face. One study which does not report this highly predictable routine of touching is that of White and Woollett (1981). In that case there were large individual differences reported in the sequence of touching and in the amount. Overall there was less touching of hands and feet than has been reported elsewhere. However, this is a British study and the parents were given their baby immediately after birth, during delivery of the placenta and while suturing took place. Typically the newborns were tightly wrapped. The differences between their results and those of previous studies may reflect the difference in the situation in which parents first encountered their newborns.

High levels of touching are also reported somewhat later when fathers were observed with their infants a few days after birth. Thus Bowen and Miller (1980) reported that fathers touched their babies 32 per cent of the time when they were observed at 12–72 hours of age. At a similar time Parke and O'Leary (1976) also recorded 32 per cent touching when fathers were with mothers and 44 per cent when they were alone. In another study, this time of fathers with their babies from 2 weeks onwards in a play setting, fathers touched 44 per cent of the time (Yogman *et al.* 1977).

In summary, when fathers are with their young babies they touch them a great deal; indeed most studies report somewhat more touching by fathers than by mothers (Parke and O'Leary 1976; White and Woollett 1981; Yogman *et al.* 1977). There is little evidence available, but it seems that touching by itself is not associated with the development of any specific skills of the part of the child (Yarrow *et al.* 1975), but it does perhaps indicate fathers' active involvement with their neonates.

Fathers' vocalizing to their young infants is another important behavior, but it has been studied less than either holding or touching. Clegg (1982) reports that in the first hour of life, half of the fathers of twins talked to their newborns. However, White and Woollett's (1981) observations suggest that in the earliest moments, while most fathers talk to some extent to their babies, they do not say very much to them (only 9 per cent of their comments were to the babies). However, they talked about their babies a great deal and indeed the newborn was the major topic of their conversation (45 per cent of their comments were about the baby).

Later, between 12 and 72 hours, talking appears to have increased; thus Bowen and Miller (1980) reported that fathers' talking to the newborn occurred for 45 per cent of the time. Parke and O'Leary

(1976) reported that fathers talked for 22 per cent of the time when mothers were present and this increased to 32 per cent in their absence. The studies that compared mothers' and fathers' vocalizations (Parke and O'Leary 1976; White and Woollett 1981) suggest that they vocalize to similar extents. Early vocalizing to infants is an important parental behavior. Infants are sensitive to and interested in human sounds and their parents' voices quickly come to attract their attention (Condon and Sandler 1974; Trevarthen 1979). In their turn, parents' language to their infants is modified; it is short, well structured and focuses on objects and events of importance to the infant. Parents also appear to time their language carefully, fitting in what they have to say with the infants' readiness to listen (Collis 1979; Schaffer 1977; Stern 1977). It is assumed that this kind of language situation provides a good context in which infants can learn the relevance and meanings of sound systems in language. It is also a good context for infants to learn to take their turns and to synchronize their behavior with that of others – both essential skills for human social interaction and language in particular. There is some evidence that children's early language contexts are associated with later language development and with later social responsivity (Elliott 1981; Snow and Ferguson 1977; Yarrow *et al.* 1975), but studies which have followed up the language development of children from the early months are rare.

Other behavior recorded in the observational studies have been smiling (Bowen and Miller 1980; Parke and O'Leary 1976; White and Woollett 1981), rocking (Parke and O'Leary 1976; White and Woollett 1981), looking (Bowen and Miller 1980; Parke and O'Leary 1976; White and Woollett 1981), imitation and feeding (Parke and O'Leary 1976). Of these behavior, only rocking has been related to the course of later development. It is claimed that rocking is associated with widespread developmental gains (Yarrow *et al.* 1975). The figures for rocking that have been observed when mothers were present are 10 per cent of time immediately after birth (White and Woollett 1981) and 11 per cent in the first three days (Parke and O'Leary 1976). However, when fathers were observed on their own, rocking increased to 34 per cent (Parke and O'Leary 1976). Both studies found fathers engaged in more rocking than mothers.

Thus, typical fathers do interact with their babies in the first weeks of life. They help with caretaking jobs although they concentrate on the clean, easy jobs such as fetching drinks and putting to bed. In some cases fathers cannot do other jobs because they are excluded by the mother. This is discussed in the next section. In addition to caretaking, fathers are willing to interact actively with their babies when they are available in the home. Thus they talk to their babies, hold them, rock them and touch them a good deal. This is the overall pattern to emerge, but obviously there are large variations from father to father. So, for instance, Woollett *et al.* (1982) and Clegg (1982) report that while nearly two-thirds of fathers held their babies immediately after birth up to a third did not. In addition there were large variations in the behavior of holding fathers. Some held for long periods, others for short periods. Some talked to the baby, rocked it and looked intensely at it, while others ignored the baby, and some took the opportunity to touch their babies while others did not.

Studies of the transition to fatherhood make it quite clear that most fathers do little to prepare themselves for parenthood other than to worry about money and their partners' health (Lewis 1980). Thus, the majority of fathers do not attend parents' evenings or childbirth classes (Lewis found that only 23 per cent attended classes). The majority do not read books and they do not take the opportunity of practising caretaking skills. Nor do they consider their changing role after the delivery. Most fathers assume that if they need to know anything mothers will tell them; therefore the majority take no active steps to become informed. Their only source of information beyond their partners is television (Lewis 1980; McKee 1980).

Those fathers who are better informed, who attend childbirth classes, read books, or practise on friends' babies might be expected to develop different roles with their own babies from unprepared fathers. However, surprisingly, few studies have addressed themselves to this issue. One study that considers whether fathers who attend classes behave differently with their children is that of Bowen and Miller (1980). They claimed that fathers who had attended childbirth classes vocalized to, looked at and smiled at their babies more than non-attending fathers during the first three days of life. However, in a later report they suggest that presence or absence at delivery outweighs the effects of parenthood classes (Miller and Bowen 1982).

Other studies show that better prepared fathers have more realistic assessments of their changing roles after birth and anticipate adjustment problems (Fein 1976; Wente and Crockenberg 1976). However, Wente and Crockenberg suggest that anticipating the changing roles does not help them to adjust to those changes. Indeed Fein makes the point that the realities of the division of parenting duties are often different from what either parent had anticipated before the delivery and in particular some fathers who had anticipated being highly involved report feeling excluded from participating. Some feel excluded because the mother imposes traditional marital roles on the couple. Because mothers assume the major responsibility for child care, they and fathers may come to see fathers as incompetent and so not encourage them to do things for the infant. Mothers who breastfeed may argue that it makes more sense for them to perform all the other tasks that go on around feeding, such as nappy changing and playing with the infant. The routines parents set up can mean that shared care is not as practicable as parents anticipated. Work constraints may also prevent fathers from participating as actively as they had planned. Because the birth of the first child is normally accompanied by the loss of the mother's income, first-time fathers, especially, may feel themselves under great pressure to work overtime or to further their careers. However, with later births, fathers may also find their participation in child care different from what they had anticipated. Some second-time fathers anticipate being as active in the care of a second child as they were with a first, but in fact find that they become more heavily involved in the care of the older child and leave most of the care of the second child to the mother (Grossman *et al.* 1980; Lamb, 1978). One aspect of preparation for parenthood can be to set up expectations which lead to disappointment if they are not met.

Preparation of another sort is sometimes given to fathers in the hospital after delivery. Some men are provided with training in hospital for simple caretaking chores, such as nappy changing and bathing. Lind (1974) has examined the effects of this sort of training on fathers' later involvement with their infants. He claimed that at three months such fathers spent more time with their children and engaged in more caretaking activities. Parke *et al.* (1980) found similar results when fathers of infants aged 3 days were shown a film that illustrated aspects of infant competence as well as basic caretaking skills.

Thus, although there is not a great deal of evidence, parenthood classes do not appear to have any major impact on the child-directed activities of fathers who attend. Training which is more directed towards helping fathers to provide everyday care for their infants and which considers the characteristics of young infants would probably be better.

Presence at delivery

Fathers are present at delivery more and more often. It is thought by many that this experience will influence their subsequent roles.

Although hospitals do not keep official records of fathers' presence at birth, information comes from interview, survey and observational data. In the United States, these studies suggest that fathers were present at 27 per cent of deliveries in 1972, but at 80 per cent in 1980 (Parke 1981). Studies in Britain suggest a similar trend; thus Woollett *et al.* (1982) reported a shift from 15 per cent fathers' presence up to 1970, to 71 per cent presence after. It is not altogether clear how many of these fathers actually witnessed the birth. Some recent studies give information on this: Boyd and Sellars (1982), on the basis of questionnaire data, reported that in 1981, 92 per cent of fathers were present during labour and 61 per cent witnessed the birth. For 1979 deliveries, White and Woollett (1981) reported 69 per cent present at the birth and 91 per cent present immediately afterwards. In her study of twin births in 1981 Clegg (1982) found that 69 per cent of fathers were present at birth and 88 per cent were present within a very few minutes. It is encouraging to see fathers present at such a high proportion of even highly medicalized births. Although at one time it appeared that middle-class fathers were more likely to be present at birth (Cartwright 1979), this is no longer so clearly the case (Entwisle and Doering 1981), but in other respects attending fathers still have different characteristics from non-attending fathers.

The medical profession is keen to see fathers present at delivery because they assume that there are long-term benefits associated with the experience. The possibility of such long-term benefits is an issue which has frequently been considered at a theoretical level. Indeed, this is the issue concerning fathers in the neonatal period that has generated most empirical studies. The majority of such studies, however, look only for very short-term effects of fathers' presence at delivery.

Most studies suggest there is at least some short-term increase in fathers' involvement with their newborns if they witness the delivery. Thus Bowen and Miller (1980) and Miller and Bowen (1982) observed fathers 12–72 hours after delivery. Fathers who were present at delivery looked, talked and smiled more at their newborns than fathers who missed the delivery. Greenberg and Morris (1974) report, on the basis of questionnaires completed by fathers between 48 and 72 hours of delivery, that fathers who were present at birth felt more comfortable holding their babies than absent fathers, but on other measures no differences were found. Another study, also using questionnaires, this time administered immediately after delivery, failed to detect any differences between attending and non-attending fathers in their feelings about the newborn baby (Cronenwett and Newmark 1974). However, being present at delivery did have an effect because this study showed that attending fathers felt more positively about the birth, about their wives and about their own role at the time. In contrast, Parke and O'Leary (1976) have conducted two studies looking at early father–child interactions. In the first study, fathers were middle class, had attended childbirth classes, were present at delivery and 68 per cent of the infants were breastfed, whereas in the second study, the fathers were lower class, had not attended childbirth classes, were not present at delivery and none of the infants were breastfed. What is noticeable about these two studies is the similarity of fathers' behavior despite their different characteristics. This study suggests that what is important for fathers is having the opportunity to interact with the child, the precise timing of the encounter being unimportant.

A little later, there are still effects of fathers' presence at delivery. Jones (1981) gave fathers questionnaires at 24–72 hours and again at 1 month. At 1 month, fathers were also observed with their infants. Like Cronenwett and Newmark, Jones found in the hours shortly after birth no differences in the expectations of attending and non-attending fathers about any future difficulty of caring for their child. However, at 1 month fathers with contact at birth were observed to interact more with the infants in terms of eye-to-eye contact, smiling, touching, kissing, cuddling, rocking and holding. Another study to use repeated questionnaires is that of Manion (1977). Questionnaires were completed by fathers shortly after delivery and again at 6 weeks. There was a significant and positive correlation between fathers' participation at the birth and their subsequent involvement in caretaking. Entwisle and Doering (1981) also reported on the impact of fathers' presence at birth and their later parenting behavior. Fathers were interviewed between 4 and 8 weeks after birth and those fathers who reported being present at birth also reported doing more for their infants, doing jobs such as changing nappies and being more involved with their infants. Finally, Cordell *et al.* (1980) interviewed fathers when their infants were 3 months old. At that time fathers who attended delivery listed more aspects of the fathers' role than non-attending fathers.

Most of the above studies report a correlation between presence at delivery and later involvement with their infants. However, fathers who choose to be present at delivery tend to have slightly different characteristics from those who choose not to be present. Attending fathers are more likely to be better educated, to be of higher socio-economic status and to have come themselves from smaller families, although the differences are not large (Bowen and Miller 1980). Consequently, fathers who are present at birth may also be more involved in other ways with their infants as a function of their general backgrounds and not because of their presence at birth. Being present at birth may be merely one indicator of this general level of involvement. One study which supports this notion is that of Entwisle and Doering (1981). They interviewed fathers, some of whom were present at birth, others who wanted to be present but were excluded by medical staff and those who were absent by their own choice. Fathers who wanted to be present but who were excluded showed even more signs of later involvement than fathers who were present; both showed considerably more involvement than fathers who were absent by choice. These results suggest that it is the fathers' intention to play an active role which ensures their later involvement as well as their presence in the delivery room. However, another factor which needs to be considered is that of expectations. Whether presence at the delivery is crucial or not may be less important than whether parents and hospitals consider it to be so. If parents think fathers' presence is important and then they are denied it because of hospital procedures or because of conflicting ideas held by doctors then they may believe that they cannot make a good relationship with their child. Thus, to understand the effects of fathers' presence at delivery we have also to know how their presence is understood by parents. For the father who is expecting to be present and who believes that his presence is important for the mother and for himself, being denied access to the delivery has different meanings and possibly different consequences than for the father who has no such beliefs or expectations. This more detailed type of analysis taking into account parental expectations has yet to be undertaken.

It would seem that presence at delivery *per se* does not ensure the future involvement of fathers, but there is some evidence that fathers' initial reactions to their newborn babies are important.

Experiences during labour and delivery

The experiences of fathers during labour and delivery vary considerably. At any one time, a father may express different and sometimes quite contradictory feelings from those he expressed earlier.

The arrival and reception at the maternity hospital or labour ward is for many an unpleasant experience. Mothers and fathers are separated at this time as mothers are prepared for the delivery. Many fathers are unprepared for this, have little notion of what is happening and so feel resentful. McKee (1980), for instance, described 38 per cent of her sample as having experienced a mixture of loneliness, confusion, anxiety, boredom and annoyance. Richman and Goldthorp (1978) refer to this as entrance trauma. One common experience of fathers during labour, and to a lesser extent during delivery, is that they feel anxious. This anxiety is associated particularly with the sight of their wives in pain, with being asked to leave while medical procedures were carried out and with being ejected from the delivery room when they had planned to stay. This anxiety is present in both those fathers who attended childbirth classes and those who did not, but is most intense in the non-prepared fathers (Gayton, reported by Beail 1982). The variation in fathers' experiences during labour and delivery are illustrated in one recent British study (Brown 1980): 10 per cent of fathers said they would rather be somewhere else, 33 per cent reported feeling stressed, but 29 per cent felt they were contributing in an important way. Other studies also report a range of different paternal experiences (Brown 1982; McKee 1980; Richman and Goldthorp 1978).

Frequently fathers express ambivalent attitudes to labour and delivery. For instance, Drähne *et al.* (1979) interviewed fathers 5 or 6 days after the delivery. Half felt tense and unsure during the first stage of labour, but this dropped to a quarter during the second stage. However, those same fathers expressed feelings of excitement and pride. More dramatically, McKee (1980) reports that the majority of the fathers she interviewed felt superfluous and redundant throughout the labour and delivery yet claimed to be of great value to their partners, offering support and companionship. Despite these ambivalent attitudes the majority of fathers would elect to be present for the next birth (Entwisle and Doering 1981; Richman *et al.* 1975). Indeed, having survived the anxieties of labour and delivery the immediate aftermath of the birth is often very positive. Some fathers now do expect a strong emotional experience and when interviewed give it as a reason for being present at birth. Of the fathers interviewed in one study 95 per cent were enthusiastic about being present (Entwisle and Doering 1981). A typical report was 'and it was a very personal and very sharing thing. For me it was extremely important. I wasn't afraid of blood or being shocked – it was an emotional thing. Indescribable.' When asked how they felt when they first knew the baby was born, 23 per cent of fathers who were present at the birth reported a peak emotional experience. None of the fathers who were not present described their reaction in this way. Moreover, mothers' ratings of absent fathers' feelings about the birth tend to underrate just how negatively fathers felt about their absence. There was no social class differences in the way men rated their feelings.

Other studies also report on fathers' positive experiences (Greenberg and Morris 1974; Oakley 1979). Oakley found that 74 per cent of fathers who stayed for the delivery were pleased that they had done so, although most agreed that it had been more of an experience than they had bargained for. Birth is literally shocking both for mothers and fathers. It is physically wearing, emotionally draining, impossible to grasp. Everyday behavior and feelings are breeched. 'When it came out, once its head was out, and it starting looking like this (this is, pink and human), this great emotional thing suddenly happened to me. I had this feeling welling up inside me. I can't put it into words. Tearful, I suppose.'

Greenberg and Morris (1974) talk about fathers as being engrossed and as feeling 'stunned, stoned, drunk, dazed, off the ground, full of energy, feeling ten feet tall, feeling different, abnormal, taken away, taken out of yourself'. Fathers also said that the birth gave them a feeling of increased self-esteem. They felt proud, bigger, more mature and older after seeing their infant for the first time. Babies make women out of girls, but for fathers, too, birth may be associated with increased social esteem and acknowledgement of their new status.

Another thing that Greenberg and Morris discuss is fathers' child-centredness; that is they felt a great interest and involvement with the newborns. Twenty-nine of the 30 fathers rated their paternal feelings as average to high; 20 said they first felt the infant was theirs immediately after birth; and 27 claimed to be able to distinguish their newborn from others. Observational studies of fathers at birth also reveal a newborn-centred response in many fathers, although they demonstrate considerable variability in this respect. Packer and Rosenblatt (1979) rated half of the fathers they observed as highly involved in that they interacted intensely with their newborn. Woollett *et al.* (1982) made similar observations: half of their fathers, all fathers of sons, were highly newborn-centred in their behavior. This revealed itself in terms of behavior such as holding the newborn for long periods, intense looking and the ignoring of comments or signs of pain and distress from the mothers. This type of infant-centredness can be very distressing for mothers as Greenberg and Morris note: 'One of the wives became angered because her husband seemed to ignore her on his visits to the hospital, spending all of his time looking at the child.' They then suggest that it is fathers who are least well prepared who are overwhelmed in this way and that good preparation minimizes it.

The expectations and experiences of fathers during labour and delivery vary considerably. These variations influence fathers' initial reactions to their newborns and they may well have long-term consequences. Only three studies provide any information about this issue. The first study by Peterson *et al.* (1979) looked at a group of 46 fathers during pregnancy, at labour and delivery, and then followed them up for the next 6 months. They obtained data prenatally on fathers' expectations of their future involvement with their infants and how they expected to react at the birth. Then they were observed at delivery and their actual reactions noted. At the same time they were interviewed about their birth experiences. Subsequently they were observed up to 6 months interacting with their infants and were interviewed about their sense of involvement and their participation in caretaking activities. They found that the best predictor of fathers' later involvement with their infants was their experience at birth. In a similar vein Manion (1977), using interview data, found a relationship between fathers' experience during labour and later involvement. Those fathers who rated themselves as participating most in the birth event were most active in caretaking up to 6 weeks. This study was based on 45 fathers.

The third study is based on a smaller number of 29 fathers (Woollett *et al.* 1982); the authors observed the initial interactions of fathers with their newborn babies in the first 20 minutes of life. Nineteen of the fathers were observed subsequently with their children up to 18 months. At birth three paternal behavior showed quite considerable variation. These were: the length of time fathers remained in the delivery room; the length of time fathers held their newborns; and the number of comments fathers directed to their newborns. These behavior were predictive of the amount of involvement of fathers with their daughters at 18 months. They were not predictive, though, of fathers' involvement with their sons. This sex difference is discussed in greater detail below, but in general fathers of boys show an elation at birth that is not necessarily predictive of their later involvement and indeed masks their likely parenting style.

These three studies show that fathers' reactions at birth are predictive of their later child-directed behavior. They do not necessarily show a causal link, although the study by Peterson *et al.* (1979) implies such a link. The relationship could exist because fathers who are likely to get involved with their children after birth are those who are also involved with them at birth. However, if this were the case it would also be expected that those fathers would anticipate being involved before the birth too. Some fathers who anticipate being involved prenatally were uninvolved at birth and beyond. Equally others who did not anticipate being involved became involved at birth and remained so. This suggests that the birth experience itself may have some effect. However, it would be wrong to overstress the importance of the fathers' birth experiences. The three studies show a partial relationship between birth experiences and later paternal involvement. They do not show that later paternal involvement can be predicted from knowledge of fathers' birth experiences; it is merely one of several predictors of their involvement. This is emphasized by the absence of a relationship between the experiences of fathers who had sons and their later involvement. In those cases fathers' high levels of involvement at birth are quickly modified by their subsequent experiences of the realities of acting as fathers of sons.

Another type of study suggesting that experiences around birth have an impact are the studies where some parents have more contact with the newborn immediately or shortly after birth than do others. Differences are then sought in the behavior of the two groups of parents. Although these studies are most commonly conducted on mothers (de Château and Wibert 1977; Kennell, Voos and Klaus 1979; Whitten 1977), the same technique has been tried out on fathers. Only one study has looked at the effect of extra contact immediately after birth. Rodhölm (1981) in a Swedish study looked at full-term babies who had been born by Caesarian section. These babies were placed routinely in an incubator for 24 hours for monitoring. One group of fathers, the contact group, were allowed to spend 10 minutes with their babies within 15 minutes of delivery before the baby was taken to an incubator. The other group of fathers, the no-contact group, did not have this brief early contact. Three months later fathers were observed in their homes playing with their babies. At this time the no-contact fathers were more likely to hold their babies in a position that did not allow for face-to-face contact and they engaged in less affectionate touching. As measured by these two behavior, the experiences of fathers at birth had an effect later. However, many other behavior (such as vocalizing or amount of holding) showed no differences between the two groups. Once again it can be seen that experiences at birth can have an effect on fathers' later child-directed behavior but that other experiences are important too.

Some bonding theorists claim that skin-to-skin contact between the parent and the newborn facilitates bonding (Hales *et al.* 1977; Klaus and Kennell 1976; Lozoff *et al.* 1977; Packer and Rosenblatt 1979). If this is so then the decision taken by fathers to hold their newborns immediately after birth may be important (Packer and Rosenblatt 1979). One study has looked particularly at this (Jones 1981). Fathers all spent time with their babies in the first hour of life: some held during that period, some did not. One month later fathers completed questionnaires and were observed in their homes interacting with their infants. The fathers who held at birth engaged in more non-verbal contact at one month, including eye-to-eye contact, smiling, touching, holding, kissing. Further support for the notion that holding is an important activity at birth comes from the Woollett *et al.* (1982) study in which length of holding at birth was predictive of the behavior of fathers of girls at 18 months. However, holding at birth accounts for only some of the variance in later paternal behavior. Jones (1981) and others have shown that features of the baby are also important; this is discussed in the next section.

Characteristics of the newborn

Newborns are not all the same; right from the start babies differ one from another in their behavior and characteristics. Perhaps the father responds to the behavior and characteristics of the baby; the variability in fathers' behavior might be a partial reflection of variability in the newborn. Newborn babies differ in a number of ways which have meaning for parents, and hence affect their initial reactions. These include sex, state and temperament.

A number of studies have revealed a preference among expectant fathers for sons (Hoffman 1977; Liebenberg 1967; Manion 1977; Oakley 1979), although this depends in part on the existing composition of the family (Hoffman 1977). In view of this clear preference it is surprising that most studies claim that at birth fathers are equally satisfied with a son or a daughter and treat the two similarly (Entwisle and Doering 1981; Greenberg and Morris 1974). However, a closer analysis of fathers' behavior reveals sex differences at birth and later in fathers' behavior to sons and to daughters.

Rubin, Provenzano and Luria (1974) asked fathers to describe their infants' behavior at 24 hours after birth. The babies were all similar in length, weight and Apgar scores, but girls and boys were described differently. Daughters were rated as soft, fine features, awkward, weak and delicate whereas sons were rated as firm, large featured, well coordinated, strong, hard and alert. These differing perceptions apparently affect fathers' behavior, as is shown by Parke and O'Leary (1976). They observed mothers and fathers interacting with their young infants between 6 and 48 hours after delivery, when there were no medical staff present. Fathers' behavior at this time varied according to the sex and birth order of the infants. First-born sons were touched and talked to more than first-born daughters and second-born sons and daughters. Mothers' behavior differed less as a function of the infants' sex and birth order. When fathers were absent, mothers touched and talked to first-born daughters more than first-born sons. However, these differences disappeared when fathers were present.

Parke and O'Leary found that fathers' reaction to their young babies was partly determined by their sex. However, these fathers were observed up to 48 hours after birth and therefore had had some time to adjust to the knowledge of their offsprings' gender. Woollett *et al.* (1982) were interested to see if fathers would respond differently to sons and daughters at birth when they had only just learned of their babies' gender. Twenty of the families observed gave birth to sons and nine to daughters. On three of the measures used fathers showed more signs of involvement with their newborn sons. They stayed longer in the delivery room; on average they stayed for an extra 3½ minutes. They held sons considerably longer than they held daughters, and they talked much more to their sons. Fathers directed six times as many comments towards sons as towards daughters. Many of these comments referred to the newborns' sex, e.g. father to sons, 'Hello little fellow, you're here now' or 'That's it, let the world know you're here mate', and fathers to daughters, 'thought you'd be a girl, you've been so obstinate'. In general mothers responded in similar ways to their sons and daughters. When fathers were present, however, mothers made more comments about their daughters than they did when fathers were absent. This did not happen with mothers of sons.

What Woollett *et al.* reported is a positive reaction of fathers to sons, but signs of disappointment if they have fathered daughters. It is fathers of boys whose behavior showed the exaggerated interest and absorption that Greenberg and Morris labelled 'engrossment'. Interestingly, in their comments about newborn babies, fathers claim to be pleased to see a girl, but they give the game away by their other behavior. In addition, mothers seem to be deliberately trying to arouse fathers' interest in their daughters by increased reference to them or to be seeking reassurance that fathers are not too disappointed; e.g. 'Did you want a boy, I wanted a girl' or 'There, you take her. Bounce her around.' There appear to be clear differences in the reactions of fathers to sons and daughters. Other observational studies of fathers at birth do not look for this early sex difference (e.g. McDonald 1978; Packer and Rosenblatt 1979; Rodhölm and Larsson 1979).

Beyond birth there is an increasing number of studies that detect differences in the ways fathers treat sons and daughters. Jones (1981) finds that girls at 1 month of age were spoken to more by their fathers than were boys. She also reports that the irritability of boys and girls affected the way they were treated, in that fathers had a more positive perception of high-irritability boys and low-irritability girls than of their opposites. In another study fathers shown a decline in their vocalizations to daughters in the first 3 months that is not apparent in their vocalizations to sons (Rebelsky and Hanks 1971). This suggests that sons retain their salience for fathers more than do daughters. Two further studies report sex differences in fathers' behavior: both are studies of holding of sons and daughters. Sons and daughters up to 5 months of age were held in different positions by their fathers, with sons being held more than daughters in a face-to-face position and daughters being held more in an across-the-body position (White *et al.* 1982). Parke and Sawin (1977) reported differences in the closeness with which fathers held sons and daughters: during the first 3 months of life sons were held further away from the body. The same study also shows that sons received more attention from fathers, a finding that is repeated with 4-month-olds (Field 1978; Rendina and Dickerscheid 1976) and with 9-month-olds (Kotelchuck 1976). It seems that the sex of the baby has an effect on fathers' reactions to them at birth and as children get older their gender continues to be important and even becomes more important.

It has been suggested that the newborns' state affects maternal behavior (Osofsky and Connors 1979). Equally the newborns' state may have an impact on the ways that fathers first make contact with them. An active, alert newborn baby is potentially more interesting and rewarding to interact with than an inactive and drowsy one. On the other hand, a relatively quiet baby might be more rewarding to interact with than one who cries all the time. A small number of studies have looked at the state of young infants as determinants of paternal role. One study examined the impact of infants' state immediately after birth (Woollett *et al.* 1982). They found that the baby's state had very little impact on the father's behavior, although many of the fathers' comments about and to their babies made reference to it; e.g. in response to a crying boy, 'Your lungs are good, aren't they?', whereas responding to a crying girl, 'She's noisy, like her mum', and making reference to a quiet girl, 'She's a nice quiet little thing, isn't she?' The comments made about the newborns' state varied according to their sex. Socialization into male and female roles can be seen to have started right from birth.

Another study (Bowen and Miller 1980) which found that infant state was not related to variability in father's behavior looked at paternal attachment behavior (looking, verbalizing, smiling, touching, holding, being in the face-to-face position) between 12 and 72 hours. These did not vary as the children's state moved through drowsy, quiet, alert, active alert and crying. Only when the babies were asleep did the incidence of these attachment behavior decline.

Finally, Jones (1981) looked at a related topic, that of individual differences in infants' temperament. The dimension Jones took was irritability. At 4 weeks irritable babies elicit more caretaking behaviours from fathers than non-irritable babies.

There are therefore differences in fathers' behavior to their babies depending on their sex and to a lesser extent on their temperamental state. These characteristics of the newborn continue to be important later. In part this is because the earliest interactions set the pattern for those that follow, but also because those features of their babies continue to have meaning for fathers.

There are a large number of individual characteristics of the newborn baby whose impact on fathers has not been examined so far. Some of these characteristics relate to family variables, e.g. position in the family, sex and age of siblings, whereas others relate more specifically to the infant itself, e.g. the infants' health, their gestation age, their activity levels, their responsiveness to stimulation, how easily they are consoled when distressed, how much they respond to being cuddled and how predictable is their behavior. Characteristics such as these have been employed in studies with mothers (Osofsky and Connors 1979; Stone *et al.* 1974), and it seems likely that they do have meaning for fathers and they are likely to respond accordingly. Clearly the babies themselves have a role to play in the early contacts they have with fathers and this ought to be an important area for future research.

THE IMPACT OF FATHERS ON MOTHER–CHILD INTERACTIONS

So far this chapter has concentrated on fathers' direct influence on their young babies by looking at the ways fathers behave towards their babies and the possible impact of those behavior. However, there is another aspect of the role of fathers that has not been discussed and that is the indirect influence fathers have on developing infants by the impact they have on mothers and others. Fathers influence the course of child development through the way they behave to mothers and others, which in turn changes the way in which mothers and others behave to the child.

This process can be seen operating during labour and delivery. One of the things that fathers do during labour is to offer the expectant mother support, to act as a mediator between the mother and the medical staff and to reduce the unfamiliarity of the setting. In these ways they may help to ease mothers' passage through labour and delivery and to enhance their emotional experience. There is some evidence that when fathers are present throughout labour mothers relax more and therefore need less medication and experience less pain (Cronenwett and Newmark 1974; Henneborn and Cogan 1975). Because these women have had less medication they are perhaps more alert and so are able to respond actively when first presented with their newborns. Thus fathers may have an indirect effect on their infants by changing the nature of the first mother–newborn encounters and therefore changing any sequelae of those encounters.

When fathers are present during labour they rub backs, hold hands, they mop brows, time contractions, breathe along with mothers and give constant encouragement and attention. They also relay mothers' needs to medical staff when necessary (Lewis 1980; McKee 1980). How effectively they do these things depends on their prior training (Perkins 1980). It seems that the most important thing is that fathers are present: simply by being there they offer support to the mothers (Cartwright 1979; Entwisle and Doering 1981; Klein *et al.* 1981; Perkins 1980). In the Klein study observations of mothers and fathers were made during the first stage of labour. Fathers were the main source of support. In particular fathers were much more likely to touch mothers than were nurses and this was something which mothers rated positively when they were asked later about the labour experience.

In addition to offering support, having the fathers present can help to enhance the emotional experience of the birth for mothers. Childbirth in hospital usually means that mothers are delivered by people they have never seen before and do not know. When they are surrounded by strangers, women are inhibited in the expression of their emotion. Having a familiar person with them enables mothers to feel less inhibited (Doering *et al.* 1980; Macfarlane 1977). This might be particularly true when the familiar person is also emotionally reactive. Thus when fathers are present, women have a stronger emotional reaction at birth and are able to relate more actively to the baby. Consequently, an enhanced emotional reaction could in its turn have long-term consequences for mother–child interaction. Here, again, fathers are having an indirect effect on the child. The presence of fathers also turns birth into more of a family event. By their comments at birth, fathers share the experience with mothers and in this way it becomes part of their common history as a couple to be talked over and relived later. In addition, through their comments to one another the couple make links between the birth and the wider family (Woollett *et al.* 1982). For instance, the baby's similarity to sisters and brothers and to grandparents was often commented upon. These comments included 'Looks like his dad', 'She's noisy like her mum', 'He's got dark hair like me' and 'Your sister was noisy too'. Mothers and fathers were equally likely to make such comments. By making such comments and also simply by being present at delivery, fathers help to turn the event of childbirth from being a largely impersonal medical event into a family event, with shared experiences, consideration of the extended family and of course support and encouragement from a familiar person.

Other examples of fathers having an impact on mothers' treatment of their newborn come from Dunn and White (1981), Parke and O'Leary (1976) and Leifer (1980). Dunn and White examined the effects of the father's presence on the mother's behavior in the minutes after the birth. Several mothers were observed both on their own and when fathers were present, and consequently it was possible to look at mothers' behavior when fathers were present and when they were absent. A father's absence arose for three reasons: arriving late, going home early or going out to telephone relatives. These absences were spread evenly over the observation period. When fathers were absent, mothers spent a slightly higher proportion of their time looking passively at the newborn than they did when fathers were present, but a lower proportion of the time actively engaged with them. Thus when fathers were present, mothers spent more time smiling at, stroking and exploring and rocking the newborn. The presence of fathers facilitated the more affective type of mother–newborn interaction. This impact of fathers on mothers' behavior was quite transitory. When fathers departed mothers reverted back to their earlier interactive style. However, although the effect is transitory it may have long-term consequences because of the timing of its occurrence.

In their study, Parke and O'Leary examined the mother's infant-directed behavior when alone with the infant and when the father was present. Observations took place in the first 3 days of life. Mothers were less likely to hold, touch, rock, talk to, imitate or feed their infants when fathers were present, but they were more likely to explore and smile at the infants. So mothers behaved differently to their babies when the fathers were present and when they were absent. Consequently, fathers were having an indirect effect on the behavior directed towards their babies.

In the third study Leifer (1980) interviewed mothers in the weeks after birth. She claims that when fathers offer emotional support to mothers during the early weeks, mothers make better adjustments to the babies and to their changed roles within the family. This she claims is particularly important if the baby is difficult.

We have seen a number of examples of fathers having an impact on the ways that mothers interact with their infants. In examining the role of the father in the neonatal period the importance of these indirect effects must not be overlooked.

FATHERS' ROLE: CONCEPTUAL ISSUES

A number of issues are raised by the fatherhood literature including the validity of the concepts of bonding, whether or not there is a common fatherhood role and how interdependent are mothers' and fathers' roles.

Bonding

The notion of bonding is of a rapid process occurring immediately after birth when parents become attached to the newborn. The concept carries with it the notion of a critical or sensitive period. There is also a commonly expressed belief that tactile contact between the parent and newborn facilitates the process. Although the notion of bonding is most commonly applied to mothers forming a relationship with the newborn (Klaus and Kennell 1976) there are also those who believe that when fathers first encounter their newborn similar unconscious mechanisms are elicited (McDonald 1978; Sasmor 1979). Increasingly, however, these assumptions are being questioned (Campbell and Taylor 1981; Lewis 1982; Svejda et al. 1980). The main arguments for a sensitive period for the formation of bonds between a parent and the newborn baby are (a) that such sensitive periods have been postulated for non-human animals, (b) newborn babies who are separated from their parents because of illness or prematurity are treated differently by their parents than are non-separated newborns (Liederman 1974), (c) mothers and fathers of normal full-term babies who are allowed an opportunity to get to know their baby immediately after birth interact more sensitively with them than do parents without this extended contact (Klaus and Kennell 1976; Rodhölm 1981). However, closer examinations of this evidence shows that the case for the concept of bonding is weak. The existence of sensitive periods in many animal species has been questioned (Bateson 1979; Novak and Harlow 1975). Equally those human studies that do show an effect of early extended contact in the main show only marginally significant effects (Klaus et al. 1972) and some studies show little or no effects (Carlsson et al.

1977; Svejda *et al.* 1980). When the results of early contact studies are examined closely many inconsistencies are apparent. Even studies that show benefits of early extended contact do not show the same benefit; there is no consistency across the studies in the behavior modified by contact. Thus Hales *et al.* (1977) reported that mothers given skin-to-skin contact with their infants immediately after birth show greater affectionate behavior at 36 hours than do control mothers. In a similar study de Château and Wiberg (1977) found no differences in affectionate behavior but did find differences in the amount of holding. These criticisms lead to the suggestion that the apparent benefits of early extended contact are not due to the contact itself, but to an awareness of the interest of the experimenters (Lewis 1982). Moreover, the apparent benefits of early extended contact have been well publicized, with the result that parents themselves expect to have such contact and believe in its effectiveness. Such expectations are themselves powerful modifiers of behavior. A final reason for being sceptical about the importance of early bonding is the observed ease with which adoptive parents make relationships with their child at a time long after any supposed sensitive bonding period (Rutter 1981). The case for a sensitive period for the establishment of bonds between the mother and the infant is therefore very weak. The case for similar bonds between the father and the infant is weaker still. There is less evidence about fathers, but it is more recent than the evidence on mothers and is therefore more likely to be contaminated by parental expectations and beliefs about a bonding process. A sensitive period for fathers could not be biologically programmed to pregnancy in the way that is possible for mothers.

Because of this belief in the importance of establishing bonds between parents and the child both parents are encouraged to have early contact with their newborns. There seem to be clear benefits associated with this experience. Parents report it as a rich emotional experience; the experience helps to promote parental confidence in their ability to cope with the newborn baby and it also helps to promote a sense of involvement in the newborn. It seems clear, however, that these benefits do not accrue because of any innate releasing mechanisms or sensitive periods. Instead the experience is beneficial because parents expect it to be beneficial and because such early contact reminds parents that the newborn is their responsibility and not that of the hospital. It seems that in giving parents extended contact with their newborns many hospitals are doing the right thing for the wrong reason.

A further consequence of the recent stress on early bonding is that parents who do not have that contact (e.g. adopting parents and parents whose infants go into special care) may feel guilty or deprived and believe that their child has been denied an important ingredient in its development. This is not true, but such beliefs can be self-fulfilling and so such parents need to be reassured that their child and their relationship with their child are not at risk. In these cases, a father may have a particular role; he can be the one who maintains contact with the newborn and who helps keep the mother and the wider family informed about it.

One corollary of the emphasis on bonding is that tremendous stress is laid on delivery and immediately after. This is reflected in the preparation of fathers. Fathers, especially first-time fathers, typically have given little thought to their role beyond delivery and to the realities of family life after birth, and have done little to prepare themselves for their role as fathers. This emphasis needs to be changed. Since parenthood classes fail to reach the majority of parents the best point to tackle this could be supportive intervention programmes such as those described by Lind (1974), Myers (1982) and Parke *et al.* (1980).

Interdependency of mothers' and fathers' roles

An implicit underlying theme throughout this chapter is that what fathers do has an impact on mothers and that what mothers do has an impact on fathers. Thus at every stage during labour, delivery and beyond fathers have an influence on mothers. This influence operates in a number of ways. First, just by being present fathers can have an impact on mothers. At labour and delivery, for instance, this is apparent in the way that mothers relax, need less medication and have shorter labours when fathers are present (Henneborn and Cogan 1975). In the hours and days after delivery the effect of the presence of fathers is apparent in the changes that occur in mothers' infant-directed behaviours (Dunn and White 1981; Parke and O'Leary 1976). Beyond the neonatal period the same process operates, as Clarke-Stewart (1978) has shown, mothers of 15–30 month-old children change their behaviour when the father is in the house even when he is not in the same room.

Second, the example fathers set can have an effect on mothers' behaviour. At birth this was apparent in the way that mothers reported a more emotional reaction when the father was present and when he was emotional too (Entwisle and Doering 1981). In the days that follow the same influence can be seen. Thus Parke and O'Leary

(1976) note that mothers hold sons more frequently after they observe fathers doing so. In a similar vein White *et al.* (1982) show that parents' holding patterns for the baby become more similar over the first 5 months of life.

Third, fathers' beliefs, attitudes, expectations and anxieties influence the way in which mothers behave towards their children. At birth this is apparent in that more anxious fathers were associated with mothers who subsequently had difficult labours. Shortly after birth it can be seen in the adjustments that women make to their new motherhood role when the father was supportive (Fein 1976; Grossman *et al.* 1980). Later on it can be seen in the way that fathers' expectations about their daughter's academic attainment influence mother–daughter interactions (Epstein and Radin 1975).

In their turn, mothers have a considerable impact on how fathers behave and so have an indirect as well as a direct effect on their children. The influence of mothers' presence on fathers' behaviour has been researched less than that of fathers' on mothers'. In the earliest days of life Parke and O'Leary (1976) report that fathers are relatively uninfluenced by the presence of mothers. Later, however, mothers' presence does have an effect on them and, for instance, inhibits their child-directed language (Golinkoff and Ames 1979).

Equally, the example mothers set for fathers has been considered less than the example fathers set for mothers, although White *et al.* (1982) and Clarke-Stewart (1978) both show effects of these examples. The influence of mothers' attitudes on fathers has been considered. Thus at labour Oakley (1979) claims that nearly half (44 per cent) of fathers who are present are there not because they want to be but because mothers want or expect them to be present. Later on the extent of their involvement in caretaking and other baby-related activities is determined at least in part by what mothers are doing already (Fein 1976; La Rossa and La Rossa 1981). Thus both parents have a direct and indirect effect on their children. Unfortunately, investigations of families have not treated them as an interdependent, dynamic system; rather mother–child interaction and father–child interaction are treated separately but in parallel. This is of course something of an advance as until recently families were considered to consist of a mother and her child. Acknowledgement of the direct and indirect effects of parents on one another takes this concept a step further. It encourages the recognition that families consist of mothers, fathers, child, sibling and others and that interactions within a family are rarely dyadic. Even when only two people are together the absent members may continue to exert their influence.

A common fatherhood role?

It is generally assumed in the literature that fathers engage in somewhat different activities from mothers and in general that they fulfil different roles from those of mothers. Thus, Lamb writes:

> Fathers and mothers both appear to be psychologically salient to their children from the time the children are infants, and they appear to adopt differentiable roles from this point on. Mothers are consistently assigned responsibility for nurturance and physical childcare, whereas fathers tend to be associated with playful interaction as well as with demands that children conform to cultural norms.

(Lamb 1981)

However, evidence for different roles has come about largely because studies have compared very specific maternal and paternal behaviours. In doing so, studies have normally failed to look for or report on points of similarity in their overall behaviours. Consequently, possibly minor differences between mothers' and fathers' behaviour are discussed and similarities underplayed.

Moreover, it is generally assumed that all fathers engage in essentially similar activities and that what distinguishes them is the extent to which they engage in those activities. Despite variability in fathers' behaviour the evidence suggests that there is a common strand in what fathers do with their infants and children. Thus even fathers who accept primary responsibility for caretaking within the family behave in a conventional paternal way (Field 1978). Moreover, there are a great many studies, both interview and observational studies, that reinforce the view that fathers help out occasionally with caretaking but that they take a major responsibility for play (Lamb 1978; Oakley 1979; Richards *et al.* 1977). So there do appear to be common elements in fathers' activities with their children. This then raises the issue of whether similarities in very specific child-directed behaviours denote similarities in the roles that parents fill in the development of their children.

There are reasons for being critical of an analysis that claims that similarities in some specific behaviours denote a common role. Just one criticism is mentioned here. A number of paternal behaviours have been studied and these are assumed to be important in defining fathers' role. These include caretaking, vocalizing, playing and holding. Normally it is the frequency of these behaviours that is considered, rather than their pacing, the context in which they occur or by whom they are initiated. Frequency may be an important measure; the willingness of parents to give their children time may be an indicator of their commitment, although it is clearly not in itself sufficient. However, the sensitivity with which these behaviours are paced to the child's needs might be a more meaningful measure. Thus two fathers may exhibit similar amounts of rough and tumble play, one in response to initiations from his child, the other initiated on the whim of the father. These two parenting styles might be superficially similar in that they involve equal amounts of play, but have very different consequences for their children because of their sensitivity to the child. Sensitivity might be reflected in a wide range of activities, e.g. talking to their children, holding, feeding or playing with them. Thus sensitivity might be the important feature rather than the activities through which it is manifested.

By assuming that similar specific behaviours denote similar parental roles and that different specific behaviours denote different parental roles, the common features of fatherhood may well have been overstressed. It is important to give consideration to individual differences in fathering. This has been a focus of the present chapter, in which we have discussed some events that are associated with variations in fathering activities. These include the reactions and behaviours of mothers, the preparation of fathers for parenthood, the presence of fathers at delivery, their emotional reactions at delivery and characteristics of their offspring.

REFERENCES

Ainsworth, M. D., Bell, S. M. and Stayton, D. J. (1974) 'Infant–mother attachment and social development: socialization as a product of reciprocal responsiveness to signals', in M. P. M. Richards (ed.) *The Integration of a Child into a Social World*, London: Cambridge University Press.

Bateson, P. P. (1979) 'How do sensitive periods arise and what are they for?', *Anim. Behav.* 27: 470–86.

Beail, N. (1982) 'The role of the father during pregnancy and childbirth', in N. Beail and J. McGuire (eds) *Fathers: Psychological Perspectives*, London: Junction Books.

Beail, N. and McGuire, J. (1982) 'Fathers, the family and society: the tide of change', in N. Beail and J. McGuire (eds) *Fathers: Psychological Perspectives*, London: Junction Books.

Bowen, S. L. and Miller, B. C. (1980) 'Paternal attachment behaviour as related to presence at delivery and pre parenthood classes: a pilot study', *Nurs. Res.* 29: 307–11.

Boyd. C. and Sellars, L. (1982) *The British Way of Birth*, London: Pan.

Brown, A. (1982) 'Fathers in the labour ward: medical and lay accounts', in

L. McKee and M. O'Brien (eds) *The Father Figure*, London: Tavistock.

Brown, I. (1980) 'Attitudes of men towards delivery and labour', *Midwife, Health Visitor and Community Nurse* 16: 278–80.

Campbell, S. B. G. and Taylor, P. M. (1981) 'Bonding and attachment: theoretical issues', in P. M. Taylor (ed.) *Parent–Infant Relationships* London: Grune and Stratton.

Carlsson, S. G., Fagerberg, H. and Horneman, G. *et al.* (1979) 'Effects of various amounts of contact between mother and child on the mother's nursing behaviours: a follow-up study', *Infant Behav. Dev.* 2: 209–14.

Cartwright, A. (1979) *The Dignity of Labour?: A Study of Childbirth and Induction*, London: Tavistock.

Clarke-Stewart, A. K. (1978) 'And daddy makes three: the father's impact on mother and young child', *Child Dev.* 49: 466–78.

Clegg, A. (1982) Personal communication.

Collis, G. M. (1979) 'Describing the structures of social interaction in infancy', in M. Bullowa (ed.) *Before Speech: The Beginning of Interpersonal Communication*, London: Cambridge University Press.

Collis, G. M. and Schaffer, H. R. (1975) 'Synchronisation of visual attention in mother–infant pairs', *J. Child Psychol. Psychiat.* 16: 315–20.

Condon, W. S. and Sander, L. W. (1974) Neonate movements in synchronized with adult speech: interactional participation and language acquisition', *Sci.* 183: 99–101.

Cordell, A. S., Parke, R. D., and Sawin, D. B. (1980) 'Fathers' views on fatherhood with special reference to infancy', *Family Relations* 29: 331–8.

Cronenwett, L. R. and Newmark, L. L. (1974) 'Fathers responses to childbirth', *Nurs. Res.* 23: 210–17.

de Château, P. and Wiberg, B. (1977) 'Long-term effects on mother–infant behaviour of extra contact during the first hour post partum, I. First observation at 36 hours', *Acta Paedia. Scand.* 66: 137–43.

Doering, S. G., Entwisle, D. R. and Quinlan, D. (1980) 'Modeling the quality of women's birth experiences', *J. Health and Social Behav.* 21: 12–21.

Drähne, A., Doch, S., König, S. and Zubke, W. (1979) 'The husband's presence at delivery – a prospective study', in L. Careriza and L. Zichella (eds) *Emotion and Reproduction (Proceedings of the Serono Symposia)*, vol. 20, New York: Academic Press.

Dunn, D. M. and White, D. G. (1981) 'Interactions of mothers with their newborns in the first half-hour of life', *J. Adv. Nurs.* 6: 271–5.

Elliott, A. J. (1981) *Child Language*, London: Cambridge University Press.

Entwisle, D. R. and Doering, S. G. (1981) *The First Birth: A Family Turning Point*, London: Johns Hopkins University Press.

Epstein, A. S. and Radin, N. (1975) 'Motivational components related to father behaviour and cognitive functioning in preschoolers', *Child Dev.* 46: 831–9.

Fein, R. A. (1976) 'The first weeks of fathering: the importance of choices and supports for new parents', *Birth and the Family J.* 32: 53–8.

Field, R. (1978) 'Interaction patterns of primary versus secondary caretaking fathers', *Developmental Psychol.* 14: 183–5.

Golinkoff, R. M. and Ames, G. J. (1979) 'A comparison of fathers' and mothers' speech with their young children', *Child Dev.* 50: 28–32.

Greenberg, M. and Morris, N. (1974) 'Engrossment: the newborn's impact upon the father', *Am. J. Orthopsychiat.* 44: 520–31.

Grossman, F. K., Eichler, L. S. and Winickoff, S. A. (1980) *Pregnancy, Birth and Parenthood*, San Francisco: Josey Bass.

Hales, D. J., Lozoff, B., Sosa, R. and Kennell, J. H. (1977) 'Defining the limits of the sensitive period', *Developmental Med. and Child Neurol.* 19: 454–61.

Henneborn, W. J. and Cogan, R. (1975) 'The effect of husband participation in reported pain and the probability of medication during labour and birth', *J. Psychosomatic Res.* 19: 215–22.

Hoffman, L. W. (1977) 'Changes in family roles, socialization and sex differences', *Am. Psychologist* 32: 644–58.

Jones, C. (1981) 'Father to infant attachment: effects of early contact and characteristics of the infant', *Res. Nurs. Health* 4: 193–200.

Kennell, J. H., Voos, D. K. and Klaus, M. H. (1979) 'Parent–infant bonding', in J. D. Osofsky (ed.) *Handbook of Infant Development*, New York: Wiley.

Klaus, M. H., Jerauld, R., Kreger, N. C., McAlpine, W., Steffa, M. and Kennell, J. H. (1972) 'Maternal attachment: importance of the first post partum days', *New Engl. J. Med.*, 286: 460–3.

Klaus, M. H. and Kennell, J. (1976) *Maternal–Infant Bonding*, St. Louis, Missouri: C. V. Mosby.

Klein, R. P., Gist, N. F., Nicholson, J. and Standley, K. (1981) 'A study of father and nurse support during labour', *Birth and the Family J.* 8: 161–4.

Kotelchuck, M. (1976) 'The infant's relationship to the father: experimental evidence', in M. E. Lamb (ed.) *The Role of the Father in Child Development*, New York: Wiley.

Lamb, M. E. (1977) 'Father–infant and mother–infant interaction in the first year of life', *Child Dev.* 48: 167–81.

Lamb, M. E. (1978) 'Influence of the child on marital quality and family interaction during the prenatal, perinatal and infancy periods', in R. M. Lerner and G. B. Spanier (eds) *Child Influences on Marital and Family Interaction: A Life-span Perspective*, New York: Academic Press.

Lamb, M. E. (1981) *The Role of the Father in Child Development*, 2nd ed., New York: Wiley.

Lamb, M. E. (1982) 'Annotation: paternal influences on early socio-emotional development', *J. Child Psychol. Psychiat.* 23: 185–90.

La Rossa, R. and La Rossa, M. M. (1981) *Transition to Parenthood: How Infants Change Families*, London: Sage.

Leifer, M. (1980) *Psychological Effects of Motherhood: A Study of First Pregnancy*, New York: Praeger.

Lewis, C. (1980) 'Father's impressions of pregnancy and childbirth', presented to the British Psychological Society, London, December.

Lewis, C. (1982) 'The observation of father–infant relationships: an "attachment" to outmoded concepts', in L. McKee and M. O'Brien (eds) *The*

Father Figure, London: Tavistock.

Liebenberg, B. (1967) 'Expectant fathers', *Am. J. Orthopsychiat.* 37: 358–9.

Liederman, P. H. (1974) 'Mothers at risk: a potential consequence of the hospital care of the premature infant', in E. J. Anthony and C. Koupernik (eds) *The Child in His Family: Children at Psychiatric Risk*, New York: Wiley.

Lind, J. (1974) 'Observations after delivery of communications between mother–infant–father', presented at the International Congress of Pediatrics, Buenos Aires, October.

Lozoff, B., Brittenham, G. M., Trause, M. A., *et al.* (1977) 'The mother–newborn relationships: limits of adaptability', *J. Paediat.* 91: 1–12.

McDonald, D. L. (1978) 'Parental behaviour at first contact with the newborn in a birth environment without intrusions', *Birth and the Family J.* 5: 123–32.

Macfarlane, A. (1977) *The Psychology of Child-birth*, London: Open Books.

McKee, L. (1980) 'Fathers and childbirth: "Just hold my hand" ', *Health Visitor* 53: 368–72.

Manion, J. (1977) 'A study of fathers and infant caretaking', *Birth and the Family J.* 4: 174–9.

Miller, B. C. and Bowen, S. L. (1982) 'Father to newborn attachment behaviour in relation to prenatal classes and presence at delivery', *Family Relations* 31: 71–8.

Myers, B. J. (1982) 'Early intervention using Brazelton training with middle-class mothers and fathers of newborns', *Child Dev.* 53: 462–71.

Novak, M. A. and Harlow, H. F. (1975) 'Social recovery of monkeys isolated for the first year of life: 1. Rehabilitation and therapy', *Developmental Psychol.* 11: 453–65.

Oakley, A. (1979) *Becoming a Mother*, Oxford: Martin Robertson.

Osofsky, J. D. and Connors, K. (1979) 'Mother–infant interaction: an integrative view of a complex system', in J. D. Osofsky (ed.) *Handbook of Infant Development*, New York: Wiley.

Packer, M. and Rosenblatt, D. (1979) 'Issues in the study of social behaviour in the first week of life', in D. Schaffer and J. Dunn (eds) *The First Year of Life: Psychological and Medical Implications of Early Experiences*, New York: Wiley.

Parke, R. D. (1981) *Fathering*, London: Fontana.

Parke, R. D., Hymel, S., Power, T. G. and Tinsley, B. R. (1980) 'Fathers and risk: a hospital based model for intervention', in D. B. Sawin, R.C. Hawkins, L. O. Walker and J. H. Penticuff (eds) *Psychosocial Risks in Infant-Environmental Transactions*, New York: Bruner/Mazel.

Parke, R. D. and O'Leary, S. E. (1976) 'Father–mother–infant interaction in the newborn period: some findings, some observations and some unresolved issues', in K. Riegel and J. Meacham (eds) *The Developing Individual in a Changing World*, vol. ii, *Social and Environmental Issues*, The Hague: Mouton.

Parke, R. D. and Sawin, D. B. (1977) 'The family in early infancy: social interaction and attitudinal analyses', paper presented to the Society for

Research in Child Development, New Orleans, March.

Perkins, E. R. (1980) 'Men on the labour ward', Leverholm Health Education Project, Occasional Paper 22, University of Nottingham.

Peterson, G. H., Mehl, L. E. and Leiderman, P. H. (1979) 'The role of some birth-related variables in father attachment', *Am. J. of Orthopsychiat.* 49: 330–8.

Rebelsky, F. and Hanks, C. (1971) 'Fathers' verbal interaction with infants in the first three months of life', *Child Development* 42: 63–8.

Rendina, I. and Dickerscheid, J. D. (1976) 'Father involvement with first-born infants', *Family Coordinator* 25: 373–9.

Richards, M. P. M., Dunn, J. F. and Antonis, B. (1977) 'Caretaking in the first year of life: the role of fathers' v. mothers' social isolation', *Child: Care, Health and Development* 3: 23–36.

Richman, J. and Goldthorp, W.O. (1978) 'Fatherhood: the social construction of pregnancy and birth', in S. Kitzinger and J. Davis (eds) *The Place of Birth*, Oxford: Oxford University Press.

Richman, J., Goldthorp, W. O. and Simmons, C. (1975) 'Father in labour', *New Society*, 16 October.

Robinson, J. P. (1977) *How Americans Use Time: A Social-psychological Analysis of Everyday Behaviour*, New York: Praeger.

Rodhölm, M. (1981) 'Effects of father–infant post partum contact on their interaction three months after birth', *Early Hum. Dev.* 5: 79–85.

Rodhölm, M. and Larsson, K. (1979) 'Father–infant interaction at the first contact after delivery', *Early Hum. Dev.*, 3: 21–7.

Rubin, J., Provenzano, F. J. and Luria, Z. (1974) 'The eye of the beholder: parents' views on sex of newborns', *Am. J. Orthopsychiat.* 43: 720–31.

Rutter, M. (1981) *Maternal Deprivation Reassessed*, Harmonsworth: Penguin.

Sasmor, J. C. (1979) 'The role of the father', in J. C. Sasmor (ed.) *Childbirth Education: A Nursing Perspective*, New York: Wiley.

Schaffer, H. R. (ed.) (1977) *Studies in Mother–Infant Interaction*, London: Academic Press.

Schaffer, H. R. and Emerson, P. E. (1964) 'The development of social attachments in infancy', *Monographs of the Society for Research in Child Development* 29 (3).

Snow, C. E. and Ferguson, C. A. (1977) *Talking to Children*, London: Cambridge University Press.

Stern, D. (1977) *The First Relationship: Infant and Mother* Glasgow: Fontana.

Stone, L. J., Smith, H. T. and Murphy, L. B. (1974) *The Competent Infant*, London: Tavistock.

Svejda, M. J., Campos, J. J. and Emde, R. N. (1980) 'Mother–infant "bonding": failure to generalize', *Child Dev.*, 51: 775–9.

Trevarthen, C. (1979) 'Communication and co-operation in early infancy: a description of primary intersubjectivity', in M. Bullowa (ed.) *Before Speech: The Beginning of Interpersonal Communication*, London: Cambridge University Press.

Wente, A. S. and Crockenberg, S. B. (1976) 'Transition to fatherhood:

Lamaze preparation, adjustment difficulty and husband–wife relationship', *The Family Coordinator* 25: 351–7.

White, D. G. and Woollett, E. A. (1981) 'The family at birth', paper presented to the British Psychological Society, London, December.

White, D. G., Woollett, E. A. and Lyon, M. L. (1982) 'Fathers' involvement with their infants: the relevance of holding', in N. Beail and J. McGuire (eds) *Fathers: Psychological Perspectives*, London: Junction Books.

Whitten, A. (1977) 'Assessing the effects of perinatal events on the success of the mother–infant relationship', in R. H. Schaffer (ed.) *Studies in Mother–Infant Interaction*, London: Academic Press.

Woollett, E. A., White, D. G. and Lyon, M. L. (1982) 'Observations of fathers at birth', in N. Beail and J. McGuire (eds) *Fathers: Psychological Perspectives*, London: Junction Books.

Yarrow, L. J., Rubinstein, J. L. and Pedersen, S. A. (1975) *Infant and Environment: Early Cognitive and Motivational Development*, New York: Halsted.

Yogman, M., Dixon, S., Tronick, E., Als, H. and Brazelton, T. B. (1977) 'The goals and structures of face-to-face interactions between infants and fathers', presented at the Biennial Meeting of the Society for Research in Child Development, New Orleans, March.

Part two

The process of development

Introduction

> The direction of development is neither from the individual to the
> social nor from the social to the individual. It is from an organism to
> a person .... That change is located as much in the infant's
> consciousness as in his interactions with others.
>
> (Kaye 1982: 205)

By what processes is the newborn so rapidly transformed from
apparent helplessness to relative social and personal competence? This
question has led to some fascinating and controversial lines of
developmental research, none more so than that by Meltzoff and
Moore (Chapter 5). Numerous studies have shown the respects in
which human infants are oriented towards human features (described
as social pre-adaptation by Schaffer, Chapter 1). What Meltzoff and
Moore appear to demonstrate is that infants are also born with
remarkable capacities for imitation, one of the principal techniques of
learning from others.

But it is not only children who are well-equipped for the task of
development. One of the features of responsive caregivers is the way
they structure the infant's environment in space and time, enabling
them progressively to acquire competence. In the second paper of
this section (Chapter 6), Kaye elaborates some features of this
cultural code for child rearing. He proposes that there are at least
seven 'parental frames', covering basic nurture and protection, guiding and providing feedback on action, serving as a model and a
memory bank, and structuring the turn-taking patterns that underlie
discourse.

But what happens when the subtle taken-for-granted processes of
interpersonal synchrony between caregiver and child break down?
This may be caused by factors within the child (for example, in cases
of autism or gross sensory impairment), or within the caregiver (for

example, in cases of maternal depression or abusive parenting). In her review of research into the effects of maternal depression (Chapter 7), Murray and Stein portray a variety of patterns of distorted relationship, the effects of which are highlighted by so-called 'perturbation studies' in which infants' reactions are observed when mothers simulate symptoms of depression. They conclude that maternal depression is not necessarily the direct cause of problems. Very often an infant's temperamental characteristics can exacerbate a caregiver's difficulties, or even contribute to the maternal depression in the first place.

These theoretical questions are taken up by Sameroff (Chapter 8). He argues that much developmental research presumes an overly simplistic, linear model of causality, especially where concepts of heredity and environment are employed. He argues that children are not passively 'affected' by their environments in a once-and-for-all way. Rather, they are themselves an active part of a complex, dynamic chain of influences. Through their own effect on their caregivers' behaviour and their selective attention to salient features of their world, they can significantly modify the effective environment for development. This 'transactional' model is of more than just theoretical interest. It has important implications for the way intervention strategies are designed, evaluated and interpreted.

REFERENCE

Kaye, K. (1982) *The Mental and Social Life of Babies*, New York: Harvester Press.

5 Cognitive foundations and social functions of imitation, and intermodal representation in infancy

Andrew N. Meltzoff and M. Keith Moore

Source: Mehler, J. and Fox, R. (eds) (1985) *Neonate Cognition: Beyond the Blooming Buzzing Confusion*, Hillsdale, N.J.: Lawrence Earlbaum Associates, pp.139–56.

INTRODUCTION

A distinction may be drawn between two different types of evolutionary change that operate in man. On the one hand, there is evolution mediated by genetic transmission; and on the other, evolution mediated by cultural transmission. The former is often called evolution in the Darwinian mode and the latter cultural or psychosocial evolution. Perhaps the best labels for differentiating between them were provided by Medawar (1957), who referred to them respectively as 'endosomatic' and 'exosomatic' evolution.

Homo sapiens profit from and rely on exosomatic evolution to a greater degree than any other species. Our everyday life and social organization have been radically altered as compared with 15th-century man's, not because of endosomatic evolution, but because of the more rapid, yet still profound process of exosomatic evolution. Most of the knowledge, traditions, and behavioral skills that we call 'culture' are passed from one generation to the next not by DNA molecules, but through nongenetic channels.

By what process(es) could nongenetic information be transferred from one generation to the next? Could imitation be one means of fulfilling such a function? Dawkins (1976), an evolutionary biologist, recently developed a detailed analogy between the role of DNA in endosomatic evolution and imitation in exosomatic evolution. He argued that just as biological information is replicated and passed on through genes, cultural information is replicated and transferred through imitation. If one accepts Dawkins' analogy, one could go on to argue that imitation provides man with a kind of Lamarckian evolutionary potential: it provides a means for passing *acquired* characteristics and behavior patterns to succeeding generations. Of course, large portions of our behavior patterns, skills, and conceptual apparatus are not gained through interaction with conspecifics at all. But some portions are; and among this subset, imitative processes may play a significant role (Bandura 1969; Bruner 1972; Piaget 1962). The importance of imitation to human development and the continuance of culture has been noted by anthropologists as well as by biologists and psychologists. Reichard (1938) pointed out that in many languages the word for 'teach' is the same as the word for 'show', because for these cultures imitative learning and teaching by example are the main pedagogical style. Vilakazi summarized the central role of imitation in the Zulu society as follows:

> The Zulu traditional system of education was mainly informal and non-institutional in the sense that there were no regular school buildings or any particular places and specific times where and when teaching took place . . . . A child learned about its culture in the home by the methods of observation, imitation and play . . . . Most of the time, Zulu life was lived in and around the kraal and it is in this setting that the child learned many items of its cultural tradition by actual participation in or direct observance of what the old people did.
>
> (Vilakazi 1962: 124)

Among the Tallensi natives in Africa, imitation is regarded as an especially efficient means of transmitting skills to the young. Fortes made the following observation about this group:

> That skill comes with practice is realized by all. When adults are asked about children's mimetic play they reply: 'That is how they learn . . . .' Rapid learning or the acquisition of a new skill is explained by *u mar nini pam*, 'he has eyes remarkably . . .'. This conception of cleverness is intelligible in a society where learning by looking and copying is the commonest manner of achieving dexterity both in crafts and in the everyday manual activities.
>
> (Fortes 1938: 13)

In some cultures children are shown adult models in situations where we might think that such exposure would be totally ineffective. Among the Navaho Indians, the power of imitative learning is exploited in ways that would surprise many of us. For example, Leighton and Kluckhohn reported that imitation is used by the Navaho to foster toilet training: 'The mother or an older sister takes the child out when she herself goes to defecate and tells the little one to imitate her position and her actions' (Leighton and Kluckhohn 1947: 35). In other cultures, learning by imitation is used in situations that we might consider too dangerous for such a strategy. A vivid example from Puerto Rican village life was provided by Steward *et al.*: 'A little girl of two sat next to her mother, who was peeling vegetables, and helped her peel, using an enormous machete as her tool. She copied her mother's manner of holding the knife very closely and used the machete with a great deal of skill' (Steward *et al.* 1956: 220). Elsewhere the author adds, 'Consequently a child develops manual skills and mastery at a comparatively early age. A three-year-old can peel a mango with a carving knife' (Steward *et al.* 1956: 145).

There has thus been little disagreement among biologists, psychologists, and anthropologists about the adaptive significance and universality of imitation in human development. In contrast, there is profound disagreement among developmentalists as to *origins* and early development of imitation in infancy. Perhaps this is to be expected. Behavior that can be lumped together into a broad category of 'imitation' in discussions of evolutionary biology or cultural anthropology begins to look more complicated when it is scrutinized and experimentally manipulated. Developmental psychologists must ask: How do we know a child is 'really' imitating rather than performing a behavior by chance? Is the capacity to imitate conspecifics part of our innate endowment, or is imitation a skill that must itself be learned? What mechanisms underlie imitation and how do they change with age? Broad arguments outlining the adaptive value of imitation do not move developmental psychologists much closer to understanding the origins and development of this ability itself.

In our laboratory we have recently completed a new series of studies investigating the origins of imitation in infancy. The results are surprising from the viewpoint of current developmental theory, if not from the more biologically orientated positions discussed above. They indicate that *Homo sapiens* have an innate capacity to imitate adult members of their species, at least in the sense that human infants are capable of imitating adult actions from the moment of birth. In this chapter we discuss our work on infant imitation, consider alternative accounts of these findings, and investigate some of the implications of these results for our theories about the beginnings of social and cognitive development in infancy.

[. . .]

ON DIFFERENTIATING IMITATIVE PHENOMENA

Of all the various acts that infants can imitate, the duplication of facial gestures is perhaps the most fascinating and difficult to explain by current development theories. Certainly, facial imitation allows the sharpest empirical test of the existing theories of imitative development.

Consider the imitation of a simple facial movement, such as mouth opening and closing. Even if we focus on the simplest situation by assuming the following three things: (1) that infants can visually resolve the adult's action, (2) that this motor movement is well within their motor capabilities, and (3) that infants are fully motivated to duplicate the adult's gesture – how is it possible for the infant to imitate this gesture?

Whereas infants can see the adult's mouth-opening display, they cannot see their own mouths. The theoretical problem is to explain how the adult's act can become 'linked' to the appropriate infant response. There seems to be no direct comparison that infants can make between the target gesture and their own behaviors. The target is picked up through visual perception, but the behavioral response cannot be visually monitored by the infant. Facial imitation thus seems to involve a kind of *cross-modal* matching in which one perceptual system (vision) provides the model against which information from a different system (proprioception) is compared. This presents a unique set of circumstances, both for the infant and for the adult theorist. In order to see just how unique facial imitation is, it is useful to compare it to manual and vocal imitation.

In both manual and vocal imitation, infants can perceive the adult model and their own behavior within the same perceptual modality and therefore should be able to compare the two. Infants can see both the adult's hand and their own hands. In principle they can visually guide their hand movements until they match the target. The same is true of vocal imitation. Infants can hear both the adult's voice and their own productions. In principle, they can use audition to monitor their vocal productions until they match the adult's. In both cases an *intramodal* matching process can be used.

[. . .]

The point of considering manual and vocal imitation is to illustrate the differences between these activities and facial imitation. The complexities of manual and vocal imitation pale in comparison to the complexities of facial imitation. In facial imitation, the infant can use neither vision nor audition to monitor his own movements. Even if we take the easiest situation outlined previously (the imitation of familiar behaviors), there is still no ready explanation for how the infant could 'link up' the model's facial gesture with a matching one of his own.

The infant may be quite familiar with feeling himself perform the act, but he can never feel the adult's act. Conversely, he may be familiar with seeing the adult's gesture, but he cannot see his own facial movements. Even when a facial gesture is both familiar to the infant and also within his motor repertoire, a profound theoretical problem still remains. *When the perception of the target and the results of production cannot be compared within the same modality, what type of experience could, even in principle, allow the infant to learn the correspondence?* This is the problem that has fascinated those of us who study facial imitation.

SOME ACCOUNTS OF FACIAL IMITATION

What are some plausible accounts of the origins of facial imitation in infancy? Three possibilities immediately suggest themselves.

First, it might be argued that the earliest instances of facial imitation are simply the result of instrumental learning. We know that young infants can be conditioned to respond to a bell or buzzer with particular head movements (Lipsitt 1969). This shows that infants can learn to link specific motor movements to a given external stimulus. There is every reason to believe that they could be shaped to treat adult mouth opening as a discriminative stimulus for mouth-opening movements of their own. [. . .]

Second, it might be argued that associative learning within the context of parent–infant interaction accounts for the origins of facial imitation in infancy. This position would need to assume that parents systematically mimic their infants' behaviors. Starting with this assumption, it could be argued that infants learn to pair their behavior with the mother's matching response during these early interactions. An 'association' would be formed on the basis of the regular temporal contiguity between the infant's actions and the adult's. [. . .]

Finally, one might adopt the Piagetian position (Piaget 1962) that instrumental and associative learning are not sufficient to account for all instances of facial imitation, and moreover that they do not account for the interesting cases. Piagetians define the interesting cases as those behaviors that can be imitated even without being part of any previous adult–infant interaction. These behaviors need not be novel in the sense that the infant has never performed them before, but only novel in the sense that the stimulus–response linkage has not been shaped up or part of any associative pairing.

[. . .]

As is well known, Piaget's findings were that facial imitation did not emerge before about 8 to 12 months as long as adult training, what he called 'pedagogical mania', was not involved. His interpretation was that infants lacked the perceptual-cognitive ability to recognize correspondences between visually and proprioceptively perceived events before this age. The onset of facial imitation, or more precisely those acts of facial imitation that were not themselves reducible to adult training, became a classic development milestone in Piagetian theory, one that indicated a fundamental reorganisation of the infant's cognitive abilities (Piaget 1962).

THE EXISTENCE OF FACIAL IMITATION IN NEONATES: AN ANOMALY FOR CURRENT THEORIES

In 1977 we reported laboratory experiments showing that 12- to 21-day-old infants could imitate one manual and three facial gestures (Meltzoff and Moore 1977). More recently these effects were replicated using a different design with newborn infants, the youngest of whom was 42 minutes old at the time of testing (Meltzoff and Moore 1983a). If neonates in the first hours of postnatal life can already imitate facial gestures, then none of the accounts considered thus far – instrumental learning, associative learning, or Piagetian cognitive development – are *necessary* conditions for the existence of this behavior. In short, the demonstration of facial imitation in neonates presents existing accounts of imitative development with a genuine anomaly that they cannot easily incorporate.

At a theoretical level, the findings force either: (1) a reconsideration of the psychological prerequisites of facial imitation (they might be simpler than anything traditionally proposed); or (2) a reconsideration of the cognitive and social capacities of neonates (they might be more sophisticated than traditionally assumed). Before examining which if either of these two resolutions is the more appropriate (see p. 122–5), it is worth reviewing some key elements in the empirical studies themselves, for the experiments were specifically designed to provide a critical test of theories of infant imitation.

Our 1977 report contained two experiments. In Experiment I, each infant was shown four gestures in a randomized order using a repeated-measures design. The gestures were lip protrusion, mouth opening, tongue protrusion, and sequential finger movements. The experiment was videotaped for subsequent analysis, and scored by observers who were kept uninformed about which adult gesture had been demonstrated in any given trial.

The observer's task was to watch the infant's response and to make a judgment as to which adult gesture the infant had been shown. This 'perceptual judgment' scoring system (Meltzoff and Moore 1983b) was utilized because we were not able to predict on a priori grounds what a neonate's imitative response would look like, if it existed. Would neonates match the form of the adult's mouth-opening gesture exactly, or would they only approximate the model and open their mouths halfway? How should we operationalize the difference between 'one' mouth opening and 'two' – should lip closure be used, or do neonates never fully seal their lips before starting their second effort? Because we did not know the answers to these and other questions about the imitative response when we began the experiment, it seemed judicious not to adopt arbitrary behavioral criteria that then might lead us to miss the effect. Our perceptual judgment system enabled unbiased observers to use the whole pattern of the response to evaluate imitation (while remaining blind to the actual experimental condition). Using this scoring system, imitation was demonstrated. (See Meltzoff and Moore 1983b for a fuller discussion of the advantages and disadvantages of the 'perceptual judgment' technique for scoring imitative responses.)

The second experiment in the 1977 paper was designed to meet three primary goals. First, because we had difficulty ensuring that all the infants in Experiment I fixated the experimenter's display, and yet the problem of imitation cannot be properly posed without fulfilling this precondition, we realized that the experiment might have underestimated the neonates' true imitative competence. We thus wanted to conduct a study that would improve our control of the infants' attention. Our idea was to equate all the infants at a given level of visual fixation before beginning the imitation test per se.

Second, because Experiment I used a perceptual judgment scoring system, we could not specify the accuracy of the imitative matches. Evidently, the infants' responses were precise enough for observers to discriminate the infants' reactions to several different types of movements within the same body region (the mouth). The results showed that the infants' imitative reactions to the lip-protrusion display were discriminably different from those to the tongue-protrusion and mouth-opening displays. Nevertheless, we could not specify exactly how far infants were protruding their lips, how often they did so, and other particulars of the nature of the imitative response. We therefore interviewed the judges and conducted further pilot testing to provide more precise operational definitions of the infants' imitative movements and then used these definitions to score the frequencies of specific behaviors in Experiment II.

Third, it was of theoretical interest to go beyond the first experiment to test whether neonates could imitate even if the target gesture had disappeared. If they could, it might imply that infants were capable of imitating on the basis of some stored model of 'representation' of the perceptually absent display (Meltzoff 1981).

We used a nonnutritive sucking technique to accomplish the goals of delaying the response and increasing our control of the infant's visual experience. The pacifier technique is depicted in Fig. 5.1. As shown, each infant was given a baseline period. Next, a pacifier was inserted into the infant's mouth and then the facial gesture was demonstrated until the infant fixated it for 15 seconds. The experimenter then stopped gesturing, assumed a passive face pose, and *only then* removed the pacifier to allow the infant to respond. The passive face pose was maintained throughout the 2½-minute response period. At the end of this period, the pacifier was reinserted and a second gesture was administered, following an identical procedure.

Because the criterion for removing the pacifier was that the infant had fixated the gesture, we could be sure that any failure to imitate was not due to inattention to the model. Because the infants in our experiment actively sucked on the pacifier while it was in their mouths – the reflexive sucking response pattern apparently taking precedence over imitative responses (Meltzoff and Moore 1977) – the procedure served to delay imitative responding until after the adult display ended.

The gestures used as models were full mouth openings and full tongue protrusions. The infant movements counted as responses were stringently defined to be isomorphic with the adult display. Infant tongue protrusion was scored only if the tongue was thrust clearly beyond the lips; and infant mouth opening was scored only if the infant fully opened his mouth. Small tongue movements or lip separations were not scored as imitative, because they did not exactly match the adult's display.

The experiment was scored from videotape by an observer who was kept uninformed about the gesture shown to the infant in any given trial. The results showed that these large tongue protrusions and full mouth openings did not occur very frequently as part of the infant's spontaneous movements during the control conditions (thus these large behaviors might not themselves be classified as 'familiar' acts, depending on one's criterion for familiar versus novel acts). More importantly, the results showed significantly more infant mouth openings after the mouth-opening demonstration than during the baseline period or after the adult tongue-protrusion demonstration. Similarly, the infants responded with significantly more tongue

Figure 5.1 The pacifier technique used to assess facial imitation in 2- to 3-week-old infants

Condition	Experimenter	Infant
Baseline exposure	Passive face	Pacifier
Baseline period (150 seconds)	Passive face	No pacifier
Experimental exposure 1	Gesture 1	Pacifier
Response period 1 (150 seconds)	Passive face	No pacifier
Experimental exposure 2	Gesture 2	Pacifier
Response period 2 (150 seconds)	Passive face	No pacifier

Note: Each infant was given a baseline period and then exposed to two adult facial gestures (mouth opening and tongue protrusion). The gestures were demonstrated to the infants while they sucked on the pacifier. The pacifier was then removed and the infants were allowed to respond during the subsequent 150-second period. The experimenter presented a passive face pose during the entire response period.
Source: Meltzoff and Moore (1977).

protrusions after the tongue-protrusion demonstration than during the baseline period or after the mouth demonstration.

In sum, the results of Experiment II showed that infants could imitate both displays even under the conditions imposed by the pacifier technique. It also went beyond the perceptual judgment system used in the first experiment and showed that the imitative pattern could be documented using the frequency of the very high-fidelity behavioral matches.

At the end of these two studies, the possibility remained that the infants had somehow learned to imitate the particular gestures shown to them during earlier interactions with their caretakers. This seemed an unlikely possibility, given the age of the subjects and the ethological description of naturally occurring interactions in home settings during the first 3 weeks of life (Whiten 1975). Nevertheless, the potential anomaly presented by these findings could easily be explained away if one chose to argue that these early imitations were based on adult training in the first 2 to 3 weeks of life.

In order to address this issue, we conducted a new study using newborn infants. All the subjects were less then 72 hours old, and the youngest was only 42 minutes old at the time of test (Meltzoff and Moore 1983a). In pilot studies we found it difficult to ensure that infants this young would visually inspect the experimenter's face. Infants cannot imitate if they do not perceive the model. Therefore, certain experimental procedures were instituted to focus the infant's attention on the adult's display. Three points are especially noteworthy and they are briefly outlined below.

First, because newborns are sensitive to ambient lighting, the room lights were extinguished. The only source of visible illumination was a small spotlight that shone on the experimenter's face. The experimenter's torso was covered by a black gown to reduce reflectance, and testing took place within a black-lined test chamber (Fig. 5.2). Second, because normal cinematic or videotape recording was impossible in such low illumination, we used an infrared-sensitive video camera to record a close-up image of the infant's face. Third, the experimenters' face was placed 25 ± 2 cm from the infant's eyes, a distance previously found effective in tests of newborn vision (Fantz 1963). Given these three procedures, the experimenter's face was the brightest object in an otherwise dark field, and the newborns seemed to stay 'on task' over the course of the 8-minute test.

We tested 40 newborns. Each infant was presented with both a mouth-opening and a tongue-protrusion gesture in a repeated-measures design, counterbalanced for order of presentation. Two 4-minute modeling periods were used (one for the mouth-opening demonstration and the other for the tongue-protrusion demonstration), and the experiment was electronically timed. There were no breaks between modeling periods or anywhere during the test. The experimenter's behavior was thus fixed from the beginning of the test the end, and not contingent upon the infant's activity. (See Meltzoff and Moore 1983a for details.)

The experimental design allowed us to distinguish between random oral movements, arousal responses, and imitation. Each infant acted as his own control. The two successive modeling periods utilized the same face, presented at the same distance, and moving at the same rate. These periods differed only with respect to the type of facial gesture presented. Within this design, imitation was demonstrated if infants responded with: (1) significantly more mouth openings to the adult mouth-opening gesture than to the tongue-protrusion gesture, and conversely (2) significantly more tongue protrusions to the tongue gesture than the mouth gesture. Such a pattern of *differential* response could not arise from a global arousal of oral movements in the presence of a moving human face, because the moving face was present in both periods.

The results provided strong support for the imitation hypothesis.

Figure 5.2 Schematic of the experimental room used to assess imitation in newborn infants under 72 hours old

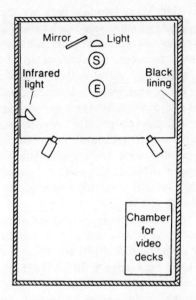

Note: The test chamber was lined with a black homogenous background. The only source of visible illumination came from the spotlight directed toward the experimenter's face (E) from behind the infant (S). This arrangement helped to direct the infants' attention towards the experimenter's face. The camera used to videotape the closeup picture of the infant's face (left) was infrared-sensitive, thus ensuring a high-resolution record of the infant's behavior for subsequent behavioral scoring. Two videodecks were housed in a sound-dampening chamber to reduce auditory distractions as much as possible.
Source: Meltzoff and Moore (1983a).

The infants produced significantly more mouth openings in response to adult mouth-opening gesture than to the tongue-protrusion gesture ($p < 0.05$, Wilcoxon test). Similarly, they produced more tongue protrusions to the tongue-protrusion gesture than to the mouth-opening gesture ($p < 0.001$).

Beyond these statistical findings, there are several interesting aspects of the morphology and temporal organisation of the imitative response that deserve mention, because they help fill in the picture of what the imitative reactions are like in these very young infants. As mentioned earlier, the infants imitate with reasonable accuracy. Our results are not based on lip quiverings or small tonguing movements inside the oral cavity. The criteria used in our behavioral scoring system (Meltzoff and Moore 1977; 1983a) ensured that only behaviors that were structurally similar to the model's were scored, and consequently the significant effects reflect a pattern in high-fidelity matches.

It is also interesting that these accurate imitative matches were not typically elicited the moment the adult presented his display. In the 1977 study, for example, we found that infants actively sucked on the pacifier while the gesture was demonstrated, and moreover that the imitative responses did not burst forth the moment the pacifier was removed. Some infants paused after pacifier removal and stared intently at the experimenter (who was now presenting the passive face pose) before beginning their imitative responding (Meltzoff 1981; Meltzoff and Moore 1977). In the newborn study, too, we observed that the response was not suddenly triggered by the adult display (Meltzoff and Moore 1983a).

Finally, when the infants began to respond, they often commenced by producing small approximations of the model and then gradually homing in on the target gesture. Their acts became more and more like the adult's act over successive efforts. We have coined the term *convergence* as a descriptor for this effect (Meltzoff and Moore 1983b). Evidently this is not a necessary aspect of response organization, because accurate imitative responses were sometimes observed after a period of rapt attention and virtually no preliminary oral movements. Nonetheless, it is of theoretical interest (discussed later) that a progressive homing in on the target – convergence – was one of the imitative patterns that presented itself.

A RESOLUTION OF THE ANOMALY: THE ROLE OF INTERMODAL REPRESENTATION IN FACIAL IMITATION

The finding that young infants, indeed newborns as young as 42 minutes old, can imitate certain simple facial gestures forces us to consider alternatives to the traditional accounts of facial imitation. Because this behavior can be elicited at birth, neither instrumental or associative learning nor the cognitive-developmental processes suggested by Piaget can be necessary conditions for such behavior.

In the 1977 paper we introduced two new alternatives that might explain this anomalous infant competence. We suggested that neonatal facial imitation might be accomplished by either: (1) an innate releasing mechanism of the type outlined by Lorenz and Tinbergen

(Tinbergen 1951); or (2) a more active intermodal matching process. The critical distinction between the releasing mechanism and active mapping views is whether the neonate does or does not use the similarity between the act seen and the act done in the course of organizing his actions. Although there are certain resemblances between these accounts (for example, that adult tuition is not involved), the distinctions between these are also important, as elaborated below.

Innate releasing mechanisms (IRM)

On the releasing mechanism account, the infant's response is a preprogrammed motor packet that is called up by a particular visual pattern (the sign stimulus). The similarity between the stimulus and the response does not enter into the equation. There is, after all, no requirement within ethological theory that a sign stimulus must be isomorphic with the fixed action pattern (FAP) it releases. In most examples of the classic sign stimulus → IRM → FAP system, the sign stimulus and the FAP do not match (Tinbergen 1951). The egg-rolling behavior of greylag geese is released by the sight of an egg, the food-begging response in newly hatched herring gull chicks is released by the mandible patch of the adult, and so forth. In these and other cases, the sign stimulus and the action pattern that is released are not isomorphic. The innate releasing mechanism is a central device that links an innately determined motor packet with a particular stimulus display. It does not require a stimulus-response isomorphism.

In fact, releasing mechanisms could just as well have accounted for the present findings if the results had been the direct opposite of what was actually found. IRMs could be invoked if it had turned out that the adult mouth-opening display elicited infant tonguing, and conversely that the tongue display elicited infant mouthing. Infants would not have to imitate but could produce any systematic motor response, and the IRM view would still be a potential explanatory concept.

The attraction of importing the IRM concept from ethology to account for infant imitation is not that it predicts, or is uniquely suited to, explaining stimulus-response isomorphisms. Rather it is that IRMs do not demand any more sophisticated perceptual-cognitive functioning that the traditional developmental theories, such as Piaget's, have already attributed to neonates. If neonatal imitation can be reduced to IRMs, then the anomaly we reported can be assimilated into existing theories simply by admitting that Piaget missed the fact that newborns imitate, but that this has no real implications for our theories of the

newborn's mind. Newborn imitation may present an empirical surprise, but it is no challenge to existing theories of infant psychology.

Active intermodal mapping (AIM)

We favor a very different interpretation of the findings of early
imitation. *In our view, this early imitation reflects a process of active
intermodal mapping in which infants use the equivalences between
visually and proprioceptively perceived body transformations as a basis
for organising their responses.* We also posit that imitation, even this
early imitation, is mediated by an internal representation of the adult's
act. The next question concerns the nature of this representation. There
are several possibilities. Our working hypothesis is that the newborn
could not be using a mental image of the adult's display in the sense of a
visual picture or iconic copy, because then again we would be left with
the problem of how infants could ever link up the 'visual image' of the
adult's act with the 'motor image' of their own movements.

We therefore have suggested that neonates are capable of picking up
'supramodal' information about the adult's movements that is then
used directly as the basis for the infant's own motor plans. Thus
conceived, the neonate's representation of the adult's act is neither
exclusively visual nor exclusively motor but rather is a non-modality-
specific description of the event. Such an internal representation
constitutes the 'model' that directs the infant's actions and against
which he matches his motor performance.

At this juncture, then, the fundamental theoretical point is whether
early imitative responses ought to be conceived of as reflecting hard-
wired stimulus-response linkages, or as a more active mapping
procedure in which the infant uses the equivalence between his own
body transformations and those of the adult as the basis for organizing
the response. These two alternative conceptions, referred to here as
'innate releasing mechanism' (IRM) and 'active intermodal mapping'
(AIM), are very different. A given behavioral pattern may reflect any
one of several different levels of organization with the organism
(Bower 1979, 1982; Bruner 1973; Kagan 1967; Piaget 1954). The
distinction we have drawn between the IRM and AIM accounts
specifies two different types of psychological organisation that might
underlie early imitation. To phrase this point in terms of the questions
posed at the outset of this chapter, these accounts provide two
different *mechanisms* that may mediate imitative behavior during the
newborn period.

We think that most of the data and observations in hand favor the

AIM account. The fact that some infants converge toward more accurate imitative matches over successive efforts is especially relevant to this theoretical issue. Such convergence can be viewed as ongoing correction by the infants, and as such suggests that they are engaged in an active matching process in which they compare the 'obtained' behavior against their representation of the 'target'. If convergence does indicate a true correction process, this would certainly be more compatible with the AIM than with the IRM account. In the classic IRM account, the sequence of motor commands would be expected to 'run off' in the absence of feedback about the status of the ongoing movements and their relation to the target (Lorenz and Tinbergen 1938).

NOTES TOWARD THE FUTURE

Intermodal representation, imitation, and the roots of social development

We are now attempting to distinguish between interesting IRM and AIM accounts experimentally. In the AIM account there is the possibility that infants could reverse the imitation effect and detect whether an adult was matching or mismatching their behavior. That is, if infants used the equivalences between their own acts and the adult's to produce imitation, they might also *recognize* when their own behavior is being imitated. This is being tested in an experiment in which the adult either performs: (1) tongue protrusions contingent on infant tongue protrusions (the case of adult matching), or (2) mouth openings contingent on infant tongue protrusions (the case of adult mismatching). The AIM view suggests that infants should react differentially to these two instances, because they can detect an intermodal equivalence in one case and not in the other. The preliminary results from this experiment are in accord with this suggestion. Infants who are being mismatched show more avoidance behaviors than do those who are being matched.

The preliminary findings are thus compatible with the idea that at some level of processing, infants can indeed compare information picked up by two different modalities (vision and proprioception). This is precisely the role of the internal representations postulated by the AIM account. There seems to be a reciprocal relationship between acts seen and acts done, and not merely simple triggering of innately organised motor patterns.

Put at a more theoretical level, what we are suggesting is that the same representational capacities that underlie the infant's imitation of adults may also allow the infant to 'run the system in reverse', as it were, and appreciate the adult's imitation of the infant. In short, the mechanisms of production can also direct perception.

There are some interesting implications of the AIM model for theories of social development. Take the problem of how infants differentiate the people from the inanimate world, how they become interested in, identify with, and become attached to tokens from the former and not the latter. If our model is correct, it raises the idea that young humans may be especially attracted to other human beings (as opposed to inanimate objects) just because it is other humans who imitate their behavior. Because neonates can recognize the equivalences between the acts they themselves perform and those performed by the adults, they have a means by which to identify with other human beings. Thus our model opens the possibility that imitation and intermodal representation, even from the earliest postnatal periods, serve an important social function in the development of the infant's self–other relations.

Summary and conclusions

It is traditionally assumed that facial imitation is a sophisticated cognitive achievement because the model and the infant's response cannot be compared within the same perceptual modality. Our demonstration of facial imitation in newborn humans under 72 hours old shows that the capacity is available at birth, and does not develop out of repeated experience in face-to-face interaction. Our working hypothesis is that human newborns have an innate ability to appreciate equivalences between their own acts and the acts they see. In our view neonates imitate by actively directing their movements to match the target gesture.

Our position can be tested in the future by (1) assessing the range of gestures that can be imitated, (2) evaluating the organization/morphology of the responses, and (3) conducting converging experiments on intermodal perception in neonates. It is our prediction that infants can imitate a variety of gestures beyond the oral movements we have tested to date; that infants' imitative responses are not rigidly fixed, stereotypic action patterns; and finally, that converging experiments will demonstrate a rich set of intermodal mappings in early infancy. Some support for the latter proposition at least has already been reported (Bower 1982; Kuhl and Meltzoff 1982; Meltzoff and Borton 1979). Pending the results of future studies, we suggest that the capacity for intermodal representation is not a late-emerging skill, but rather a basic starting point for infant psychological development. Armed with an innate capacity for intermodal representation and imitation, the human newborn is provided with a firm foundation and powerful tools for subsequent cognitive and social development.

REFERENCES

Bandura, A. (1969) 'Social-learning theory of identificatory processes', in D. A. Goslin (ed.), *Handbook of Socialization Theory and Research*, Chicago: Rand McNally.

Bower, T. G. R. (1979) *Human Development*, San Francisco: W. H. Freeman.

Bower, T. G. R. (1982) *Development in Infancy* (2nd ed.), San Francisco: W.H. Freeman.

Bruner, J. S. (1972) 'Nature and uses of immaturity', *American Psychologist* 27: 1–22.

Bruner, J. S. (1973) 'Organization of early skilled action', *Child Development* 44: 1–11.

Dawkins, R. (1976) *The Selfish Gene*, New York: Oxford University Press.

Fantz, R. L. (1963) 'Pattern vision in newborn infants', *Science* 140: 296–7.

Fortes, M. (1938) 'Social and psychological aspects of education in Taleland', Memorandum XVII of the International Institute of African Languages and Cultures, Oxford: Oxford University Press.

Kagan, J. (1967) 'On the need for relativism', *American Psychologist* 22: 131–42.

Kuhl, P. K. and Meltzoff, A. N. (1982) 'The bimodal perception of speech in infancy', *Science* 218: 1138–41.

Leighton, D. and Kluckhohn, C. (1947) *Children of the People*, Cambridge, Mass.: Harvard University Press.

Lipsitt, L. P. (1967) 'Learning capacities of the human infant', in R. J. Robinson (ed.) *Brain and Early Behavior Development in the Fetus and Infant*, New York: Academic Press.

Lorenz, K. and Tinbergen, N. (1938) 'Taxis and instinctive behavior pattern in egg-rolling by the greylag goose', in K. Lorenz (ed.) *Studies in Animal and Human Behavior* (1970) (vol. 1), trans. R. Martin, Cambridge, Mass.: Harvard University Press.

Medawar, P. B. (1957) *The Uniqueness of the Individual*, London: Methuen.

Meltzoff, A. N. (1981) 'Imitation, intermodal coordination, and representation in early infancy', in G. Butterworth (ed.) *Infancy and Epistemology*, Brighton: Harvester Press.

Meltzoff, A. N. and Borton, R. W. (1979) 'Intermodal matching by human neonates', *Nature* 282: 403–4.

Meltzoff, A. N. and Moore, M. K. (1977) 'Imitation of facial and manual gestures by human neonates', *Science* 198: 75–8.

Meltzoff, A. N. and Moore, M. K. (1983a) 'Newborn infants imitate adult facial gestures', *Child Development* 54: 702–9.

Meltzoff, A. N. and Moore, M. K. (1983b) 'The origins of imitation in infancy: paradigm, phenomena, and theories', in L. P. Lipsitt (ed.) *Advances in Infancy Research* (vol. 2), Norwood, N.J.: Ablex.

Piaget, J. (1954) *The Construction of Reality in the Child*, New York: Basic Books.

Piaget, J. (1962) *Play, Dreams, and Imitation in Childhood*, New York: Norton.

Reichard, G. (1938) 'Social life', in F. Boas (ed.) *General Anthropology*, Boston: D. C. Heath.

Steward, J. H., Manners, R., Wolf, E., Seda, E., Mintz, S., and Scheele, R. (1956) *The People of Puerto Rico*, Urbana, Ill.: University of Illinois Press.

Tinbergen, N. (1951) *The Study of Instinct*, New York: Oxford University Press.

Vilakazi, A. (1962) *Zulu Transformations: A Study of the Dynamics of Social Change*, Pietermaritzburg: University of Natal Press.

Whiten, A. (1975) 'Neonatal separation and mother–infant *interaction*', paper presented at the meeting of the International Society for the Study of Behavioral Development, Guildford, July.

6　The parental frame

Kenneth Kaye

Source: Kaye, K. (1982) *The Mental and Social Life of Babies*, Harvester Press, Chapter 5.

You see, really and truly, apart from the things anyone can pick up (the dressing and the proper way of speaking and so on), the difference between a lady and a flower girl is not how she behaves, but how she's treated. I shall always be a flower girl to Professor Higgins, because he always treats me as a flower girl, and always will; but I know I can be a lady to you, because you always treat me as a lady, and always will.

(George Bernard Shaw, *Pygmalion*, 1916)

[. . .]

This article will describe some observations of interaction between infants and adults. I shall try to show that infants learn to play the roles of system members because adults place them in situations where the skills they lack are performed for them. Parents, especially, keep up many of the essential features of their own side of the interaction despite the infant's deficiencies as a partner. By taking his role for him, they also demonstrate that role. Gradually, they relinquish it to him as he shows signs of being able to take it on.

SHARED MEANING THROUGH JOINT DOING

In the recent literature on mother–infant interaction some intriguing consistencies appear. The observations made by many investigators, across a variety of situations and ages, call attention to the way parents organise time and space for their infants.

After eight weeks or so when social smiling is well established, the mother may spend long periods eliciting smiling in her infant. During such periods the infant is held on the mother's lap facing her and supported by her arms or is placed in an infant seat. The mother smiles and vocalizes to the infant and moves her head rhythmically towards and away from his face. The infant first responds by rapt attention, with a widening of his eyes and a stilling of his body movements. Then his excitement increases, body movements begin again, he may vocalize and eventually a smile spreads over his face. At this point he turns away from his mother before beginning the whole cycle once again. Throughout this sequence the mother's actions are carefully phased with those of the infant. During the infant's attention phase the mother's behavior is restrained but as his excitement increases she vocalizes more rapidly and the pitch of her voice rises. At the point when he is about to smile her movements are suddenly reduced, as if she was allowing him time to reply. However, not all mothers behave in this way. Some subject their infants to a constant and unphased barrage of stimulation. The infant is given no pauses in which to reply and he seems totally overwhelmed by his mother. Instead of playing this game for long periods, he is quickly reduced to fussing and crying and shows sustained and prolonged turning away from the mother's face.

(Richards 1971: 37–8)

This example shows how the successful mother creates a microcosm or 'frame' within which schemas can function. All parents do this in one form or another much of the time, but since none can do it perfectly all the time difficulties will sometimes arise.

It may seem contradictory to say that mothers organise the world for their infants and also to say, as Richards says above, that interaction is a matter of mothers' adjustment to their babies. Yet this is not a contradiction. The consequence of that adjusting is that the infant experiences a mirroring and magnifying of his arousal, attention to his vocalization or facial expression, and then a reaction to it. When a parent fails to be responsive in these ways, the infant experiences no differentiation of the message-sending and message-receiving roles. When adults do allow their own behavior to be temporally organized by the infant's, they are really assimilating his cycles of attention and arousal to the adult world's cycles of speaking and listening, gesturing and observing. So the adults' adjustment is in fact a form of socialization. They construct a consistently organised social world around the infant, teaching him to punctuate the flow of experience.

Alan Fogel (1976), in a case study of one mother's face-to-face play with her son in 12 videotaped sessions from 5 to 13 weeks, found that the mother's continual gaze was a kind of frame within which her infant's gaze could wander and return. This is the same kind of frame a

Figure 6.1 'Framing' relationship of infant's attention, mother's exaggerated facial expressions (smiling, nodding, raised eyebrows, etc.), and infant's vocalizations, smiles, wide-open mouth, etc.

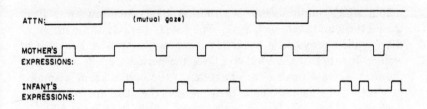

Source: Adapted from Fogel (1976).

Figure 6.2 Proportion of time mothers spend in different facial activities and proportion of time infants spend attending to mothers' faces, in the face-to-face play situation

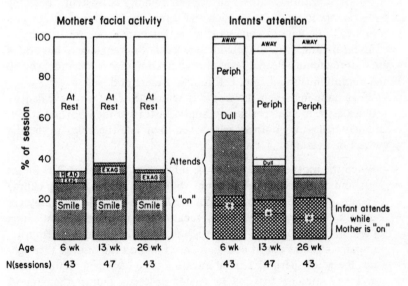

Note: *level the cross-hatched area would have been equal to, by chance.
Source: Kaye and Fogel (1980).

mother uses in holding her infant at the breast while he sucks and pauses (Kaye 1977), and later when the toddler returns to the mother after each exploratory foray into the wider world (Ainsworth 1967). Within the periods of mutual gazing, Figure 6.1 shows Fogel's findings regarding the relation between baby's and mother's mouth movements.

The larger study by Kaye and Fogel (1980) confirmed what Fogel had concluded from his case study: when the mothers did not have their babies' attention they typically waited. They continued talking to the infants and watching them. They provided a temporal frame within which infants were free to shift their attention away from the mothers and then back again. The babies' periods of attention-to-mother then provided a frame for their own expressive behavior as well as for that of the mothers. Over the period from 6 weeks to 6 months, we saw three clear changes: (1) the babies spent a smaller proportion of time looking at their mothers (i.e., the 'on' to 'off' ratio declined within the frame provided by mother) (Figure 6.2); (2) mothers, rather than trying to resist this trend, became even more selective about fitting their own expressions within the frame of the babies' 'on' time (also seen in Figure 6.2); (3) babies began to take the role of initiators of greetings during these frames within frames rather than merely responders. In summary, by adjusting to the on-off cycles of infant attention, mothers succeed in creating consistent, recurring mini-sequences of events, which the infant in turn responds to and comes to anticipate in consistent ways. Intrinsic processes (the cycles of attention and arousal) provide one level of organization, but adults use that to create a deeper level of organization that is extrinsic, social, and communicating – long before it is understood.

What happens when the frame is removed? This was revealed by Tronick *et al.* in an experimental study. Instead of their normal active, attentive behavior, mothers were asked to violate the 'rules' in specific ways. For example:

> When the mother is in profile the infant acts differently. The infant sits and watches her. He seldom smiles but makes cooing, calling vocalizations and often leans forward in his seat. He also may cry but the cries seem faked. This vocalizing is interspersed with long periods of intense looking at the mother. The infant's orientation remains straight ahead and with gaze fixed on the mother throughout the whole period. The infants do not go into the greeting phase and they often get fussy as the session proceeds. Our mothers report that a similar type of performance often happens while they are driving their car and unable to maintain an *en face* position with their infants.
>
> (Tronick *et al.* 1979: 364)

These frames are spatial as well as temporal. The behavior of mother and baby during the time frame takes place in a segment of space, and conversely the space marked off by their gaze directions constrains their behavior during a segment of time. Here are some more examples of behavioral space–time frames created by mothers:

> To apply the name 'Give and Take' to the exchange of objects between a mother and her three-month-old infant is somewhat of a misnomer. For early instances of Give and Take are more properly glossed as 'offering and grasping' and appear notoriously one-sided: the burden of the exchange resting heavily on mother. Characteristic of this early period of exchange is mother's utilization of an array of attentional devices that make up the 'offering' and 'giving' phase of the Give and Take. This phase is often quite lengthy with the mother (M) maneuvering the object in a space approximately 12 to 24 inches in front of the child (C). M's manipulation of objects is frequently accompanied by verbal highlighting, primarily in the form of interrogatives and tag questions: 'Do you want this?' 'You want your rattle, don't you?' Moreover, the object being offered provides an additional source of stimulation for C. With the brightly coloured, noisy rattle, for example, M has an ideal object with which to capture and sustain his attention. Frequently she is observed shaking the rattle, looming it close to C's face, gently rubbing it up and down C's stomach – such endless variety in technique has the common purpose of activating C and, perhaps more importantly, M 'sees' him as taking his 'turn' in the 'game'.
>
> (Bruner 1977: 283)

Mothers appear to have a good idea of whether the pointing gesture is meaningful to their infant. Many mothers of nine-month-old babies (and also of younger ones whom we brought to the laboratory) reported that normally they simply do not attract their babies' attention to objects at a distance but rather bring them to the child. This resulted in two mothers being replaced in the sample, because throughout the session they repeatedly got up from their seats for long periods in order to attract the baby's attention to toys by playing with them and by pulling them towards him, despite instructions to remain seated.

An attempt to observe mothers of much younger babies (four–six months) was abandoned because, when obliged to attract the attention of babies at this age to distal objects, the mothers pointed in a completely different way. They spent a lot of their time placing a finger in front of the babies' eyes, clicking their fingers, and slowly drawing the hand towards the object. It was observed that, in desperation, these mothers might even physically turn the babies' head in the direction of the finger. Such behavior we termed 'cueing,' i.e. providing additional cues to the point . . . .

The mothers of 14-month-olds cued less and the cues they used tended to be of a less forceful nature. Their behavior largely consisted of a quick tap on the hand or arm — a very effective method of indicating to a child that his mother is about to do something to which she wants him to attend.

(Murphy and Messer 1977: 334)

At 0;9 (16) [9 months, 16 days] [Jacqueline] discovers more complex signs during a meal than previously. She likes the grape juice in a glass but not the soup in a bowl. She watches her mother's activity. When the spoon comes out of the glass she opens her mouth wide, whereas when it comes from the bowl, her mouth remains closed. Her mother then tries to lead her to make a mistake by taking a spoon from the bowl and passing it by the glass before offering it to Jacqueline. But she is not fooled. At 0;9 (18) Jacqueline no longer needs to look at the spoon. She notes by the sound whether the spoonful comes from the glass or from the bowl and obstinately closes her mouth in the latter case. At 0;10 (26) Jacqueline also refuses her soup. But her mother, before holding out the spoon to her, strikes in against a silver bowl containing stewed fruit. Jacqueline is fooled this time and opens her mouth due to not having watched the move and to having depended on the sound alone.

(Piaget 1952: 249)

With babies in the second and third month, most mothers we have filmed played games that involved touching the infant's body, like pat-a-cake with the hands, bouncing the legs, shaking the cheeks, prodding the nose or stomach. Gradually, it would seem the mother herself is accepted as a game object as she mirrors the infant's acts of expression. After this the play incorporates objects that the infant has accepted as foci for interest. We found that by 6 months these games via objects, or with parts of the mother's body treated as objects, became the infant's preferred form of play. Then, at 9 or 10 months, they started the deliberately co-operative form of interest in objects which transforms play into exchange of act of meaning.

(Trevarthen and Hubley 1978: 212)

The parade of examples could go on and on. I will conclude with an author who has traced explicitly how joint symbolic reference to objects, 'shared meaning' is made salient to the 1-year-old child because of a framework of exchange established by parents.

In the primitive phase, the reaching of the child is effective through the mother's acting upon her interpretation of its significance, but the child has no cognizance of this essential role that the mother plays and of those aspects of his own behavior that are instrumental in securing her co-operation. In passing from the primitive phase to the gestural the child becomes *aware* of the communicative aspect of his own behavior, which has always been there in reality. In other words, whereas before there was co-ordination of activity, i.e., communication, the child was not aware of the relation between his own activity and his mother's monitoring of it. In a far-reaching cognitive restructuring he gains insight into the consequences of his own activity and the 'mechanics' of the situation he finds himself in. A gesture, in this case the reach, emerges as a gesture because it is not simply produced in order to get an object, but in order to produce an effect on another in order to get an object.

(Clark 1978: 249)

Our concern here is with the role that all of the mothers just described seem to have been playing with respect to their infants' differentiation of skills. So we will now turn to two theories referred to as the inside-out and outside-in theories.

The parental frames help us to be more specific about the outside-in metaphor. The parents do not work on the infants' skills with pruning shears or with much contingent reinforcement. Actual praise and criticism are surprisingly infrequent, and when they occur they may be quite nonspecific or even contradictory. The same is true of verbal instructions. Instead, the parent relies on the infant's intrinsic abilities to differentiate his own skills gradually, as needed. However, that does not occur orthogenetically either. It occurs as a result of the way parents organise the world of objects and events. The differentiation process itself may be intrinsic, but the order to which the schemas adapt is only one of many possible orderings of the world. It is an ordering selected by parents to a greater extent than psychologists have realized.

Some theories have emphasized the early construction of a mental reality in adaptation to physical reality – to universal, logical truths about things – and some have discussed the socialization of children into cultural norms, especially after they begin to use language. What

136   *The process of development*

we have only recently come to understand is that the physical world too – the world of objects, motion, time, and space – is presented to infants in a socially structured way. The 'social construction of reality' is not only a social consensus among language users about how things should be described and conceptualized. It is literally a construction, by social means, of microcosms that are the physical reality to which infants adapt. The spatial settings and anticipatable temporal patternings provide essential frames for cognitive development.

TYPES OF ADULT 'FRAMES' FOR CHILD BEHAVIOR

Contrary to Watson's (1925) classic boast, the parent does not have unlimited power to shape the child into any kind of adult imaginable. There are plenty of intrinsic constraints upon the course of development. But contrary to Werner and Kaplan (1963) and to Piaget (1952), those intrinsic functions fall far short of orthogenesis. The possible paths are varied and world-dependent. Growth depends upon the reduction of a potential chaos to an assimilable order, with just moderate degrees of novelty and variety.

There are many ways in which parental behavior structures the world so as to facilitate the infant's own processes of differentiation. The idea of frames is borrowed from Goffman's (1974) analysis of the context-dependency of social interaction and from Fogel's (1976) analysis of the multiply-imbedded levels of behavioral contexts in the mother–infant face-to-face situation. We can identify a number of different types of frames that adults provide for children. These types can be defined and exemplified functionally, without reference to specific modalities of behavior, ages of children, or situations.

In the *nurturant frame*, adults nourish, comfort, clean, console and fondle infants. As obvious and non-controversial as these functions are, they have occupied an inordinate amount of attention among students of child development. Perhaps this is because parents have been found to differ, across and within cultures, in the time and energy they devote to these various activities. However, performing them at some level is universal and unavoidable.

An important point about nurturance in the early months is that it often carries its own guaranteed concordance between parent and infant goals. So long as the mother realizes that her newborn is hungry, no formal communication is required in order to establish a cooperative endeavor (he does not have to be told to suck when she puts him to the breast). To some extent, this continues to be true. The toddler frightened by a stranger or injured by a fall finds immediate consolation without having to explain his problem. The nurturant frame is perhaps the most reliable channel for parent–infant intersubjectivity.

The *protective frame* is one that adults provide in a general sense by keeping the infant within earshot and by keeping dangerous objects out of his reach, as well as in a very specific sense by creating bounded spaces within which new accomplishments can be tried. For example, few parents would try to teach a child to dive by standing beside him at water's edge, urging him to plunge in. We stand in the water, an inch or two beyond where the child will hit, and promise to catch him. The child's daring depends upon trusting the adult, and the child's survival (psychologically if not biologically) depends upon the adult keeping that promise.

It is interesting to note how varied are the forms that the protective frame takes. There are the physical restraints of high chairs, playpens, cradle boards, etc. But there are also the ways in which adults restrict their discussion of certain topics, alter the rules of games so as to give the child an edge, and control the behavior of older siblings if the latter themselves do not spontaneously adopt a protective frame.

As with nurturance, protection is a dimension of cross-cultural and individual variation. But again as with nurturance, despite variation in the extent of protectiveness of any particular kind, the existence of the protection function in general is universal. It is merely expressed differently in different families and cultures. Protection is always relative. Parents do not normally try to protect the child completely – that would mean keeping him out of the water, not letting him play with older children, etc. We are as quick to condemn each other for being overprotective parents as for being underprotective. This fact shows that the function of the protective frame is to allow the child to go a little way, just not too far, beyond his competence.

We can also see examples of this frame in animals. Sometimes it comes close to human forms. I watched an orangutan mother in the Lincoln Park Zoo play a tickling game with her 2-month-old. As he hung by one hand from a horizontal bar, she made an elaborate show of being about to tickle him under that arm. When she did so, he would double up his body and switch to the other hand, sometimes getting hold of the bar and sometimes missing it but catching the mother's forearm. This went on for 15 minutes. I noticed that the mother always had one hand below her infant, not touching him but close enough to grab him when (as happened only once) he let go before getting a good grip with the other hand. The adaptive value of this maternal caution was obvious, for there was nothing else to catch the baby's fall but the concrete floor 30 feet below.

In the *instrumental frame*, an adult carries out what appears to be the infant's intention. For example, left to his own devices a 3-month-old swipes ineffectually toward a rattle placed upon a table. However, should he happen to be seated in someone's lap, within a minute or so the rattle is likely to be moved closer to his hand or turned so that his finger will hook its handle on the next swipe. The important difference between this kind of intervention and either the nurturant or the protective frame is that here an adult is acting on behalf of what she perceives as the infant's own goals, whereas nurturant or protective frames are merely for his benefit, without regard to his goals.

The instrumental frame, then, consists of the adult monitoring the infant's behavior (usually in relation to objects), interpreting the infant as having a certain intention, and partially or completely fulfilling that intention. Perhaps it is not immediately apparent that this is important for the development of the infant's skills. In fact, it may seem to be counterproductive, 'overprotective', for it would seem to prevent the infant from learning to do things for himself. Let us postpone that question for a few moments.

The same parental act can serve several different functions. We can see in the very earliest nurturant activities the beginnings of the instrumental frame: In nursing her baby, while obviously providing nourishment and pleasure, a mother also closes the gap between her breast and the infant's rooting mouth, just as she will later close the gap between the rattle and his groping hand. In addition to providing a nurturant and an instrumental frame, the nursing mother encircles her baby protectively with her arm and simultaneously tries to prevent his swallowing too much air or breathing too little.

The *feedback frame* provides more consistent or more salient consequences to the child, for his own action, than the physical world itself would provide. For example, touching an electric cord or playing close to the fire do not usually result in pain. But the parent's 'No!' serves to shape the infant's behavior so that the potentially dangerous consequences need never be felt. On the positive side, praise or parental delight can signal success in a task where the actual performance was not really good enough to attain its objective. Or the parent, by putting the rattle nearer the infant's hand, can make an inadequate reach a successful one, leaving its refinement for later. This is one way, then, that an instrumental completion is instructive: when it reinforces one or more constituents of the needed skill.

The feedback frame often overlaps with the instrumental frame;

which is just what we should expect. When subschemas can be performed with minimal attention, the skill learner can focus upon the problem of combining subskills into higher-order skills. We see adults breaking tasks down into manageable subtasks all the time; one example already discussed was the detour task, in which most mothers brought the toy out to the open area at least once, as if to suggest to the baby that the hand on that side should do the reaching instead of the hand that was blocked by the plexiglass. We have seen 24-month-olds use a similar strategy in teaching 18-month-olds how to obtain a cookie from a puzzle box (Poppei 1976), so it is clearly not a 'maternal' frame so much as a natural human reaction to another person's incompetence.

The effectiveness of both the instrumental and the feedback frame may depend as much upon timing as upon consistency. Experimental studies of infants' ability to learn the contingent effects of their own behavior show that, when feedback is delayed by as little as 3 seconds, infants are unable to learn the contingency. This is true even of 6- to 8-month-olds (Millar and Watson 1979). Behavior modification techniques, whether used by operant psychologists in the last 20 years, circus trainers in the last couple of thousand years, or human parents for perhaps a million years, involve the instrumental frame (simplifying the task) as much as the feedback frame (reinforcement).

In the foregoing examples, more is involved than the parent merely making the physical consequences of certain actions salient to the infant. The most important thing is that social consequences are introduced even into nonsocial actions. 'Good girl!' someone shouts, and a simple product of maturation and solitary practice is marked as a social occasion. Similarly, parents' 'No!' or 'Hot!' when the child approaches too near the fire (which must occur a hundred times for every one time a child actually gets burned) does more to build the edifice of approving and disapproving caretakers, and to lay the foundation for perception of self, than it teaches about physical safety.

The *modeling frame* occurs when an adult performs some action and then waits for the child to try to imitate it. As we shall see, this can and does occur in a turn-taking pattern, alternating many trials by the infant with many demonstrations by the adult (Pawlby 1977), or it may involve isolated trials on different occasions. Imitative attempts will often elicit feedback. On the other hand, inadequate goal-directed actions will often elicit adult demonstrations. In fact, when the adult carries out some action the infant seems to have been attempting, this instrumental frame provides a model for imitation whether the adult was intending to do so or not.

To illustrate, let us go back to the example of the rattle. I am holding a 3-month-old in my lap. She stares at the toy about 6 inches in front of her on the table. Her fingers scrabble on the table surface, then she extends her arm toward the toy but, with her fist closed, knocks it a few inches away. I reach for it and move it back to where it was. I have no lesson plan, in fact I act without really thinking. I don't care much whether the baby succeeds. I enjoy watching her clumsy failures, but I cannot do that when the toy is out of her reach. So I move it back. Yet in doing so, I have demonstrated the correct way to reach and grasp the rattle. Adults perform dozens of demonstrations like that for infants every day without realizing it. And when I watch quietly for the next attempt, though not thinking about it as a matter of imitation because I have not thought of what I just did as having provided a model, I am nonetheless providing a modeling frame.

Patiently waiting for the infant to make a trial might seem unlikely to be effective, in view of the infant's short-term memory problems. However, his very short memory for contingencies – failing to see event Y as contingent upon X unless it comes within a second or two of X – is not due to any deficiency in short-term memory in general. In habituation, classical conditioning, and object permanence, all of which processes are involved in imitation, short-term memory increases greatly from 2 to 6 months (Watson 1967; Millar and Watson 1979; Fitzgerald and Brackhill 1976). The result is that imitation becomes more powerful than operant learning, and consequently adults prefer trying to show the infant how to do things as opposed to 'shaping' his behavior.

The modeling frame serves social functions at the same time it suggests new ends and means to the child. Given the opportunity to play with an object being manipulated by an adult or with an identical copy of it that is closer to him, the infant passes by the copy in favor of the one that seems to interest the adult (Eckerman, Whatley and McGehee 1979). So he is not merely imitating; he is allowing the adult to establish joint focus upon a common topic (Bruner 1977). At the same time, he makes himself into a person among persons; imitation ceases to be a matter of assimilating features of isolated acts and begins to be an exchange of roles in a continuing dialogue with others.

The *discourse frame* creates a conversation-like exchange, not necessarily involving vocalizations. Discourse begins when the two partners' actions are still not equivalent in any respect. If the parent discovers that blowing 'raspberries' or puffing air at baby's tummy will elicit a laugh, and if the parent then repeats the action, which then elicits another laugh, what results is a dialogue. The structure it has in the parent's mind or seems to have to an observer can lead us to ascribe more sophisticated interacting to the infant than is really warranted by the facts. All he is doing, at first, is laughing in response to each tickle.

Of course, the longer sequence soon becomes the routine, so that the 5-month-old expects and anticipates the parent's repetition in response to his own laugh. This expectation is revealed in his reaction, a questioning look and a tentative chuckle, when the parent does *not* do the next trial. So the infant has some expectation of the normal sequence. But he is still not the one responsible for it. And long after he is taking turns in a verbal conversation it will still be up to adults to ensure that those turns constitute connected discourse.

One of the ways the discourse frame is used is to manipulate the child's play. Adults pose demands in the form of questions and indirect suggestions, so that the child's turn in the turn-taking sequence can often take the form of demonstrating comprehension, of mastering a toy, and later of using language (Schaffer and Crook 1979; Garvey 1977; Kaye and Charney 1981).

Finally (though I do not claim this list is exhaustive), there is the *memory frame*. To the extent the parent has shared experiences with the infant – knows what objects have intrigued him, what he has been able and unable to do with them, what he has imitated, what feedback he has received from objects and from people – the parent can use that information in making choices about what to offer, what to do for the infant, what to demonstrate, what kind of feedback to use, and so forth. In short, the adult's memory, especially to the extent that it is a *shared memory* with the infant, itself provides a frame organizing the infant's subsequent experiences.

By shared memory I do not mean that the information is encoded or represented in the same way, nor that it has the same meaning to both people. I mean that they have shared experiences, which usually take different forms in their different memories. That is precisely why the adult's memory provides a useful frame for the infant's activity, because the adult has often a symbolic representation of what the infant represents in a sensorimotor schema.

Any of these frames can, but need not, take the form of a *game*. I have avoided the term, because besides the connotation of conscious enjoyment, it also suggests that the two (or more) participants take turns and that they follow rules. In adult–infant interaction, a game is any routinized interaction in which the *adult* takes turns and pretends that the infant is taking turns, follows rules and pretends that the infant is aware of them and acts as though they both are enjoying it.

142   *The process of development*

Although games, strictly defined, account for a relatively small proportion of mothers' time with their babies (Gustafson, Green and West 1979), they have been the subject of dozens of studies in recent years. The reason for this interest is that what is true of the readily identified games like 'peek-a-boo' or 'pat-a-cake' is true of parental frames in general, or at least true of a great many activities that cannot be called games in any specific sense. 'Taking turns' is one of the threads that tie together games, discourse (verbal as well as preverbal), my own studies, and much of the literature on the interaction of infants with their elders.

REFERENCES

Ainsworth, M. (1967) *Infancy in Uganda*, Baltimore: Johns Hopkins Press.
Bruner, J. (1977) 'Early social interaction and language acquisition', in H. R. Schaffer (ed.) *Studies in Mother–Infant Interaction*, London: Academic Press.
Clark, R. (1978) 'The transition from action to gesture', in A. Lock (ed.), *Action, Gesture and Symbol: The Emergence of Language*, New York: Academic Press.
Eckerman, C., Whatley, J. and McGehee, L. J. (1979) 'Approaching and contacting the object another manipulates: a social skill of the 1-year-old', *Developmental Psychology* 15: 585–93.
Fitzgerald, H. and Brackhill, Y. (1976) 'Classical conditioning in infancy: development and constraints', *Psychological Bulletin* 83: 353–76.
Fogel, A. (1976) 'Gaze, face and voice in the development of the mother–infant face-to-face interaction', Ph.D. dissertation, University of Chicago.
Garvey, C. (1977) 'The contingent query: a dependent act in conversation', in M. Lewis and L. Rosenblum (eds) *Interaction, Conversation, and the Development of Language*, New York: Wiley.
Goffman, E. (1974) *Frame Analysis: An Essay on the Organization of Experience*, New York: Harper & Row.
Gustafson, G., Green, J. and West, M. (1979) 'The infant's changing role in mother–infant games: the growth of social skills', *Infant Behavior and Development* 2: 301–8.
Kaye, K. (1977) 'Toward the origin of dialogue', in H. R. Schaffer (ed.) *Studies in Mother–Infant Interaction*, London: Academic Press.
Kaye, K. and Charney, R. (1981) 'How mothers maintain "dialogue" with two-year-olds', in D. Olson (ed.) *The Social Foundations of Language and Thought*, New York: Norton.
Kaye, K. and Fogel, A. (1980) 'The temporal structure of face-to-face communication between mothers and infants', *Developmental Psychology* 16: 454–64.
Millar, W. and Watson, J. (1979) 'The effect of delayed feedback on infant learning reexamined', *Child Development* 50: 747–51.
Murphy, C. and Messer, D. (1977) 'Mothers, infants, and pointing: a

study of a gesture', in H. R. Schaffer (ed.) *Studies in Mother–Infant Interaction*, London: Academic Press.

Pawlby, S. (1977) 'Imitative interaction', in H. R. Schaffer (ed.), *Studies in Mother–Infant Interaction*, London: Academic Press.

Piaget, J. (1952) *The Origins of Intelligence in Children*, New York: International Universities Press (originally published in French, 1936).

Poppei, J. (1976) 'Toddlers' use of peer imitation for problem-solving', Ph.D dissertation, University of Chicago.

Richards, M. (1975) 'Social interaction in the first weeks of human life', *Psychiatry, Neurology, and Neurochirurgy* 14: 35–42.

Schaffer, H. R. and Crook, C. K. (1979) 'Maternal control techniques in a directed play situation', *Child Development* 50: 989–96.

Trevarthen, C. and Hubley, P. (1978) 'Secondary intersubjectivity: confidence, confiding, and acts of meaning in the first year', in A. Lock (ed.) *Action, Gesture, and Symbol: The Emergence of Language*, New York: Academic Press.

Tronick, E., Als, H. and Adamson, L. (1979) 'Structure of early face-to-face communicative interactions', in M. Bullowa (ed.) *Before Speech: The Beginning of Interpersonal Communication*, Cambridge: Cambridge University Press.

Watson, J. (1967) 'Memory and contingency analysis in infant development', *Merrill-Palmer Quarterly* 13: 55–76.

Watson, J. B. (1925) *Behaviorism*, New York: Norton.

Werner, H. and Kaplan, B. (1963) *Symbol Formation*, New York: Wiley.

7 The effects of postnatal depression on mother–infant relations and infant development

Lynne Murray and Alan Stein

Studies of the impact of parental depression on preschool and school-aged children have consistently reported a variety of adverse effects. For example, there have been findings of raised levels of psychiatric disturbance, greater insecurity in attachment relationships and impairments in attention and lowered I.Q. (Weissman *et al.* 1972; Gamer *et al.* 1977; Cohler *et al.* 1977; Welner *et al.* 1977; Grunebaum *et al.* 1978; McKnew *et al.* 1979; Weissman *et al.* 1984; Cox *et al.* 1987b).

Epidemiological research carried out in the last decade has shown that approximately 10 per cent of women suffer from non-psychotic depression in the first few months following childbirth. This prevalence rate contrasts with that for postpartum psychotic episodes which, while more severe, occur rarely, affecting only one or two per thousand women. In cases of non-psychotic depression with postnatal onset all the characteristics of depression occurring at other times are presented, with irritability, anxiety, concentration impairments, and depressive mood and thoughts being prominent (Nott 1987; Cooper *et al.* 1988; Murray and Carothers 1990). All these features of depression may exert a profound effect on interpersonal relationships, including that established with the infant. Moreover, it is common for some level of symptoms to persist for at least a year beyond childbirth. Since it is the case that, in most cultures, the mother constitutes the infant's primary social environment in these first months, the issue of the effects on the rapidly developing infant of depression occurring at this time is one of special clinical concern. In addition to the clinical significance of the impact of postnatal depression, the study of infancy in the context of a disturbed or pathological family environment can be valuable in elucidating the role of interpersonal relations in the developmental process. This article reviews studies that have been carried out in recent years to address both these clinical and theoretical issues.

MATERNAL REPORTS

Several studies have made indirect child assessments by interviewing mothers, often some years after an episode of postnatal depression, about their child's current behaviour. Zajicek and de Salis (1979) interviewed women who had experienced symptoms in the postnatal period that were either of a severity to produce impairments in daily functioning and relationships, or were subjectively distressing but not incapacitating. At 27 months the children of these women were reported to be fearful, to have eating problems and to have difficulties in bladder control. Uddenberg and Englesson (1978), using very similar case definitions to those described above, found that the 4½-year-old children of women who had suffered from postpartum mental disturbance were described as being troublesome, uncontrollable and prone to temper tantrums.

Williams and Carmichael (1985) conducted a study of the effects of maternal depression on infants in a poor, multi-ethnic community in Melbourne, Australia. Amongst the primiparous mothers in their sample, those who became depressed reported significantly more difficulties than non-depressed mothers. Two principal patterns of disturbance were found. First, several mothers reported that there had been a failure to establish a relationship or routine pattern of management with the baby whilst on the postnatal ward. On their return home, the infant was said to cry persistently, feed poorly, sleep irregularly and only for brief periods, and to be difficult to soothe. This situation itself appeared to cause depressive symptoms in the mothers, who became frustrated and angry with their infants. Second, for other mothers, infant sleeping, feeding and crying difficulties developed only after the onset of the depressive episode some weeks following delivery. Again, a vicious cycle of impaired communication became established. This picture of marked difficulties in infant care and behaviour applying where the infant was an only child contrasted with that obtaining where there were older children in the family. In these circumstances there was no increase in reports of infant behavioural disturbance. Indeed, in a substantial proportion of cases, the depressed mothers were protective of their infants, and had a good relationship with them. However, significant levels of behaviour problems were found instead amongst the older preschool siblings.

These studies point to an increased risk of child behavioural disturbance, and difficulties in the mother–child relationship, where there has been psychiatric disturbance in the months following delivery. However, it should be borne in mind that many of the women taking part in the research described above were depressed at the time of interview. Current maternal depression may influence the outcome of these studies in two ways. First, there may be a direct effect of current symptoms on child functioning, making if difficult to determine the effect of postnatal depression. Second, the mother's current depression may colour her perceptions of the child's behaviour, and hence lead to over-reporting of problems. Thus some caution is required when considering the findings of this series of studies.

A carefully analysed study was carried out by Ghodsian *et al.* (1984), in which account was taken of current symptoms when evaluating the impact on the child of depression occurring during the three and a half years after the birth. Mothers were psychiatrically assessed at 4, 14, 27 and 42 months, and, on all but the first occasion, they were interviewed about their child's behaviour. No effects were found of depression occurring in the first 4 months. However, there was evidence that depression occurring at 14 months had an independent effect on later behaviour problems.

Wrate *et al.* (1985) interviewed women who had participated in a prospective study of postnatal depression when their children were 3 years old. As in the study carried out by Ghodsian *et al.*, the data were analysed to take account of current depression, and again no increase in child behavioural disturbance was reported by mothers who had suffered from a postnatal depressive episode. However, women who had had mild depressive symptoms in the postnatal period did report more difficulties. This apparently paradoxical outcome seemed to arise from the fact that those women who had suffered from mild symptoms of depression in the postnatal period had earlier shown far greater anxiety about their maternal role, and had often gone on later to have depressive episodes that focussed on anxieties about the child.

Using a similar design to that adopted by Wrate *et al.*, Caplan *et al.* (1989) followed up women who had taken part in a study of depression occurring after childbirth (Kumar and Robson 1984). When the children were 4 years old mothers who were currently depressed reported more child behavioural difficulties. The association seemed to be mediated by disturbed family interactions, since reports of such difficulties were also related to marital conflict and paternal psychiatric history. However, as in the studies of Ghodsian *et al.* and Wrate *et al.*, no relationship was found between reported child disturbance and clinical depression occurring in the postnatal period.

Evidence from these indirect studies indicates, therefore, that while there have been several reports of an increase in later behavioural disturbance associated with episodes of postnatal depression, when account is taken of current symptoms and the pattern of family relationships, no effects of postnatal depression per se are found on these particular dimensions of child outcome.

DIRECT STUDIES OF OLDER CHILDREN

Two studies have been completed in recent years that have the advantage of making direct assessments of children whose mothers had suffered from depression during the postnatal period. In the first study Cogill *et al.* (1986) examined child cognitive functioning using the same cohort as Caplan *et al.* above. At 4 years, children whose mothers had been depressed during the first postnatal year had significantly lower scores on the McCarthy Scales of cognitive development than children whose mothers had not been postnatally depressed. These differences could not be accounted for by current maternal depression.

The second study, carried out by Stein *et al.* (1990), highlights the processes that might cause this lower cognitive functioning. This study investigated the relationship between maternal postnatal depressive disorder and later mother–child interactions. They observed two groups of mothers and infants during home assessments when the infants were 19 months old. The index group consisted of mothers who had had a depressive disorder during the postnatal year. By 19 months half of these mothers had made a full recovery. The control group consisted of mothers who had been free from depression since the child's birth.

The main significant findings from the observational studies were that, compared with the controls, depressed mothers interacted less with their children, and showed less facilitation (positive contribution to their child's activity). Their children, in turn, showed less affective sharing (smiling and showing toys to the mother, or smiling and vocalizing during joint play), and greater distress during a planned brief departure of the mother from the room. Similar, but reduced, effects were seen in the subgroup of families in which the mothers had been depressed postnatally, but were no longer so at the 19-month follow-up.

It is important to note that the index group of mothers had experienced significantly more marital difficulties and social problems that mainly concerned housing and finance. Regression analysis revealed that these difficulties were the most powerful predictors of the quality of mother–child interaction at 19 months. However, an additional, independent contribution was made by maternal depression, both in the first few months and at the time of assessment. In contrast to research based on maternal reports of child behavioural disturbance, these direct studies indicate that maternal depression in the postpartum period may be associated with later lowered scores on cognitive assessments, and with less harmonious and mutual mother–child interactions. The way in which these specific adverse outcomes arise in the context of postnatal depression remains to be established, and differing interpretations of their development can be advanced. Thus, taking an 'environmental discontinuity' perspective, it could be argued that adverse infant and child outcome arises as a function of current difficulties in maternal communication. Evidence consistent with this hypothesis is, for example, the finding that significant problems in interpersonal functioning in intimate relationships persist in those who have suffered from depression even through periods of remission (Weissman and Paykel 1974). Alternatively, psychoanalytic theory has been taken up by some researchers who propose something akin to a sensitive period in early infancy, the experience of seriously distorted interpersonal contacts at this stage being held sufficient to bring about later impairments in functioning (Stern 1985). A third, 'dynamic interactionist' or 'transactional' model, drawing on the tradition of developmental embryology (Waddington 1957), suggests that characteristics of both environment and infant exert influences, and that their impact in turn modifies subsequent experience. For example, an unresponsive, depressed mother may provoke withdrawal and avoidance in the infant that then renders subsequent communication difficult, even though the mother may be ready to resume a more appropriate form of contact once she has recovered (see Robertson 1963 for a case study where such a process is apparent). These alternative models of the developmental process are discussed in some detail by Sameroff (1989). In order to resolve such issues, detailed prospective, longitudinal evidence about the developing relationship between the depressed mother and her infant, and the course of infant progress, is required. To date, however, little such evidence is available.

Nevertheless, a few studies have been carried out in recent years in which assessments have been made of early interactions between depressed mothers and their babies. These are reviewed below, along with evidence from developmental psychology about the development of mother–child relations in non-clinical populations. When considered together, these two lines of research provide some indication of the routes by which both deviant and favourable outcome may be brought about.

DIRECT STUDIES OF EARLY MOTHER—INFANT INTERACTIONS

Normal Populations

Over the last 20 years a large body of evidence has accumulated from developmental psychology about the interpersonal functioning of infants. One finding to emerge from this work is that very early on there is a propensity to be attracted to human forms. Some time ago Fantz (1963) had demonstrated that 2-month-olds prefer looking at face-like rather than scrambled visual arrays, and this has since been confirmed for newborn infants (Goren *et al.* 1975; Dziuranwiec 1987). Neonates seem not only to be attracted to faces or face-like stimuli, but are also capable of discriminating and imitating particular facial configurations, for example tongue protrusion (Meltzoff and Moore 1977) and various emotional expressions (Field *et al.* 1982; Field 1985).

In the auditory modality it has been shown that infants will orient selectively to the source of human speech when just an hour old (Alegria and Noirot 1978). Preferential responsiveness to the sound of the human voice compared to non-human sounds of the same pitch and intensity, and to the female rather than the male voice has been demonstrated in newborn infants by Friedlander (1970) and by Eisenberg (1975).

Leslie (1984) found that 6-month-olds could discriminate the characteristics of human action patterns carried out in relation to objects from equivalent physical effects generated by objects alone, and this has been confirmed for infants of 15 weeks in pilot work (Leslie, personal communication). Results such as these suggest that the infant's preferential responsiveness to the attributes of persons cannot be reduced to a simple attraction for certain salient physical properties such as motion, high-contrast visual forms or particular sound frequencies. Rather, it seems to be the case that the human infant is predisposed to respond to human qualities as special categories of experience.

In addition to the general responsiveness to human attributes there is a tendency in the infant rapidly to develop a preference for the particular qualities of the person caring for him. Selective responsiveness to the mother's face appears to be established shortly after birth (Field 1985; Bushnell *et al.* 1989). Preference for maternal speech has been demonstrated in experiments which show that infant sucking rate on a dummy fitted with a pressure transducer set up to drive a tape recording is increased to produce the mother's rather than a stranger's voice (de Casper and Fifer 1980; Mehler *et al.* 1978). By 6 days infants will turn towards their mother's breast pad more than to the breast pad of another lactating woman (McFarlane 1975). Finally, infants are also able to distinguish their mother from a stranger holding and carrying them in the dark, showing a more relaxed and moulded posture with their mother (Widmer–Robert–Tissot 1981).

This fundamental propensity for human contact and for the establishment of specific relationships is further elaborated in the period 6 weeks to 3 months. At a time before effective reaching and independent mobility are established, infants will, when alert and content, attend for prolonged periods to an adult who is gentle and responsive. During such contacts a complex repertoire of gestures, lip and tongue movements, and facial expressions is displayed. Together with the largely unconscious adaptations that are made by the adult partner – e.g., gentle head movements, expressive and rhythmical speech – a conversation-like form is achieved. This phase is considered by many researchers to be the most essentially social in infancy: it is termed the period of 'core relatedness' by Stern (1985) and that of 'primary intersubjectivity' by Trevarthen, both terms reflecting the fact that communication at this time typically has no other referent than the feelings and intentions of the two partners, and appears to be satisfying as an end in itself.

A number of studies have been carried out to explore infant sensitivity to the quality of adult communication at this time. In this research the mother's normal interactions with her infant are experimentally disrupted and the infant's response carefully monitored. The first of a series of studies to examine the infant's reaction to an unresponsive partner was carried out by Wolff (1969). Three-week-old infants who, when fussing, were presented with a silent, nodding face, began to cry; crying ceased when the face withdrew. Carpenter and colleagues (Carpenter *et al.* 1970; Carpenter 1974) reported distress and avoidance in infants under 2 months upon the presentation of their mother, still-faced and silent before them, and this behaviour profile has since been reported in a number of studies (Brazelton *et al.* 1975; Tronick *et al.* 1978; Murray 1980; Murray and Trevarthen 1985). Papousek and Papousek (1975) arranged further forms of distortion to the way in which the mother was presented: infants lost interest in the mother if a perspex screen with horizontal stripes was placed between them. In the same study infants were found actively to avoid the mother if she attempted to engage them following an 'incomprehensible' disappearance, such as leaving the room in the dark; no such response was seen if the departures were conducted in a natural fashion in full view of the infant.

In another series of studies examining infant sensitivity to perturbations in the mother–child relationship, Murray (Murray 1980; Murray and Trevarthen 1985) made the important distinction between 'naturalistic' and 'unnatural' perturbations. They found that a naturalistic disruption to maternal behaviour (the mother being interrupted and engaged in conversation with the experimenter for a brief period) led to a quietening of infant behaviour, but did not provoke distress. However, if an unnatural disruption was arranged, for instance if the mother adopted a still, blank face, or if the timing of the mother's communication was put out of phase with infant behaviour, then different and distressed patterns of infant response were provoked. In the blank face condition infants very quickly appeared disturbed: a form of response resembling protest was first seen, the infant making thrashing movements and frowning at the mother. Subsequently a phase of avoidance occurred, the infant turning away from the mother with a drooping posture, often becoming self-absorbed in hand regard or in fingering the clothes. When maternal responses were set out of phase with infant activity by means of a closed-circuit television system infant avoidance was again provoked, along with the appearance of confusion: the infant made short, darting glances at the mother's face, and then turned away, frowning. In each case the particular form of infant behaviour – quietening, distress, withdrawal or confusion – seemed appropriate to the ongoing disruption, and indeed, appeared to serve a regulatory role within the interaction by bringing about a change in the quality of maternal response. Thus, mothers often commented on the infant's distressed behaviour following the perturbation, and became more solicitous and concerned. The impact of the infant on the quality of the mother's communication was further demonstrated when the infant's behaviour was put out of phase with the mother's in the same closed-circuit television system described above. Significant differences in the form and content of the mother's 'baby-talk' were found according to the presence or absence of infant responsiveness (Murray and Trevarthen 1986).

This body of research with young infants illustrates the idea that infants are preadapted to engage with other people and to develop specific attachments, as is proposed within attachment theory (Bowlby 1974–80; Ainsworth *et al.* 1978). But it also shows that very young infants are highly sensitive to the form of their interpersonal contacts: interactions of a particular kind are sought, and if these are not forthcoming then reactions are provoked that entail significant alterations in affective state and attention. Complex repertoires of action and expression are evident, and these appear to serve in the regulation of maternal communication.

This work, using experimental distortions of maternal communication to explore infant sensitivities, has been developed in recent years specifically to explore the effects of disturbed communication arising in the context of depression. In an initial study Cohn and Tronick (1983) examined the effects of simulated depression on the infant. As in the experiments in which the mother was required to become blank-faced and unresponsive, 3-month-old infants reacted by protesting and becoming wary and avoidant when their mothers behaved as though depressed.

Clinical populations

Field and colleagues (Field 1984; Field *et al*. 1985; 1988) have conducted a series of studies comparing brief (three-minute sequences) videotaped interactions between depressed and non-depressed mothers with their 3-month-old babies. Although the scoring procedures differed somewhat between the various studies, a consistent pattern of results emerged. Depressed mothers were far less active, making fewer vocalizations, touching the baby less and showing fewer positive facial expressions. Furthermore, their behaviour was less contingent on that of the infants, and there was little game-play. The infants of the depressed mothers themselves showed 'depressed' behaviour: they were fussy, discontented and avoidant, and, like their mothers, made fewer positive facial expressions and vocalizations, and were less active. In the most recent study in this series it was found that the depressed mothers' infants generalized this interactive style to other situations, being less positive and active when presented with a non-depressed adult.

Further work with clinical populations has been carried out by Cohn *et al*. (1986) and Lyons-Ruth *et al*. (1986). They video-recorded both structured mother–infant interactions (where the mother was asked to play face-to-face with the infant) and those occurring spontaneously in the home. These assessments were carried out from 6 to 12 months postpartum in a population where women had been identified by healthcare workers as having significant difficulties in the management of their babies. A large proportion of these women were subsequently identified as being depressed. As in the studies conducted by Field *et al*., interactions between the depressed mothers and their infants were, on the whole, less harmonious than those obtaining in the authors' previous research with non-clinical populations. In the 6-month structured face-to-face interactions, Cohn *et al*. identified four styles of depressed maternal interactive behaviour. The first, the 'disengaged' pattern, resembled that already described in the literature: mothers were withdrawn, and 'slouched back in their chairs, turned away from the infant, or spoke to the baby in an expressionless voice with little facial expression' (Cohn *et al.* 1986: 36). A second group, described as 'mixed', did attempt to engage with their babies, using many eliciting techniques seen in normal samples. However, like the disengaged group, they showed low levels of positive affect, and were not able to play. Unlike previous descriptions of depressed maternal behaviour, almost half the mothers in this sample were categorized as 'intrusive': they showed low proportions of positive expression, and high levels of anger, frequently poking or pulling at their infants. All three of these subgroups of mothers failed to respond contingently to infant behaviours. Finally, there were depressed women who appeared to have positive relations with their infants.

The infants of the depressed women were themselves withdrawn and showed very little positive affective expression during the interactions; it was also found that the particular form of infant response related to maternal style. Thus, infants of 'disengaged' mothers showed a great deal of protest behaviour; whereas maternal intrusiveness tended to provoke infant avoidance. The authors found that both maternal and infant styles seen in the structured interactions carried over to a large extent to their spontaneous behaviour, although the intrusive mothers tended to become somewhat withdrawn when left to determine the extent of their involvement with the infant.

In a follow-up study of these same mother–infant pairs, along with additional cases from the same population, assessments were made of infant development, the quality of interactions and of attachment to the mother. In naturalistic observations of the mothers' behaviour at home at 12 months it was found that the depressed women were significantly more angry and controlling in relation to their infants than non-depressed controls. Maternal depression was also significantly related to lowered infant scores on both the physical and mental indices of the Bayley Scales of development, even after controlling for the effects of maternal I.Q. The effects of depression on infant attachment were less clear-cut. Severely depressed women had infants who were insecure and ambivalent. However, the infants of mildly depressed women tended to be securely attached. It should be noted that some caution is required when considering these data, since the population was not a random community sample but was specifically selected on the basis of problems identified in the mother–child relationship. Nevertheless, this work is important in providing detailed documentation of the variability in the quality of relations between depressed mothers and their infants, and of the links between maternal interactive style and infant behaviour.

Preliminary data from a prospective study of depressed and control women and their infants, drawn from a large random community sample in Cambridge (Murray 1990; Murray and Marwick 1990), also reveal significant effects of depression on the quality of the mother's communication with her infant. An analysis of the content of the mothers' speech to the infant at two months showed that, compared with non-depressed mothers, those who were depressed were far more self-oriented, critical and controlling. These features of 'motherese' (Snow, p. 195–210 of this volume) were independent of the severity of symptoms and timing of onset; however, they were far more likely to occur where the episode of depression was the first in the woman's experience, where the feelings of depression seemed to centre on difficulties in adapting to motherhood, rather than on stresses unrelated to childbearing. Voice quality, too, was altered in depressed women, who showed far fewer of the specific features that normally occur in maternal speech to infants. As in the work of Cohn *et al.* (1986) and Lyons-Ruth *et al.* (1986) outlined above, there were also indications that, within the case group, there was a relation between the style of interaction at 3 months and later performance on developmental tasks: thus, infants were successful on tests of object constancy at 9 months where maternal speech during the 3-month interactions had been focussed on infant experience, but failed where speech had been mother-centred (Murray 1990).

The role of infant variables

It is clear from this review of studies that have made direct observations of relations between depressed mothers and their infants that in a large proportion of cases the adaptations to infant characteristics that are normally made by mothers when interacting with their babies do not occur. In turn, infant behaviour departs from the usual pattern of responsive and positive engagement. One issue raised by this evidence of early deviations in the profile of infant behaviour is that of the possible role of infant temperament. It might be argued, for example, that infants who are inherently 'difficult' and unresponsive contribute both to deviations in maternal interactive style, and even to depression in the mother. Indeed, with regard to the impact on interactive style, it was found in the study carried out by Field *et al.* (1988) that, when the non-depressed experimenter interacted with infants of depressed mothers, their own behaviour became less positive and expressive than when interacting with infants of non-depressed mothers. In the closed-circuit television experiment described on p. 151 Murray found that if infant behaviour was set out of phase with the mother's, maternal speech style came to resemble that found in depressed populations (Murray and Trevarthen 1986).

Evidence consistent with the impact of difficult infant temperament on depression itself derives from several sources. Cutrona and Troutman (1986) assessed infant temperament at 3 months, using crying records, maternal reports and direct observations of the infants in the home. They found that maternal depression was far more likely to persist where the infant was difficult to soothe and cried excessively. Similarly, Whiffen and Gotlib (1989) found that depressed mothers perceived their 2-month-old infants as being more difficult to care for and more bothersome than did non-depressed mothers; and independent assessments by the experimenter showed the depressed mothers' infants to be more tense, less content, and as deteriorating more quickly during cognitive testing. This evidence alone is not, of course, conclusive, since it could be the case that these infants became 'difficult' over the first 2 to 3 months through the process of being with a depressed mother. Direct assessments of infants are required in the neonatal period in order to resolve this issue.

Other researchers have found that stressful postpartum events specifically related to the infant are predictors of maternal depression and depressive symptomatology. O'Hara *et al.* (1984) carried out a prospective study of postnatal depression and found that perinatal events with longer term consequences, such as the baby having health problems during the first few months of life, were the only significant life-stress variables to predict depression. However, not all perinatal problems pose risks for later depression; other studies have found that complications occurring in the immediate perinatal period that are shortlived play little or no role in the aetiology of postpartum depression (Stein *et al.* 1989).

SUMMARY OF RESEARCH FINDINGS AND IMPLICATIONS FOR POLICY

It is clear that although psychiatric and behavioural disturbance in the child is not a likely outcome, relations between depressed mothers and their babies are, on the whole, markedly different from those obtaining in non-clinical populations. Although the particular form of disengagement may vary, interactions are generally characterized by a lack of positive affect and mutual responsiveness. Furthermore, there is evidence to suggest that the infant's cognitive development and security of attachment to the mother may be adversely affected in the longer term. This evidence from clinical populations linking the nature of early interactions to later infant performance is consistent with that obtained in very different areas of infant research. For example, it has been found that the quality of maternal interactive behaviour is associated with infant performance on habituation tasks (Lewis and Goldberg 1969; Bornstein 1984; Bornstein and Tamis 1986). Together, these lines of study underline the importance of human relationships in the developmental process, and this in turn carries implications for policy. The following sets out, by way of example, some of the ways in which research in developmental psychology and the area of postnatal depression can suggest directions for the development of practice in obstetric and primary healthcare. First, intervention strategies are suggested with respect to the identification of those who are vulnerable. Second, implications of research for secondary prevention and treatment are considered.

Detection of depression and vulnerability

Antenatal identification of vulnerable women

Epidemiological research suggests that it may be possible to identify those at risk of postnatal depression before delivery, a cluster of risk factors having been found in a number of studies. Thus a poor marital relationship, severe social and economic stress, and lack of a close, confiding relationship and a previous psychiatric history have consistently been found to be associated with episodes of postnatal depression (see O'Hara and Zekoski 1988; and Cooper *et al.* 1989 for reviews), thus affording the obstetric team some opportunity for allocating resources to those who are identified as vulnerable at the time of antenatal clinic contact. One key area for future research is the development of a suitable tool for accurate, routine identification of those at risk on the basis of antenatal factors.

Identification of vulnerability on the postnatal ward

No matter how refined the instruments developed for antenatal clinic administration, predictions based on antenatal risk factors will never be wholly accurate. Furthermore, as noted above, events following the child's birth may play a significant role in the onset of maternal emotional disturbance. Close attention is still required therefore on the postnatal ward, where many of the difficulties experienced by the woman who is vulnerable to depression may become evident, before the onset of a full clinical episode. Thus, in addition to the factors that can be identified during the antenatal period and stresses relating to the infant health, the following areas may be worthy of particular attention:

1 Maternal response to the infant at delivery

Although it is now acknowledged that a large minority of women do not experience an immediate rush of intense positive feeling for their infant at delivery but develop such affection gradually over the first few days (Robson and Kumar 1980), it is found that those who become postnatally depressed are far more likely to have responded negatively to their infants at birth. For example, in the study carried out by Murray (1990), 47 per cent of those who had a postnatal depressive episode, compared to 22 per cent of those who did not, experienced feelings about their infants at this time which ranged from ambivalent to strongly negative. This association was found to hold independently of the method of delivery. These moments of first contact, therefore, may serve to provide the obstetric team with information that is pertinent to the future progress of the mother's relationship with her baby. Clearly, it would be very misguided to make judgments about a mother's capacity to form a warm and close relationship with her child solely on the basis of the response at the time of birth; however, strong, adverse maternal reactions to the infant at delivery may alert staff to maternal vulnerability. Such identification could be of benefit if follow-up is sensitively managed.

2 Feeding difficulties

While just as many women who later become depressed intend to breastfeed their infants as do other mothers, the majority give up by 8 weeks (Cooper *et al.* 1989). Although it has been suggested by some researchers that hormonal changes implicated in weaning may provoke the depressive episodes, evidence for this interpretation of the association between ceasing to feed and depression in unconvincing. Both the study of Cooper *et al.* and that of Murray, showed that in the majority of cases the onset of full depressive symptoms preceded weaning. However, although weaning itself may not be causal in relation to depression, difficulties associated with feeding that culminate in weaning may well play a role in contributing to its onset, as do other difficulties associated with infant care. The inception of problems of this nature may well be detectable on the postnatal ward, where feeding difficulties are frequently experienced amongst those who later become depressed.

3   Severe 'blues'

Several studies have found that severe feelings of low mood and tearfulness, usually experienced in mild form on about the fourth day after delivery by a large proportion of mothers, are associated with the occurrence of a full depressive episode postpartum (Paykel *et al.* 1980). As with response at delivery and the presence of feeding difficulties, such reactions may be detectable by obstetric staff during routine care on the postnatal ward.

4   Absence of confiding relationships

As noted above, one of the most important risk factors for postnatal depression is the absence of social support, and in particular a close, confiding relationship. In addition to any reports that the mother might give at the point of antenatal contact, the lack of visitors on the postnatal ward, or else a strained quality of contact when visits are made, may provide vigilant staff with indications of difficulties in this area.

Identification of postnatal depression in the community

In the event that the precursors of depression are not identified antenatally or on the postnatal ward, consideration of the role of the health visitor in the detection of depression is required. In spite of the considerable input of resources from the primary care team to address the needs of mothers and young infants in the early postnatal months it is estimated that only a quarter of those who become depressed at this time are identified (Hennessy 1985). Cox and colleagues recently have developed a simple, self-report questionnaire to detect postnatal depression in community samples (Cox *et al.* 1987a). Items are carefully worded to take account of the somatic and practical consequences of parturition, and thus the scale avoids confounding these effects with symptoms of depression. The questionnaire is highly acceptable to mothers and its validity has been established on a large, unselected postnatal sample (Murray and Carothers 1990). Its routine use at the time of a 6-week postnatal check, therefore, is recommended.

Secondary prevention and treatment

Clinical trials are required, comparing different forms of intervention, in order to establish the most effective treatment for postnatal depression. Even more work needs to be carried out to evaluate methods of improving the mother–baby relationship in the context of depression; models of mother–infant interactions based on developmental theory (see Sameroff 1989) can be used to suggest different therapeutic approaches, and the outcome of different treatments can then, in turn, be used to modify theory. The following outlines recent developments in the treatment of postnatal depression and disturbances in the mother–baby relationship.

Addressing the context of motherhood: non-directive counselling

This approach takes the mother and her situation as the focus for treatment. Studies have shown repeatedly, as outlined earlier, that the lack of social support, and in particular of a close confiding relationship, is strongly associated with postnatal depression. One possible approach to the treatment of the mother–infant relationship is, therefore, to bring about a change in the circumstances of support in order to provide a different context for mothering. A study has recently been published in which health visitors were trained to give non-directive counselling to depressed mothers, rather than routine care (Holden *et al.* 1989). Maternal depressive symptoms remitted significantly more quickly in women who received counselling, although the effects on the mother–infant relationship and on infant development were not evaluated. It remains to be established whether such changes in maternal mood are sufficient to bring about an alteration in the pattern of mother–infant interaction when this has not been a key element in treatment. Nevertheless, the implications of this preliminary work for the development of practice merit further consideration. In addition to its replication and development in the community, one should consider the extension of this research to practice on the postnatal wards where obstetric staff are in a unique position, working with women around the time of delivery and the subsequent postpartum days, to accommodate the research findings in their routine care. The study carried out by Holden *et al.* suggests that a supportive, counselling approach may very profitably complement the practical advice and training that constitutes the core of post-natal care. Such an approach, which could be directed in particular to those who are identified as vulnerable, could address the very difficulties which have been found to be predictors of depression, such as feelings of failure and helplessness when having difficulties feeding, or abandonment when there are no visitors. All this, of course, requires commitment on the part of the relevant professions to give emotional aspects of childbirth their place in the clinical agenda and, therefore, the training curriculum.

Focus on maternal dynamics

In addition to the lack of confiding relationships and social support associated with postnatal depression, a consistent finding in the literature has been a difficulty in the depressed mother's reaction to her own mother. Researchers with a psychoanalytic orientation have naturally paid close attention to such issues when considering problems encountered in the transition to motherhood and in infant care. The psychodynamic approach assumes that unresolved conflicts from earlier patterns of relationships may be stirred up by the infant, and become expressed in disturbances in mother–infant interactions. Although psychodynamic approaches have traditionally taken the individual as the focus for therapy, recent developments of work in this area (Fraibert 1980; Lieberman and Pawl 1988; Cramer and Stern 1988) have incorporated the infant and the mother–infant relationship in the treatment process. These researchers suggest that exploration of the source of difficulties, and of the way in which they find expression in the current mother–infant relationship, can bring about a resolution of conflicts and change the pattern of interaction. A number of successfully treated cases are reported in this literature, but this line of work requires more systematic appraisal and appropriate development of service resources.

Mother-infant interaction treatment

As with the recent developments of psychodynamic theory described above, this treatment approach focuses on the mother–infant relationship, rather than on one of the partners in the interaction alone (Stern 1985; Aarts 1989). Typically, mother–infant interactions are videotaped by the therapist/researcher, and then the mother and therapist work through the tape together. Using evidence from developmental psychology about the structure of interactions, the mother is helped through picture-by-picture analysis of the video material to become aware of the patterning of both problematic and successful interactions. While this treatment has been used successfully in the Netherlands as an alternative to institutional care for disturbances of the mother–infant relationship, it has not been employed systematically with postnatally depressed mothers and their infants.

CONCLUSION

The rapidly developing infant is entirely dependent upon, and experiences the world through, those who care for him. In our culture this care is usually undertaken by the mother. If the mother becomes depressed it is very likely that the way in which she handles her infant and presents the world to him will be altered. The research that has been conducted to date suggests that while psychiatric disorder is unusual amongst these children in their later years, there is a significantly increased risk of difficulties in the relationship with the mother and of problems in the child's attachments in general. The possibility of some effects on cognitive development has also been raised.

It is, therefore, important for obstetric staff and those responsible for mothers and infants in the postnatal months to be aware both of the possibility of postnatal depression and of risk factors for the condition; in particular, the lack of social support, especially a confiding relationship, socio-economic hardship, early difficulties between mother and infant, a temperamentally difficult infant, and possibly persistent feeding difficulties may all act as provoking factors. Recent research suggests that the provision of support and counselling may be beneficial to mothers, and may thus help to protect the infant. In addition, research findings on mother–infant relations have been used to develop psychodynamic and cognitive-interaction treatments that take the mother–infant relationship as the unit for therapy. However, further research is required to establish how best to assist vulnerable women in the context of both obstetric and primary care.

REFERENCES

Aarts, R. (1989) Paper presented to the Seminar on Alternatives to Institutional Placement for Children, Israel, 12-19 March.

Ainsworth, M. D., Blehar, M. C., Waters, E. and Wall, S. (1978) *Patterns of Attachment: A Psychological Study of the Strange Situation*, New Jersey: Erlbaum.

Alegria, J. and Noirot, E. (1978) 'Neonate orientation behaviour towards the human voice', *Early Human Development* 1: 291-312.

Bornstein, M. H. (1984) 'Infant attention and caregiver stimulation: two contributions to early cognitive development', paper presented at the International Conference on Infant Studies, New York.

Bornstein, M. H. and Tamis, C. (1986) 'Origins of cognitive skills in infants', paper presented at the International Conference on Infant Studies, Los Angeles.

Bowlby, J. (1974) *Attachment*, Harmondworth: Penguin.

Bowlby, J. (1979) *Separation: Anger and Anxiety*, Harmondsworth: Penguin.

Bowlby, J. (1980) *Loss: Sadness and Depression*, Harmondsworth: Penguin.

Brazelton, T. B., Tronick, E. Z., Adamson, L., Als, H. and Wise, S. (1975) 'Early mother–infant reciprocity', in M. Hofer (ed.) *Parent–Infant Interaction*, Amsterdam: Elsevier.

Bushnell, I. W., Sai, F. and Mullin, J. T. (1989) 'Neonatal recognition of the mother's face', *British Journal of Developmental Psychology* 7: 3-15.

Caplan, H. R., Cogill, S. R., Alexandra, H., Robson, K. M., Katz, R. and Kumar, R. (1989) 'Maternal depression and the emotional development of the child', *British Journal of Psychiatry* 154: 818-23.

Carpenter, G. C. (1974) 'Visual regard of moving and stationary faces in early infancy', *Merrill Palmer Quarterly* 20: 181-94.

Carpenter, G. C., Tecce, J. S., Stechler, G. and Friedman, S. (1970) 'Differential behaviour to human and humanoid faces in early infancy', *Merrill Palmer Quarterly* 16: 91-108.

Cogill, S. R., Caplan, H. R., Alexandra, H., Robson, K. M. and Kumar, R. (1986) 'Impact of maternal postnatal depression on cognitive development of young children', *British Medical Journal* 292: 1165-7.

Cohler, B. J., Grunebaum, H. U., Weiss, J. L., Garner, E. and Gallant, D. H. (1977) 'Disturbance of attention among schizophrenic, depressed and well mothers and their young children', *Journal of Child Psychology and Psychiatry and Allied Disciplines* 18: 115-35.

Cohn, J. F. and Tronick, E. Z. (1983) 'Three month-old infants' reactions to simulated maternal depression', *Child Development* 54: 185-93.

Cohn, J. F., Matias, R., Tronick, E. Z., Connell, D. and Lyons-Ruth, D. (1986) 'Face-to-face interactions of depressed mothers and their infants', in E. Z. Tronick and T. Field (eds) *Maternal Depression and Infant Disturbance*, San Francisco: Jossey-Bass.

Cooper, P. J., Campbell, E. A., Day. A., Kennerley, H. and Bond, A. (1988) 'Non-psychotic psychiatric disorder after childbirth: a prospective study of prevalence, incidence, course and nature', *British Journal of Psychiatry* 152: 799-806.

Cooper, P. J., Murray, L. and Stein, A. (1989) 'Postnatal depression', in A. Seva (ed.) *European Handbook of Psychiatry and Mental Health*.

Cox, J. L., Holden, J. M. and Sagovsky, R. (1987a) 'Detection of postnatal depression: development of the 10-item Edinburgh Postnatal Depression Scale', *British Journal of Psychiatry* 150: 782-6.

Cox, A. D., Puckering, C., Pound, A. and Mills, M. (1987b) 'The impact of maternal depression of young children', *Journal of Child Psychology and Psychiatry and Allied Disciplines* 28: 917-28.

The effects of postnatal depression 163

Cramer, B. and Stern, D. N. (1988) 'Evaluation of change in mother–infant brief psychotherapy: a single case study', *Infant Mental Health Journal* 9: 20.

Cutrona, C. E. and Troutman, B. R. (1986) 'Social support, infant temperament and parenting self efficacy: a mediational model of postpartum depression', *Child Development* 57: 1507–18.

De Casper, A. J. and Fifer, W. P. (1980) 'Of human bonding: newborns prefer their mothers' voices', *Science* 208: 1174–6.

Dziuranwiec, S. (1987) 'Neonates' attention to faces', in V. Bruce, H. Ellis and A. Young (eds) *Developmental Aspects of Face Recognition*, unpublished report on ESRC Workshop, Grange-over-Sands.

Eisenberg, R. B. (1975) *Auditory Competence in Early Life: The Roots of Communicative Behavior*, Baltimore: University Park Press.

Fantz, R. L. (1963) 'Pattern vision in newborn infants', *Science* 140: 296–7.

Field, T. M. (1984) 'Early interactions between infants and their post partum depressed mothers', *Infant Behaviour and Development* 7: 517–22.

Field, T. M. (1985) 'Neonatal perception of people: motivational and individual differences', in T. M. Field and N. A. Fox (eds) *Social Perception in Infants* 31–52, Norwood, New Jersey: Ablex.

Field, T., Healy, B., Goldstein, S., Perry, S. and Bendell, D. (1988) 'Infants of depressed mothers show "depressed" behaviour even with nondepressed adults', *Child Development* 59: 1569–79.

Field, T., Sandberg, D., Garcia, R., Vega Lahr, N., Goldstein, S. and Guy L. (1985) 'Prenatal problems, postpartum depression and early mother–infant interactions', *Developmental Psychology* 12: 1152–6.

Field, T. M., Woodson, R., Greenberg, R. and Cohen, D. (1982) 'Discrimination and imitation of facial expressions by neonates', *Science* 218: 179–81.

Fraiberg, S. (1980) *Clinical Studies in Infant Mental Health: The First Year of Life*, London: Tavistock Publications.

Friedlander, B. (1970) 'Receptive language development in infancy', *Merrill Palmer Quarterly* 16: 7–51.

Gamer, E., Gallant, D., Grunebaum, H. U. and Cohler, B. J. (1977) 'Children of psychotic mothers', *Archives of General Psychiatry* 34: 592–7.

Ghodsian, M., Zajicek, E. and Wolkind, S. (1984) 'A longitudinal study of maternal depression and child behaviour problems', *Journal of Child Psychology and Psychiatry and Allied Disciplines* 25: 91–109.

Goren, C. G., Sarty, M. and Wu, P. Y. K. (1975) 'Visual following and pattern discrimination of face-life stimuli by newborn infants', *Pediatrics* 56: 544–9.

Grunebaum, H. U., Cohler, B. J., Kauffman, C. and Gallant, D. H. (1978) 'Children of depressed and schizophrenic mothers', *Child Psychiatry and Human Development* 8: 219–28.

Hennessy, D. A. (1985) 'Should Health Visitors also care for mothers?, in P. J. Hawthorne (ed.) *Proceedings of the RCN Research Society Annual Conference*, University of Nottingham.

Holden, J. M., Sagovsky, R. and Cox, J. L. (1989) 'Counselling in a general practice setting: controlled study of health visitor intervention in treatment of postnatal depression', *British Medical Journal* 298: 223–6.

Kumar, R. and Robson, K. M. (1984) 'A prospective study of emotional disorders in childbearing women', *British Journal of Psychiatry* 144: 35–47.

Leslie, A.M. (1984) 'Infant perception of a manual pick up event', *British Journal of Developmental Psychology* 2: 19–32.

Lewis, M. and Goldberg, S. (1969) 'Perceptual cognitive development in infancy: a generalised expectancy model as a function of the mother-infant interaction', *Merrill Palmer Quarterly* 115: 82–100.

Lieberman, A. F. and Pawl, J. H. (1988) 'Clinical applications of attachment theory', in J. Belsky and T. Nezworski (eds) *Clinical Implications of Attachment*, New Jersey: Erlbaum.

Lyons-Ruth, K., Zoll, D., Connell, D. and Grunebaum, H.U. (1986) 'The depressed mother and her one-year-old infant', in E. Z. Tronick and T. Field (eds) *Maternal Depression and Infant Disturbance*, San Francisco: Jossey-Bass.

McFarlane, J. (1975) 'Olfaction in the development of social preferences in the human neonate', in M. Hofer (ed.) *Parent-Infant Interaction*. Amsterdam: Elsevier.

McKnew, P. H., Cyrtryn, L., Efron, A. M., Gershon, E. S. and Bunney, W. E. (1979) 'The offspring of parents with affective disorders', *British Journal of Psychiatry* 134: 148–52.

Mehler, J., Bertoncini, H. and Barniere, M. (1978) 'Infant recognition of mother's voice', *Perception* 7: 491–7.

Meltzoff, A. N. and Moore, M. K. (1977) 'Imitation of facial and manual gestures by human neonates', *Science* 198: 73–5.

Murray, L. (1980) 'The sensitivities and expressive capacities of young infants in communication with their mothers', Ph.D. thesis, University of Edinburgh.

Murray, L. (1990) 'The impact of maternal depression on infant development', paper presented at the Convegno Internazionale dal Nascere Aldivenire nella Realita e Nella Fantasia, Turin: Italy.

Murray, L. and Carothers, A. D. (1990) 'The validation of the Edinburgh Postnatal Depression Scale on a community sample', *British Journal of Psychiatry* (in press).

Murray, L. and Marwick, H. (1990) 'Effects of depression on voice quality in maternal speech to infants', manuscript in preparation.

Murray, L. and Trevarthen, C. B. (1985) 'Emotional regulation of interactions between two-month-olds and their mothers', in T. M. Field and N. A. Fox (eds) *Social Perception in Infants*, Norwood, New Jersey: Ablex.

Murray, L. and Trevarthen, C. B. (1986) 'The infant's role in mother-infant communications', *Journal of Child Language* 13: 15–29.

Nott, P. N. (1987) 'Extent, timing and persistence of emotional disorders following childbirth', *British Journal of Psychiatry* 151: 523–7.

O'Hara, M. W. and Zekoski, E. M. (1988) 'Postpartum depression: a comprehensive review', in R. Kumar and I. F. Brockington (eds)

Motherhood and Mental Illness, London: John Wright.
O'Hara, M. W., Neunaber, D. J. and Zekoski, E. M. (1984) 'A prospective study of postpartum depression: prevalence, course and predictive factors', *Journal of Abnormal Psychology* 93: 158–71.
Papousek, H. and Papousek, M. (1975) 'Cognitive aspects of preverbal social interaction between human infants and adults', in E. Hofer (ed.) *Parent–Infant Interaction*, Amsterdam: Elsevier.
Paykel, E. S., Emms, E. M., Fletcher, J. and Rassaby, E. J. (1980) 'Life events and social support in puerperal depression', *British Journal of Psychiatry* 136: 339–46.
Robertson, J. (1963) 'Mother–infant interaction from birth to 12 months: two case studies', in B. M. Foss (ed.) *Determinants of Infant Behaviour*, vol. 3, London: Methuen.
Robson, K. and Kumar, R. (1980) 'Delayed onset of maternal affection after childbirth', *British Journal of Psychiatry* 136: 347–53.
Sameroff, A. J. (1989) 'The social context of development', in N. Eisenberg, *Contemporary Topics in Developmental Psychology*, New York: Wiley.
Stein, A., Cooper, P. J., Campbell, E. A., Day, A. and Altham, P. E. M. (1989) 'Social adversity and perinatal complications: their relation to postnatal depression', *British Medical Journal* 298: 1073–4.
Stein, A., Gath, D., Boucher, J., Bond, A., Day, A. and Cooper, P. J. *et al.* (1990) 'The relationship between postnatal depression and mother–child interactions', under revision for *British Journal of Psychiatry*.
Stern, D. N. (1985) *The Interpersonal World of the Infant: A View from Psychoanalysis and Developmental Psychology*, New York: Basic Books.
Tronick, E. Z., Als, H., Adamson, L., Wise, S. and Brazelton, T. B. (1978) 'The infants' response to entrapment between contradictory messages in face-to-face interaction', *Journal of the American Academy of Child Psychiatry* 17: 1–13.
Uddenberg, N. and Englesson, I. (1978) 'Prognosis of postpartum mental disturbance. A prospective study of primaparous women and their 4-year-old children', *Acta Psychiatrica Scandinavica* 58: 201–12.
Waddington, C. H. (1957) *The Strategy of the Genes*, London: Allen & Unwin.
Weissman, M. M. and Paykel, E. S. (1974) *The Depressed Woman*, Chicago and London: University of Chicago Press.
Weissman, M. M., Paykel, E. S. and Klerman, G. L. (1972) 'The depressed woman as a mother', *Social Psychiatry* 7: 98–108.
Weissman, M. M., Prusoff, B. A., Gammon, G. D., Merinkangas, K. R., Leckman, J. F. and Kid, K. K. (1984) 'Psychopathology in the children (6–18) of depressed and normal parents', *Journal of the American Academy of Child Psychiatry* 23: 78–84.
Werner, Z., Welner, A., Donald, M., McCrany, B. A. and Leonard, M. A. (1977) 'Psychopathology in children of inpatients with depression', *Journal of Nervous and Mental Disease* 164: 408–13.
Whiffen, V. E. and Gotlib, I. H. (1989) 'Infants of postpartum depressed mothers: temperament and cognitive status', *Journal of Abnormal Psychology* 98(3): 1–6.

Widmer–Robert–Tissot, C. (1981) 'Les modes de communication du bébé: postures, mouvements et vocalises', in Delachaux and Niestlé (eds) *Actualites Pedagogiques et Psychologiques*, Paris: Neuchatel.

Williams, H. and Carmichael, A. (1985) 'Depression in mothers in a multi-ethnic urban industrial municipality in Melbourne. Aetiological factors and effects on infants and pre-school children', *Journal of Child Psychology and Psychiatry and Allied Disciplines* 26: 277–88.

Wolff, P. H. (1969) 'The natural history of crying and other vocalizations in early infancy', in B. M. Foss (ed.) *Determinants of Infant Behaviour*, vol. 4, London: Methuen.

Wrate, R. M., Rooney, A. C., Thomas, P. F. and Cox, J. L. (1985) 'Postnatal depression and child development: a 3-year follow-up study', *British Journal of Psychiatry* 146: 622–7.

Zajicek, E. and de Salis, W. (1979) 'Depression in mothers of young children. Family Research Unit, *Child Abuse and Neglect* 146: 622–7.

8 The social context of development

Arnold J. Sameroff

Source: Eisenberg, N. (ed.) (1987) *Contemporary Topics in Developmental Psychology*, New York: Wiley.

Theories of development have varied in the emphasis they place on contributions the characteristics of the person and characteristics of the environment make to later behavior. While this debate can be treated as merely an academic discussion, it has important ramifications for the utilization of vast amounts of social resources. From intervention efforts that cost millions of dollars to the educational system that costs billions, practitioners rationalize their efforts on the basis of scientific knowledge. One of the major flaws in such knowledge is an inadequate conceptualization of the environment. Bronfenbrenner and Crouter (1983) have traced the history of empirical investigations of the environment and shown how theoretical limitations have placed limits on the sophistication of research paradigms. The goal of this presentation is to expand upon our understanding of the environment in order to lay a basis for more complex paradigms in both research and practice.

The significance of nature and nurture for development can be viewed from two perspectives. The first is whether they make a contribution at all and the second is whether these contributions are active ones or passive ones. Riegel (1978) placed models of development into four categories reflecting various combinations of passive and active persons and environments. In the passive person–passive environment category he placed mechanistic theories that arose from the empiricist philosophy of Locke and Hume in which combinations of events that occur in the environment in the presence of observers are imprinted into their minds. This view has been the basis for learning theories in which factors such as the continuity, frequency, or recency of stimuli determine how they will be coded into the receiving mind.

In a second category the passive person is combined with an active environment. In this category are Skinnerian approaches to behavior modification in which the conditioner actively structures the input to alter the person's behavior in particular directions, but in which the person is assumed to make no contribution to the outcome independent of experience.

The third category contains the concept of the active person but retains the passive environment. In this grouping fall the cognitive theories of Piaget and the linguistic views of Chomsky. Piaget sees the person as an active constructor of knowledge based on experience with the environment. The environment is a necessary part of development, but has no active role in structuring thought or action. Similarly, Chomsky sees language development as the person's application of innate linguistic categories to linguistic experience. The organization of that experience is not a determinant of language competence.

In the fourth category are models that combine an active person and an active environment. Riegel sees these models as deriving from Marx's interpretations of the dialectical nature of development in which the actions of the individual change reality, and then, in turn, the changes in reality affect the behavior of the individual. Sameroff and Chandler (1975) captured this process in their transactional model of development. In this view developmental outcomes are not a product of the initial characteristics of the child or the context or even their combination. Outcomes are the result of the interplay between child and context across time, in which the state of one affects the next state of the other in a continuous dynamic process.

Arguments over appropriate theories have important implications for both research and clinical strategies. Unless one understands how development proceeds, there is little basis for attempts to alter it, through either prevention or intervention programs. The conclusion that I will work toward is that both nature and nurture are necessary for any developmental process and that the contributions of both are not only active, but interactive and transactive as well.

Attempts to intervene in development have been based on stable models of child development. In these views, if a child is doing well or poorly early in life, he or she would be expected to continue to do well or poorly later on. As an example, children who were identified early in life as being at developmental risk from biological circumstances, such as birth complications, were thought to have generally negative behavioral outcomes later in life. On the contrary, longitudinal research in this area has demonstrated that the majority of children suffering from such biological conditions did not have intellectual or social problems later in life (Sameroff and Chandler 1975). On the other hand, early interventionists believed that getting children to perform well early in life would lead to them performing well throughout childhood. The early childhood education movement as exemplified in the Head Start program was designed to improve the learning and social competence of children during the preschool years with the expectation that these improvements would be maintained into later life. However, follow-up research of such children has found only minimal intellectual gains being maintained into adolescence (Zigler and Trickett 1978), although there were reduced rates of grade retention and need for participation in special education programs and improved maternal attitudes toward school performance (Lazar and Darlington 1982).

In both domains early characteristics of the child are frequently overpowered by factors in the environmental context of development. Where family and cultural variables have fostered development, children with severe perinatal complications have been indistinguishable from children without complications. When these variables have hindered development, children from excellent preschool intervention programs developed severe social and cognitive deficits. Thus while a continuous view of developmental functioning makes intuitive sense, it has not been borne out by empirical investigations.

As will be seen, all development seems to follow a similar model. In this view outcomes are never a function of the individual taken alone or the experiential context taken alone. Behavioural competencies are a product of the combination of an individual and his or her experience. To predict outcome, a singular focus on the characteristics of the individual, in this case the child, will frequently be misleading. What needs to be added is an analysis and assessment of the experiences available to the child.

DEVELOPMENTAL MODELS

Ancient theorists interpreted development as an unfolding of intrinsic characteristics that were either preformed or interacted epigenetically (Sameroff 1983; see Figure 8.1). This model was countered by an environmental model of discontinuity in which each stage of development was determined by the contemporary context analogous to Riegel's (1978) passive person–active environment category. If the context remained the same the child remained the same. If the context changed, the child changed (see Figure 8.2).

An interactionist position combined these two as in Figure 8.3. Here continuity is carried by the child but moderated by possible discontinuities in experience. Anastasi (1958) is credited with the important

Figure 8.1 Deterministic constitutional model of development (C1 to C4 represent state of the child at successive points in time)

interactionist conceptual breakthrough in pointing out that development could not occur without an environment. There is no logical possibility of considering development of an individual independent of the environment. Continuity could not be explained as a characteristic of the child because each new achievement was an amalgam of characteristics of the child and his or her experience. Neither alone would be predictive of later levels of functioning. If continuities were found it was because there was a continuity in the relation between the child and the environment, not because of continuities in either taken alone.

More recent conceptualizations of the developmental model have incorporated effects of the child on the environment posited by Rheingold (1966) and Bell (1968). These dynamic interactionist (Thomas *et al.* 1968) or transactional models (Sameroff and Chandler 1975) add to the independent contributions of child and environment, characteristics of the environment that are conditioned by the nature of the child. Different characteristics of the child will trigger different responses from the environment (see Figure 8.4).

In Figure 8.4 there is a continuity implied in the organization of the child's behavior by the series of arrows from C1 to C2 to C3. What is still missing from this model is a sense of continuity in the organization of the environment that would be indicated by a series of arrows from E1 to E2 to E3. The characterization of this organization will be contained in what follows.

Recently, I reviewed at length the dynamic, dialectical interplay between individual and context in not only development, but evolution as well (Sameroff 1983). Two points from this review are pertinent to this discussion. The first is that no organism ever existed outside of an environment. The classic chicken-and-egg paradox is a dialectical truism. The fertilized egg contains the genotype but also an organized biochemical environment with which the genotype interacts.

Figure 8.2 Deterministic environmental model of development (E1 to E4 represent experiential influences at successive points in time)

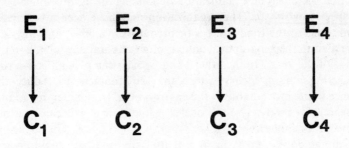

Figure 8.3 Interactionist model of development

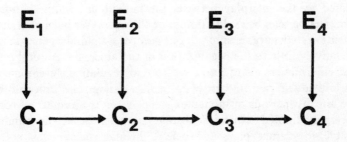

Figure 8.4 Reciprocal interaction model of development

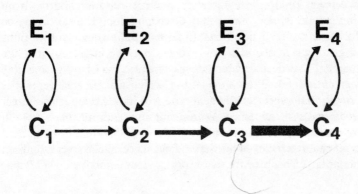

This cytoplasmic environment was not produced by the genome it contains. Each species evolved in intimate relationship to some environment. The second point is that environments are organized. In evolution there was an organization of existing forms into which each new species had to fit. The organization may have been a biological one in terms of the food sources or predators available, or a physical one related to the geographic context, or a temporal one related to the seasons of the year. On the other hand, species can play an active role in selecting among niches within that environment to reduce the variance in life attributable to the environment. In summer, an animal can search for relatively cool locales, while in winter it can seek out relatively warm ones.

In human development, as well, there is an organised environment. Someone needs to feed, protect, and provide warmth to infants. There is a cultural code in each society that provides an agenda of experiences for the developing child aimed at producing an adult suitable to fill a role in that society. Behavioral development is regulated by the interplay between the individual and the cultural system. Neither can be said to dominate the other. We have paid a lot of attention to the organization of one control system, the genetic one, but relatively little to the organization of the other, the cultural one.

The environment takes an active role in regulating development. Most individuals can only grow up to fill existing roles in a culture. There are vast periods of human existence when the number of roles were highly limited, either in absolute number or in the number available to certain parts of society. Feudal society was not a meritocracy. Serfs, no matter what their talents, could not fill intellectual or political roles in their societies.

To the extent that roles are open to individuals, there are usually selection systems to determine who would be most appropriate for available positions in the existing social organisation. Academic tests allow certain children to enter or prevent certain children from entering certain tracks, but so may discrimination. The same may be true for athletic or artistic efforts. In these situations the contributions of the genotype to the selection process may be large, but it is the environment that decides which developmental tracks are permissible for a given individual. In a society in which artistic achievement is proscribed, that aspect of the genotype will have little positive effect on developmental outcomes. Within our own culture there are still major restrictions the environment places on individual development based on characteristics other than talent. Race, social status, and sex are examples of such restrictive criteria. Bronfenbrenner (1977) has cogently argued that a much more sophisticated analysis of the ecological environment is necessary. In his view the understanding of human development requires the examination of multiperson systems of interaction that go beyond the immediate setting into larger social contexts.

Extending the work of Lewin (1936) on the individual's participation in multiple contexts, Bronfenbrenner (1977) proposed a hierarchical model of environmental organization encompassing microsystems, mesosystems, exosystems, and macrosystems. This model has been productive in permitting empirical investigations in a variety of cognitive and personality domains (Bronfenbrenner and Crouter 1983). The *microsystem* is the immediate setting of a child in an environment with particular features, activities, and roles. The *mesosystem* comprises the relationships between major settings at a particular point in an individual's development. The *exosystem* is the next higher level in which the mesosystem settings are embedded, including, for example, the world of work and neighbourhoods. The *macrosystem* comprises the overarching institutional patterns of the culture including the economic, social, and political systems of which the micro-, meso-, and exosystems are concrete expressions.

Bronfenbrenner's model reflects the complexity of the human context at any point in time. For the purposes of this discussion, the focus will be on the lifelong coherence of environmental influences rather than an analysis of the multiple influences within a single period of development.

TRANSACTIONAL MODEL

A model of development that included both the child and the child's experiences extended through time was suggested by Sameroff and Chandler (1975). Within this 'transactional model', the development of the child was seen as a product of the continuous dynamic interactions of the child and the experience provided by his or her family and social context. What was innovative in the transactional model was the emphasis placed on the effect of the child on the environment, so that experiences provided by the environment were not independent of the child. The child by its previous behavior may have been a strong determinant of current experiences. In Figure 8.5 one can see a concrete example of such a transactional outcome. The arrows implying continuities in child and environment have been eliminated in this figure in order to emphasize the interplay between child and caregiver.

Figure 8.5 Example of transactions leading to poor developmental outcome

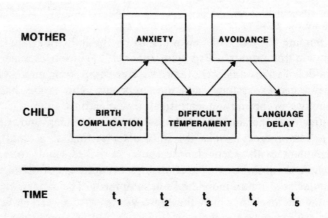

A complicated childbirth may have made an otherwise calm mother somewhat anxious. The mother's anxiety during the first months of the child's life may have caused her to be uncertain and inappropriate in her interactions with the child. In response to such inconsistency the infant may have developed some irregularities in feeding and sleeping patterns that give the appearance of a difficult temperament. This difficult temperament decreases the pleasure that the mother obtains from the child and so she tends to spend less time with the child. If there are no adults interacting with the child, and especially speaking to the child, the child may not meet the norms for language development and score poorly on preschool language tests. In this case the outcome was not determined by the complicated birth nor by the mother's consequent emotional response. If one needed to pick a cause it would be the mother's avoidance of the child, yet one can see that such a view would be a gross oversimplification of a complex developmental sequence.

When attempts are made to operationalize transactional processes within a specific research design the data are rarely as simple as the figure would indicate. Crockenberg and Smith (1982) examined the relation of infant and mother characteristics to the development of infant temperament and mother–infant interaction during the first 3 months of life. Mothers' responsive attitudes and infant behavior were measured during the newborn period. Mothers with responsive and flexible attitudes responded more quickly when their 3-month-old infants cried, and their infants spent less time fussing and crying. There was no significant contribution of neonatal irritability to the amount of child crying at 3 months. On the other hand, time required to calm down was not related to maternal attitudes and was related to newborn irritability. In other words, crying at 3 months was not a consequence of the initial characteristics of the child, but time to calm down was. Amount of time crying was a function of the subsequent caregiving experiences, and time to calm down was not. From the infant's side a transaction had occurred: the state of the child was changed as a function of the environment. There was also evidence in this study that the behavior of the mother was changed by the specific characteristics of the child. Alert infants had mothers who spent more time in contact with them, and mothers of irritable females responded more quickly to fussing and crying than mothers of irritable males. The mother's behavior was sensitive to both the behavioral and physical characteristics of the child. The evidence for transactional processes in this study is an example of the multidimensional nature of both maternal and child behavior. Depending on the antecedent and outcome measures and the ages of assessment, different relations will be found, some giving strong evidence for transactions and others not.

Observations of families in natural settings provide insights into possible causal sequences in development, but definitive evidence can only be produced by attempts to manipulate developmental variables (Bronfenbrenner 1977). Experimental manipulations designed to illuminate transactional processes have not been frequent as yet. Bugental and Shennum (1984) assessed beliefs about causes of caregiving outcomes for a group of mothers who were then placed in interaction situations with children who had been trained to be more or less responsive and assertive. Short-term transactions were identified in some conditions where mothers responded differently as a function of the combination of their attributions and the actual behavior of the child. Other research projects have been directed at long-term transactions resulting from massive intervention programs.

Zeskind and Ramey (1978, 1981) examined the effects of an intensive early intervention program on the development of a group of fetally malnourished infants. Intervention began at 3 months and included social work, medical and nutritional services, and an educational curriculum. Children attended the program approximately 8 hours a day, 5 days per week, during the whole year. A control group received similar social work and medical and nutritional services but did not participate in the educational program. Comparisons were made in the later functioning of lower-SES underweight (i.e., low ponderal index) infants, half of whom participated in the educational program and half of whom did not. As a group, the infants without educational intervention declined in DQ from 3 to 18 months of age and continued to score lower on tests at 36 months of age. However, within that group the low ponderal index babies showed a much greater decline into the retarded range. These lower DQs were associated with lower levels of maternal involvement. In contrast, in the group of families that received educational intervention, the malnourished infants who had scored significantly lower than the rest of the group at 3 months were doing as well as the others by 18 months. Zeskind and Ramey (1981) concluded that the educational program had interrupted the negative transaction found in the control group. Where low social status mothers would usually be put off by the characteristics of a fetally malnourished infant, contributing to a worsening developmental outcome, intervention fostered the relationship between mother and child, thereby leading to an above-average outcome within this sample.

Biological basis of developmental models

The transactional model despite its novel name is in reality not a novel model. It is merely a new emphasis on some very old traditions in developmental theory, specially theories of the dialectic in history and philosophy. A more cogent referent is theory and research in biology, where transactions are a recognized essential part of any developmental process.

In the study of embryological development, for example, there are continuous transactions between the phenotype and the genotype (Ebert and Sussex 1970; Waddington 1957). A simple view of the action of genes is that they produce the parts that make up the organism. A brown eye gene may be thought to produce a brown eye. In reality there is a much more complex process of mutual determinism. The material in the fertilized egg cell will turn on or off specific genes in the chromosomes. The turned-on genes will initiate changes in the biochemicals in the cell. These changed biochemicals will then act back on the genetic material turning on or off more genes in a continuous process usually producing an adult organism.

In certain circumstances one has the illusion of a linear relationship between a particular gene and a particular feature of the phenotype, as in the case of eye color. In reality, however, there is never a linear determinism because of the complexity of biological processes. What then creates the illusion? The answer is in the regulatory system that buffers development, what Waddington (1957) described as canalization. Within all the complex interactions between genotype and phenotype is a regulatory system that monitors the developmental changes to ensure that they stay within defined bounds. This regulatory system and the bounds are the result of an evolutionary process that occurred across myriad generations, that now ensures a particular outcome.

With eye color the system is hidden since it is so tightly buffered (i.e., regulated) that if one knows the structural genes one can predict the outcome. However, there are some simple examples where the regulatory system is quite evident. In the case of identical twins, a single fertilized cell splits in two. Shouldn't the result be two half-sized children? The genetic regulatory system ensures that this is not the outcome. Compensations are made so that the resulting infants will all be of normal size. In the case of genetic dominance the result for a homozygous individual is the same as for a heterozygous one. If there are two brown eye genes, the eyes are no browner than if there were only one. A regulation has occurred.

A more complex example is the result of the translocation in Down's syndrome. Here in the meiotic process of forming a germ cell there is a breakage in a chromosome such that in one of the resulting germ cells there is too much genetic material and in the other there is too little. In the cell with too much, the Trisomy 21 condition, regulations can occur that compensate for much of the anomalous genetic condition. A child is born that looks in large part like other human infants. In the case of the germ cell in which there is too little, regulation fails and the zygote is aborted. Another perspective is that regulation succeeded in the aborted cell and failed in the trisomy cell, but that issue will not be dealt with in this presentation.

Regulatory systems

When thinking in terms of the biological model, one has to think about a system with two levels, the developing organism and a superordinate regulatory system. In biology the regulatory system for physical outcomes is found in the genetic code. For behavioral outcomes there is also a system that regulates the way human beings fit into their society. This cultural code is directed at the regulation of cognitive and social–emotional processes so that the individual will be able to fill some social role defined by society including the reproduction of that society.

The genetic code has two properties that permit it to maintain its superordinate regulatory role. It is transmitted as an organized system through time from one individual to another, and it is not affected by the individual action of those that carry it. The cultural code has the same two properties. It is transmitted through time as an organized system from one individual to another (Berger and Luckmann 1966), and it is not affected by the individual action of those that carry it. The cultural code can be changed by groups of individuals who combine to produce formal changes in legislation or informal changes in customs. The banding together of parents of handicapped children to alter laws about segregated educational systems is an example of a formal change, whereas the greater role of men in modern child-rearing in conjunction with the liberation of women from the home is an example of an informal change.

The cultural code can be broken down into sets of regulatory functions that operate across different magnitudes of time. The longest cycle is associated with *macro-regulations* that are a culture's 'developmental agenda'. The developmental agenda is a series of points in time when the environment is restructured to provide different experiences to the child. Age of weaning, toilet training, schooling, initiation rites, and marriage are coded differently in each culture, but provide the basis for socialization in each culture. The validity of such agendas is not in their details but in the fact that the culture is successfully reproduced in generation after generation of offspring.

On a shorter time base are *mini-regulations* that refer to the caregiving activities of the child's family. Such activities are feeding children when they awaken, changing diapers when they are wet, and keeping children warm. Both the mini- and macro-regulations are known to acculturated members of society and can be transmitted from member to member and generation to generation.

On the shortest time base are *micro-regulations*, which refer to the momentary interactions between child and character that others have referred to as *behavioral synchrony* or *attunement* (Field 1979; Stern 1977). Micro-regulations are a blend between the cultural and biological codes because many of these activities appear naturally and even without awareness. These include the caregiver's smiling responses to an infant's smile or possibly the matching of vocal and movement patterns between caregiver and child (Condon and Sander 1974).

Although the cultural code can be conceptualized independently of the child, changes in the abilities of the child are major triggers for regulatory changes and in all likelihood were major contributors to the evolution of the code. In most cultures formal education begins between the ages of 6 and 8 (Rogoff 1981), when most children have attained the cognitive ability to learn from such formalized experiences. On the other hand, informal education can begin at many different ages depending on the culture's attributions to the child. The Digo and Kikuyu are two East African cultures that have different beliefs about infant capacities (deVries and Sameroff 1984). The Digo believe that infants can learn within a few months after birth and begin socialization at that time. The Kikuyu wait until the second year of life before they believe serious education is possible. During the first year they keep their infants swaddled.

Given this understanding of the regulatory system for psychological development, what implications will it have? The primary application will be in the analysis of problems of deviant development. On the caregiver's side one must analyze the factors that caused regulation to fail. These would include such factors as parents not knowing the cultural code or knowing the code but being unable to use it because of other demands for their time and resources. Such other demands may include the need to be away from the home to make a living, life event stresses that interfere with their caregiving, or mental illness that diverts their attention from their children's needs to their own.

On the child's side the parents may know the cultural code and even have the time and resources to use it but be confronted by a child who does not fit the code. A child with a handicap, one born prematurely, or one with a difficult temperament would present such problems. Within this model deviancy will be the outcome of a stress on the regulatory system. The prevention of deviancy will be a function of the identification of that stress, whether it comes from the child, the parents, or perhaps the larger social context.

The caregiving environment has evolved to provide normative experiences for the normative child. Should a child be born who does not fit the normative pattern, then new regulations must be made to restore the child to the appropriate developmental trajectory. The activation of these new regulations requires transactions in which the environment is sensitive to individual differences in the children raised in that environment.

APPLYING THE TRANSACTIONAL MODEL

At the outset I raised the issue of the importance of developmental models for targeting interventions in children's lives. At this point we can examine how an understanding of development in terms of regulatory systems would affect intervention strategies.

When one begins to assess the effect of environments on child development a wide variety of risk factors are apparent. The most obvious of these is social status. Socioeconomic factors have been consistently related to cognitive (Broman *et al.* 1975; Golden and Birns 1976) and social–emotional competence (Hollinghead and Redlich 1957; Sameroff *et al.* 1982). Social status is only a summary variable that incorporates a variety of risk factors that exert both independent and interactive influences on outcomes. We (Sameroff *et al.* 1987) have shown that the developmental outcomes for young children are multiply determined. No single factor was always present or always absent in cases where high levels of social–emotional and intellectual incompetency were found. When one searches for factors that can be easily altered to improve the outcome for such children the list is short. Certain of these variables are enduring characteristics of the family – for instance, minority status and family size – whereas others are not in the usual domain of intervention – for example, stressful life events and marital status. Another set is highly unlikely to change – for example, occupation and educational level. What is left is the coping skills of the parents. These include the psychological variables of mental health, parental perspectives, and parent–child interaction patterns. These coping skills are what we have described above as the cultural code, the social regulatory system that guides children through their development and buffers them from those aspects of the broader environment with which they are not yet able to cope by themselves.

The basic developmental model in which transactional processes between child and environment are combined with continuities in each can be seen in Figure 8.6. There is a set of arrows leading from the child's initial state (C1) to the child's state at succeeding points in time. This dimension refers to the continuity of competency within the child. As children increase in age the line gets thicker as they learn more and more skills for taking care of themselves and buffering themselves from stressful experiences. There is another set of arrows leading from the environment's initial state (E1) to the environment's state at succeeding points in time. The relevant environmental factors for the present discussion are the parents' understanding of the cultural code and their competency at regulating their child's development. The sets of vertical arrows refer to the actions of parents on children and conversely of children on parents.

Intervention strategies must focus on the vertical arrows that mediate the transactional regulatory functions. These strategies fall into two categories affecting, respectively, the upward and downward

Figure 8.6 Social regulatory model of development

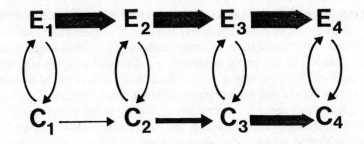

arrows. The upward arrows reflect the effect of the child on the parents. Their effects can be moderated by either changing the child or changing the parents' interpretation of the child. The downward arrows reflect the effect of the parents on the child. Parent effects can be similarly altered by either changing the parents or changing the child's interpretation of the parents. In early childhood this last category is not feasible given the limited cognitive abilities of the child, so the following analysis will be based on the first three possibilities. For simplicity I have labeled these the 'three R's' of intervention – remediation, redefinition, and reeducation.

Remediation

The strategy of remediation is the traditional prevention mechanism aimed at repairing or changing the child. Within the traditional medical model (Engel 1977), this strategy is based on the idea that the psychological development of the child is determined by the child's biological state. Thus by repairing biology one can normalize psychological functioning. Although there are many physical conditions for which such an approach may be valid – for example, intestinal or cardiac anomalies – the vast majority of behaviorally disordered children are the result of transactional processes. In such cases the intervention strategy is to change the child's effect on the parental regulating system.

Malnutrition in infancy may be a good example of how this strategy operates. Although there was an early assumption that malnutrition in infancy affected later intelligence adversely because of reductions in the number of brain cells, longitudinal studies with appropriate control groups have shown that lower later intelligence in malnourished infants is the consequence of their poor environments, not their poor biology (Read 1982). Cravioto and DeLicardie (1979) found that the behavioral effects of malnutrition were most prevalent in families in which the mothers were passively traditional in their child care and provided little stimulation to their children. In a naturalistic study Winick *et al.* (1975) compared two groups of Korean children who had suffered severe malnutrition as infants. One group was raised by their parents in Korea and scored very poorly on psychological tests given during adolescence. The second group was adopted by middle-class US parents who had no knowledge that the children had suffered from malnutrition as infants. The adopted group scored as well as or better than their US contemporaries when tested.

Transactional effects of infant malnutrition were hypothesized to be the result impaired attentional processes, reduced social responsiveness, heightened irritability, inability to tolerate frustration, low activity level, reduced independence, and diminished affect (Barrett, Radke-Yarrow and Klein 1982). Lester (1979) is cited by Barrett and colleagues as suggesting that:

> such effects may occur within a synergistic system where the malnourished infant is less successful at engaging caretakers in interaction and, in turn, is responded to less often and with less sensitivity, resulting in a failure to develop normal patterns of social interaction. If so, we should suspect that insufficient nutrition early in life would be associated with poor interpersonal skills and general lack of responsiveness in later childhood.
>
> (Barrett *et al.* 1982: 542)

Based on these hypotheses, Barrett and colleagues (1982) compared a group of children who had received caloric supplementation during infancy with a group that did not. The results were that better nutrition was associated with greater social responsiveness, more expression of affect, greater interest in the environment, and higher activity level at school age.

Food supplementation of young infants interrupted the transaction by which their low energy levels failed to stimulate their parents to engage in adequate socialization. The failure to develop normal patterns of social interaction, especially with peers, found for the malnourished control group was prevented in the supplemented group.

Remediation as an intervention does not tamper with the cultural code, that is, the parental regulatory system. It changes the child to fit better whatever the normative code is. For older children both biochemical and behavioral approaches to remediation have been used. Hyperactive children who disturb their parents and teachers are very frequently given medication to quiet them down. Such children as well as those with conduct disorders can be given behavior therapies to modify their behavior so that they will be less likely to elicit negative responses from others in their social context. Such positive changes may be possible for some behavioral problems but are less successful with other problems such as handicaps or difficult temperaments. One cannot easily make a blind child see or a spina bifida child walk. One cannot easily stop some babies from having irregular sleeping and eating habits or from having high levels of endogenously determined crying. In these cases another strategy must be used to prevent later disabilities – redefinition.

Redefinition

In order for a transactional regulation to occur the parent must define the child as being deviant. In the case of a child with a severe motor problem the parent identifies the child as abnormal and may decide that the usual regulatory function – that is, normal child rearing – is not possible. In some such cases the parent may try to convince society that the child cannot be maintained in the family and must be reared in a completely different setting – that is, an institution – with an appropriate abnormal child-rearing program for their abnormal child. In other cases the parents may accept the responsibility for the physical care of their child but expect little in the way of a satisfactory psychological relationship with the child (Roskies 1972).

The prevention effort with such families is directed at a *redefinition* of the situation, at identifying for the parents the possibilities for normal child rearing within what appears to be a deviant situation. In the case of a child with motor handicaps the redefinition may involve a refocus on the possibility of normal cognitive and social–emotional development. In the case of a retarded child, such as one with Down's syndrome, the redefinition may involve a focus on the normal sequencing of development, albeit at a slower pace.

The redefinitions allow the family to admit the child to their caregiving system. They allow the parents to see that they can indeed raise the child within the caregiving system they already know. They may need to learn some special skills for feeding or positioning the child, but these are only variations of what they would have done with a nonhandicapped child. In the case of temperamental problems, the redefinitions may be simpler. When a colicky child who cries most of the time may be perceived as emotionally deviant, the redefinition takes the form of indicating that colic is only an extreme on a normal dimension of individual differences (Chess 1966). Crying babies need not become mentally ill adults or even crying adults. Admittedly, it is a greater strain on the regulatory system to raise a handicapped or colicky infant, but this does not mean that the regulatory system is not adequate for this purpose.

The strategy of redefinition is to intervene so that the parents will use their existing regulatory system to guide the child toward normative developmental outcomes. It prevents the initial biological deficit from being converted into a later behavioral abnormality. In systems terminology, it prevents a cycle of positive feedback that would have amplified the deviation by placing the child in an abnormal child-rearing context such as an institution.

Redefinition is a reasonable strategy when the parents have a normal child-rearing capacity, when they know the cultural code. But if the parents don't know this code, if they are not aware of how to raise a child at all, then redefinition would be an insufficient prevention strategy.

Reeducation

The third strategy – reeducation – simply refers to teaching parents how to raise children. Its purpose is to teach the cultural code that regulates the child's development from birth to maturity. The most obvious target for such prevention efforts is adolescent mothers. An increasing proportion of children are being born to teenage, unmarried mothers who have few intellectual, social, or economic resources for raising their children. In these cases the intervention is aimed at training them how to be mothers and in some cases fathers. There are few normative strategies among these parents, and the child's survival is more a function of the child's resiliency or the supporting social network than the parents' abilities (McDonough 1985).

Other populations include parents of children at high risk because of either psychosocial or biological factors. One technique that has proven fruitful for such interventions is the demonstration of how to elicit infant behaviors by an expert. Widmayer and Field (1981) compared three groups of low-income teenage mothers with pre-term infants. Mothers in one group watched the administration of the Brazelton Neonatal Behavioral Assessment Scales and were trained to administer an adaptation of the scales during their babies' first month. Mothers in another group were only trained to administer the adaptation. Mothers in the third group did neither. Observations of later mother–child interactions saw improvements in the intervention groups, and the infants scored higher on developmental assessments at 12 months of age. These very needy parents seemed to benefit greatly from a targeted 1-month intervention program. An interesting question was whether such interventions would also benefit less needy mothers.

The effects of similar interventions were examined in several studies of middle-class mothers of healthy full-term babies. One study compared three groups of mothers who either watched a demonstration of the Brazelton examination, watched a standard physical examination of their baby, or were routinely discharged (Liptak *et al.* 1983). Three months later the group that saw the Brazelton demonstration spent more time playing with, looking at, and talking to their infants, but the authors felt that these were not highly significant differences. In all three groups over 90 per cent of the parents were married, living together, had attended childbirth education classes, and the father had been present during delivery. The power of the procedure is evident in the fact that any differences were found at all in this low-risk sample.

While adolescent parents may be an easily identified target for education efforts, there is a similar problem even among middle-class professional parents. There are many fathers and mothers who have had no experience taking care of siblings when growing up and who are separated from their own parents who provide the child-rearing training in more traditional societies. The difference between these two kinds of parents is that the middle-class professionals usually will seek out the information to educate themselves in how to raise a child whereas teenage mothers usually will not. In both cases information and training are necessary to equip the parents with the cultural code. For some parents, having the information available will be sufficient; for others, more intrusive educational efforts are necessary to prevent developmental deviances.

UNDERSTANDING ENVIRONMENTS

The preceding discussion has been aimed at understanding the complexity of contextual influences on development. A case was made that the environment is an active force in shaping outcomes. However, the shaping force is constrained by the state and potentialities of the individual (Sameroff 1983). In an attempt to incorporate both aspects in a coherent model of development, the utility of the transactional model for designing programs to prevent cognitive and social-emotional problems was explored. The development of these problems has been interpreted as deviations in a child-rearing regulatory system. The prevention of these problems has been defined as the adjustment of the child better to fit the regulatory system or the adjustment of the regulatory system better to fit the child. Within this regulatory framework transactions are ubiquitous. Wherever parents change their way of thinking about or behaving toward the child as a result of something the child does, a transaction has occurred. Most of these transactions are normative within the existing cultural code and facilitate development. Intervention only becomes necessary where these transactions are nonnormative. A normative event for which society is prepared is the family's registering the child in school. Society responds by changing a large part of the child's environment by the provision of a new physical environment – the school – new regulators of socialization – the teachers – and a new social network – the classmates. A nonnormative event for which society may or may not be prepared is when the parent seeks a professional for help with a deviant child. The degree of help that can be provided is a function of society's awareness of how development is regulated and the availability of resources for intervening.

In sum, models that focus on singular causal factors are inadequate for either the study or manipulation of developmental outcomes. The evolution of living systems has provided a regulatory model that incorporates feedback mechanisms between the individual and regulatory codes. These cultural and genetic codes are the context of development. By appreciating the workings of this regulatory system we can obtain a better grasp of the process of development.

REFERENCES

Anastasi, A. (1958) 'Heredity, environment, and the question, "How?" ', *Psychological Review* 65: 81–95.

Barrett, D.E., Radke-Yarrow, M. and Klein, R.E. (1982) 'Chronic malnutri- tion and child behavior: Effects of early caloric supplementation on social and emotional functioning at school age', *Child Development* 18: 541–56.

Bell, R.Q. (1968) 'A reinterpretation of the direction of effects in studies of socialization', *Psychological Review* 75: 81–95.

Berger, P.L., and Luckmann, T. (1966) *The Social Construction of Reality*, Garden City, NY: Doubleday.

Broman, S.H., Nichols, P.L. and Kennedy, W.A. (1975) *Preschool IQ: Prenatal and Early Developmental Correlates*, Hillsdale, NJ: Erlbaum.

Bronfenbrenner, U. (1977) 'Toward an experimental ecology of human development', *American Psychologist* 32: 513–31.

Bronfenbrenner, U. and Crouter, A. C. (1983) 'The evolution of environmental models in developmental research', in P.H. Mussen (gen. ed.), W. Kessen (vol. ed.) *Handbook of Child Psychology*, vol. 1: *History, Theories, and Methods*, New York: Wiley.

Bugental, D.P. and Shennum, W.A. (1984). ' "Difficult" children as elicitors and targets of adult communication patterns: an attributional–behavioral transactional analysis', *Monographs of the Society for Research in Child Development* 49 (Whole No. 205)

Chess, S. (1966) 'Individuality in children: its importance to the pediatrician', *Journal of Pediatrics* 69: 676–84.

Condon, W.S. and Sander, L.W. (1974) 'Synchrony demonstrated between movements of the neonate and adult speech', *Child Development*, 45: 456–62.

Cravioto, J. and DeLicardie, E.R. (1979) 'Nutrition, mental development, and learning'. in F. Falhner and J.M. Turner (eds) *Human Growth*, vol. 3: *Neurobiology and Nutrition*, New York: Plenum.

Crockenberg, S.B. and Smith, P. (1982) 'Antecedents of mother–infant interaction and infant irritability in the first three months of life', *Infant Behavior & Development* 5: 105–19.

deVries, M.W. and Sameroff, A.J. (1984) 'Culture and temperament: influences on temperament in three East African societies', *American Journal of Orthopsychiatry* 54: 83–96.

Ebert, J.D. and Sussex, I.M. (1970) *Interacting Systems in Development* (2nd ed.), New York: Holt, Rinehart & Winston.

Engel, G. L. (1977) 'The need for a new medical model: a challenge for biomedicine', *Science* 196: 129–36.

Field, T.M. (1979) 'Interaction patterns of preterm and term infants', in T.M. Field, A.M. Sostek, and H.H. Schuman (eds) *Infants Born at Risk: Behavior and Development*, New York: SP Medical and Scientific Books.

Golden, M. and Birns, B. (1976) 'Social class and infant intelligence', in M. Lewis (ed.) *Origins of Intelligence: Infancy and Early Childhood*, New York: Plenum.

Hollingshead, A.B. and Redlich, F.C. (1957) *Social Class and Mental Illness: A Community Study*, New York: Wiley.

Lazar, I. and Darlington, R. (1982) 'Lasting effects of early education: a report from the consortium for longitudinal studies', *Monographs of the Society for Research in Child Development* 47 (Whole No. 195).

Lester, B.M. (1979) 'A synergistic process approach to the study of prenatal malnutrition', *International Journal of Behavioral Development* 2: 377–94.

Lewin, K. (1936) *Problems of Topological Psychology*, New York: McGraw-Hill.

Liptak, G.S., Keller, B.B., Fieldman, A.W. and Chamberlin, R.W.

(1983) 'Enhancing infant development and parent–practitioner interaction with the Brazelton Neonatal Assessment Scales', *Pediatrics* 72: 71–8.

McDonough, S.C. (1985) 'Intervention program for adolescent mothers and their offspring', *Journal of Children in Contemporary Society* 17: 67–76.

Read, M.S. (1982) 'Malnutrition and behavior', *Applied Research in Mental Retardation* 3: 279–91.

Rheingold, H.L. (1966) 'The development of social behavior in human infant', in H.W. Stevenson (ed.), 'Concept of development', *Monographs of the Society for Research in Child Development* 31(5) (Whole No. 107).

Riegel, K.F. (1978) *Psychology, Mon Amour: A Countertext*, Boston: Houghton Mifflin.

Rogoff, B. (1981) 'Schooling and the development of cognitive skills', in H.C. Triandis and A. Heron (eds) *Handbook of Cross-Cultural Psychology: Developmental Psychology* (vol. 4) Boston: Allyn & Bacon.

Roskies, E. (1972) *Abnormality and Normality: The Mothering of Thalidomide Children*, Ithaca, NY: Cornell University Press.

Sameroff, A.J. (1983) 'Developmental systems: contexts and evolution', in P.H. Mussen (gen. ed.), W. Kessen (vol. ed.) *Handbook of Child Psychology* vol. 1 *History, Theories, and Methods*, New York: Wiley.

Sameroff, A.J., and Chandler, M.J. (1975) 'Reproductive risk and the continuum of caretaking casualty', in F.D. Horowitz, M. Hetherington, S. Scarr-Salapatek and G. Siegel (eds) *Review of Child Development Research* (vol. 4), Chicago: University of Chicago Press.

Sameroff, A.J., and Seifer, R. (1983, April) *Sources of Continuity in Parent–Child Relationships*, paper presented at the meeting of the Society for Research in Child Development, Detroit.

Sameroff, A.J., Seifer, R., Barocas, B., Zax, M., and Greenspan, S. 'I.Q. scores of 4-year-old children: social–environmental risk factors', *Pediatrics*, in press.

Sameroff, A.J., Seifer, R., and Zax, M. (1982) 'Early development of children at risk for emotional disorder', *Monographs of the Society for Research in Child Development* 47(7) (Serial No. 199).

Stern, D. (1977) *The First Relationship: Infant and Mother*, Cambridge, Mass.: Harvard University Press.

Thomas, A., Chess, S., and Birch, H. (1968) *Temperament and Behavior Disorders in Children*, New York: New York University.

Waddington, C.H. (1957) *The Strategy of the Genes*, London: Allen & Unwin.

Widmayer, S.M., and Field, T.M. (1981) 'Effects of Brazelton demonstrations for mothers on the development of preterm infants', *Pediatrics* 72: 711–14.

Winick, M., Meyer, K., and Harris, R. (1975) 'Malnutrition and environmental enrichment by early adoption', *Science* 190: 1173–5.

Zeskind, P.S. and Ramey, C.T. (1978) 'Fetal malnutrition: an experimental study of its consequences for infant development in two caregiving environments', *Child Development* 49: 1155–62.

Zeskind, P.S. and Ramey, C.T. (1981) 'Preventing intellectual and interactional sequelae of fetal malnutrition: a longitudinal, transactional, and
synergistic approach to development', *Child Development* 52: 213-18.

Zigler, E. and Trickett, P. K. (1978) 'I.Q., social competence, and evaluation of early childhood intervention programs', *American Psychologist*
33: 789-99.

Part three

Relationships and early learning

Introduction

> . . . human competence is both biological in origin and cultural in the means by which it finds expression. . . . We must ask not only about capacities, but also about how humans are aided in expressing them in the medium of culture.
>
> (Bruner 1983: 23)

The next four chapters explore the significance of early relationships for children's learning, with particular emphasis on language acquisition and use. The problem of how virtually all children master a skill as complex as their mother-tongue has attracted a great deal of research attention. As the quotation from Bruner makes clear, while it is tempting to follow Chomsky and propose an inborn 'Language Acquisition Device' (LAD), it is also important to identify the respects in which children's early social relationships function as a 'Language Acquisition Support System' (LASS).

Snow's observations of mothers and young children have been very influential in this regard (Chapter 9). The concept of 'motherese' has been widely used to encapsulate such characteristic features as shorter length of utterance, grammatical simplification, repetition and distinctive intonation. How far these are necessary conditions for language learning, and how far merely enabling conditions for the young child is a matter of some debate.

The chapter by Schieffelin and Ochs (Chapter 10) offers a very different perspective, based largely on ethnographic work in Papua New Guinea. They argue that because researchers share the same cultural context as their subjects they have been blind to the respects in which 'motherese' is culture-specific rather than a species-characteristic support system for early learning. Rabain-Jamin begins her chapter (Chapter 11) by rehearsing this issue, and then goes on to report the results of a study of language use in a play situation, comparing French with West African mothers living in Paris.

In the final chapter (Chapter 12), Bruner steps back from these particular cases of cultural variation in human learning and teaching. This is an edited version of his landmark paper on 'the evolution of educability'. Drawing extensively on primate as well as human research, Bruner highlights the importance of observational learning, tool use, play, language and instruction, in progressively releasing learning from the constraints of a particular context, amplifying the potential for transmitting knowledge and skill, especially with the modern spread of literacy and schooling.

REFERENCE

Bruner, J. (1983) *Child's Talk*, Oxford: Oxford University Press.

9 The language of the mother-child relationship

Catherine E. Snow

Source: Rogers S. (ed.) (1976)*The Don't Speak Our Language – Essays on the Language World of Children and Adolescents*, London: Edward Arnold.

By the time children of four or five years go off to school, they know a great deal about the language they speak and about using that language to communicate with others. The process of acquiring this knowledge is, for most children, very fast, relatively painless, and seemingly automatic, so it often goes unnoticed how much time and effort the children themselves and their older caretakers invest in the process. It is the purpose of this paper to look at some of the events and experiences in infancy and early childhood which may contribute to the acquisition of linguistic and communicative skills. These events and experiences include:

1 'Conversation-like' interactions in early infancy.
2 Having one's first communicative efforts responded to.
3 Receiving linguistic input of a simplified and repetitive nature.
4 Having adults respond to one's signals that their communicative efforts are ineffective.

Whether any or all of these experiences is crucial to normal language development must be further studied.

One of the principles which underlies the view of language acquisition presented here is that language acquisition is the result of an interaction between caretaker (usually, in societies with which we are familiar, the mother) and child in which both play an active role. The role of the child in initiating and in terminating the interaction, in pacing and directing it, and in determining its nature and content is as great as or greater than that of the mother. The mother's contribution to the interaction is that she is uniquely aware of and sensitive to the child's needs, interests and abilities, and to his special communicative devices. She is therefore in the best position to engage in appropriately paced and mutually interesting interactions with her child.

Reference is continually made in the following discussion to the mother–child relationship, because the mother is the primary caretaker and most constant companion of the young child in the societies where most of the research referred to here has been performed. There is no intention to imply that only the biological mother can perform the caretaker function, nor that she is the best person to perform this function, nor even that one single person can perform it better than two or several.

HOW MOTHERS AND INFANTS COMMUNICATE

One of the first steps in the child's acquisition of the ability to communicate is learning to signal. Children learn very early that cries of pain, of hunger, and of discomfort are effective in summoning an adult and in changing the situation. Babies in the first three months of life cry more when the mother is far away; by one year they cry more when she is nearby. They have learned that crying communicates and that the addressee must be present for the communication to be effective (Bell and Ainsworth 1972). Mothers report that they can distinguish different types of cries from one another as early as one month after the baby is born. This assertion is, in fact, probably not true. But it is nonetheless revealing that mothers think it is true, precisely because this means that they are treating their babies, even at this age, as communicating beings (Eveloff 1971). As such, mothers set the stage for real communication, creating a situation in which the babies are encouraged to participate actively as soon as they are able to. Similarly, the first time the baby smiles at his mother she can interpret this as communicating that she is recognized as someone special – an attitude which will greatly support later communicative interactions.

But there is a second aspect of the infant's communication system. Infants learn at a very early age that there are rules governing communicative interactions, e.g. that communication involves give and take and that the participants must take turns. Infants seem to have mastered the *form* of communicative interactions long before they can do anything about introducing content to those interactions.

Infants' first experience of communicative interactions comes in the form of 'conversation-like interactions'. What exactly are conversation-like interactions? One example is the 'protoconversation' (Bateson 1971), an interaction sequence which looks very much like conversation between two adults, in that (a) the two participants look at each other, (b) only one of them talks at a time, (c) when one stops talking, the other begins almost immediately, and (d) each listens to the other. But a typical adult conversation follows lines like the following:

A: Hi, how are things?
B: Well, I got fired last week.
A: Oh dear.
B: But I got a new job.
A: Oh yeah? Is it working out?
B: Pretty well. It's hard work, but twice the salary of the other place.
A: Hey, have they got an opening for me?

whereas a typical protoconversation consists of:

M: What you gonna say?
B: (babbles)
M: Huh?
B: (babbles)
M: Oh dear.
B: (babbles)
M: You gonna be a good boy today?
B: (babbles)
M: (laughs) You're not?

The baby could not contribute much in the way of content to this interaction (quoted from Bateson 1971); he was only three months old and did not have much to say yet. But he *was able* to sustain an interaction that had many of the characteristics of adult conversations.

Similarly, sequences of gazing at each other by mothers and babies can be described by the same mathematical model used to describe adults talking to each other (Jaffe, Stern and Perry 1973).

It would seem that babies, long before the onset of speech, have general rules for communicative interactions. These rules have the chance to develop or be learned because babies are born with a strong tendency to be interested in 'talking, moving faces'. When awake, babies tend to quieten down and pay attention when their mothers come within sight and or start to talk (Jones and Moss 1971). This quiet, attentive baby is then ripe to engage in a conversation-like interaction with his mother. If he happens to vocalize while his mother is looking at him or talking to him, she is quite likely to respond with more talking or with attention of some other kind. By the age of three months, babies' productions of vocalizations can be increased if their vocalizations are rewarded by social responses (being touched, spoken to, or looked at) (Jones and Moss 1971). So all that is needed to create a protoconversation is a baby that is interested in talking adults and an adult who is interested in vocalizing babies. The product of these complementary interests is a child who approaches the language-learning situation with a great deal of knowledge about how to use the language he has not yet learned.

It is of course the case that some adults are less interested in vocalizing babies than others. Fathers, for instance, tend to interact with their infants, and to talk to them, much less than mothers do, an average of 38 seconds per day according to one American study (Rebelsky and Hanks 1971). This is of course partly a question of opportunity in societies where fathers go to work and mothers stay home. But it is also no doubt a question of cultural norms; women are supposed to be more interested in babies, and are supposed to show their interest and affection more openly, than men. It is acceptable for women to do 'silly' things like talking to infants who are clearly too young to understand. This is somewhat less acceptable for men, and not at all to be expected of them. Therefore infants are mostly dependent on their mothers to teach them about interacting.

But there also exist cultures and subcultures which put little value on interacting with infants. Even two cultures as similar as middle-class America and middle-class Holland differ considerably in their norms for interacting with infants. Dutch mothers tend to believe that young babies should be fed on schedule, should sleep a great deal, should not be overstimulated with crib toys or play sessions, and should not be spoiled (Rebelsky 1967).

As a consequence of these culturally determined child-rearing norms, Dutch babies (at least up to an age of three months) have considerably less interaction with their mothers than American babies, and the interactions that do occur tend to be initiated and scheduled by the mother rather than the baby. Dutch mothers show much less tendency to respond to fussing or crying babies than do American mothers, nor do they exploit openings for conversation-like interactions as often. Nonetheless, Dutch babies do grow up normally and do learn to talk. Does this mean that mother–infant interaction at a few months of age has no effect in later language acquisition? Nobody knows, because no one has directly related the speed or ease of language learning in children from different child-rearing cultures to the opportunities for prelinguistic conversation-like interactions within the cultures. However, it has been shown that the IQ scores of eight- to ten-month-old infants whose mothers were restrictive and engaged in a little physical or verbal contact were lower than those of infants whose mothers were permissive and engaged in much verbal and physical contact. This difference was found even within a group of middle-class mothers, all of whom provided fully adequate and loving maternal care (Beckwith 1971). This effect of maternal style on IQ strongly suggests that maternal style in first several months of life could also affect the course of language acquisition which occurs a year and a half later.

Just as Dutch mothers think it is overstimulating to play too much with their young infants, lower-class American mothers think it is ludicrous to talk to somewhat older children (Tulkin and Kagan 1972). Middle-class mothers tend to report of their prelinguistic children that they 'can't talk very well yet, but she understands everything I say to her'. This belief is probably as incorrect as the belief that one-month-old babies produce distinguishable cries, and it may well support the child's learning to communicate in a similar way. Because mothers believe their children can understand them, they talk to them. Because they believe their children are already learning to talk, they teach them words and play verbal games with them. Thus the child can start learning language as soon as his cognitive capacities allow him to, and even before that time he has had much practice in listening to language and in learning that spoken words carry messages. He is thus acquiring the communicative skills which make the job of acquiring linguistic skills much easier. The lower-class child whose mother thinks him (probably correctly) too young to talk or to understand misses a huge chunk of experience which may well speed up the language acquisition process.

HOW MOTHERS TALK TO CHILDREN

We have in the first section discussed generally how mothers interact with their infants. We have seen that such factors as responding to an infant's crying, providing him with toys, playing with him, looking at him, talking to him, and responding when he smiles or vocalizes, all play a role in early mother-infant interactions, and may have an effect on the later development of language. We will now look more specifically at one aspect of mother-child interaction that intuitively would seem to be the most important for language development - how mothers talk to their children.

The issue of how mothers talk to their children has become very important to the study of developmental psycholinguistics because of its relevance to the nativism-empiricism controversy. Nativists such as Chomsky and others see language as a process of unfolding or discovery; they stress how complicated a system language is, that attempts to teach non-humans to talk have failed, that the process of language development is very similar for all children no matter what language they are learning, that language development is closely related to maturational milestones for innate motoric development, and that the structure of the linguistic system is not directly derivable from a list of utterances. The first and last points are really central to the argument; not only is language a very complex system, but it is a system whose structure is obscured in the spoken language we hear, which is often confused, garbled, poorly constructed, and inadequately organized. Because the language they hear gives them so little real information about the structure of the language which they will have to learn, children must have innate linguistic abilities which enable them to recognize the underlying structure despite the confusing input. That is, according to the nativists.

The empiricists or behaviourists point out that although adult language is a complex system, the language children learn to speak is considerably simpler. Furthermore, they say, the language children hear is not garbled, confused or misleading – it is very well organised to be quite transparent in structure even to a young child. Empiricists emphasize that environmental factors play an important role in how quickly and how well children learn to talk, and that language acquisition takes a long time and is characterized by much explicit teaching on the part of the mother and implicit practice on the part of the child. According to the empiricists all this means that language is learned just as other skills are learned. Innate characteristics which are prerequisite to that learning may exist, but then they are general characteristics like being social, finding human beings interesting, wishing to be able to communicate, recognizing that objects can be categorized, etc., not specific linguistic universals like knowing that sentences have subjects and predicates, or knowing that there are different grammatical classes of words. It is not our purpose here to discuss the nativist–empiricist controversy at length – nor would that be very fruitful, since both positions are more 'ways of looking at things' than they are statements of truth. The controversy is important in the present context primarily because it has been the motivation for detailed description of the speech of mothers to their babies and young children by experimenters seeking to support the empiricist claims. These data will provide the basis for the discussion to follow.

BABY-TALK

The phenomenon of baby-talk – 'It's an itsy-bitsy cutie-pie, isn't it? – is one which we all recognize and occasionally shudder at. Baby-talk is a phenomenon which belongs to the culture of child-raising; in some cultures it is considered the appropriate way to address small children. In other cultures it is seen as demeaning and potentially harmful to the child. Nonetheless, despite cultural norms, it is probably safe to say that all cultures have some baby-talk forms. Baby-talk has, furthermore, some characteristics which are very similar no matter what the adult language is. Consonant cluster simplification or substitution, for example, is typical of baby-talk in English (*tummy* for stomach) as well as in Dutch (*noepie* for *snoepje*, sweetie), Comanche American Indian (*píhI* for *kwíhI*, wife, and *pánA* for *kwánA*, smell) and Papiamentu Spanish (*panu* for *aeroplanu*, airplane).

Syllable reduplication and onomatopoetic or rhyming words are also common (English: *yum-yum* for delicious, *itsy-bitsy* for little; Dutch: *woef-woef* for dog; French: *do-do* for dormir; Comanche: *tutú* for train; Berber: *duddu* for *udi*, butter; and the ubiquitous *pipi* for urinate). There is a tendency to use diminutive endings widely (English: –ie or –y, as in *doggie* and *nappy*; Dutch: –ie or –je; Comanche: –cí as in *haicí*, friend) (Bynon 1968; Casagrande 1968; Ferguson 1964). Pronouns show certain deviations from normal usage, e.g., 'Are we hungry?' for 'Are you hungry?', 'Isn't it a cute baby?' for 'Aren't you a cute baby?' and 'Mamma's going now' for 'I'm going now' (Wills 1974). The voice is pitched higher than normal in baby-talk, and the normal intonation patterns are greatly exaggerated.

In terms of grammatical structure and content, the speech addressed to babies up to about a year of age is widely variant. Some mothers produce quite complicated monologues, though maintaining baby-talk intonation patterns, probably on the assumption that the baby will not understand anyway. Other mothers adapt the content and the structural characteristics of their speech to the baby's limited abilities very early (Phillips 1973). Examples of monologues that might be produced by these two kinds of mothers follow:

1 And what are we gonna do when daddy gets home? Maybe we should go buy a big steak at the supermarket and grill it outdoors on the barbecue. Hmm? Would you like that?
2 Pretty baby. It's such a pretty baby. How is pretty baby today? Hungry? Are you hungry? Do you want your bottle? We'll go get you a bottle. Just a minute. Wait just a minute.

In neither of these cases would the mothers really expect the baby to understand, or to respond. The first mother has chosen to think aloud about reasonable adult topics, whereas the second has limited her topics to baby-oriented ones, and has produced grammatically much simpler sentences.

SEMANTIC RESTRICTIONS

This variation and free choice in the sometimes quite complicated monologues disappears by the time the baby is eighteen months old; at that time all mothers – indeed, all adults – address children in a grammatically very simple way about a severely restricted set of topics. These topics can be described as limited to 'everydayness', the 'here-and-now', concrete concepts (Phillips 1973). Mothers tend to talk to children about what the children themselves are doing, about the objects they are looking at, holding, or playing with, about what is going on around them. Discussions about what happened yesterday or what will happen tomorrow are relatively infrequent, and if they do occur tend to be practised routines of the following sort:

M: Who is coming next week?
C: Santa Claus
M: What will he ride in?
C: Sleigh
M: And what is he bringing?
C: Toys
M: Who are the toys for?
etc.

The fact that mothers limit the topics of their conversations with children to a fairly small set of shared experiences may be crucial in the development of language. A theory of language acquisition has been presented which is based on precisely this assumption – that children can learn to talk only because the meaning of the vast majority of utterances they hear is obvious. This theory, which has been called the theory of Semantic Primacy, sees the language development process as one led and controlled by the child's cognitive development (see Macnamara 1972). Children first learn to understand the world, to identify objects, to categorize, to recognize cause and effect; once the children have recognized and understood the important facts about reality, they can begin to correlate certain facts or states or occurrences with certain maternal utterances. Thus, a mother's sentence 'That is a dog' can provide information to a child about (1) the appropriate word for a concept and (2) the syntactic form for sentences with a labelling function. But the child could not use that information, would not be able to understand nor process it, if he did not already have the concept for which he was searching for aname. The majority of mothers' utterances can be seen as having this sort of function, namely describing events which the child has just experienced and thereby giving him names for his concepts, e.g. 'Your milk is all gone' to a child who has just emptied his glass, 'Daddy's coming home' as the car pulls into the driveway, or 'It is time for lunch' as the child is placed in his high chair. Mothers' utterances can be seen as the linguistically simplest description of the most salient aspects of the current situation. Mothers say what their children are most likely to be thinking about any situation. Thus does the meaning of maternal utterances remain transparent, and does the child have a chance to learn how his own thoughts must be expressed in the adult language.

No one has ever directly tested the Semantic Primacy theory of language acquisition, nor would it be morally feasible to test it by, for example, giving a child as his only linguistic input four hours a day of reading from the *Encyclopedia Britannica*. However, there is some evidence that children whose 'ways of organizing the world', as revealed in the first fifty words they choose to learn, do not match their mothers' views of the world, as revealed in the kinds of words they use most often, learn language with greater difficulty than children whose mothers' cognitive organizations do match their own (Nelson 1973). Thus, it would seem that children start with a set of concepts for which they search for names in the linguistic input. If their mothers think the same kinds of concept important, then they will naturally provide the correct names in the course of their comments on what is happening around the child. But if the mother has different ideas about what is important – if she, for example, persists in commenting 'He says bow-wow' about a picture of a dog, while the child wants to know the name for the class of dogs, – then the child's language acquisition will be slowed down.

Linguistic input to children is, thus, usually characterized by being semantically interpretable: that is, able to be understood by the child at any given level of development; in those cases where it is not entirely interpretable, language acquisition is impeded. But mothers' speech to children has other striking characteristics besides its here-and-nowness. It is also grammatically very simple, is highly redundant, with the same thing being said in many different ways, and shows particular intonation patterns. These characteristics will be treated in the following sections.

GRAMMATICAL SIMPLICITY

There are many different ways of measuring grammatical simplicity in speech – but on all the different measures used in several different studies of mothers' speech to children, mothers speak more simply to children than to adults, and more simply to younger children than to older children (see Broen 1972; Phillips 1973; Remick 1972; Snow 1972a). Mean or average length of utterance, which is the most generally used and perhaps most useful measure of linguistic complexity in young children, is always in the range three to eight words per utterance in speech addressed to two-year-old children, whereas for older children and adults it ranges from eight to ten. Mean length of utterances in itself says nothing, of course, about precisely what makes sentences long and complex. A more detailed analysis of those structures that make sentences long and complex, such as subordinate clauses and co-ordinations, reveals that they are either very infrequent or entirely absent in the speech of mothers to young children.

Other optional structures in sentences, such as adjectives, adverbs and prepositional phrases of various sorts, are used in mothers' speech, but at a rate of one or at most two per sentence. In general, sentences are pared down to one idea, and that idea is expressed as simply as possible in terms of grammar.

A large number of the sentences addressed by mothers to their young children are 'labelling sentences', of the form 'That is a ———' or 'This is a ———'. These sentences are, of course, of the utmost grammatical simplicity. Mothers also use imperatives a great deal when talking to two-year-olds – and there is some indication that lower-class mothers use them more often than middle-class mothers (Snow *et al.* 1974). Imperatives can be very simple sentences, e.g. 'Get your gloves', 'Pick up the dollie', and 'Drink your milk'. Questions, which at least in English are quite complex to produce, are used much more often in speech to two-year-olds than with older children or adults (Sachs, Brown and Salerno 1972; Snow *et al.* 1974); however, it is to a large extent fairly simple questions which are posed, most often: 'What is that?' These questions, which are quite simple grammatically, are nonetheless sometimes quite complex in that the communicative force is very different from what it would be in adult language. 'What is that?' for example, which would be used to an adult as a request for information, is almost exclusively used to children in situations in which the speaker knows the answer perfectly well, i.e. with a tutorial function. Similarly, 'Are your hands clean?' when addressed to a child means 'Wash your hands' and 'Are you sleepy?' very often means 'You're sleepy!'

Many aspects of the grammatical simplicity of maternal speech are clearly a result of the semantic limitations discussed above. Discussions of the here-and-now make no reference to the past or future, so the tense system is largely limited to the present, and temporal subordinate clauses such as 'When you have done this, go and do . . . .' are also unnecessary. Describing what is going on at the moment requires minimal use of subordinate clauses introduced by *if*, *unless*, *because*, *although*, or *as a result of*. Grammatical functions are limited to the bare minimum – subject, verb, direct object, place adverbials, and a few more. New ones are added only as the child shows the ability to understand them and the need to use them himself.

REDUNDANCY

Mothers talking to two-year-olds never seem to say anything just once. Words and phrases as well as whole sentences are repeated again and again. The type–token ratio, a measure of the diversity of vocabulary used in a text or conversation, has been found to be in the range .3 to .5 for speech to two-year-olds, as compared to .5 to .7 in speech to adults (Broen 1972; Phillips 1973). Children hear a relatively small number of words over and over again – a fact which must help them immensely in the difficult task of segmenting the stream of speech they hear into meaningful units. Furthermore, children hear phrases from sentences repeated out of context and in new contexts, as in the following passage:

Put the red truck in the box. The red truck. That's right, in the box. Put it in the box. Come on, the red one. The red one. In the box. Put it in there.

Nativists in the language-acquisition controversy have long contended that children must have built-in information about language, because they would otherwise never analyse for themselves the complex hierarchical organization of sentences, represented by some linguists in tree diagrams, as in Figure 9.1. Repetition sequences like that shown in Figure 9.1, however, could serve to isolate constituents of the sentence, and then to show how smaller constituents added together make up larger constituents, as in Figure 9.2.

Repetition is not all of this constituent-juggling type, of course. Sometimes it consists of a mother saying one thing in several ways, presumably because the child shows insufficient responsiveness to or comprehension of the original version. This production of paraphrases

Figure 9.1 Linguistic tree diagram

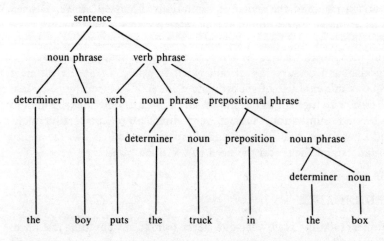

Figure 9.2 Linguistic tree showing the build-up of constituents

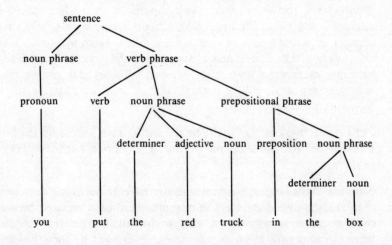

is clearly controlled by one of the major principles of mother–child interaction: the child must understand what is said to him. Children are not allowed not to understand; and their comprehension is ensured (a) by trying to express only simple ideas, (b) by phrasing the simple ideas in simple ways, and (c) by carefully monitoring the child's response so that they can be said a different way if the first seems ineffective.

INTONATION PATTERNS OR PROSODY

As in baby-talk, mothers' speech to children is higher pitched than normal speech, and shows an exaggerated intonation pattern (Garnica 1974; Remick 1972). The higher pitch is probably used because it attracts children's attention. In fact, even very young babies are more attentive to a female than to a male voice (Brazelton, quoted in Korner 1973). It may be that the attraction of a high-pitched voice for children is built-in, or it may be that they learn that high-pitched speech is addressed to them and that they should listen. It is in either case a very handy mechanism; it means that children know what is for them, and that they do not even have to try to figure out what adults are saying to each other in the early stages of language acquisition. If no such mechanism existed for making 'child-speech' clearly distinguishable from 'adult-speech', children might try to learn to talk on the basis of highly inappropriate linguistic data, the relatively complex speech of adults to adults, and might become quite confused in the process.

The exaggerated intonation contour typical of adult–child speech has two potential functions:

1 It causes the content words in the sentence to be even more heavily stressed than normal. It is, of course, the content words, not the unstressed grammatical function words, which are crucial to the child in deciphering the message. Thus, the exaggerated intonation is a way of making the semantic content of the speech clearer.
2 The exaggerated contour makes it easier for the child to correlate syntactic form with meaning. Questions, imperatives, and statements are made very highly recognizable sentence types, since the intonation pattern associated with each is even more distinctive than in normal speech. Thus, the child can recognize on prosodic grounds what kind of sentence is being offered, and can then search for the syntactic markers (word order, wh-words, or whatever) which occur in conjunction with each intonation pattern.

HOW CHILDREN INFLUENCE THEIR MOTHERS

All of these modifications in mothers' speech for young children – the restriction of semantic content, the redundancy, the intonation, the grammatical simplification – are adjusted to the level of the child. Though a child of two and a child of three will both be addressed with modified speech styles, the speech addressed to the two-year-old will be even simpler and more redundant so that the same thing is said in more than one way, than the speech addressed to the three-year-old. How do mothers know exactly what level of speech to produce for their children at every age and at every stage of development? They know because the children tell them, using various cues of less or greater subtlety.

Children become less attentive when the speech addressed to them does not show the normal characteristics of maternal speech (Snow 1972b; Dale, personal communication).

They become less likely to respond when the sentences addressed to them begin with words they do not know (Shipley, Gleitman and Smith 1969). Furthermore, children of course share with adults certain techniques for modifying the speaker's style – such as saying 'What?' or 'Huh?' or 'This one?' or other such explicit expressions of noncomprehension. Adults seem to be very sensitive to all these various cues from children, and to keep modifying their speech styles until the inattention, the lack of comprehension, and the questioning disappear. Thus, the production of appropriately modified speech styles for young children is the result of a process of interaction based on mutual expectations to communicate on the part of both mother and child.

The child's tendency to stop listening when speech becomes too complex has a second effect, besides that of causing the adult to change his speech style. The child's attentional system functions as a filter which passes only appropriate linguistic data. Sentences which begin with unfamiliar words, sentences whose syntactic form is indecipherable and whose semantic content is unclear, never get through the filter. Thus, an adult who is exceptionally unskilled in adjusting his speech to the abilities of the child, or who is unusually obtuse in picking up the child's signals of inattention and noncomprehension, will not be able to retard the child's language acquisition process. The inappropriate sentence, which might have confused the child and complicated his language-learning task, simply does not get through.

LEARNING TO TALK

By the time children are four to five years old, they have learned to talk well enough to use language in much the same way adults do – for transferring information and ideas, for making contact with other people, and for inducing others to do what you want them to do. This achievement is possible because the child has learned a great deal about language as a means of communication, and about language as an abstract system characterized by complicated and sometimes arbitrary rules of syntax and morphology. This second kind of learning – learning the rules of syntax – is dependent on the first kind, and gives relatively little trouble precisely because the first kind has already taken place, at least partially.

Children come to the language-learning situation with the expectation that meaningful things will be said to them, and mothers fulfil that expectation beautifully. Similarly, mothers expect their children to try to communicate, and respond immediately to any behaviour that can be interpreted as communicative. Thus arises an interaction which leads to true communication, and which along the way provides the model opportunity for learning the rules of grammar.

REFERENCES

Bateson, M. C. (1971) 'Epigenesis of conversational interaction', paper presented to the Society for Research in Child Development, Minneapolis.

Beckwith, L. (1971) 'Relationships between attributes of mothers and their infants' IQ scores', *Child Development* 42: 1083–98.

Bell, S. M. and Ainsworth, M. (1972) 'Infant crying and maternal responsiveness', *Child Development* 43: 1171–90.

Broen, P. A. (1972) 'The verbal environment of the language-learning child', American Speech and Hearing Association Monograph 17, December.

Bynon, J. (1968) 'Berber nursery language', Transactions of the Philological Society: 107–61.

Casagrande, J. B. (1968) 'Comanche Baby Talk', *International Journal of American Linguistics* 14: 11–14.

Eveloff, H. (1971) 'Some cognitive and affective aspects of early language development', *Child Development* 42: 1895–1907

Ferguson, C. A. (1964) 'Baby talk in six languages', in J. J. Gumperz and D. Hymes (eds) 'The ethnography of communication', *American Anthropologist* 66(6) 2: 103–14.

Garnica, O. (1971) 'Some prosodic characteristics of speech to young children', paper presented at Conference on Language Input and Acquisition, Boston, September.

Jaffe, J., Stern, D. and Perry, J. (1973) ' "Conversational" ' coupling of gaze behavior in prelinguistic human development', *Journal of Psycolinguistic Research* 2: 321–30.

Jones, S. and Moss, H. (1971) 'Age, state, and maternal behavior associated with infant vocalisations' *Child Development*, 42: 1039–52.

Korner, A. F. (1973) 'Early stimulation and maternal care as related to infant capabilities and individual differences', *Early Child Development and Care* 2: 307–27.

Macnamara, J. (1972) 'Cognitive basis of language learning in infants', *Psychological Review* 79: 1–13.

Nelson, K. (1973) 'Structure and strategy in learning to talk', Society for Research in Child Development Monograph 141, 38(1) and (2).

Phillips, J. (1973) 'Formal characteristics of speech which mothers address to their young children', Ph.D thesis, Johns Hopkins University.

Rebelsky, F. (1967) 'Infancy in two cultures', *Nederlands Tijdschrift voor Psychologie* 22: 27-36.

Rebelsky, F. and Hanks, C. (1971) 'Fathers' verbal interactions with infants in the first three months of life', *Child Development* 42: 63-8.

Remick, H. (1972) 'Maternal speech to children during language acquisition', paper presented at International Symposium of First Language Acquisition, Florence, Italy.

Sachs, J., Brown, R. and Salerno, R. (1972) 'Adults' speech to children', paper presented at International Symposium on First Language Acquisition, Florence Italy.

Shipley, E., Gleitman, L. and Smith, C. (1969) 'A study in acquisition of language: free responses to commands', *Language* 45: 322-42.

Snow, C. E. (1972a) 'Mothers' speech to children learning language', *Child Development* 43: 549-65.

Snow, C. E. (1972b) 'Young children's responses to adult sentences of varying complexity', paper presented at International Conference of Applied Linguistics, Copenhagen.

Snow, C. E., Arlman-Rupp, A., Hassing, Y., Jobse, J., Joosten, J. and Vorster, J. (1974) 'Mothers' speech in three social classes', unpublished paper, Institute for General Linguistics, University of Amsterdam.

Tulkin, S. and Kagan, J. (1972) 'Mother-child interaction in the first year of life', *Child Development* 43: 31-42.

Wills, D. D. (1974) 'Participation deixis in English and Childish', paper presented at Conference on Language Input and Acquisition, Boston, September.

10 A cultural perspective on the transition from prelinguistic to linguistic communication

Bambi B. Schieffelin and Elinor Ochs

Source: Golinkoff, R. M. (ed.) (1983) *The Transition from Prelinguistic to Linguistic Communication*, Hillsdale, N.J.: Erlbaum.

ETHNOGRAPHIC ORIENTATION

To most middle-class Western readers, the descriptions of verbal and non-verbal behaviors of middle-class caregivers with their children seem very familiar, desirable, and even natural. These descriptions capture in rich detail what does go on in many middle-class households, to a greater or lesser extent. The characteristics of caregiver speech (baby-talk register) and comportment that have been specified are highly valued by members of white middle-class society, including researchers, readers, and subjects of study. They are associated with good mothering and can be spontaneously produced with little effort or reflections. As demonstrated by Shatz and Gelman (1973), Sachs and Devin (1976), and Andersen and Johnson (1973), children as young as 4 years of age can speak and act in these ways when addressing small children.

From our research experience in other societies as well as our acquaintance with some of the cross-cultural studies of language socialization (Blount 1972; Bowerman 1981; Fischer 1970; Hamilton 1981; Harkness 1975; Harkness and Super 1977; Heath 1983; Miller 1982; Philips 1982; Schieffelin and Eisenberg 1984; Scollon and Scollon 1981; Stross 1972; Ward 1971; Wills 1977), the general patterns of caregiving that have been described in the psychological literature on white middle class are neither characteristic of all societies nor of all social groups (e.g., all social classes within one society). We would like the reader, therefore, to reconsider the descriptions of caregiving in the psychological literature as *ethnographic descriptions*.

By ethnographic, we mean *descriptions that take into account the perspective of members of a social group, including beliefs and values that underlie and organise their activities and utterances.* Ethnographers rely heavily on observations and on formal and informal elicitation of members' reflections and interpretations as a basis for analysis (Geertz 1973). Typically the ethnographer is not a member of the group under study. Further, in presenting an ethnographic account the researcher faces the problem of communicating world views or sets of values that may be unfamiliar and strange to the reader. Ideally such statements provide a set of organising principles that give coherence and an analytic focus to the behaviors described.

Psychologists who have carried out research on verbal and non-verbal behavior of caregivers and their children draw on both of the methods articulated above. However, unlike most ethnographers, typically the psychological researcher *is* a member of the social group under observation. (In some cases, the researcher's own children are the subjects of study.) Further, unlike the ethnographer, the psychologist addresses a readership familiar with the social scenes portrayed.

That researcher, reader, and subjects of study tend to have in common a white middle-class literate background has had several consequences. For example, by and large, the psychologist has not been faced with the problem of cultural translation, as has the anthropologist – there has been a tacit assumption that readers can provide the larger cultural framework for making sense out of the behaviors documented. A consequence of this in turn is that the cultural nature of the behaviors and principles presented is not explicit. From our perspective, *language and culture as bodies of knowledge, structures of understanding, conceptions of the world, collective representations, are both extrinsic to and far more extensive than any individual could know or learn. Culture encompasses variation in knowledge between individuals, but such variation, while crucial to what an individual may know and to the social dynamic between individuals, does not have its locus within the individual.* Our position is that culture is not something that can be considered separately from the accounts of caregiver–child interactions; it is what organizes and gives meaning to that interaction. This is an important point, as it affects the definition and interpretation of the behaviors of caregivers and children. How caregivers and children speak and act towards one another is linked to cultural patterns that extend and have consequences beyond the specific interactions observed. For example, how caregivers speak to their children may be linked to other institutional adaptations to young children. These adaptations in turn may be linked to how members of a given society view children more generally (their 'nature', their social status and expected comportment) and to how members think children develop.

We are suggesting here that sharing of assumptions between researcher, reader, and subjects of study is a mixed blessing. In fact, this sharing presents a *paradox of familiarity*. We are able to apply without effort the cultural framework for interpreting the behavior of caregivers and young children in our own social group; indeed as members of a white middle-class society, we are socialized to do this very work, that is interpreting behaviors, attributing motives, and so on. The paradox is that in spite of this ease of effort, we can not easily isolate and make explicit these cultural principles. As Goffman's work on American society has illustrated, articulation of norms, beliefs, and values is often possible only when faced with violations, that is with gaffes, breaches, misfirings, and the like (Goffman 1963, 1967; Much and Shweder 1979).

Another way to see the cultural principles at work in our own society is to examine the ways in which *other* societies are organized in terms of social interaction and in terms of the society at large. In carrying out such research, the ethnographer offers a point of contrast and comparison with our own everyday activities. Such comparative material can lead us to reinterpret behaviors as cultural that we have assumed to be natural. From the anthropological perspective, every society will have its own cultural constructs of what is natural and what is not. For example, every society has its own theory of procreation. Certain Australian Aboriginal societies believe that a number of different factors contribute to conception. Von Sturmer (1980) writes that among the Kugu–Nganychara (West Cape York Peninsula, Australia) the spirit of the child may first enter the man through an animal that he has killed and consumed. The spirit passes from the man to the woman through sexual intercourse, but several sexual acts are necessary to build the child. (See also Montagu 1937; Hamilton 1981.) Even within a single society, there may be different beliefs concerning when life begins and ends, as the recent debates in the United States and Europe concerning abortion and mercy killing indicate. The issue of what is nature and what is nurture (cultural) extends to patterns of caregiving and child development. Every society will have (implicitly or explicitly) given notions concerning the capacities and temperament of children at different points in their development (see, for example, Ninio 1979; Snow, de Blauw and van Roosmalen 1979; Dentan 1978). The expectations and responses of caregivers will be directly related to these notions.

TWO DEVELOPMENTAL STORIES

At this point, using an ethnographic perspective, we will recast selected behaviors of white middle-class caregivers and young children as pieces of one 'developmental story'. The white middle-class 'developmental story' that we are constructing is based on various descriptions available, and focuses on those patterns of interaction (both verbal and non-verbal) that have been emphasized in the literature. This story will be compared with another developmental story: the Kaluli (Papua New Guinea), a society that is strikingly different.

One of the major goals in presenting and comparing these developmental stories is to demonstrate that communicative interactions between caregivers and young children are culturally constructed. In our comparisons, we will focus on three facts of communicative interaction: (1) the social organisation of the verbal environment of very young children; (2) the extent to which children are expected to adapt to situations or that situations are adapted to the child; and (3) the negotiation of meaning by caregiver and child. We first present a general sketch for each social group and then discuss in more detail the consequences of the differences and similarities in communicative patterns in these two groups.

These developmental stories are not timeless, but rather are linked in complex ways to particular historical contexts. Both the ways in which caregivers behave towards young children and the popular and scientific accounts of these ways may differ at different moments in time. The stories that we present represent ideas currently held in the two social groups.

The two stories show that there is more than one way of becoming social and using language in early childhood. All normal children will become members of their own social group. But the process of becoming social including becoming a language user is culturally constructed. In relation to this process of construction, every society has its own developmental stories that are rooted in social organization, beliefs, and values. These stories may be explicitly codified and/ or tacitly assumed by members.

Anglo-American white middle-class developmental story

Middle class in Britain and the United States covers a broad range of white-collar and professional workers and their families, including lower-middle-, middle-middle-, and upper-middle-class strata. The literature on communicative development has been largely based on middle-middle- and upper-middle-class households. These households tend to consist of a single nuclear family with one, two, or three children. The primary caregiver almost without exception is a child's natural or adopted mother. Researchers have focused on communicative situations in which one child interacts with his or her mother. The generalizations proposed by these researchers concerning mother–child communication could be an artifact of this methodological focus. However, it could be argued that the attention to two-party encounters between a mother and her child reflects the most frequent type of communicative interaction to which most young middle-class children are exposed. Participation in two-party as opposed to multi-party interactions is a product of many considerations, including the physical setting of households, where interior and exterior walls bound and limit access to social interaction.

Soon after an infant is born, many mothers will hold their infants in such a way that they are face-to-face and will gaze at them. Mothers have been observed to address their infants, vocalize to them, ask questions, and greet them. In other words, from birth on, the infant is treated as a *social being* and as an *addressee* in social interaction. The infant's vocalizations, physical movements, and states are often interpreted as meaningful and will be responded to verbally by the mother or other caregiver. In this way, proto-conversations are established and sustained, along a *dyadic, turn-taking* model. Throughout this period and the subsequent language-acquiring years, caregivers treat very young children as communicative partners. One very important procedure in facilitating these social exchanges is the mother's (or other caregiver's) act of *taking the perspective of the child*. This perspective is evidenced in her own speech through the many simplifying and affective features of baby-talk register that have been described and through the various strategies employed to identify what the young child may be expressing.

Such perspective-taking is part of a much wider set of accommodations by adults to young children. These accommodations are manifested in several domains. For example, there are widespread material accommodations to infancy and childhood in the form of cultural artifacts designed for this stage of life, that is baby clothes, baby food, miniaturization of furniture, and toys. Special behavioral accommodations are coordinated with the infant's perceived needs and capacities, for example, putting the baby in a quiet place to facilitate and insure proper sleep; 'babyproofing' a house as a child becomes increasingly mobile, yet not aware of or able to control the consequences of his own behavior. In general, *situations and the language used in them are adapted or modified to the child* rather than the reverse. Further, the child is a *focus of attention*, in that the child's actions and verbalizations are often the *starting point* of social interaction with more mature persons.

While developmental achievements such as crawling, walking, and first words are awaited by caregivers, the accommodations noted above have the effect of keeping the child dependent on and separate from the adult community for a considerable period of time. The child is protected from certain experiences which are considered harmful (e.g. playing with knives, climbing stairs), but such protection delays his knowledge and developing competence in such contexts.

The accommodations of white middle-class caregivers to young children can be examined for other values and tendencies. Particularly among the American middle class, these accommodations reflect a *discomfort with the competence differential* between adult and child. The competence gap is reduced by two strategies. One is for the adult to simplify her or his speech to match more closely what the adult considers to be the verbal competence of the young child. Let us call this strategy the *self-lowering* strategy, following Irvine's (1974) analysis of intercaste demeanor. A second strategy is for the caregiver to interpret (Brown 1973) richly what the young child is expressing. Here the adult acts as if the child were more competent than his behavior more strictly would indicate. Let us call this strategy the *child-raising* strategy. Other behaviors conform to this strategy, such as when an adult cooperates in a task with a child but treats that task as an accomplishment of the child.

For example, in eliciting a story from a child, a caregiver will often cooperate with the child in the telling of the story. This cooperation typically takes the form of posing questions to the child, such as 'Where did you go?', 'What did you see?', and so on, to which the adult knows the answer. The child is seen as telling the story even though she or he is simply supplying the information the adult has preselected and organised (Ochs, Schieffelin and Platt 1979; Schieffelin and Eisenberg 1984; Greenfield and Smith 1976). Bruner's (1978) descriptions of scaffolding, in which a caregiver constructs a tower or other play object, allowing the young child to place the last block, are also good examples of this tendency. Here the tower may be seen by the caregiver and others as the child's own work. Similarly, in later life, caregivers playing games with their children may let them win, acting as if the child can match or more than match the competence of the adult.

A final aspect of this white middle-class developmental story concerns the willingness of many caregivers to interpret unintelligible or partially intelligible utterances of young children (cf. Ochs 1982). One of the recurrent ways in which interpretation is carried out is for the caregiver to offer a paraphrase (or 'expansion' (Brown and Bellugi 1964; Cazden 1965)), using a question intonation. This behavior of caregivers has continuity with their earlier attributions of intentionality directed towards ambiguous utterances (from the point of view of the infant). For both the prelinguistic and language-using child, the caregiver provides an explicitly verbal interpretation. This interpretation or paraphrase is potentially available to the young child to affirm, disconfirm, or modify.

Through exposure to and participation in these clarification exchanges, the young child is being socialized into several cultural patterns. The first of these is a way of recognizing and defining what constitutes unintelligibility, that an utterance or vocalization may in fact not be immediately understood. Second, the child is presented with the procedures for dealing with ambiguity. Through the successive offerings of possible interpretations, the child learns that more than one understanding of a given utterance or vocalization may be possible. The child is also learning who can make these interpretations, and the extent to which they may be open to modification. Finally the child is learning how to settle upon a possible interpretation and how to show disagreement or agreement. *This entire process socializes the child into culturally specific models of organizing knowledge, thought, and language.*

A kaluli developmental story

The Kaluli people (population approximately 1200) are an example of a small-scale, nonliterate egalitarian society (Schieffelin 1976). Kaluli, most of whom are monolingual, speak the Kaluli language, a non-Austronesian verb-final ergative language. They live in the tropical rain forest on the Great Papuan Plateau in the Southern Highlands of Papua New Guinea. Kaluli maintain large gardens and hunt and fish in order to obtain protein. Villages are composed of 60–90 individuals who traditionally lived in one large longhouse that had no internal walls. Currently, while the longhouse is maintained, many families are living in smaller dwellings so that two or more extended families may live together. It is not unusual then for at least a dozen individuals of different ages to be living together in one house which consists essentially of one semi-partitioned room.

Men and women utilize extensive networks of obligation and reciprocity in the organisation of work and sociable interaction. Everyday life is overtly focused around verbal interaction. Kaluli think of and use talk as a means of control, manipulation, expression, assertion, and appeal. It gets you what you want, need, or feel owed. Talk is a primary indicator of social competence and a primary way to be social. Learning how to talk and become independent is a major goal of socialization.

For the purpose of comparison and for understanding something of the cultural basis for the ways in which Kaluli act and speak to their children, it is important to first describe selected aspects of a Kaluli developmental story which I have constructed from various kinds of ethnographic data. Kaluli describe their babies as helpless, 'soft' (*taiyo*), and 'having no understanding' (*asugo andoma*). They take care of them, they say, because they 'feel sorry for them'. Mothers, who are primary caregivers, are attentive to their infants and physically responsive to them. Whenever an infant cries it is offered the breast. However, while nursing her infant, a mother may also be involved in other activities, such as food preparation, or she may be engaged in conversation with individuals in the household. Mothers never leave their infants alone and only rarely with other caregivers. When not holding their infants, mothers carry them in netted bags which are suspended from their heads. When the mother is gardening, gathering wood, or just sitting with others, the baby will sleep in the netted bag next to the mother's body.

Kaluli mothers, given their belief that infants 'have no understanding' never treat their infants as partners (speaker/addressee) in dyadic communicative interactions. While they greet their infants by name and use expressive vocalizations they rarely address other utterances to them. Furthermore, mothers and infants do not gaze into each other's eyes, an interactional pattern that is consistent with adult patterns of not gazing when vocalizing in interaction with one another. Rather than facing their babies and speaking to them, Kaluli mothers tend to face their babies outwards so that they can be seen by, and see others that are part of the social group. Older children greet and address the infant and in response to this, the mother while moving the baby, speaks in a high-pitched nasalized voice 'for' the baby. Triadic exchanges such as the one shown in Figure 10.1 is typical of these situations.

When a mother takes the speaking role of an infant she uses language that is well-formed and appropriate for an older child. Only the nasalization and high pitch mark it as 'the infant's'. When speaking

Figure 10.1 Example of a triadic exchange

Mother	Abi
(Abi to baby)	¹Bage!/do you see my box here?/do you see it?/do you see it?/
(high nasal voice talking as if she is the baby, moving the baby who is facing Abi):	
²My brother, *I'll* take half, my brother.	
(holding stick out)	³Mother, give him half/give him half/ mother, my brother – here, here take half/X/
(in a high nasal voice as baby):	
⁴My brother, what half do I take? What about it, my brother, put it on the shoulder!	
⁵(to Abi in her usual voice): 'Put it on the shoulder'.	
(Abi rests stick on baby's shoulder)	
⁶There, carefully put it on. (stick accidentally pokes baby) Feel sorry, stop.	

Notes: Mother is holding her infant son Bage (3 months). Abi (35 months) is holding a stick on his shoulder in a manner similar to that in which one would carry a heavy patrol box (the box would be hung on a pale placed across the shoulders of the two men). (Transcription conventions follow Bloom and Lahey (1978).)

as the infant to older children, mothers speak assertively, that is, they never whine or beg on behalf of the infant. Thus, in taking this role the mother does for the infant what the infant cannot do for itself, appear to act in a controlled and competent manner, using language. These kinds of interactions continue until a baby is between 4–6 months of age.

Several points are important here. First, these triadic exchanges are carried out primarily for the benefit of the older child and help create a relationship between the two children. Second, the mother's utterances in these exchanges are not based on, nor do they originate with anything that the infant has initiated – either vocally or gesturally. Recall the Kaluli claim that infants have no understanding. How could someone with 'no understanding' initiate appropriate interactional sequences?

However, there is an even more important and enduring cultural construct that helps make sense out of the mother's behaviors in this situation and in many others as well. Kaluli say that 'one cannot know what another thinks or feels'. Now, while Kaluli obviously interpret and assess one another's available behaviors and internal states, these interpretations are not culturally acceptable as topics of talk. Individuals often talk about their own feelings (I'm afraid, I'm happy, etc.). However, there is a cultural dispreference for talking about or making claims about what another might think, what another might feel, or what another is about to do, especially if there is no external evidence. As we shall see, these culturally constructed behaviors have several important consequences for the ways in which Kaluli caregivers verbally interact with their children, and are related to other pervasive patterns of language use which shall be discussed below.

As infants become older (6–12 months) they are usually held in the arms or carried on the shoulders of the mother or an older sibling. They are present in all on-going household activities, as well as subsistence activities that take place outside the village in the bush. During this time period babies are addressed by adults to a limited extent. They are greeted by a variety of names (proper names, kinterms, affective and relationship terms) and receive a limited set of both negative and positive imperatives. In addition, when they do something they are not to do, such as reach for something that is not theirs to take, they will often receive such rhetorical questions such as 'Who are you?!' (meaning 'not someone to do that') or 'It is yours?!' (meaning 'it is not yours') to control their actions by shaming them (*sasidiab*). What is important to stress here is that the language addressed to the preverbal child consists largely of 'one-liners' which call for no verbal response. Either an action or termination of an action is appropriate. Other than these utterances, very little talk is directed to the young child by the adult caregiver.

This pattern of adults not treating infants as communicative partners continues even when babies begin babbling. Kaluli recognize babbling (*dabedan*) but say that this vocal activity is not communicative and has no relationship to speech that will eventually emerge. Adults and older children occasionally repeat vocalizations back to the young child (ages 12–16 months) reshaping them into the names of persons in the household or into kinterms, but they do not say that the baby is saying the name nor do they wait for or expect the child to repeat those vocalizations in an altered form. In addition, vocalizations are not generally treated as communicative and given verbal expression. Nor are they interpreted by adults, except in one situation, an example of which follows.

When a toddler shrieks in protest at the assaults of an older child, mothers will say 'I'm unwilling' (using a quotative particle) referring to the toddler's shriek. These were the only circumstances in which mothers treated vocalizations as communicative and provided verbal expression for them. In no other circumstances in the four families in the study did adults provide a verbally expressed interpretation of a vocalization of a preverbal child. Thus, throughout the preverbal period very little language is directed to the child, except for imperatives, rhetorical questions, and greetings. A child who by Kaluli terms has not yet begun to speak is not expected to respond either verbally or vocally. What all of this means is that in the first 18 months or so very little sustained dyadic verbal exchange takes place between adult and infant. The infant is only minimally treated as an addressee, and is not treated as a communicative partner in dyadic exchanges. One immediate conclusion is: the conversational model that has been described for many white middle-class caregivers and their preverbal children has no application in this case. Furthermore, if one defines language input as language directed to the child then it is reasonable to say that for Kaluli children who have not yet begun to speak, there is very little. However, this does not mean that Kaluli children grow up in an impoverished verbal environment and do not learn how to speak. Quite the opposite is true. The verbal environment of the infant is rich and varied, and from the very beginning the infant is surrounded by adults and older children who spend a great deal of time talking to one another. Furthermore, as the infant develops and begins to crawl, engage in play activities, and other independent actions, these actions are frequently referred to, described, and commented upon by members of the household speaking to one another especially by older children. Thus, the ongoing activities of the preverbal child are an important topic of talk between members of the household, and this talk about the here-and-now of the infant is available to the infant, though only a limited amount of talk is addressed to the infant. For example, in referring to the infant's actions, siblings and adults use the infant's name or kinterm. They will say, 'Look at Seligiwo! He's walking'. Thus the child may learn from these contexts to attend to the verbal environment in which he or she lives.

Every society has its own ideology about language, including when it begins and how children acquire it. The Kaluli are no exception. Kaluli claim that language begins at the time when the child uses two critical words, 'mother' (*nɔ*) and 'breast' (*bo*). The child may be using other single words, but until these two words are used, the beginning of language is not recognized. Once a child has used these words, a whole set of inter-related behaviors is set into motion. Kaluli claim once a child has begun to use language he or she then must be 'shown how to speak' (Schieffelin 1979). Kaluli show their children language in the form of a teaching strategy which involves providing a model for what the child is to say followed by the word ɛlɛma, an imperative meaning 'say like that'. Mothers use this method of direct instruction to teach the social uses of assertive language (teasing, shaming, requesting, challenging reporting). However, object labeling is never part of an ɛlɛma sequence, nor does the mother ever use ɛlɛma to instruct the child to beg or appeal for food or objects. Begging, the Kaluli say, is natural for children. They know how to do it. In contrast, a child must be taught to be assertive through the use of particular linguistic expressions and verbal sequences.

A typical sequence using ɛlɛma is triadic, involving the mother, child (between 20-36 months), and other participant(s). Figure 10.2 gives an example. *In this situation, as in many others, the mother does not modify her language to fit the linguistic ability of the young child. Instead her language is shaped so as to be appropriate (in terms of form and content) for the child's intended addressee.* Consistent with the ways she interacts with her infant, what a mother instructs her young child to say usually does not have its origins in any verbal or nonverbal behaviors of the child, but in what the mother thinks should be said. The mother pushes the child into ongoing interactions that the child may or may not be interested in, and will at times spend a good deal of energy in trying to get the child verbally involved. This is part of the Kaluli pattern of fitting (or pushing) the child into the situation rather than changing the situation to meet the interests or abilities of the child. Thus, mothers take a directive role with their young children, teaching them what to say so that they may become participants in the social group.

In addition to instructing their children by telling them what to say in often extensive interactional sequences, Kaluli mothers pay attention to the form of their children's utterances. Kaluli will correct the phonological, morphological, or lexical form of an utterance or its pragmatic or semantic meaning. Since the goals of language acquisi-

Figure 10.2 Example of a triadic exchange using ɛlɛma

---

¹Mother → Wanu → > Binalia:[a]
Whose is it? say like that.

²whose is it?!/

³Is it yours?! say like that.

⁴is it yours?!/

⁵Who are you?! say like that.

⁶who are you?!/

⁷Mama → Wanu → > Binalia:
Did you pick (it)?! say like that.

⁸did you pick (it)?!/

⁹Mother → Wanu → > Binalia:
My G'ma picked (it)! say like that.

¹⁰my G'ma picked (it)!/

¹¹Mama → Wanu → > Binalia:
This *my G'ma* picked! say like that.

¹²this *my G'ma* picked!/

Notes: Mother, daughter Binalia (5 years), cousin Mama (3½ years), and son Wanu (27 months) are at home, dividing up some cooked vegetables. Binalia has been begging for some but her mother thinks that she has had her share. (Transcription conventions follow Bloom and Lahey (1978).)
[a] → = speaker → addressee.
→> = addressee →> intended addressee.

tion include a child becoming competent, independent, and mature-sounding in his language, Kaluli use no baby-talk lexicon, for they said (when I asked about it) that to do so would result in a child sounding babyish, which was clearly undesirable and counter-productive. The entire process of a child's development, of which language acquisition plays a very important role, is thought of as a hardening process and culminates in the child's use of 'hard words' (Feld and Schieffelin 1982).

The cultural dispreference for saying what another might be thinking of feeling has important consequences for the organization of dyadic exchanges between caregiver and child. For one, it affects the ways in which meaning is negotiated during an exchange. For the Kaluli the responsibility for clear expression is with the speaker, and child speakers are not exempt from this. Rather than offering possible interpretations or guessing what a child is saying or meaning, caregivers make extensive use of clarification requests such as 'huh?' and 'what?' in an attempt to elicit clearer expression from the child. Children are held to what they say and mothers will remind them that they in fact have asked for food or an object if when given it they don't act appropriately. Since responsibility of expression does lie with the speaker, children are also instructed with ɛlɛma to request clarification (using similar forms) from others when they do not understand what someone is saying to them.

Another important consequence of not saying what another thinks is the absence of adult expansions of child utterances. Kaluli caregivers will put words into the mouths of their children but these words originate from the caregiver. However, caregivers do not elaborate or expand utterances initiated by the child. Nor do they jointly build propositions across utterances and speakers except in the context of sequences with ɛlɛma in which they are constructing the talk for the child.

All of these patterns of early language use, such as the lack of expansions or verbally attributing an internal state to an individual, are consistent with important cultural conventions of adult language usage. The Kaluli very carefully avoid gossip and often indicate the source of information they report. They make extensive use of direct quoted speech in a language that does not allow indirect quotation. They utilize a range of evidential markers in their speech to indicate the source of speakers' information – for example, whether something was said, seen, heard, or gathered from other kinds of evidence. These patterns are also found in early child speech and, as such, affect the organization and acquisition of conversational exchanges in this small-scale egalitarian society.

A DISCUSSION OF THE DEVELOPMENTAL STORIES

We propose that infants and caregivers do not interact with one another according to one particular 'biologically designed choreography' (Stern 1977). There are many choreographies within and across societies. Cultural systems as well as biological ones contribute to their design, frequency, and significance. The biological predispositions constraining and shaping social behavior of infants and caregivers must be broader than thus far conceived in that the use of eye gaze, vocalization and body alignment are orchestrated differently in the social groups we have observed. As noted earlier, for example, Kaluli mothers do not engage in sustained gazing at, or elicit and maintain direct eye contact with, their infants as such behavior is dispreferred, associated with witchcraft.

Another argument in support of a broader notion of biological predisposition to be social, concerns the variation observed in the participant structure of social interactions. The literature on white middle-class child development has been orientated, quite legitimately, towards the two-party relationship between infant and caregiver, typically infant and mother. The legitimacy of this focus rests on the fact that this relationship is primary for infants within this social group. Further, most communicative interactions are dyadic in the adult community. While the mother is an important figure in the Kaluli developmental story, the interactions in which infants are participants are typically triadic or multi-party. As noted, Kaluli mothers will organise triadic interactions in which infants and young children will be oriented away from their mothers towards a third party.

This is not to say that Kaluli caregivers and children do not engage in dyadic exchanges. Rather, the point is that *such exchanges are not accorded the same significance as in white middle-class society.* In white middle-class households that have been studied the process of becoming social takes place predominantly through dyadic interactions, and social competence itself is measured in terms of the young child's capacity to participate in such interactions. In Kaluli [. . .] households, the process of becoming social takes place through participation in dyadic, triadic, and multi-party social interactions, with the latter two more common than the dyad.

From an early age, Kaluli children must learn how to participate in interactions involving a number of individuals. To do this minimally requires attending to more than one individual's works and actions, and knowing the norms for when and how to enter interactions, taking into account the social identities of at least three participants. Further, the sequencing of turns in triadic and multi-party interactions has a far wider range of possibilities vis-à-vis dyadic exchanges and thus requires considerable knowledge and skill. While dyadic exchanges can only be ABABA . . ., triadic or multi-party exchanges can be sequenced in a variety of ways, subject to social constraints such as speech act content and status of speaker. For Kaluli children, triadic and multi-party interactions constitute their earliest social experiences and reflect the ways in which members of these societies routinely communicate with one another.

CONCLUSIONS

This chapter contains a number of points but only one message – that the process of acquiring language and the process of acquiring socio-cultural knowledge are intimately linked. In pursuing this generalization, we have formulated the following proposals:

The specific features of caregiver speech behavior that have been described as simplified register are neither universal nor necessary for language to be acquired. White middle-class and Kaluli children, become speakers of their languages within the normal range of development and yet their caregivers use language quite differently in their presence.

The use of simplified registers by caregivers in certain societies may be part of a more general orientation in which situations are adapted to young children's perceived needs. In other societies, the orientation may be the reverse – that is, children at a very early age are expected to adapt to requirements of situations. In such societies, caregivers direct children to notice and respond to others' actions. They tend not to simplify their speech and frequently model appropriate utterances for the child to repeat to a third party in a situation.

The cross-cultural research raises many questions. The extent to which we are developing culturally specific theories of development needs to be considered. To add to what we know we must examine the prelinguistic and linguistic behaviors of the child of the ways in which they are continually and selectively affected by the values and beliefs held by those members of society who interact with the child.

It is tempting to speculate about what differences these differences make. Cross-cultural research invites that. However, at this point in our research it seems premature to focus on answers. Instead we prefer to use these data to generate questions – questions that will suggest new ways to think about language acquisition and socialization. And when we identify a new phenomenon or find old favorites missing – such as the absence of expansions and lack of extensive modified speech to the child in diverse societies – we must identify the socio-cultural factors that organize and make sense of communicative behaviors. Because these behaviors are grounded in culturally specific norms we can expect that the reasons for the 'same' phenomenon will be different.

While biological factors play a role in language acquisition, socio-cultural factors have a hand in this process as well. It is not a trivial fact that small children develop in the context of organized societies. Cultural conditions for communication organise even the earliest interactions between infants and others. Through participation as audience, addressee, and/or 'speaker', the infant develops a range of skills, intuitions, and knowledge enabling him or her to communicate in culturally preferred ways. The development of these competencies is an integral part of becoming a competent speaker.

REFERENCES

Anderson, E. S. and Johnson, C. E. (1973) 'Modifications in the speech of an eight-year-old to younger children', *Stanford Occasional Papers in Linguistics* 3: 149–60.
Bloom, L. and Lahey, M. (1978) *Language Development and Language Disorders*, New York: Wiley.
Blount, B. (1972) 'Aspects of socialization among the Luo of Kenya', *Language in Society* 235–48.
Bowerman, M. (1981) 'Language development', in H. C. Triandis and A. Heron (eds) *Handbook of Cross-Cultural Psychology*, vol. 4. *Developmental Psychology*, Boston, Mass.: Allyn & Bacon.
Brown, R. (1973) *A First Language: The Early Stages*, Cambridge, Mass.: Harvard University Press.
Brown, R. and Bellugi, U. (1964) 'Three processes in the child's acquisition of syntax', *Harvard Educational Review* 34: 133–51.
Bruner, J. S. (1978) 'The role of dialogue in language acquisition', in A. Sinclair, R. J. Jarvella and W. J. M. Levelt (eds) *The Child's Conception of Language*, New York: Springer-Verlag.
Cazden, C. (1965) 'Environmental assistance to the child's acquisition of grammar', unpublished Ph.D. dissertation, Harvard University.
Dentan, R. K. (1965) 'Notes of childhood in a nonviolent context: the Semai case', in A. Montagu (ed.) *Learning Non-Aggression: The Experience of Nonliterate Societies*, Oxford: Oxford University Press.
Feld, S. and Schieffelin, B. B. (1982) 'Hard talk: a functional basis for Kaluli discourse', in D. Tannen (ed.) *Analyzing Discourse: Talk and Text,* Washington, D.C.: Georgetown University Press.
Fischer, J. (1970) 'Linguistic socialization: Japan and the United States', in R. Hill and R. Konig (eds) *Families in East and West*, The Hague: Mouton.
Geertz, C. (1973) *The Interpretation of Cultures*, New York: Basic Books.
Goffman, E. (1963) *Behavior in Public Places*, New York: Free Press.
Goffman, E. (1967) *Interaction Ritual: Essays on Face-to-Face Behavior*, Garden City, New York: Anchor Books.
Greenfield, P. M. and Smith, J. H. (1976) *The Structure of Communication in Early Language Development*, New York: Academic Press.
Hamilton, A. (1981) 'Nature and nurture: Aboriginal childrearing in north-central Arnhem land', Institute of Aboriginal Studies, Canberra.

Harkness, S. (1975) 'Cultural variation in mother's language', in W. von Raffler-Engel (ed.) *Child Language, Word* 27: 495–8.

Harkness, S. and Super, C. (1977) 'Why African children are so hard to test', in L. L. Adler (ed.) *Issues in Cross-Cultural Research. Annals of the New York Academy of Sciences* 285: 326–31.

Heath, S. B. (1983) *Ways with Words: Language, Life and Work.* London: Cambridge University Press.

Irvine, J. (1974) 'Strategies of status manipulation in the Wolof greeting', in R. Bauman and J. Sherzer (eds) *Explorations in the Ethnography of Speaking*, New York: Cambridge University Press.

Miller, P. (1982) *Amy, Wendy and Beth: Learning Language in South Baltimore*, Austin, Tex.: University of Texas Press.

Montagu, A. (1937) *Coming into Being among the Australian Aborigines: a Study of the Procreative Beliefs of the Native Tribes of Australia*, London: Routledge.

Much, N. and Shweder R. (1979) 'Speaking of rules: The analysis of culture in breach', in W. Damon (ed.) *New Directions for Child Development: Moral Development* 2, San Francisco, California: Jossey-Bass.

Ninio, A. (1979) 'The naive theory of the infant and other maternal attitudes in two subgroups in Israel', *Child Development* 50: 976–80.

Ochs, E. (1982) 'Talking to children in Western Samoa', *Language in Society* 11: 77–104.

Ochs, E., Schieffelin, B. B. and Platt, M. (1979) 'Propositions across utterances and speakers', in E. Ochs and B. B. Schieffelin (eds) *Developmental Pragmatics*, New York: Academic Press.

Philips, S. (1982) *The Invisible Culture*, New York: Longman, Inc.

Sachs, J. and Devin, J. (1976) 'Young children's use of age-appropriate speech styles', *Journal of Child Language* 3: 81–98.

Schieffelin, B. B. (1979) 'Getting it together: an ethnographic approach to the study of the development of communicative competence', in E. Ochs and B. B. Schieffelin (eds) *Developmental Pragmatics*, New York: Academic Press.

Schieffelin, B. B. (1981) 'A developmental study of pragmatic appropriateness in word order and case marking in Kaluli', in W. Deutsch (ed.) *The Child's Construction of Language*, London: Academic Press.

Schieffelin, B. B. and Eisenberg, A. (1984) 'Cultural variation in children's conversations', in R. L. Schiefelbusch and J. Pickar (eds) *Communicative Competence: Acquisition and Intervention*, Baltimore, Md.: University Park Press.

Schieffelin, E. L. (1976) *The Sorrow of the Lonely and the Burning of the Dancers*, New York: St Martins Press.

Scollon, R. and Scollon, S. (1981) 'The literate two-year old: the fictionalization of self. Abstracting themes: a Chipewyan two-year-old', in R. O. Freedle (ed.) *Narrative, Literacy and Face in Interethnic Communication*, vol. VII: *Advances in Discourse Processes*, Norwood, N. J.: Ablex.

Shatz, M. and Gelman, R. (1973) 'The development of communication skills: modifications in the speech of young children as a function of listener' *Monographs of the Society for Research in Child Development* 152, 38 (5).

Snow, C., de Blauw, A. and van Roosmalen, G. (1979) 'Talking and playing with babies: the role of ideologies of childrearing', in M. Bullowa (ed.) *Before Speech: The Beginnings of Interpersonal Communication*, Cambridge: Cambridge University Press.

Stern, D. (1977) *The First Relationship: Infant and Mother*, Cambridge, Mass.: Harvard University Press.

Stross, B. (1972) 'Verbal processes in Tzeltal speech socialization', *Anthropological Linguistics* 14(1).

von Sturmer, D. E. (1980) 'Rights in nurturing', unpublished M.A. thesis, Australian National University, Canberra.

Ward, M. (1971) *Them Children: A Study in Language Learning*, New York: Holt, Rinehart & Winston.

Wills, D. (1977) Culture's cradle: social structural and interactional aspects of Senegalese socialization, unpublished Ph.D. dissertation, University of Texas, Austin.

11 Culture and early social interactions: the example of mother–infant object play in African and native French families

Jacqueline Rabain-Jamin

Source: *European Journal of Psychology of Education* (1989) 4: 295–305.

One of the aims of cross-cultural research on parental behaviour and child development, as is the case in anthropology, is to go beyond inventories of disparities to arrive at universals of human behaviour. Universals are not always easy to detect. It is argued here that applying a linguistic model to parental behaviour differentiating pancultural structures from morphological variants may be a powerful tool in this regard. Ethnological accounts of child-rearing practices first drew attention to the variety of forms of parent–child interactions. Across cultures the number of caregivers, amount of physical contact, presence of toys, and the social representation of the child all constitute variables which shape the context in which exchanges take place.

In traditional African societies, for example, the mother plays a central but non-exclusive role in caregiving. Mothers may delegate some of their child care duties to older children or to adult kin when their children are as young as 5 months (Leiderman and Leiderman 1977; Lallemand 1976). Education, i.e. the process of training in which culture, ideas and technique are transmitted to the child (Bohannan 1963), is the responsibility of the extended family. Thus the transmission of knowhow and values is more broadly based than in a strictly parental system, as well as more fully integrated into daily life than is the case in Western societies (Greenfield 1972; Scribner and Cole 1973).

However, regardless of culture, infants come into the world with approximately the same biological equipment and abilities: the environment furnishes the appropriate stimuli for the development of these abilities. In Africa as in New Guinea, in Geneva as in New Delhi, people who care for babies know how to use their capacities to attend to the sounds and speech addressed to them. People know how to tease out a smile, calm a baby through physical contact, song and rocking, and notice when a baby has learned to wait for certain events to reoccur and makes attempts to have control over the physical and social environment (Super 1981).

On this basis, a number of researchers have come to the conclusion, that despite variants in child-rearing practices, a few variables truly differentiate cultures, and that at least prior to age 2, child development is mainly dependent upon biological factors (Kagan 1981). According to this point of view, there are only variations in developmental timing.

Other researchers have challenged that view and stress differences in development and behaviour which they ascribe to environmental influences and the broad range of teaching/learning situations (Bril and Sabatier 1986; Kilbride and Kilbride 1980; Landau 1982). The debate remains wide open, since there are few studies on infant development on this point.

A better vantage point on these positions can be gained by distinguishing between two central issues: parental behaviour and forms of child rearing/teaching, and second, the development of skills and knowledge in the child. No a-priori direct relations can be assumed to exist between the two. Studies have shown that in all societies, parents tend to promote those specific forms of activity in their offspring that coincide with societal values and the entire constellation of social behaviours. For instance, in African societies, close physical contact is reinforced more than object-mediated relationships (Rabain 1979). However, it would be erroneous to conclude that these child-rearing practices, which make use of some behavioural capacities in infants, will result in the development of specific skills. At best this may be true in cases, for example, of certain types of crafts which if taught early enough result in the acquisition of highly specialized skills.

Beyond the question of their impact on the development of certain forms of knowledge and/or skills, child-rearing practices clearly affect social behaviours. The fact that parents emphasize one type of activity over another in early social exchanges can have long-term effects and even create obstacles later on in adulthood for individuals who are confronted with other social models – for example, in another culture.

Thus theoretical models characterizing the complex links between parental behaviours and child development need to be elaborated. Scribner and Cole (1973) made this point clear when they state that there is a simultaneous need for a theory of skill development and a theory of the role of educational processes in skill shaping. A number of studies on school-age children have shown that the activities which are solicited as part of the physical and/or social environment of a given culture may lead to the development of specialized skills. For example, Dasen and Heron (1981) indicate that the notion of space in Inuit (Eskimos of Canada) children, and quantity in the Baoule (Ivory Coast) which are mastered earlier by children of these cultures are precisely those areas of knowledge which are valued positively by the society itself. Few works on this theme have dealt with infancy, with the exception of the study on Baoule 6–30-month-olds (Dasen *et al.* 1978). Dasen *et al.* (1978) argue that their findings are indicative of structural universality in sensorimotor development.

Other studies have also shown that cultural differences in teaching contexts are apparent from early childhood. One of the most striking examples of this can be found in African societies which place enormous importance on early physical manipulations such as infant massage and a whole range of postural and vestibular stimulations infants receive from physical contact with family members. These stimulations have a positive effect on motor development which is apparent during the first year of life (Bril and Sabatier 1986; Hopkins and Westra 1988a; Rabain-Jamin and Wornham 1987). Other inter-actional features which are specific to these cultures, such as the importance of speaker status and the relatively low value attached to objects in child–adult exchange (Rabain 1979), have a social impact and tend to orient learning towards social rather than technological skills (Mundy-Castle 1974; Dasen *et al.* 1985).

In the present paper, data from studies on parental behaviour in early social exchange will be examined. These findings will help formulate a number of questions concerning the impact of parental behaviour on child development, bearing in mind that current state-of-the-art research cannot provide definitive answers.

Cultural underpinnings in early social interactions

Only a small number of studies using structured paradigms and observation techniques affording valid comparisons have focused on contexts for early social exchange. Several works have investigated mother–child interaction in specific cultural settings (Field *et al.* 1981; Leiderman *et al.* 1977). Over the last 15 years there has been an increase in investigations of early mother–infant interaction, providing theoretical models for the study of certain skills involved in social development and the acquisition of communicative competence (Bruner 1975).

Dixon *et al.* (1981) observed the Gusii of Southern Kenya, an agricultural society, in face-to-face exchange situations between mothers and infants 2–12 weeks old). This group has strict rules governing gaze, as is common in Africa. The results differentiate structural and universal features of exchange (emotional states and their cyclic acceleration and deceleration patterns, conjoint and disjoint phases) from culturally specific ones. Dixon *et al.* report that Gusii mothers exhibit the same universal behaviours with respect to stereotyped forms of approach, avert, and play phases, and the same modulation of voice and gaze used to sustain the infant's attention.

They also draw attention to differences in phase duration in the Gusii: mothers have shorter play episodes; phases are more frequent and quicker. They look away from the infant more often than American mothers and avoid build-ups of affect which raise the level of excitement in the child. High-intensity phases are not amplified upon since in Gusii culture the goal is smooth and even interaction. Dixon *et al.* (1981) conclude that specific cultural expectations produce differences in face-to-face exchanges, but maintain that there is a basic interactional structure corresponding to a universal awareness of infants' perceptual capacities.

The various cultural norms governing adult interaction in terms of gaze and forms of address are almost universally suspended in the case of mother–infant interaction. The repertoire of caretaker–infant interaction is thought to be biologically programmed [. . .] and includes seeking eye contact, stereotyped forms of approach to the baby, changes in facial expression and the use of 'motherese'.

Jahoda (1986) points out that a number of recent studies have challenged the universality of this paradigm. Relevant data may however suggest that there are only variants in the basic modes of exchange. Schieffelin and Ochs (1983) report that the Kaluli mothers of Papua New Guinea rarely have visual contact with their babies during vocal exchange because gaze is associated with witchcraft. Instead of seeking out face-to-face exchanges with their infants, mothers turn them towards a third individual to achieve triadic exchange. In this triadic situation mothers modify their intonation patterns to talk to a third party 'for' the baby. These ethnographic data do not disconfirm the hypothesis that there are universal forms of parental intervention which promote the development of the infant's communicative competence. They simply indicate that cultures have different preferences, or variants, in their ways of eliciting attention in the infant and stimulating him for future exchanges.

Although certain types of verbal exchanges appear to be universal, such as explicit instructions concerning forms of expression and/or content, not all societies have recourse to the same set of procedures for addressing children or for the socialization of language activities (Schieffelin and Ochs 1986).

The context in which linguistic exchange takes place varies from culture to culture. Studies which have contrasted informal education found in traditional societies with formal education found in Western ones have stressed the fact that informal education places emphasis on learning through observation and imitation and does not require the use of questions (Fortes 1938; Greenfield and Lave 1982). In contrast, formal types of education are heavily oriented towards learning through verbal exchange and questions. Language and culture are acquired through interactive routines, some of which are universal whereas others are specific to a given social context. For example, Ervin-Tripp and Strage (1985) point out that whereas in most societies children are taught people's names, societies which place emphasis on literacy tend to teach children more object labels. The way in which caregivers in Western societies help children participate in verbally recalled events and activities (Bruner 1975) has also received attention. It is more than likely these practices can be found in other cultures, but in other contexts (Schieffelin and Ochs 1986).

Dixon, LeVine, Richman and Brazelton (1984) compared mother–infant interactions in middle-class Americans and in the Gusii of Kenya on a teaching task from 6 to 25 months. They report pronounced differences in verbal behaviour of the mother and type of control over the child. Gusii mothers tend to control their infants visually more than verbally. They use physical contact and physical control to orient the infant towards the task. Gusii mothers use a high amount of instructions and do not encourage the child through praise. In contrast, American mothers provide verbal encouragement and their mode of teaching includes a considerable amount of remarks on the child's mood as well as reflections on the child's actions.

Cultural preservation and immigration

The few studies in this area have compared different cultural groups living in their natural environments. Other studies have investigated ethnic minorities living in the United States (Field *et al.* 1981). In Europe, only a handful of investigations have been carried out on immigrant populations. The number of foreign workers has increased steadily in Europe since the latter part of the nineteenth century, with fluctuations due to the economic situation of the moment. Their number has been sharply curtailed in France since 1974 but a large number of wives legally joined their husbands. Thus temporary, economically-motivated immigration became stable, permanent emigration.

Changes in immigrants' behaviour reflect the value and prestige they assign to models held by the host country. A study conducted in Paris on West African families shows that in the area of child care, bottle feeding is perceived as an outward manifestation of integration into modern society. In contrast, traditional forms of behaviour such as long-term breastfeeding may be preserved as a means of reaffirming the traditional identity (Rabain-Jamin and Wornham 1987). African mothers express some degree of resistance to Western child-rearing practices. They fear that their children will no longer be educated in the values of the extended family and will not acquire the rules of social exchange that govern community life. In the area of parental behaviour, observations of children of recent African immigrants in Paris provides evidence for the relative stability of interactive routines. At the age of 6 months, 90 per cent of mother–infant exchange time is spent in physical contact, in contrast to French children of the same age (around 30 per cent, see Bril and Zack 1989); at 10 months the figure is 60 per cent. Object play accounts for 7 per cent of exchange time at 6 months, and 52 per cent at 10 months, but mothers initiate object play or spontaneously take part only 10 per cent of the time at this age (Rabain-Jamin and Wornham 1989). Finer analyses of emigration-related changes and the problems of culture clash deserve attention in future studies, as does research on the difficulties children and families experience with regard to schooling and the acquisition of knowledge.

OBJECT PLAY IN AFRICAN AND FRENCH FAMILIES LIVING IN PARIS

For purpose of illustration, the study presented here compares interactive styles of French mothers and African mothers (living in Paris) in an object play situation with their 10–15-month-olds. The aim of this study is to show how differences in verbal and non-verbal interactive routines in these two groups of mothers draw on cultural specificities involving both the status of objects and the language situations which are privileged in the two cultural contexts.

The decision to observe French and African mothers in a play situation with objects was motivated by research showing that the way in which the mother structures her child's exploration is indicative of her ability to adapt to the child's level of development. Her degree of responsiveness is thought to promote cognitive development (Belsky *et al.* 1980; Riksen-Walraven 1978). However, the many studies on play have almost all been conducted on American or European samples. Nevertheless, maternal expectations concerning their children's development, and their beliefs as to the role of caregivers differ across cultures (Hopkins and Westra 1988b; Keller *et al.* 1984; Ninio 1979). Culturally distinct value systems may thus have an impact on the fundamental processes of social interaction.

Since a comparison of mother–infant interactions in a free-play situation would have produced too broad a range of differences between the two groups (in organization of space, availability of toys, participation of others), a more structured situation centred around objects provided by the observer was selected to test in a controlled fashion for specific differences in mothers' interactive styles. Nevertheless, it is impossible to disregard the fact that the situation in itself had a radically different meaning for each of the two cultures. French mothers, regardless of social class, do not find it strange to play for a period of ten minutes with their child. Being available and giving the child toys to play with is viewed positively. In African societies this is a relatively unusual situation and it is considered to be fairly impolite to neglect conversation between adults and to devote oneself for such a long period of time in this way to one's child.

Forty mother–child dyads (composed ot two groups of children aged 10 and 15 months with ten dyads per cultural group at each age) took part in the experiment. The sample of mothers was selected from a child consultancy file of a health centre located in the 20th district of Paris, and from the files from a day care centre in the same vicinity. The group of African mothers was homogeneous: all came from West African countries (Senegal, Mali, Mauritania), had not received any formal education in Africa, and had lived in Paris for less than ten years. Their husbands were blue-collar workers. A small number of these women (20 per cent) spoke French fairly well. A Senegalese interpreter competent in Bambara, Soninke and Toucouleur was present during the sessions. The French families had either working-, middle-, or upper-middle-class backgrounds.

The ten-minute observation sessions were conducted in the mothers' homes. A set of toys was placed on the floor. For the 10-month-olds, the set was composed of a rattle, a pot, a stick, a brush and comb, an empty box of hard candies, and a pink panther. For the 15-month-old group the rattle was replaced by three rolls of cardboard, two other sticks, and a spoon. The mother was asked to sit down next to the

Table 11.1 Verbal and non-verbal behaviours in French and African mothers (mean percentages and standard deviations)

			Age			
			10 months		15 months	
			Fr.	Afr.	Fr.	Afr.
	Only	M	24.3*	49.0	14.1**	35.2
	non-verbal	SD	16.9	24.3	12.5	12.4
Objects	Non-verbal	M	37.0*	24.8	41.2*	32.4
	+ verbal	SD	8.3	11.9	5.7	10.9
	Only	M	29.0**	12.1	39.2**	15.7
	verbal	SD	11.5	8.3	13.2	10.8
Infant's body third parties	Only verbal	M	9.7	14.1	5.5**	16.7
		SD	7.9	10.8	3.9	9.1

Note: t significant at .05 (*); .01 (**).

child and play with the child. Due to the African mother's reticence about being filmed, in part due to the current immigration policy in France (problems of illegality) and fear of becoming a 'media event', mother–child exchanges were audio-recorded for both groups and a thoroughly trained observer coded the mothers' and children's actions sequentially.

The data were classified into four mutually exclusive categories characterizing the mother's behaviour in the object play situation: (a) non-verbal behaviour. Non-verbal behaviour was defined as object-related gestures and actions that were not produced in conjunction with verbal exchanges (e.g. the mother places the comb silently in the child's visual field); (b) joint verbal and non-verbal behaviour. The mother elicits a response from the child on both the sensorimotor and verbal levels (e.g. the mother holds out the comb and says 'Comb your hair'); (c) verbal object-related behaviour. The mother comments on the child's actions, describes an object, gives an instruction, asks a question, without intervening herself (e.g. the mother watches the child take the comb and says to him 'It's a comb'; (d) verbal non-object-related behaviour: maternal speech on topic other than the objects (the infant's body, third parties, etc).

Non-verbal exchanges were significantly higher in African mothers in the 10-month-old group and in the 15-month-old group (Table 11.1). In contrast, French mothers made more joint non-verbal and verbal utterances than African mothers with their children at both ages. This is also the case for purely verbal utterances at 10 and at 15 months. In the 15-month-old group, however, African mothers tended to make more verbal utterances than French mothers concerning third parties and the infant's body.

Maternal utterances were analyzed by partitioning them into segments bounded by pauses or changes in intonation. Utterances were classified as descriptive, directive or expressive (i.e. reflecting pragmatic intent, see Searle 1969) on the basis of classifications of speech acts described in Feider and Saint-Pierre (1987). The descriptive category covers all the utterances made by mother about the child or the objects whether objective ('It's a cup') or based on subjective judgment ('You're tired'). The directive category was divided into four subcategories: request for attention ('Look'), direct request for action ('Take the comb'), indirect request for action ('Are you going to comb mommy's hair?') and request for information ('Where are its eyes?'). The expressives were all conventional expressions serving to establish or maintain contact (Hello; thank you).

The major differences between the two groups of mothers are related to the relative frequency of two categories of mother speech: descriptive utterances and requests for action (Table 11.2). French mothers use many more descriptives than African mothers at both 10 and 15 months. In contrast African mothers make more direct requests for action at both ages. At 15 months French mothers use more indirect requests for action which are often formulated as questions, and at 10 months tend to use more requests for information.

One of the most striking findings of this study is the preponderance of non-verbal behaviours in African mothers during exchanges with their children. These decrease as the child grows older but still predominate at 15 months. Purely verbal utterances concerning objects only show a significant increase in the French mothers, reaching a level comparable to that observed in American mothers (Power 1985). In African mothers, verbal object-related exchange remains dependent longer on the concrete physical context and relies more heavily on gestures. A number of authors have interpreted this as a characteristic of oral societies which differentiates them from societies with written traditions, where there is a greater reliance on verbal messages (Greenfield 1972).

Table 11.2 French and African mothers' utterances (mean percentages and standard deviations)

		Age			
		10 months		15 months	
Utterances		Fr.	Afr.	Fr.	Afr.
Descriptive	M	45.6**	21.9	41.9**	21.9
	SD	14.3	6.4	11.6	16.1
Directive	Attention-getting	M	14.6	14.0	11.0	8.7
		SD	7.4	4.7	8.7	7.3
	Direct request for action	M	18.6**	51.2	15.5**	48.6
		SD	11.6	13.7	13.0	23.5
	Indirect request for action	M	5.8	5.3	13.9*	7.4
		SD	4.5	6.3	6.6	7.1
	Request for information	M	10.6	6.9	12.8	9.8
		SD	5.0	4.2	5.6	8.9
Expressive	M	4.8	0.7	5.4	3.5
	SD	4.9	2.2	3.9	6.3

Note: t significant at .05 (*); .01 (**).

THE ROLE OF VERBAL AND NON-VERBAL INTERACTION

In all cultures, mother–infant verbal exchanges are highly contextualized. During the preverbal period, non-verbal information provided by a caregiver helps the child increase his understanding of purely linguistic messages (Zukow *et al.* 1982). The sensorimotor context of the exchange provides the framework in which capacities for joint attention (Bruner 1975) develop as well as the notion of the orderliness of interaction (Goffman 1974). Although non-verbal messages are crucial to the success of early communication, unaccompanied gestures remain fairly ambiguous in that speech is dissociated from action. Banging a stick on a box is a more ambiguous gesture than calling a child by his first name to attract his attention or requesting him to carry out a specific action.

What are the techniques mothers use to attract children's attention to objects and to encourage them to perform certain actions at the age of 10 to 15 months? These have been described by a number of authors

(Schaffer and Crook 1979; Power 1985) and appear to be comparable in the groups studied here. Future work may indicate variations in the incidence of these techniques. The three major (and most likely universal) techniques are: drawing attention to an object, asking to have an object, and showing the child its properties.

Means of focussing the child's attention on the object vary in precision (placing an object in the child's focal range is less ambiguous than striking one object against another) but this means of designating an object is relatively unspecific as to the type of action. Some mothers of 10-month-olds, regardless of cultural background, may not intend to get their children to produce a highly specific object-related action when the material is elementary. Here non-verbal behaviour may be sufficient. French mothers, however, still tend to intervene verbally here and even more so when the object is one of the 'educational toys' that are common place in French households.

Typical behaviours in African mothers, such as attracting the child's attention to objects by drumming, are part of infant attention-getting routines and are dissociated from verbal exchanges. Other forms of behaviour are specific to mothers in this cultural group, such as tossing an object at a distance (often towards another person) to encourage the child to make trips to and fro. They are indicative of the value attributed to motility and the exploration of a social space which may be related to the responsibility for errand-running that very young children are expected to carry out in these cultures.

African mothers tend to respond less to children's initiatives with objects and to respond more to children's glances towards a third party, vocalizations, or changes in posture. One possible explanation is that African mothers assign communicative intent to these visual and vocal behaviours and feel they require a response, an intent they do not react to on the same level when the child's behaviour is object-centered.

In their verbal exchanges with their children, French like American mothers (Murphy and Messer 1972), tend to use descriptive utterances involving object labels, descriptions of their properties, and reflections. The topic can also be the child's ongoing actions, which thus constitutes a system of redundancy between the verbal and non-verbal registers. In contrast, comments and descriptive utterances are infrequent in African mothers, and when they do occur, are listener- rather than object-oriented, i.e. the child is the subject and discourse appears to be directed towards the listener rather than to the object.

The Dixon *et al.* (1984) comparisons of mother–child interactions in middle-class Americans and in the Gusii of Kenya indicate a high frequency of instructions in Gusii mothers. These instructions are almost entirely composed of requests for action. In the present study, the type of action governs the type of message. The object is rarely identified or labelled ('It's a comb') in its own right, but is rather used to specify an action scheme or a use ('Give me the comb').

The most immediate explanation for the differences in verbal behaviour between the two groups would be to attribute them to differences in socio-economic status and the mothers' level of education. Several studies on mothers' teaching strategies have reported comparable differences (Bee *et al.* 1969; Hess and Shipman 1965; Laosa 1980; Steward and Steward 1973). However, Dixon *et al.* (1984), who compared the behaviour of American mothers and the Gusii of Kenya, obtained findings which refute this assumption. Gusii mothers, in contrast to American mothers with low levels of education, do not give ambiguous orders to their children nor is feedback low. Rather, their messages are clear, and their responses to infant behaviour are contingent and positive. The low incidence of verbal exchanges found in Gusii mothers, which places them on the same level as Mexican–American mothers studied by Steward and Steward (1973), can be accounted for by the fact that in both contexts direct imitation appears to be the most efficient form of learning (Greenfield 1972).

CONCLUSION

Early education in traditional African societies and the emigrant context studied here places prime value on the infant's motor and social behaviour. This results in encouraging exploratory activities that enhance cognitive development per se which at this age is not, in contrast to motor and social activities, subject to parental expectations, explanations and reinforcements. As one African mother put it, 'We give toys (to children) to play with. You give them toys to teach, for the future. We feel that children learn better when they are older'. Thus, the primary function of object-related exchanges seems less to teach the children something about efficient actions on the physical world – which they discover by themselves through exchanges with peers of older siblings who put objects into circulation – than to encourage the act of giving and exchanging with others.

Attention and communication behaviour are oriented toward social objects, and the most valued linguistic situations are those which involve social interchange, as can be seen in the litany of names used to rock the baby and the playful dialogues visitors initiate when questioning the child (Rabain-Jamin 1988).

French mothers' interactions with their children are illustrative of tight connections between verbal and non-verbal behaviour. Action is the basis or anchor point for verbal exchange; and this repetition or verbal redundancy yields discourse-on-actions which to a certain extent distances the action and allows for a generalization process to take place. In contrast, African mothers' interactions with their infants present less verbal 'scaffolding' (Bruner 1975) of non-verbal behaviour, which appears primarily when the context is favourable to this type of exchange and is centred on objects. This type of interaction allows for a greater 'disjunction' or separation of non-verbal and verbal communication. As part of their culture, African mothers are used to performing actions in a social environment where, much more than in France or in Europe in general, modes of social exchange established through discourse, and the value ascribed to physical presence (both in proximity, bearing and posture) solicit as much as they define the child as a genuine social partner.

In emphasizing verbal exchange in day-to-day situations which focus less on ongoing actions through descriptions of their characteristics and their organization in time than on relationships between people and social events, African cultures do not assign the spoken word with the educational function of structuring and planning activities in the here-and-now. In mother–infant exchanges, directive utterances are less centered on the technical side of an action, its sequencing, and steps than on what is acceptable, what fits with societal norms. These differences in emphasis can best be rendered by examples: 'Do that, that's good, you must answer your mother (or your uncle, or X)' an African mother might say. 'Do that, that's the way it works', a European mother is likely to say. African mothers seek to obtain actions from their children through a direct request-and-response pattern. European mothers tend to obtain actions from their children through a relationship which is more mediated by stressing the object and its properties.

African cultures place value on a specific type of adaptation. Even young children must fulfill a role in their social universe, recognize sibling rank and kinship position and carry out actions which serve the community. The models generated by the school system correspond to other types of obligations which are strongly affected by a temporal perspective. In school, as Bruner (1964) points out, theoretical presentation precedes execution of action. The scholastic model trains children to anticipate actions, and plan ahead. When they enter the school system children raised in 'traditional' environments will have to conform to these requirements, which may be in sharp contrast or contradiction with the adaptation model valued by the community.

REFERENCES

Bee, H.L., Van Egeren, L.F., Streissguth, A.P., Nyman, B.A., and Leckie, M.S. (1969) 'Social class differences in maternal teaching strategies and speech patterns', *Developmental Psychology* 1: 726–34.

Belsky, J., Goode, M.K. and Most, R.K. (1980) 'Maternal stimulation and infancy exploratory competence: cross-sectional, correlational, and experimental analyses', *Child Development* 51: 1163–78.

Bohannan, P. (1963) *Social Anthropology*, New York: Holt, Rinehart & Winston.

Bril, B. and Sabatier, C. (1986) 'The cultural context of motor development: postural manipulations in the daily life of Bambara babies (Mali)', *International Journal of Behavioral Development* 9: 1–15.

Bril, B. and Zack, M. (1989) 'Analyse comparative de "l'emploi du temps postural" de l'enfant de la naissance à la marche (France – Mali)', in J. Retschitzki, M. Bossel-Lagos and P. Dasen (eds) *Contributions à la Recherche Interculturelle*, Actes du 2ème Colloque de l'ARIC, Paris: L'Harmattan.

Bruner, J.S. (1975) 'The ontogenesis of speech acts', *Journal of Child Language* 2: 1–19.

Dasen, P.R. (1988) 'Cultures et développement cognitf. La recherche et ses applications', in R. Bureau and D. de Saivre (eds) *Apprentissages et Cultures. Les Manières d'Apprendre*, Paris: Karthala.

Dasen, P.R., Dembele, B., Ettien, K., Kabran, K., Kamagaté, D., Koffi, K.A., and N'Guessan, A. (1985) ' "N'gouélé", l'intelligence chez les Baoulé' *Archives de Psychologie* 53: 293–324.

Dasen, P.R. and Heron, A. (1981) 'Cross-cultural tests of Piaget's theory', in H.C. Triandis and A. Heron (eds) *Handbook of Cross-Cultural Psychology*, vol. 4: *Development Psychology*, Boston: Allyn & Bacon.

Dasen, P.R., Inhelder B., Lavallee M. and Retschitzki J. (1978) *Naissance de l'intelligence chez l'enfant baoulé de Côte d'Ivoire*, Berne: Hans Huber.

Dixon, S.D., LeVine, R.A., Richman, A. and Brazelton, T.B. (1984) 'Mother–child interaction around a teaching task: an African–American comparison', *Child Development* 55: 1252–64.

Dixon, S., Tronick, E., Keefer, C. and Brazelton, T.B. (1981) 'Mother–infant interaction among the Gusii of Kenya', in T. Field, A. Sostek, P. Vietze and P.H. Leiderman (eds) *Culture and Early Interaction*, Hillsdale, N.J.: Erlbaum.

Ervin-Tripp, S. and Strage A. (1985) 'Parent–child discourse', in *Handbook of Discourse Analysis*, vol. 3, London: Academic Press.

Feider, H. and Saint-Pierre, M. (1987) 'Etude psycholinguistique des capacités pragmatiques du langage chez les enfants de 5 à 10 ans', *Revue Quebecoise de Linguistique* 16: 163–88.

Field, T.M., Sostek, A.M., Vietze, P., and Leiderman, P.H. (eds) (1981) *Culture and Early Interaction*, Hillsdale, N.J.: Erlbaum.

Fortes, M. (1938) 'Social and psychological aspects of education in Taleland', London: International African Institute, *Supplement to Africa* 11(4): also in J.S. Bruner, A. Jolly and K. Sylva (eds) *Play, Its Role in Development and Evolution* (1976) Harmondsworth, Middlesex: Penguin Books.

Goffman, E. (1974) *Frame Analysis*, New York: Harper Colophon Books.

Greenfield, P.M. (1972) 'Oral and written language: the consequences for cognitive development in Africa, the United States and England', *Language and Speech* 15: 169–78.

Greenfield, P.M., and Lave, J. (1982) 'Cognitive aspects of informal education', in D.A. Wagner and H.W. Stevenson (eds) *Cultural Perspectives on Child Development*, San Francisco: Freeman. (French translation in *Recherche, Pédagogie et Culture* (1979) 8: 16–35.)

Hess, R.D. and Shipman, V. (1965) 'Early experience and the socialization of cognitive modes in children', *Child Development* 34: 869–86.

Hopkins, B. and Westra, T. (1988a) 'Maternal handling and motor development: an intracultural study', *Genetic, Social and General Psychology Monographs* 114: 379–408.

Hopkins, B and Westra, T. (1988b) 'Maternal expectations and motor development: some cultural differences', *Developmental Medicine and Child Neurology* (in press).

Jahoda, G. (1986) 'A cross-cultural perspective on developmental psychology', *International Journal of Behavioral Development* 9: 417–37.

Kagan, J. (1981) 'Universals in human development', in R.H. Munroe, R.L. Munroe and B.B. Whiting (eds) *Handbook of Cross-Cultural Human Development*, New York: Garland.

Keller, H.D., Miranda D., and Ganda, G. (1984) 'The naive theory of the infant and some maternal attitudes: a two-country study', *Journal of Cross-Cultural Psychology* 15: 165–79.

Kilbride, P.L. (1980) 'Sensorimotor behavior of Baganda and Samia infants: a controlled comparison', *Journal of Cross-Cultural Psychology* 11: 131–52.

Lallemand, S. (1976) 'Génitrices et éducatrices mossi', *L'Homme* 16: 109–24.

Landau, R. (1982) 'Infant crying and fussing: findings from a cross-cultural study', *Journal of Cross-Cultural Psychology* 13: 427–44.

Laosa, L.M. (1980) 'Maternal teaching strategies in Chicano and Anglo-American families: the influence of culture and education on maternal behavior' *Child Development* 51: 759–65.

Leiderman, P.H. and Leiderman, G.F. (1977) 'Economic change and infant care in an East African agricultural community', in P.H. Leiderman, S.R. Tulkin and A. Rosenfeld (eds) *Culture and Infancy: Variations on the Human Experience*, New York: Academic Press.

Leiderman, P.H., Tulkin, S.R. and Rosenfeld, A. (eds) (1977) *Culture and Infancy: Variations on the Human Experience*, New York: Academic Press.

Leiderman, P.H., Tulkin, S.R. and Rosenfeld, A. (eds) (1977) *Culture and Infancy: Variations on the Human Experience*, New York: Academic Press.

Mundy-Castle, A.C. (1974) 'Social and technological intelligence in Western and non-Western cultures', *Universita (University of Ghana)*, 4: 46–52.

Murphy, C.M. and Messer, D.J. (1977) 'Mothers, infants and pointing: a study of a gesture', in H.R. Schaffer (ed.), *Studies in Mother–Infant Interaction*, London: Academic Press.

Ninio, A. (1979) 'The naive theory of the infant and other maternal attitudes in two sub-groups in Israel', *Child Development* 50: 976–80.

Power, T.G. (1985) 'Mother- and father–infant play: a developmental analysis', *Child Development* 56: 1514–24.

Rabain, J. (1979) *L'enfant du Lignage: du Sevrage a la Classe d'Age chez les Wolof du Sénégal*, Paris: Payot.

Rabain-Jamin, J. (1988) 'Tradition et appretissage', in R. Bureau and D. de Saivre (eds), *Apprentissages et Cultures: les Manieres d'Apprendre*, Paris: Karthala.

Rabain-Jamin, J. and Wornham, W.L. (1987) 'Child care practices among West African families living in Paris', presented at the meeting of the International Society for the Study of Behavioural Development, Tokyo, Japan, July.

Rabain-Jamin, J. and Wornham, W.L. (1989) 'Pratiques de soin et interaction mère-enfant dans un contexte d'émigration', in J. Retschitzki, M. Bossel-Lagos and P. Dasen (eds) *Contributions à la Recherche Interculturelle*, Actes du 2ème Colloque de l'ARIC, Paris: L'Harmattan.

Riksen-Walraven, J. (1978) 'Effects of caregiver behavior on habituation rate and self-efficacy in infants', *International Journal of Behavioral Development* 1: 105–30.

Scribner, S. and Cole, M. (1973) 'Cognitive consequences of formal and informal education', *Science* 182: 553–9.

Schaffer, H.R and Crook, C.K. (1979) 'Maternal control techniques in a directed play situation', *Child Development* 50: 989–96.

Schieffelin, B.B. and Ochs, E. (1983) 'A cultural perspective on the transition from prelinguistic to linguistic communications', in R.M. Golinkoff (ed), *The Transition from Prelinguistic to Linguistic Communication*, Hillsdale, N.J.: Erlbaum.

Schieffelin, B.B., and Ochs, E. (1986) *Language Socialization Across Cultures*, Cambridge: Cambridge University Press.

Searle, J.R. (1969) *Speech Acts: An Essay in the Philosophy of Language*, Cambridge: Cambridge University Press.

Steward, M. and Steward, D. (1973) 'The observation of Anglo-, Mexican-, and Chinese-American mothers teaching their young sons, *Child Development* 44: 329–37.

Super, C.M. (1981) 'Cross-cultural research on infancy', in H.C. Triandis and A. Heron (eds) *Handbook of Cross-Cultural Psychology*, vol. 4: *Developmental Psychology*, Boston: Allyn & Bacon.

Zukow, P.G., Reilly, J. and Greenfield, P.M. (1982) 'Making the present absent: facilitating the transition from sensorimotor to linguistic communication', in K.E. Nelson (ed.) *Children's Language*, vol. 3, Hillsdale, N.J.: Erlbaum.

12 Nature and uses of immaturity

Jerome S. Bruner

Source: *American Psychologist* (1972) 27(8).

To understand the nature of any species fully, we need to know more than the ways of its adults. We need to know how its young are brought from initial, infantile inadequacy to mature, species-typical functioning. Variation in the uses of immaturity tells much about how adaptation to habitat is accomplished, as well as what is likely to happen given a change in habitat. The nature and uses of immaturity are themselves subject to evolution, and their variations are subject to natural selection, much as any morphological or behavioural variant would be.

One of the major speculations about primate evolution is that it is based on the progressive selection of a distinctive pattern of immaturity. It is this pattern of progressive selection that has made possible the more flexible adaptation of our species. Too often this pattern is over-explained by noting that human immaturity is less dominated by instinct and more governed by learning.

Because our ultimate concern is with the emergence of human adaptation, our first concern must be the most distinctive feature of that adaptation. This feature is man's trait, typical of his species, of 'culture using', with all of the intricate set of implications that follow. Man adapts (within limits) by changing the environment, by developing not only amplifiers and transformers for his sense organs, muscles and reckoning powers, as well as banks for his memory, but also by changing literally the properties of his habitat. Man, so the truism goes, lives increasingly in a man-made environment. This circumstance places social burdens on human immaturity. For one thing, adaptation to such variable conditions depends heavily on opportunities for learning, in order to achieve knowledge and skills that are not stored in the gene pool. But not all that must be mastered can be learned by direct encounter. Much must be 'read out' of the culture pool, things learned and remembered over several generations:

knowledge about values and history, skills as varied as an obligatory natural language or an optional mathematical one, as mute as using levers or as articulate as myth telling. Yet, though there is the gene pool, and though there exist direct experience and the culture as means for shaping immaturity, none of these directly prepares for the novelty that results when man alters his environment. That flexibility depends on something else.

Yet it would be a mistake to leap to the conclusion that, because human immaturity makes possible high flexibility in later adjustment, anything is possible for the species. Human traits were selected for their survival value over a 4–5 million-year period, with a great acceleration of the selection process during the last half of that period. There were crucial, irreversible changes during that final man-making period – recession of formidable dentition, doubling of brain volume, creation of what Washburn and Howell (1960) have called a 'technical–social way of life', involving tool and symbol use. Note, however, that *hominidization* consisted principally of adaptations to conditions in the Pleistocene. These preadaptations, shaped in response to earlier demands of the habitat, are part of man's evolutionary inheritance. This is not to say that close beneath the skin of man is a naked ape, that 'civilization' is only a 'veneer'. The technical–social way of life is a deep feature of the species adaptation.

But we would err if we assumed *a priori* that man's inheritance places no constraint on his power to adapt. Some of the preadaptations can be shown to be of no present use. Man's inordinate fondness for fats and sweets no longer serves his individual survival well. And human obsession with sexuality is plainly not fitted for survival of the species now, however well it might have served to populate the upper Pliocene and the Pleistocene. But note that the species responds typically to these challenges by technical innovation rather than by morphological or behavioural change. This is not to say that man is not capable of controlling or, better, transforming behaviour. Whatever its origin, the incest taboo is a phenomenally successful technique for the control of certain aspects of sexuality – although its beginning among the great apes (van Lawick-Goodall 1968) suggests that it may have a base that is rooted partly in the biology of propinquity, a puzzling issue. The technical innovation is contraception, which dissociates sexuality from reproduction. What we do not know, of course, is what kinds and what range of stresses are produced by successive rounds of such technical innovation. Dissociating sexuality and reproduction, for example, may produce changes in the structure of the family be re-defining the sexual role of women, which in turn may alter the authority pattern affecting the child, etc. Continuous, even accelerating, change may be inherent in such adaptation. If this is so, then there is an enormous added pressure on man's uses of immaturity for instruction. We must prepare the young for unforeseeable change – a task made the more difficult if severe constraints imposed by human preadaptations to earlier conditions of life have created rigidities.

EVOLUTION OF EDUCABILITY

Le Gros Clark's (1963) *échelle des êtres* of the primates runs from tree shrews through the prosimian lorisformes, lemuriformes, and related forms through the New World and Old World monkeys, through the hylobates such as the gibbon, through the great apes, through the early hominids like *Australopithecus* and *Homo habilis* and other small-brained predecessors, terminating in the modern form of *Homo sapiens* with his 1300-cubic-centimetre brain. Closing the gap between great apes and modern man is, of course, a complex and uncertain undertaking, particularly where behaviour is concerned, for all that remains are palaeontological and archaeological fragments, and little by way of a behaviour record. But there are inferences that can be made from these fragments, as well as from the evolution of primate behaviour up to the great apes. Enough is known to suggest hypotheses, though no conclusions. Such as *échelle des êtres* is bound to be only a metaphor, since contemporary species are only approximations to those that existed in the evolutionary tree. But it can tell us something about change in the primate order. We propose to use it where we can to make inferences, not so much about preadaptations to earlier conditions that characterize our species, but rather more to assess crucial changes that have been recurring in immaturity. My interest is in the evolution of educability.

I am not primarily a student of pre-human primates. I have brought the materials of primate evolution together to understand better the course of human infancy and childhood, its distinctiveness or species typicality. I propose to go back and forth, so to speak, between primate phylogeny and human ontogeny, not to establish any shallow parallel between the two, but in the hope that certain contrasts will help us see more clearly. If indeed the fish will be the last to discover water, perhaps we can help ourselves by looking at some other species.

Specifically, I should like to look at several issues whose resolution might be of particular help. The first of these has to do with the nature and evolution of social organisation within a species and how this may affect the behaviour of the immature. The second has to do with the structure of skill and how the evolution of primate skill almost inevitably leads to tool using. We must then pause to consider the nature of tool using and its consequences. That matter in turn leads us directly to the roles of both play and imitation in the evolution of educability. Inevitably, we shall deal with that distinctly human trait, language: what it is and how its emergence drastically alters the manner in which we induct young into the species.

My emphasis throughout is principally on the evolution of intellect – problem solving, adaptation to habitat, and the like. But it will soon be apparent that, to use the jargon (Bloom 1956), one cannot easily separate the cognitive from the conative and the affective. I have been told that the Chinese character for *thinking* combines the character for *head* and the character for *heart*. Pity it does not also include the character for *others* as well, for then it would be appropriate to what will concern us. At the end, I try to deal with the question of what can be done better to equip the young for coping.

Any species depends, as we know from the work of the last half century (e.g. Mayr 1963), on the development of a system of mutuality – a set of mechanisms for sharing a habitat or territory, a system of signalling that is effective against predators, dominance relations that are effective without being pre-empting (Chance 1967), a system of courtship with matching mating releasers (Tinbergen 1953), etc. There is, at the lower end of the primate line, a considerable amount of rather fixed or linear structure about such mutuality. Behaviour repertoires are limited in prosimians and in monkeys, and the combinatorial richness in their behaviour is not great (see Jolly 1966), though one can make a case for their goodness of fit to habitat conditions (as Hinde 1971, has). Even where there is, within a given species, an increased variety in behaviour produced by enriched or more challenging environments – as in the contrast between urban and forest-dwelling rhesus monkeys (Singh 1969) or among Japanese macaques tempted by new foods introduced in their terrain (Itani 1958) – the difference is not towards variability or loosening of social structure, but towards the incorporation of new patterns into the species-typical social pattern. Action patterns that are altogether fixed prevail; and *play*, that special form of violating fixity, is limited in variety, early and short-lived, and irreversibly gone by adulthood – a matter to which I shall return.

There are notably fixed limits for the young of these species; and as the animal grows from infant to juvenile to adult – transitions usually marked by conspicuous changes in appearance and coat colour –

social induction into the group is effected rapidly, usually by the quick response of a young animal to the threat of attack by an older animal in the troop. The sharply defined oestrous receptivity of the adult female almost assures that the young animal will be rejected and made virtually self-sufficient within a year. It is this sharply defined receptivity that also creates a scarcity economy in sexual access and leads to such a close link between male dominance and sexual access – perhaps the most notable source of linear, tight social structure virtually throughout the monkeys and prosimians. The comfort-contact system of mother and infant, involving not only initial nursing but also hair holding and grasping by the young for protection in flight and for sheer comfort, is obviously of great importance in prosimians, New World and Old World monkeys. But as Dolhinow and Bishop (1970) have remarked, we must be careful about exaggerating it. Harlow's (e.g. 1959) pioneering studies do show that a macaque made solely dependent on a terry-cloth or wire-mesh mother surrogate is more backward than one dependent on a real mother. Yet, for all that, twenty minutes of play daily with peers in a play cage obliterates the difference between the three groups – another of Harlow's (Harlow and Harlow 1962) findings. Note by way of contrast that a three-year-old chimpanzee deprived of a mother modelling the skilled act of fishing for termites seems not to be able to master the act later, even if among peers who are succeeding.

LOOSENING THE PRIMATE BOND

Probably the first step toward loosening the initially tight primate bond is the development of what Chance (1967) has referred to as an 'attentional structure' within the group. Rather than behaviour patterns leading to constant interaction and mutual release of agonistic patterns, there is instead a deployment of attention in which the dominant animal is watched, his behaviour is anticipated, and confrontation is avoided. One of the major things that induction into a tightly organized Old-World monkey group means, then, is an enormous investment in attention to the requirements of the troop – mating, dominance, food foraging, etc. There is, so to speak, little attentional capacity left for anything else.

The great apes represent a crucial break away from this pattern toward a far more relaxed one, and as we shall see in a moment, the effect on the young is striking. All three of the great ape species are virtually free of predators. None of them defends a territory. None of them has a troop structure nearly as well defined and rigidly maintained as, say, the least rigid Old-World species, if such a phrase makes sense. In the gorilla, the orang-utan, and the chimpanzee, male dominance does not preclude copulation between a subdominant male and a female in the presence of the dominant male. It is even difficult, in fact, in the case of chimpanzee and orang-utan to define a dominant male in the monkey sense (cf., e.g. Goodall 1965; Reynolds 1965; Schaller 1964). Indeed, the route to dominance may even involve a superior technological skill. Note the increased deference paid to a male in the Gombe Stream Reserve who had learned to produce an intimidating din by banging two discarded tin cans together (van Lawick-Goodall 1968). Thus, too, while oestrous marks the period of maximum receptivity in which the female initiates sexual activity, her availability to a male may in fact continue even into the first two months of pregnancy (Reynolds 1965). Doubtless the achievement of a 600–700-cubic-centimetre brain in great apes also contributes to the further evolution of cerebral control of sexual behaviour of which Beach (1965) has written. The spacing of infants is over three years apart, on average, and the bond between mother and infant, particularly in the chimpanzee, remains active for as long as five years (van Lawick-Goodall 1968).

One concomitant of the change is the decline in fixed patterns of induction into the group. There is much less of what might be called training by threat from adults or actual punishment by adults of a juvenile who has violated a species-typical pattern. The prolonged infant–mother interaction includes now a much larger element of play between them, often initiated by the mother and often used to divert an infant from a frustration-arousing situation.

What appears to be happening is that, with the loosening of fixed bonds, a system of reciprocal exchange emerges, the structure of which is at first difficult to describe. [. . .] There can be little doubt that primate evolution is strongly and increasingly characterized by such reciprocal exchange. The trend probably pre-dates the emergence of hominids. In an article in 1971, Trivers said:

> During the Pleistocene, and probably before, a hominid species would have met the preconditions for the evolution of reciprocal altruism: long life span, low disperal rate; life in small, mutually dependent, stable, social groups (Lee and DeVore 1968; Campbell 1966); and a long period of parental care. It is very likely that dominance relations were of the relaxed, less linear form characteristic of the baboon (Hall and DeVore 1965).

(Trivers 1971: 45)

As Gouldner (1960) reminded us a decade ago and as new studies on remaining hunter–gatherers reassert (Lee and DeVore 1968), there is no known human culture that is not marked by reciprocal help in times of danger and trouble, by food sharing, by communal nurture of the young or disabled, and by the sharing of knowledge and implements for expressing skill. Lévi-Strauss (1963) posited such exchanges as the human watershed and classified them into three types: one involving the exchange of symbols and myths and knowledge; another involving the exchange of affectional and affiliative bonds, including the exchange of kin women in marriage to outside groups for political alliances, with this rare resource preserved by an incest taboo; and finally an exchange system for goods and services. The pressures in such primate groups would surely select traits consonant with reciprocity, leading to self-domestication by the selection of those capable of 'fitting in'. The incessant aggressiveness of the linear pattern would wane gradually.

What accompanies these changes is a marked transformation in ways of managing immaturity. The maternal buffering and protection of the young not only lengthens materially but undergoes qualitative changes. Several of these have been mentioned: a much prolonged period dominated by play: increased participation in play by adults, especially though not exclusively, by the mother; decline in the use of punishment and threat as modes of inducting the young into the pattern of species-typical interactions. The most important, I believe, is the appearance of a pattern involving an enormous amount of observation of adult behaviour by the young, with incorporation of what has been learned into a pattern of play (Dolhinow and Bishop 1970; Hamburg 1968; Hayes and Hayes 1952; Köhler 1925; Reynolds 1965; Rumbaugh 1970; van Lawick-Goodall 1968; Yerkes and Yerkes 1929). Though psychologists are chary about using the term imitation, because of the difficulty of defining it, virtually all primatologists comment on the enormous increase in imitation found in chimpanzees in contrast to Old-World monkeys (where there is genuine doubt whether imitation in any common-sense meaning of the term occurs at all). After its first appearance at about 17 months of age, this pattern of observing and imitating takes up much of the time of infants and young juveniles – watching social interaction, watching the care of the young, watching copulation, watching agonistic displays, watching instrumental or tool behaviour. Such observation requires free attention on the part of the young; and, indeed, the incorporation of observed behaviour in play occurs most usually during the more relaxed periods in the life of the group. It was Köhler (1925), in his classic *The Mentality of Apes*, who commented initially on the intelligent rather than the mechanical or slavish nature of imitative behaviour in anthropoids – how the sight of another animal solving a problem is used not to mimic but as a basis for guiding the observer's own problem solving or goal striving. He used the term 'serious play' (Köhler 1925: 157), and the literature since the early 1920s bears him out (e.g. Dolhinow and Bishop 1970; Hamburg 1968). In a word, the chimpanzee adult serves not only as a buffer or protector or 'shaper' for the young but as a model – though there is no indication of any intentional modelling or of behaviour that is specifically 'demonstrational'.

To summarize briefly, the emergence of a more flexible form of social bonding in primate groups seems to be accompanied by the emergence of a new capacity for learning by observation. Such learning indeed may be necessary if not sufficient for transmission of culture. But that gets ahead of the argument still to be made; for there is still an enormous gap to be accounted for between the behaviour of a grouping of great apes, however flexible, and the mode of structuring of a human society, no matter how simple it may be.

OBSERVATIONAL LEARNING

There are many facets to observational learning (I cautiously continue to avoid the term *imitation*). There is ample evidence that many mammals considerably less evolved than primates can benefit from exposure to another animal carrying out a task; for example, the classic study of cats by Herbert and Harsh (1944) demonstrates improvement in escape from a puzzle box by cats who have seen other animals escape – and more so if the cats observed were still inexpert at the task. Whether they are learning the possibility of getting out of the box, the means for doing so (by displacing a bar), or whatever, observation helps. [. . .]

But this is quite different from the sort of 'serious play' to which Köhler referred. Consider an example:

I would call the following behaviour of a chimpanzee imitation of the 'serious play' type. On the playground a man has painted a wooden pole in white colour. After the work is done he goes away leaving behind a pot of white paint and a beautiful brush. I observe the only chimpanzee who is present, hiding my face behind my hands, as if I were not paying attention to him. The ape for a while gives much attention to me before approaching the brush and the paint because he has learned that misuse of our things may have serious consequences. But very soon, encouraged by my attitude, he takes the brush, puts it into the pot of colour and paints a big stone which happens to be in the place, beautifully white. The whole time the ape behaved completely seriously. So did others when imitating the washing of laundry or the use of a borer.

(Köhler 1925: 156–7)

I consider such behaviour to be dependent on two important prerequisites both amenable to experimental analysis:

The first *is the ability to differentiate or abstract oneself from a task*, to turn around on one's own performance and, so to speak, see oneself, one's own performance as differentiated from another. This involves self-recognition in which one, in some way, is able to model one's *own* performance on some selected feature of another's performance. [. . .]

The second prerequisite for observation learning is [. . .] *construction of an action pattern by the appropriate sequencing of a set of constituent sub-routines to match a model* (Lashley 1951). Observing the development of skilled, visually directed manipulatory activity in human infants and children, one is struck repeatedly by the extent to which such activity grows from the mastery of specific acts, the gradual perfecting of these acts into what may be called a modular form, and the combining of these into higher-order, longer-range sequences. Flexible skilled action may almost be conceived of as the construction of a sequence of constituent acts to achieve an objective (usually a change in the environment) while taking into account local conditions [. . .]

EFFECT OF TOOLS

We must consider now the question of tools and their use, and what effect this evolutionary step may have had on the management of immaturity.

Chimpanzee survival does not depend on the use of sticks for fishing termites or on the use of crushed leaves as drinking or grooming sponges. As Jane Lancaster put it in a closely reasoned article on tool use, there is 'a major change from the kind of tool use that is incidental to the life of a chimpanzee to the kind that is absolutely essential for survival of the human individual' (Lancaster 1968: 62). Yet, in spite of the absence of 'obligatory pressures', chimpanzees use tools optionally in an extraordinary variety of ways: for eating, drinking, self-cleaning, agonistic displays, constructing sleeping platforms, etc. Nor is it some accident of morphology:

The hands of monkeys and apes are equally suited to picking up a stick and making poking or scratching movements with it but differences in the brain make these much more likely behaviour patterns for the chimpanzee.

(Lancaster 1968: 61)

I would like to make the rather unorthodox suggestion that in order for tool using to develop it was essential to have a long period of optional, pressure-free opportunity for combinatorial activity. By its very nature, tool using (or the incorporation of objects into skilled activity) required a chance to achieve the kind of wide variation upon which selection could operate.

Dolhinow and Bishop made the point most directly. Commenting first that 'many special skills and behaviours important in the life of the individual are developed and practised in playful activity long before they are used in adult life' (Dolhinow and Bishop 1970: 142), they then note that play 'occurs only in an atmosphere of familiarity, emotional reassurance, and lack of tension or danger'. Schiller reported, 'with no incentive the chimpanzee displayed a higher variety of handling objects than under the pressure of a lure which they attempted to obtain' (Schiller 1952: 186). He reported, actually, that attempting to direct play by reinforcing chimpanzees for play behaviour had the effect of inhibiting play.

FUNCTIONS OF PLAY

Play appears to serve several centrally important functions. First, it is a means of minimizing the consequences of one's actions and of learning, therefore, in a less risky situation. This is particularly true of social play, where, by adopting a play face or a 'galumphing gait' (Miller 1973) or some other form of metacommunication (Dolhinow and Bishop 1970), the young animal signals his intent to play. Now, so to speak, he can test limits with relative impunity:

There are many rules of what can and cannot be done in a troop, and most of these are learned early in life, when the consequences of violating them are less severe than later on.

(Dolhinow and Bishop 1970: 148)

Second, play provides an excellent opportunity to try combinations of behaviour that would, under functional pressure, never be tried.

The tendency to manipulate sticks, to lick the ends, to poke them into any available hole are responses that occur over and over again in captive chimpanzees. These responses are not necessarily organized into the efficient use of sticks to probe for objects, but they probably form the basis of complex motor patterns such as termiting.

(Lancaster 1968: 61)

[. . .]

Various writers (Dolhinow and Bishop 1970; Loizos 1967; van Lawick-Goodall 1968) are convinced that the mastery of complex tool skills among subhuman anthropoids depends not only on observation learning but also on whether or not they take place in the close setting of the infant–mother interaction. Reference was made in passing to one of the infants in the Gombe Stream Reserve, Merlin, who lost his mother at age 3 and was 'taken over' by older siblings. He mastered neither termiting nor nest building, skills that apparently require repeated observation.

Van Lawick-Goodall (1968) made it clear in her detailed reporting why such repeated opportunity to observe and play is necessary; mastery of a complex skill like termiting is a complex process of mastering *features* of the task – a non-mimicking approach – and then combining the mastered features. There is, for example, mastery of pushing a stick or grass into an opening, though initially this will be done without regard to appropriate rigidity of the probe or appropriate diameter, or appropriate length. It will be played with as a past skill once mastered – as Flint (2.8 years, who had started at play termiting) pushing a grass stalk through the hairs of his leg. And sheer repetition will provide the familiar routinization that permits an act to be combined with other acts to meet the complex requirement of a stick of a particular diameter and rigidity, pushed in a particular way, withdrawn at a particular angle at a certain speed, etc. A comparable set of observations on human infants by Wood *et al.* (1976) shows the importance of skill to 3–5-year-olds in enabling them to benefit from demonstrations of how to put together an interlocking set of blocks to make a pyramid. Unless the child can master the subroutines, the demonstration of the whole task is about as helpful as a demonstration by an accomplished skier is to a beginner. As with the young chimps, so too with the young children: they take selectively from the demonstration those features of performance that are within the range of their capacity for constructing skilled acts. They are helped, but the process is slow.

One very crucial feature of tool skills in chimpanzees as in humans is the trying out of variants of the new skill in different contexts. Once

Köhler's (1925) ape Sultan had 'learned' to use a stick to draw in food, he tried using it very soon for poking other animals, for digging, and for dipping it through an opening in a cesspool. Once Rana had learned to climb up stacked boxes to get a suspended piece of fruit, she rapidly tried her new climbing routine on a ladder, a board, a keeper, and Köhler himself – most often forgetting the fruit in preference for the combinatory activity *per se*. [. . .]

The play aspect of tool use (and, indeed, complex problem solving in general) is underlined by the animal's loss of interest in the goal of the act being performed and by its preoccupation with means – also a characteristic of human children. Consider the following episode:

> Hebb recounted how a chimpanzee he tested solved problems for banana slice incentives. On one particular day, she arranged the banana slice rewards in a row instead of eating them! Apparently, she had solved the problems for their own sake. 'I was out of bananas, but I offered her another problem . . . she solved the problem: opened the correct box and put a slice of banana into it. I took it out and then set the box again . . . I ended up with thirty slices of banana'.
>
> (Rumbaugh 1970: 56)

A far cry from reinforcement in any conventional sense!

Köhler's (1925) account contains an interesting happening. He gave a handful of straw to one animal who tried to use it to draw in an out-of-reach piece of fruit. Finding the straw too flexible, the animal doubled it up, but it was too short, so he abandoned the effort. Modification is systematic, most often directed to features relevant to the task, and is combinatorial. It follows first constructions or first efforts at copying a model. But it appears first in play, not in problem solving.

PLAY IN RELATION TO TOOL USE

I have described these play activities at great length because I believe them to be crucial to the evolution of tool using – steps that help free the organism from the immediate requirements of its task. Play, given its concomitant freedom from reinforcement and its setting in a relatively pressureless environment, can produce the flexibility that makes tool using possible. At least two laboratory studies, one by Birch (1945) and the other by Schiller (1952), indicate the necessity of initial play with materials in order for them to be converted to instrumental ends. They both used problems involving the raking in of food with sticks of varying length – before and after an opportunity to play with sticks. Few succeeded before play. Observed during play, Birch's animals were seen to explore increasingly over three days the capacity of the sticks to lengthen an arm. When put back into the test situation, all of these animals solved the problem within half a minute. Perhaps, as Loizos (1967) has suggested, it is the very exaggeration and lack of economy of play that encourage extension of the limits.

Looked at logically, play has two crucial formal patterns: one consists of a function and its arguments; the other, an argument and the functions into which it can fit. A ball or a stick are fitted into as many acts as possible; or an act, climbing, is performed on as many objects to which it can be applied appropriately. This pattern, I would speculate, is close to one of the universal structures of language, predication, which is organised in terms of topic and comment:

John has a hat
John is a man
John jumps the fence, or

Brush the hat
Wear the hat
Toss the hat.

It is interesting that the language play after 'lights out' of the 3-year-old, reported by Ruth Weir (1962) in her remarkable book *Language in the Crib*, takes precisely such a form. And I will not be the first to comment that the simultaneous appearance in man of language and tool using suggests that the two may derive from some common programming capacities of the enlarging hominid nervous system.

[. . .]

To summarize once again, the great ape possesses manipulative subroutines that are practiced, perfected and varied in play. These are then put together clumsily and selectively to meet the requirements of more extended tasks, very often in response to observing an adult in a stable and relaxed setting. The imitation observed is akin to imitation by a child of an adult speech model: the child's output is *not* a copy of the adult's; it has its own form even though it is designed to fill the same function. These initial acts are then modified in a systematic manner to fulfil further requirements of the task. The acts themselves have a self-rewarding character. They are varied systematically, almost as if a play to test the limits of a new skill. A baboon living in the same habitat as the chimpanzee is as eager to eat termites as is the latter; yet he shows none of these capacities even though he is seen to observe the chimpanzee exercising them often. He, too, is equipped with a good pair of hands. Note that there is an association between play and tool use, and that the natural selection of one, tools, led to the selection of the other as well, in the evolution of the hominids and man.

ADULTS AS MODELS

Neither among chimpanzees nor in the infinitely more evolved society of hunter-gatherers is there much direct intervention by adults in the learning of the young. They serve principally as models and as sources of the necessary affection (Bruner 1965). Among the primates, there is very little intentional pedagogy of any kind. [. . .]

There may, however, be something like 'tutor proneness' among the young – an increased eagerness to learn from adults. One study suggests how such tutor proneness may come about. Rumbaugh *et al.* (1972) are training chimpanzees and orang-utans under the following conditions. One group receives tutoring modelling on a variety of tasks; each task is presented on each new encounter in the form of a new embodiment of the problem. A second group gets the same problems, but each time in the same form, so that this group is essentially repeating. The third group is presented the materials used by the others, but the human tutor model neither presents them as tasks nor models the solutions as in the first two instances. The tasks are mechanical puzzles, packing fitted containers within each other, searching for a hidden object, transporting an object to another part of the room, extracting candy from a container, etc. The reward is some combination of task completion and the tutor's approval. A preliminary finding of this work-in-progress is of particular interest. The apes in the more challenging first condition are the ones most likely to wait for the tutor to provide a clue before beginning on their own.

Does it then require a certain level of challenge and novelty to create tutor proneness in primates? Schaller remarked of the gorillas he observed in the Congo,

> Why was the Australopithecus, with the brain capacity of a large gorilla, the maker of stone tools, a being with a culture in the human sense, while the free-living gorilla in no way reveals the marvellous potential of its brain? I suspect that the gorilla's failure to develop further is related to the ease with which it can satisfy its needs in the forest. In its lush realm there is no selective advantage for improvement. . . . The need for tools . . . is more likely in a harsh and marginal habitat where a premium is placed on an alert mind. . . .
>
> (Schaller 1964: 232)

And the same view was voiced by Yerkes and Yerkes (1929) in their classic work on the great apes, as well as by Vernon Reynolds (1965) who, in a penetrating article on the comparative analysis of selection pressures operating on chimpanzees and on gorilla, concluded:

> Finally, we may briefly consider the contrast in temperaments between these two anthropoid species. Comparative behaviour studies in the past often stressed this difference. Tevis (1921), for instance, wrote, 'In mental characteristics there is the widest difference between the two apes that we are considering. The chimpanzee is lively, and at least when young, teachable and tameable. The gorilla, on the other hand, is gloomy and ferocious, and quite untameable' (p. 122). It is possible to suggest an explanation for this contrast between the morose, sullen, placid gorilla, and the lively, excitable chimpanzee. The difference seems to be most clearly related to the difference in social organisation and foraging behaviour. The herbivorous gorilla is surrounded by food: the more intensively it feeds, the slower it travels; its survival needs are easily met, and it is protected from predators by the presence of powerful males. Here there is no advantage to any form of hyper-activity except in threat displays and the charge of the big male, which is a hyper-aggressive behaviour form. Chimpanzee survival, on the other hand, depends heavily on the fluidity of social groups and the ability to communicate the whereabouts of food by intense forms of activity (wild vocalizing and strong drumming). Moving rapidly about the forest, meeting up with new chimpanzees every day, vocalizing and drumming, and locating other chimpanzees by following their calls, are the basic facts of chimpanzee existence. Here an advantage may be seen in having a responsive, expressive, and adaptable temperament. Hyperactivity is the chimpanzee norm in the wild, and with it goes a volatile temperament.
>
> (Reynolds 1965: 704)

But here we encounter a seeming contradiction. The evolutionary trend we have been examining seems to have placed a major emphasis on a combination of developments: a relatively pressure-free environment with its concomitant increase in play, exploration and observation; and at the same time, a certain challenge in the requirements of adaptation to a habitat. [. . .]

I believe that Desmond Morris (1964) has a resolution for this apparent dilemma – that, on the one hand, a non-pressureful habitat seems crucial and, on the other, challenge is significant. He made the distinction between two modes of adaptation to habitat: *specialist* and *opportunist* – the squirrel versus the rat, certain exclusively forest-dwelling monkeys like the vervet or green versus the adaptable rhesus (cf. Hinde 1971). Non-specialists depend on high flexibility rather than on morphology or behavioural specialization. Aristarchus said it well and provided Isaiah Berlin (1953) with a famous book title: 'The fox knows many things; the hedgehog knows one big thing.'

One can only speculate that the evolution of intellectual processes in the primate stock from which man descended was in the direction of opportunism and away from specialism. It could be argued, indeed, that the original stock, as far as intellect goes, was closer to chimpanzee than to either of the contemporary pongids, though Rumbaugh (1970) believed that in certain forms of intellectual performance there are striking parallels between man and orang-utan. The argument for opportunism seems in fact essential to account for the rapid fanning out of the evolved species to such a variety of habitats.

INSTRUCTIONAL INTERACTION BETWEEN ADULTS AND YOUNG

What can be said of 'instruction' of the young in the protohominids and early man? Alas, nothing definite. But contemporary 'simple' societies, hunter-gatherers, provide certain clues. No matter how constraining the ecological conditions, there is among such people an expansion in adult–child instructional interaction, both quantitatively and qualitatively, of a major order. Although one cannot reconstruct the Pleistocene hunter-gatherer by reference to such isolated hunter-gatherers as the contemporary !Kung Bushmen, their practices do suggest something about the magnitude of the change. !Kung adults and children play and dance together, sit together, participate in minor hunting together, join in song and story-telling together. At frequent intervals, moreover, children are the objects of intense rituals presided over by adults – minor, as in the first haircutting, or major, as when a boy kills his first Kudu buck and undergoes the proud but painful process of scarification. Children also are playing constantly at the rituals, with the implements, tools and weapons of the adult world. However, in tens of thousands of feet of !Kung film prepared by the Marshalls (see Bruner 1966), one virtually never finds an instance of teaching taking place outside the situation where the behaviour to be learned is relevant. Nobody teaches away from the scene, as in a school setting. Indeed, there is nothing like a school.

Often the adult seems to play the role of inducting the young into novel situations that, without the presence of a protecting and familiar adult, would be frightening – as in extended trekking, in witchcraft ceremonials, and in many other spheres where the child comes along and participates to the limit that he is able. This induction to the margin of anxiety, I believe, starts very early. A study by Sroufe and Wunsch (1972) provides a hint of just how early that may be. The study sets out to explore what makes human infants laugh. From four months (when laughing first appears in reliable and recognizable form) into the second year of life, the sufficient stimulus for laughter becomes increasingly distal – at first being principally tactile and close visual (e.g., tickle plus looming), with incongruities following later, as when the mother adopts an unusual position such as crawling on all fours. Note, however, that at all ages the capers most likely to produce laughter when performed by the mother are the ones most likely to produce tears when performed by a stranger. The mother seems able to bring the young, so to speak, to the edge of terror. King (1966) has suggested that this feature of mothering is universal; that among birds as well as mammals, the presence of the mother reduces fear of novel stimuli and provides the assurance necessary for exploratory behaviour. But it is only among humans that the adult *introduces* the novel, inducts the young into new, challenging, and frightening situations – sometimes in a highly ritualistic way, as with the *rites de passage*.

There is little question that the human young (and the young of the primates generally) are quite ready to be lured by the novel, given even the minimum adult reassurance. 'Neophilia' is what Desmond Morris (1967) calls it. Such readiness of novelty may even be attested to by a superiority, at least among the great apes and man, of the young over the old in detecting or extracting the rules and regularities in new situations. At least one laboratory study (Rumbaugh and McCormack 1967) has even found a *negative* correlation between age and the ability to master learning-set problems – tasks that have a common principle but a new embodiment on each presentation, like 'pick the odd one when two are alike and one is different'. But note that it is in man only that adults arrange play and ritual for children that capitalize on this tendency.

It is obvious that the play and ritual in which young and adult humans are involved are saturated heavily with symbolism. Though the kind of mastery play I have been at some pains to describe in the preceding discussion is still a feature of human play, there is added to it now an extraordinary range of play forms that have as their vehicle the use of *symbols* and *conventions* – two terms that will concern us in due course. Not only are sticks, so to speak, used as arrows or spears or even as novel and unusual tools, they may be used now in a symbolic way that transcends utility – as horses, for example, when put between the legs (Vygotsky 1933) or giant trees when propped up in the sand. The prop or 'pivot' or toy (it is difficult to name the stick) is not used as a *utilitandum* (as, say, Khroustov's chimpanzee used a separated splinter to poke food out of a tube) but as a point of departure from the present perceptual situation. Though the stick must have some feature that is horselike (it must at least be 'go-between-the-leggable'), it must now also fit into an imaginary situation. It is for this reason that the great Russian psychologist Vygotsky used the term pivot: the stick is a pivot between the real and the imagined.

Once the symbolic transformation of play has occurred, two consequences follow. Play can serve as a vehicle for teaching the nature of a society's conventions, and it can also teach about the nature of convention *per se*. David Lewis (1969) defined a convention as an agreement about procedure, the procedure itself being trivial, but the agreement not. We drive to the right, or we exhibit a red light to port and a green to starboard. And it is evident immediately that a linguistic-cultural community depends on an easy and fluent grasp of convention on the part of its members. Symbolic play, whatever function it may serve for the individual child in working through his own problems or fulfilling his wishes at the fantasy level, has an even more crucial role in teaching that child fluency with rules and conventions.

[. . .]

USING SYMBOLIC MEANS: LANGUAGE

Having gone this far into symbolic play, I now turn to language in order to be more precise about what is involved when symbolic means are used for preparing the human young for culture. Higher primate skill, as I have described it, has about it certain language-like properties. Skilled action, like language, has paraphrases and a kind of grammar. But there is also a communicative function of language; and it is this function, in all probability, that determines many of its design features (cf. Hockett 1960). I have emphasized the similarity between action and the structure of language in order to propose a critical hypothesis: the initial use of language is probably in support of and closely linked to action. The initial structure of language and, indeed, the universal structure of its syntax are extensions of the structure of action. Syntax is not arbitrary; its cases mirror the requirements of signalling about action and representing action: agent, action, object, location, attribution and direction are among its cases. Whatever the language, the agent-action-object structure is the form soon realized by the young speaker. Propositions about the evolution of language are justly suspect. I offer this hypothesis not on the basis of evolutionary evidence but on developmental grounds. For what the child himself shows us is that initial development of language follows and does not lead his development of skill in action and thought. It is only *after* a distinction has been mastered in action that it appears in initial language; and when it first does so, it is referenced by paraphrase of previously learned words or phrases (cf. Slobin 1971). Piaget put it succinctly; 'language is not enough to explain thought, because the structures that characterize thought have their roots in action and in sensorimotor mechanisms that are deeper than linguistics' (Piaget 1967: 98). This is not to say that once a language has been mastered to a certain level (unfortunately, not easily specifiable), it cannot then be used to signal properties of action and events that up to then had *not* been mastered by the child. It is in this sense that language can in fact be used as a medium for instruction (see Bruner *et al.* 1966). [. . .]

At the onset of speech, then, language is virtually an outgrowth of the mastery of skilled action and perceptual discrimination. These abilities sensitize and almost drive the child to linguistic development. De Laguna (1963, originally published 1927) remarked that the most likely evolutionary explanation of language lies in the human need for help, crucial to the 'social-technical way of life' that is distinctly human (cf. Washburn and Howell 1960). De Laguna went on:

> Once we deliberately ask the question: What does speech do? What objective function does it perform in human life – the answer is not far to seek. Speech is the great medium through which human co-operation is brought about. It is the means by which the diverse activities of men are co-ordinated and correlated with each other for the attainment of common and reciprocal ends.
>
> (De Laguna 1963: 19)

Having said that much, we must next note that with further growth, the major trend is a steadfast march *away* from the use of language as an adjunct of action or as a marker for representing the immediate experience. If in the beginning it is true (Block, cited in De Laguna 1963: 89–90) that 'a substantive does not denote simply an object but all the actions with which it is in relation in the experience of the child', it is soon the case that language in the human comes increasingly to be free of the context of action. Whereas 'to understand what a baby is saying, you must see what the baby is doing', nothing of the sort is true for the adult. This brings us to the famous De Laguna dictum, the implications of which will concern us for the remainder of this article.

> The evolution of language is characterized by a progressive freeing of speech from dependence on the perceived conditions under which it is uttered and heard, and from the behaviour which accompanies it. The extreme limit of this freedom is reached in language which is written (or printed) and read. For example, it is quite indifferent to the reader of these words, under what physical conditions they have been penned or typed. This represents, we repeat, the extreme limit of the process by which language comes to be increasingly independent of the conditions of its use.
>
> (De Laguna 1963: 107)

We need not pause long on a comparison of language as it is acquired and used by man and by chimpanzee – notably by the chimpanzee Washoe (Gardner and Gardner 1971; Ploog and Melnechuk 1971). For one thing, Washoe's language acquisition is not spontaneous, and she can be seen from the film record to be both reluctant and bored as a language learner. There is neither the play nor the drive of the human child, the *Funktionslust* (Bühler 1934), that keeps the child exploring and playing with language. [. . .] In a word, chimpanzee use of a taught form of human speech is strongly tied to action, beyond which it tends not to go either spontaneously or by dint of teaching effort.

On the other hand, the development of language in humans not only moves in the direction of becoming itself free of context and accompanying action, it also frees the attention of the user from his immediate surroundings, directing attention to what is being said rather than to what is being done or seen. In the process, language becomes a powerful instrument in selectively directing attention to features of the environment represented by it.

With respect to the first of these, language processing goes on in its very nature at different levels. We process the phonological output of a speaker, interpret his syntax, hold the head words of imbedding phrases until the imbedded phrase is completed and the tail is located to match the head word, etc. At the same time, we direct attention to meanings and to references. The acts of language [. . .] free attention from control by immediate stimulation in the environment. [. . .]

To summarize then, though language springs from and aids action, it quickly becomes self-contained and free of the context of action. It is a device, moreover, that frees its possessor from the immediacy of the environment, not only by pre-emption of attention during language use but by its capacity to direct attention towards those aspects of the environment that are singled out by language.

I have gone into this much detail regarding early language because it is a necessary preliminary to a crucial point about the management of immaturity in human culture. I have commented already on the fact that in simple, hunter-gatherer societies there is very little formal teaching outside the sphere of action. The child is not drawn aside and told how to do it; he is shown while the action is going on, with language as an auxiliary and as a marker of action – an aid in calling attention to what is going on that is relevant. Over and beyond that, the principal use of language was probably some mix of guiding group action and giving shape to a belief system through myths and incantations, as Susanne Langer (1969) has long proposed. I rather suspect that increasing technology imposed an increasing demand on language to represent and store knowledge in a fashion to be helpful outside the immediate context of original use. L. S. B. Leaky (personal communication, April 1966) suggested that once stone instruments came to be made to match a pattern rather than by spontaneous breaking, as in fabricating an Acheulean pebble tool with a single-face-edge, *models* could be fashioned and kept. He has found excellent, obsidian-grained hand axes at Olduvai that appear never to have been used; he speculates that they were 'models for copy', with a religious significance as well.

But an inert model is a poor thing; it is, in effect, an end state, something to be attained with no intervening instruction concerning means. Language does better than that, and it is interesting to see the extent to which magic becomes mixed with practice and imitation in a primitive technology. A good example is afforded by the boat building and inter-island navigation of the pre-literate Puluwat Islanders in the Marshalls [. . .] described in rich detail by Gladwin (1970) in a book entitled *East is a Big Bird*. Theirs is a system in which East is marked by Altair at horizon elevation, distance by a common-sense speed-estimating method, with distance 'logged' by noting the supposed parallax of islands at different distances over the horizon. Final homing on an island is accomplished by noting the direction of end-of-day nesting flights of boobies and frigate birds. And the lot is peppered with sundry omens given by weeds and sea turtles and the feel of things. I happen to be a navigator myself. I am impressed not only that the system works but that it is genuinely a *system*; it ties together means and ends. The framework of the system can be *told*; however, without language it would be impossible, for the ingredients of the system involve reference to the absent or invisible, to the possible, to the conditional, and even (I suspect) to the knowingly false (the white lies all navigators must tell to keep the trustful sailors trusting). There must have been hunting systems and seasonal marking systems of this sort, representable outside the setting of action, in use by very early man – probably much earlier than heretofore suspected (cf. Marshack 1972).

Increasingly, then, language in its decontextualized form becomes among human beings the medium for passing on knowledge. And, of course, the emergence of written language – a very recent innovation from an evolutionary point of view – gives this tendency still further amplification. Once this mode of transmitting knowledge has become established, the conditions for the invention of school – a place where teaching occurs – are present. School is a very recent development in evolutionary terms, even in historical terms. [. . .]

FROM 'KNOWING HOW' TO 'KNOWING THAT'

As soon as schools, pedagogues, and the storing of decontextualized information received legitimacy – and it was probably the written word that accomplished this legitimization – the emphasis shifted from *knowing how* to *knowing that*. Even growth becomes re-defined in accordance with the shift – the adult 'having' more knowledge, that is, 'knowing about' more things. We have even come to define the needs of infancy in these terms, as 'the need for experience' (rather than, as Bowlby 1969, noted, in terms of the need for love and for predictability). Knowledge in some way becomes a central desideratum. And when, as in the United States, attention turns to the children of the under-privileged and the exploited, their difficulty is likely to be, and indeed in this case was, attributed to 'cultural deprivation'. Hence, an 'enriched environment' was prescribed much as if the issue were avitaminosis. Dewey (1916) referred early to this diagnosis as the 'cold-storage' ideal of knowledge and, of course, attacked it vigorously.

But this is too simple, for in fact there is great power inherent in decontextualized knowledge – knowledge represented in a form that is relatively free from the uses to which it is to be put or to which it has been put in the past. It is not too serious an over-simplification to say that it is precisely such a process of reorganizing knowledge into formal systems that frees it of functional fixedness. By using a system of notation that re-defines functional requirements in formal terms, far greater flexibility can be achieved. Rather than thinking in terms of 'hammers', with all of their associated conventionalized imagery, one thinks instead in terms of force to be applied in excess of a certain level of resistance to be overcome. It is, in effect, the way of science to render the problem into this form in order to make the solving of *particular* problems mere instances of much simpler general problems and thereby to increase the range of applicability of knowledge. Why should the Puluwatan navigator struggle with such a set of complexities as I have described, when all it gets him is competence over a few hundred miles of ocean, and a shaky competence at that! He would be more accurate and more general, as well as more flexible, if he learned to take the elevation of a heavenly body, note the time, and reduce the sight to the easily solved spherical triangle of the western navigator. Such a system would serve him anywhere.

But there are two problems (at least!) in this ideal of efficient formal knowledge rather than implicit knowledge, to use Polanyi's (1958) phrase. The first grows out of the point already made about skill and its de-emphasis. That de-emphasis comes out of what I believe to be a misplaced confidence in the ease with which we go from *knowing that* to *knowing how*. It is not easy; it is a deep and perplexing problem. Let me call it the effectiveness problem. Just as deep is a second problem: it may well be that the message of decontextualization and formal structure is implicitly anti-fantasy and anti-play. Call this the engagement problem. The two together – effectiveness and engagement – bring us to the heart of the matter.

With respect to effectiveness, it is probably a reasonable hypothesis that as technology advances, the effector and the energy components of industrial activity become increasingly remote from human empathy; neither the arm nor the hand any longer give the models for energy or for artificing. Energy and the tool kit become, for planning purposes, black boxes, and the major human functions are *control* and the *organization* of work. There is a spiral. It becomes possible to talk about the conduct of work almost without reference to skill or vocation – wheat production and steel production and gross national product and energy production and balance of payments. With work and competence presented in that mode, the young become more and more remote from the nature of the effort involved in running a society. Vocation, competence, skill, sense of place in the system – these become more and more difficult for the young to fathom – or, for that matter, for the adult. It is difficult for the child to say what he will do or what he will 'be' as an adult. Effectiveness becomes elusive.
[. . .]

School, separated from work which itself has grown difficult to understand, becomes its own world. As McLuhan (1964) insists, it becomes a medium and has its own message, regardless of what is taught. The message is its irrelevance to work, to adult life. For those who wish to pursue knowledge for its own sake, this is not upsetting. But for those who do not or cannot, school provides no guide – only knowledge, the relevance of which is clear neither to students nor to teachers. These are the conditions for alienation and confusion. [. . .]

I do not propose to become gloomy. Surely human culture and our species are in deep trouble, not the least of which is loss of heart. But much of the trouble is real: We are degrading the biosphere, failing to cope with population, permitting technology to degrade individuality, and failing to plan. Many of the experimental and often radical efforts of the young represent, I believe, new variants of ancient, biologically rooted modes by which the young characteristically work through to maturity. And a great many of these efforts are in response to the new conditions we have been at such pains to describe – a rate of change faster than can be transmitted intergenerationally with concomitant likelihood of disastrous consequences. Let me conclude with a closer analysis of this point and, in so doing, come to what was referred to above as the problem of engagement.

A great many of the world's schools are conventional and dull places. They do not foster much productive play and little of what Jeremy Bentham (1840), in his *Theory of Legislation*, called 'deep play' and condemned as irrational and in violation of the utilitarian ideal. By deep play, Bentham meant play in which the stakes are so high that it is irrational for men to engage in it at all – a situation in which the marginal utility of what one stands to win is clearly less than the marginal disutility of what one stands to lose. Bentham proposed, good utilitarian that he was, that such play should be outlawed. But as the anthropologist Geertz commented in his close analysis of cock-fighting in Bali, 'despite the logical force of Bentham's analysis men do engage in such play, both passionately and often, and even in the face of law's revenge' (Geertz 1972: 667). Deep play is playing with fire. It is the kind of serious play that tidy and even permissive institutions for educating the young cannot live with happily, for their mandate from the society requires them to carry out their work with due regard for minimizing chagrin concerning outcomes achieved. And deep play is a poor vehicle for that.

[. . .]

There is ample reason to believe that the present forms of deep play point to a thwarted, backed-up need for defining competence, both individually and socially, to oneself and to others. Recall that in most previous cultural eras, adults provided challenge and excitement and a certain sense of muted terror for the young by induction into rituals and skills that had momentous consequences. Engagement was built into the system. One knew the steps to growing up, both ritually and in terms of skill.

If adult life ceases to be comprehensible, or begins to be less a challenge than a drag, then engagement is lost – but only for a while. I have the impression of something new emerging. What takes the place of the deposed, incomprehensible, or worn-out competence figure, the classical adult image of skill? [. . .] I believe that gradually there is emerging a new form of role bearer – the *intermediate generation* – adolescents and young adults who take over the role of acting as models. They exist visibly in context. Their skills and vocation are proclaimed, miniaturized to appropriate size, and personalized. I should like to propose that such an intermediate generation is a response to the crisis of a change rate that goes faster than we can transmit from generation to generation.

[. . .]

I do not think that intermediate models are a transitory phenomenon. I believe that we would do well to recognize the new phenomenon and to incorporate it, even make it easier for the young adult and later juvenile to get more expert at it. Nobody can offer a blueprint on how an intermediate generation can help ready the less mature for life in an unforseeably changing world. [. . .] But letting the young have more of a hand in the teaching of the younger, letting them have a better sense of the dilemmas of society as a whole, these may be part of the way in which a new community can be helped to emerge. What may be in order is a mode of inducting the young by the use of a more communal system of education in which each takes responsibility for teaching or aiding or abetting or provoking those less able, less knowledgeable, and less provoked than he.

It was in the universities that these current matters first surfaced – a long way from the high savannas of East Africa where we began our quest for an understanding of immaturity and its uses. One becomes increasingly shaky the closer one comes to man in his contemporary technological society. I would urge only that in considering these deep issues of educability we keep our perspective broad and remember that the human race has a biological past from which we can read lessons for the culture of the present. We cannot adapt to everything, and in designing a way to the future we would do well to examine again what we are and what our limits are. Such a course does not mean opposition to change but, rather, using man's natural modes of adapting to render change both as intelligent and as stable as possible.

REFERENCES

Bartlett, F. C. (1958) *Thinking: An Experimental and Social Study*, New York: Basic Books.

Beach, F. (1965) *Sex and Behavior*, New York: Wiley.

Bentham, J. (1840) *The Theory of Legislation*, Jordan, Boston: Weeks.

Berlin, I. (1953) *The Hedgehog and the Fox*, New York: Simon & Schuster.

Birch, H. G. (1945) 'The relation of previous experience to insightful problem-solving', *J. Comp. Physical. Psychol.* 38: 367–83.

Block, S. C. (1972) 'Early competence in problem-solving', in K. Connolly and J. S. Bruner (eds) *Competence in Early Childhood*, CIBA Foundation Conference, London: Academic Press.

Bloom, B. (ed.) (1956) *Taxonomy of Educational Objectives*, New York: McKay.

Bowlby, J. (1969) *Attachment and Loss*, vol. 1, London: Hogarth Press.

Bruner, J. S. (1965) 'The growth of mind', *Amer. Psychol.* 20: 1007–17.

Bruner, J. S. (1966) *Toward a Theory of Instruction*, Cambridge, Mass.: Harvard University Press.

Bruner, J. S. (1970) *Poverty and Childhood*, Detroit: Merrill-Palmer Institute.

Brunner, J. S., Goodnow, J.J. and Austin, G. A. (1956) *A Study of Thinking*, New York: Wiley.

Bruner, J. S., Greenfield, P. M. and Olver, R. R. (1966) *Studies in Cognitive Growth*, New York: Wiley.

Bruner, J. S. and Koslowski, B. (1972) 'Preadaptation in initial visually guided reaching', *Perception* 1.

Bühler, K. (1934) *Sprachtheories*, Jena.

Chance, M. R. A. (1967) 'Attention structure as the basis of primate rank orders', *Man* 2: 503–18.

Clark, W. E. LeGros (1963) *The Antecedents of Man: An Introduction to the Evolution of the Primates*, New York: Harper & Row.

Cole, M. and Bruner, J. S. (1971) 'Cultural differences and inferences about psychological processes', *Amer. Psychol.* 26: 867–76.

Denenberg, V. H. (ed.) (1970) *Education of the Infant and the Young Child*, London: Academic Press.

Dewey, J. (1916) *Democracy and Education*, New York: Macmillan.

Dolhinow, P. J. and Bishop, N. (1970) 'The development of motor skills and social relationships among primates through play', *Minn. Symp. Child Psychol.*

Geertz, C. (1972) 'Deep play: notes on the Balinese cockfight', *Daedalus* 101: 1–38.

Gladwin, T. (1970) *East is a Big Bird*, Cambridge, Mass.: Harvard University Press.

Goodall, J. (1965) 'Chimpanzees of the Gombe Stream Reserve', in

I. DeVore (ed.) *Primate Behavior: Field Studies of Monkeys and Apes*, New York: Holt, Rinehart & Winston.

Gouldner, A. (1960) 'The norm of reciprocity: a preliminary statement', *American Sociological Review* 25: 161–78.

Hall, K. R. L. and DeVore, I. (1965) 'Baboon social behavior', in I. DeVore (ed.) *Primate Behavior: Field Studies of Monkeys and Apes*, New York: Holt, Rinehart & Winston.

Hamburg, D. (1968) 'Evolution of emotional responses: evidence from recent research on non-human primates', *Science and Psychoanalysis* 12: 39–54.

Harlow, H. F. (1959) 'Love in infant monkeys', *Sci. American* 200: 68–74.

Harlow, H. F. and Harlow, M. K. (1962) 'The effect of rearing conditions on behavior', *Bulletin of the Menninger Clinic* 26: 213–24.

Hayes, K. J. and Hayes, C. (1952) 'Imitation in a home-raised chimpanzee', *J. Comp. Physiol. Psychol.* 45: 450–9.

Herbert, M. J. and Harsh, C. M. (1944) 'Observational learning in cats', *J. Comp. Physiol. Psychol.* 37: 81–95.

Hinde, R. A. (1971) 'Development of social behavior', in A. M. Schrier and F. Stollnitz (eds) *Behavior of Nonhuman Primates*, vol. 3, London: Academic Press.

Hockett, C. D. (1960) 'The origins of speech', *Sci. American*.

Itani, J. (1958) 'On the acquisition and propagation of a new food habit in the natural group of the Japanese monkey at Takasakiyana', *Primates* 1: 84–98.

Jolly, A. (1966) *Lemur Behavior: A Madagascar Field Study*, Chicago: University of Chicago Press.

King, D. L. (1966) 'A review and interpretation of some aspects of the infant–mother relationship in mammals and birds', *Psychological Bulletin* 65: 143–55.

Köhler, W. (1925) *The Mentality of Apes*, London: Routledge & Kegan Paul.

Laguna, G. A. de (1963) *Speech: Its Function and Development*, Indiana: Indiana University Press. (Orig. publ. 1927.)

Lancaster, J. B. (1968) 'On the evolution of tool-using behavior', *American Anthropologist* 70: 56–66.

Langer, S. (1969) *Philosophy in a New Key*, Cambridge, Mass.: Harvard University Press. (Revised edition: orig. publ. 1942.)

Lashley, K. S. (1951) 'The problem of serial order in behavior', in L. A. Jeffress (ed.) *Cerebral Mechanisms in Behavior: The Hixon Symposium*, New York: Wiley.

Lawick-Goodall, J. van (1968) 'The behavior of free living champanzees in the Gombe Stream Reserve', *Anim. Behav. Monog.* 1: 165–301.

Lee, R. B. and DeVore, I. (eds) (1968) *Man the Hunter*, Chicago: Aldine.

Levi-Strauss, C. (1968) *Structural Anthropology*, London: Allen Lane.

Lewis, D. (1969) *Convention*, Cambridge, Mass.: Harvard University Press.

Loizos, C. (1967) 'Play behaviour in higher primates: a review', in D. Morris (ed.) *Primate Ethology*, London: Weidenfeld & Nicholson.

Luria, A. R. and Yudovich, F. Y. (1959) *Speech and the Development of*

Mental Processes in the Child, Staples Press.

McLuhan, M. (1964) *Understanding Media*, London: Routledge & Kegan Paul.

Marshack, H. (1972) *The Roots of Civilization*, New York: McGraw-Hill.

Mayr, E. (1963) *Animal Species and Evolution*, Cambridge, Mass.: Harvard University Press.

Miller, S. N. (1973) Ends, means and galumphing: some leitmotifs of play', *American Anthropologist* 75.

Morris, D. (1964) 'The response of animals to a restricted environment', *Symp. Zool. Soc.* 13: 99–118.

Morris, D. (ed.) (1967) *Primate Ethology* London: Weidenfeld & Nicholson.

Piaget, J. (1967) *Six Psychological Studies* (ed. D. Elkind), New York: Random House.

Piaget, J. (1971) *Structuralism*, London: Routledge & Kegan Paul.

Ploog, D. and Melnechuk, T. (1971) 'Are apes capable of language?', *Neurosciences Research Program Bulletin* 9: 600–700.

Polanyi, J. (1958) *Personal Knowledge*, Chicago: University of Chicago Press.

Popper, K. (1954) *Nature, Mind and Modern Science*, London: Hutchinson.

Premack, D. (1971) 'On the assessment of language competence in the chimpanzee', in A. M. Schrier and F. Stollnitz (eds) *Behavior of Nonhuman Primates*, vol. 4, London: Academic Press.

Reynolds, V. (1965) 'Behavioral comparisons between the chimpanzee and the mountain gorilla in the wild', *American Anthropologist* 67: 691–706.

Rumbaugh, D. M. (1970) 'Learning skills of anthropoids', in *Primate Behavior*, vol. 1, London: Academic Press.

Rumbaugh, D. M. and McCormack, C. (1967) 'The learning skills of primates: a comparative study of apes and monkeys', in D. Stark, R. Schneider, and J. H. Kuhn (eds) *Progress in Primatology*, Stuttgart: Fischer.

Rumbaugh, D. M., Riesen, A. H. and Wright, S. C. (1972) 'Creative responsiveness to objects: a report of a pilot study with young apes', privately distributed paper from Yerkes Laboratory of Psychobiology, Atlanta, Georgia.

Schaller, G. (1964) *The Year of the Gorilla*, London: Collins.

Schiller, P. H. (1952) 'Innate constituents of complex responses in primates', *Psych. Rev.* 59: 177–91.

Singh, S. D. (1969) 'Urban monkeys', *Sci. American* 221: 108–15.

Slobin, D. (1971) 'Cognitive prerequisites of language', in W. O. Dingwall (ed.) *Developmental Psycholinguistics: A Survey of Linguistic Science*, University of Maryland Linguistics Program, College Park.

Sroufe, L. A. and Wunsch, J. P. (1972) 'The development of laughter in the first year of life', *Child Development* 43: 1326–44.

Tinbergen, N. (1953) *The Herring Gull's World: A Study of the Social Behaviour of Birds*, London: Collins.

Trivers, R. (1971) 'The evolution of reciprocal altruism', *Quart. Rev. Biol.* 46: 35–57.

Vygotsky, L. S. (1933) 'Play and its role in the mental development of the child', *Soviet Psychology* 3(5): 62–76.

Washburn, S. L. and Howell, F. C. (1960) 'Human evolution and culture' in S. Tax (ed.) *The Evolution of Man*, Chicago: University of Chicago Press.

Weir, R. H. (1962) *Language in the Crib*, Mouton, The Hague.

Werner, H. and Kaplan, B. (1963) *Symbol Formation*, New York: Wiley.

Wood, D. J., Bruner, J. S. and Ross, G. (1976) 'The role of tutoring in problem solving', *Journal of Child Psychology and Psychiatry*, 17: 89–100.

Yerkes, R. M. and Yerkes, A. W. (1929) *The Great Apes: A Study of Anthropoid Life*, New Haven: Yale University Press.

Part four

The construction of identity

Introduction

> The self . . . is essentially a social structure, and it arises in social experience.
>
> (Mead 1934: 150)

Children don't just acquire human skills and competencies in the context of relationships with their parents, siblings, peers and other caregivers. Most importantly, they learn who they are. The chapters in Part four examine some of the processes through which identity is constructed, with a particular emphasis on one of the most salient dimensions – gender.

Lloyd and Duveen (Chapter 13) summarize ingenious research illustrating how cultural markers such as a baby's dress are more significant than biological sex in determining how adults behave towards a 'boy' or a 'girl'. As gender differences emerge in, for example, children's styles of play, parents appear to systematically amplify their significance, in a transactional process similar to that discussed by Sameroff (Chapter 8). Observing children up to 4 years of age, Lloyd and Duveen offer evidence of gender-related aspects of the social world being gradually internalized, and represented in their speech and pretend play.

The chapter by Berman (Chapter 14) focuses on a particular dimension of gender, namely caregiving and responsiveness to babies. This work links back to themes developed earlier in this volume, especially by White and Woollett (Chapter 4), concerning the origins of gender differences in parenting. She observed 2- to 7-year-old children in an experimental situation where they were asked to look after a baby, and found that there was a striking gender difference linked to age, with older girls engaging in substantially more interaction with the baby than either older boys or younger children.

The general issue of children's relationships with other children (peers and siblings) has received relatively little research attention, with a few notable exceptions – for example, Dunn and Kendrick (1982). The single activity they are most likely to engage in is play, especially pretend play. In the final chapter of this volume (Chapter 15) Fein takes G. H. Mead's theoretical framework as the starting point for exploring young children's very considerable skill in perspective-taking, shifting effortlessly between roles, displaying sophisticated knowledge about the rules of social behaviour and expressing subtle and appropriate emotions, yet at all times working within a meta-framework of pretence, signalled by the exclamation 'We're only playing'. In play we can see some of the processes through which children construct a differentiated sense of self in social context.

REFERENCES

Dunn, J. and Kendrick, C. (1982) *Siblings: Love, Envy and Understanding*, Cambridge, Mass.: Harvard University Press.
Mead, G. H. (1934) *Mind, Self and Society*, Chicago: University of Chicago Press.

13 The reconstruction of social knowledge in the transition from sensorimotor to conceptual activity: the gender system

Barbara Lloyd and Gerard Duveen

Source: Gellatly, A. *et al.* (1989) *Cognition and Social Worlds*, Oxford: Oxford University Press, pp. 83–98.

INTRODUCTION

This presentation is, like Gaul, divided into three parts. First we consider the interpretations of experience and knowledge which shape the presentation of the main material. The principal province is an account of a series of studies over the past decade exploring the development of children's knowledge of gender. Finally we examine the contribution this material might make to the developmental study of social cognition.

We use our recent theoretical statement on social gender identity as a framework for presenting the empirical material (Duveen and Lloyd 1986). We have deliberately eschewed the more traditional search for sex differences and employed instead a semiotic approach, viewing gender as a system of signs. From this perspective the results of a number of studies are interrogated in order to demonstrate how young children gain access to this sign system in which the relationships between signifiers and signifieds are socially agreed and arbitrary.

The gender system is a particularly fruitful model to consider in the context of a discussion of cognition and social worlds. It is amenable to semiotic analysis for at least two reasons: first, all societies employ biological sex differences in an obligatory and ubiquitous semiotic system in which social representations of gender are the signified, and second, in all societies it is necessary for individuals to acquire social gender knowledge and to create for themselves a social gender identity.

The data which we present have been gathered in quasi-naturalistic settings; we brought mothers to our laboratory to play with unfamiliar infants, and we arranged that preschool friends play together in our observation room. We used these tactics, not only because we are trained in the quantitative and empirical traditions of academic psychology, but also because we believed that it would be difficult to collect sufficient naturalistic evidence to comment upon the relevant psychological issue in the acquisition of a social gender identity.

In this introductory section we will pose some psychological questions which have guided the collection and analysis of our data on gender understanding. The second and major section is an account of the development of social identities from birth until four years of age. This is not intended as a review of published studies; rather the evidence from other research will be invoked only when it makes a particularly salient point about an issue on which our own data are silent.

As developmental psychologists who focus on gender we have pre-empted an answer to the question Robert Siegler posed in the title of his book *Children's Thinking: What Develops?* We assert that what develops is a social gender identity. Infants are born with a biological sex which is used as a signifier in assigning them to a social gender category. This category is part of a partially arbitrary but consensually agreed gender system. This system resides in the members of a particular society as a shared set of beliefs about the nature, behaviour, and value of females and males. Individuals, both adults and older children, realize the gender system in their social gender identities when interacting with each other and in interaction with infants.

The developmental problem which this view poses is: how do infants enter into this system? Initially the social gender identities of infants are held by adults and older children; it is they who locate the infant within a social world and whose representations function as scaffolding or indices for infants seeking order in their social worlds. Eventually infants internalize their society's gender system.

The psychological questions we seek to address concern this process. As Piagetians we can describe this development as the emergence of the semiotic function, by which Piaget meant that children become capable of representing objects and events in their absence, and are able to use these representations to regulate their activity. Thus infants move from regulation in terms of the social gender identities of others and those which others ascribe to them to being able to invoke a social gender identity when interacting with others. In familiar Piagetian language this is described as the construction of representational knowledge from indexical or sensorimotor knowing.

Vygotskian psychology offers another framework within which to pose questions about the acquisition of gender understanding and a social gender identity. The world of the infant is, *par excellence*, an interpersonal one as Winnicott (1945) noted long ago. Thus the development of a social gender identity from birth to four years can be examined as an example of interiorization, semiotic relations moving from the interpersonal plane to the intrapersonal plane.

At its most general, the question is whether data collected about a particular aspect of social life can inform our understanding of the development of children's thinking.

THE DEVELOPMENT OF A SOCIAL GENDER IDENTITY

Birth

Birth is the starting point for an account of the development of social gender identities because it is the moment in which biological characteristics are invoked to assign the new individual to a gender category. Although legal definitions of paternity have changed, and it is no longer necessary to specify whether a child is born in wedlock, it is still mandatory, where births are registered, to declare whether an infant is male or female. The procedure is relatively straightforward: assignment is made on the basis of dimorphic, physical criteria. In rare instances, where the external genitalia are ambiguous, further investigations designed to assess genetic sex are undertaken through examination of cells taken from the lining of the mouth. Assignment may be relatively straightforward, but the consequences of this assignment are complex and enduring.

The physical characteristics of infants are crucial in assignment to a gender category, but it is the socially shared beliefs about the nature, behaviour, and value of males and females which guide interaction with the newborn. This gender system operates before birth and, it has been suggested, may influence parental decisions about abortion when the genetic sex of the fetus is known. There is no doubt that the social gender system is operative once the biological sex of the newborn is announced. The biological sex assigned to infants is interpreted by parents in terms of the gender system; it becomes a sign signifying gender characteristics.

Within hours of birth parents of first borns are reported to describe their daughters as significantly more beautiful, small, and cute while fathers describe their sons as firmer, larger featured, more alert, stronger, and better co-ordinated (Rubin *et al.* 1974). As the male and female infants in this study did not differ in birth weight, birth length, or Apgar scores, it is social gender identities functioning as ideal types which organize parents' perceptions of their first-born children.

In the first year

A further example of the use which adults make of their access to social gender identities is to be found in our cross-dressing studies undertaken with 6-month-old infants (Smith and Lloyd 1978; Smith, unpublished thesis 1982). In a series of studies we have systematically observed mothers playing for 10 minutes with one of our unfamiliar 6-month-old infants, two boys and two girls. The dress of each infant varied so that half the time they were presented as being assigned to the gender congruent with their biological sex, and half the time as the other gender. In these exchanges the mothers knew only the baby's gender differentiated name, i.e. Jane or John, and could observe that the infant was wearing either a ruffled dress and socks or a 'babygro'. They were unaware that there might be a discrepancy between gender and biological sex. The mothers' choice of an initial toy for the baby matched the baby's ascribed social gender identity. Regardless of the biological sex of the infant, when the infant was presented as a boy mothers were likely to offer the hammer or rattle, but when the same infant was presented as a girl the doll was the favourite toy to be offered first. Across the 10-minute observation period the clear gender-based toy choice of mothers was moderated by infants' interest and, as this interest was not yet differentiated, gender did not influence significantly the length of time the gender marked toys were used.

Other aspects of the behaviour of mothers were also influenced by the ascribed social gender identity of the infants. Although there were no measured differences in the motoric behaviour of the two girl and two boy babies who participated in the study, mothers' responses to the babies varied in terms of the presentational social gender identity of the baby. When named and dressed as boys mothers offered all infants more verbal encouragement to gross motor activity. In addition, when the babies were presented as boys rather than as girls mothers responded to their gross motor activity with further stimulation. With a baby dressed as a girl this behaviour often led to efforts to soothe and calm the infant. At six months, therefore, infants experience gender-specific play outcomes; although they have no direct access to the sign system which regulates gender, their participation in pleasurable play routines is regulated by adult choices made on the basis of the infant's ascribed social gender identity.

The beginning of the second year

In the second year infants begin to manifest their social gender identities through preferences for different play routines. In a well-known study, Golberg and Lewis (1969) observed 13-month-olds playing for 15 minutes in a room with their mothers and reported gender differences in time spent playing with toys and in related behaviour. Girls spent significantly more time playing with blocks, a peg board, and two toys with faces, a cat and a dog. Girls were observed spending significantly more time sitting and combining toys and boys more time being active and banging. Goldberg and Lewis asserted that girls chose toys which involved more fine motor than gross motor co-ordination. Although mothers were instructed to watch their children's play and to respond to it in any way they desired, mothers' feedback to girls and boys was not compared. These results are interpreted as evidence of gender differentiation originating with the infant. The toys afford different possibilities for activity, and it is the infant's preference for particular play routines or activity which result in differential amounts of time spent playing with the various toys.

In two partial replications in our laboratory Caroline Smith (unpublished thesis 1982) observed 13-month-olds playing for 10 minutes with a similar array of toys. In her first study the mallet was the only toy which provided evidence of statistically significant gender-differentiated use, and in the second no single toy was used differentially.

Smith also measured gross motor play and fine motor-manipulative play with toys. Gross motor play, including bang, shake, throw, and push, occurred more than five times as much as manipulative, which included fit, place, and handle. Quantitatively boys engaged in more of the former and girls in more of the latter, but in the first study only the gender difference in gross motor play was statistically significant. The view that toys afford different possibilities for play is supported by Smith's observation that differences in duration of play with particular toys are confounded with the differences in styles of play. She observed that boys spent a significantly greater proportion of the time they were in contact with the mallet banging it.

Smith added a condition in her second study; after the initial 10-minute period mothers were asked to play actively with their 13-month-olds for a further 10 minutes. Although only one significant gender difference in toy use was reported in either condition, there were clearer differences in types of activity. Again boys engaged in significantly more gross motor play and girls in significantly more fine motor manipulative play with toys. But the participation of mothers had a highly significant and gender-specific effect on styles of play. The gross motor play of boys (but not of girls) increased significantly when mothers engaged actively in play. Though the manipulative play of girls (but not of boys) increased in frequency, the effect failed to reach conventional levels of significance ($P < 0.09$). It appears that the 13-month-old's mother amplifies the child's developing social gender identity.

In order to understand the nature of mother–child interaction Smith also examined children's first action after their mothers brought a toy to their attention. Children's social gender identity did not predict whether they would make a response nor whether they would hold the toy to themselves. However, boys were significantly more likely to use the toy in some gross motor activity such as banging or hitting, and there was a trend in the direction of girls using the toy to engage in manipulative activity.

In interaction with their mothers, the behaviour of 13-month-olds is regulated in terms of their social gender identity. The mechanisms which govern this gender regulation are unclear. Somewhat surprisingly, in view of the work with 6-month-olds, Smith found no difference in the frequency with which mothers of boys and mothers of girls joined in their children's gross motor play.

In discussing development in the first year, we suggest that mothers may contribute to the development of gender-differentiated patterns of sensorimotor activity through their active influence on infants' practical activity, by their encouragement of and reward for gender-appropriate toy choice and play style. If this hypothesis is well grounded, it may be that by 13 months this gender regulation is already a well-established feature of children's practical activity, with the consequence that active influence by the mother is no longer necessary. Over a shorter time span, six to nine months, Vandell and Wilson (1987) showed that infants who engaged in proportionally longer turn-taking sequences with their mothers at six months engaged in proportionally longer sequences with a sibling at nine months. Interaction with mother may encourage the development of sensorimotor routines just as it facilitates the development of social interaction skills and language (Bruner 1975).

Developmental changes from the second year through the fourth year

From around the beginning of the second year, infants begin to manifest a social gender identity in their styles of play and related choice of objects for motoric activity (see pp. 285–6). The second year is a time of major changes, and these have important implications for the expression of a social gender identity. Increasing mobility and the use of language in communication provide new media for the expression of social gender identities. Money and Ehrhardt (1972) have suggested, on the basis of their evidence showing that sex reassignments undertaken between 18 months and 3 or 4 years are unlikely to have successful outcomes, that a gender identity is already formed by the time children begin to speak. Where, formerly, it was adults and older children who exercised regulation of infants' activities in terms of gender, these new competencies may facilitate the child's internalization of gender regulation. The process of this internalization can be traced through the development of children's social interactions with their peers and their play with toys.

To illustrate some of these changes we present data from two studies which included children from 18 months to 4 years (Duveen and Lloyd 1988; Lloyd 1987; Lloyd and Smith 1985; Lloyd *et al.* 1988). All the children in the samples walked confidently and had begun to speak.

Language and social gender identities

Alongside locomotor changes in the second year there are major sensorimotor and cognitive/linguistic developments. Modern studies of language acquisition based upon the speech corpora of a very few children (e.g. Brown 1973) have not focused on gender, but the superior linguistic development of girls in the preschool years is a widely accepted generalization in the field of sex differences (Maccoby and Jacklin 1975; Coates 1986). Results may not always yield statistically significant effects but the direction of findings consistently favours girls. More interesting from the perspective of the infant's construction of a social gender identity is Lieberman's (1967) report that even before the appearance of speech infants adapt the pitch of their voices to the pitch of the person they are addressing; the pitch used with fathers is lower than that addressed to mothers. Although Lieberman's results are limited, they suggest that in the first year infants are already becoming sensitive to features which mark the gender of the person with whom they interact.

Our own linguistic recognition and production data from 18 months onwards suggest that this knowledge of gender quickly finds other means of expression as children gain access to the linguistic code. When children of 18 to 23 months were shown photographs of a man and a woman *or* a girl and a boy they could select the pictures which corresponded to the gender-marked nouns *man*, *lady*, *daddy*, *mummy*, *boy*, and *girl*, 60 per cent of the time. In the 3- to 4-year-old groups recognition was virtually perfect, 99 per cent. These same children found the matching of photographs to the pronouns *she*, *he*, *her*, and *him* much more difficult; the youngest children responded infrequently and then were rarely correct although the oldest children were correct 95 per cent of the time.

Children's ability to produce the same terms was also tested in the context of a recognition task. Once the child selected the photograph which matched the given noun the child was then asked to name the other picture. The children's replies were scored along four dimensions – gender, age, part of speech, and precise complement. Thus, after choosing the picture which matched the term *lady*, a child was expected to supply the word, *man*. The scoring procedure was such that the word *daddy* would not be scored as totally correct. The increasingly adequate performance across the age range is scarcely surprising. In part this can be explained by the very strict criteria of the task and the failure of many of the youngest children to respond at all. More interesting to consider is the finding that when errors did occur, gender confusion accounted for only 2.4 per cent and age confusion 3.5 per cent. Even the youngest children were able to categorize according to social dimensions of gender and age; it is the other dimensions of the linguistic code, part of speech and particular complement, which they found more difficult.

Play and social gender identity

Observing gender-marked play

The same children whose linguistic development was reported in the previous section were observed and video-recorded while playing for six minutes with mothers and familiar peers in a room which contained a variety of gender-marked toys. Parents of local primary school children rated an array of toys described in published reports as appropriate objects for girls and boys. The female-marked toys selected on the basis of the parental ratings were irons and ironing boards, comb, brush, and mirror sets, large white hats, shopping bags, saucepans and stove top, and baby dolls and cradle. The male-marked toys were a sit-and-ride fire engine, construction trucks, firemen's hats, briefcases, pegbenches with hammers, and guns. Crayons and paper were also available but they were not reported to be or rated as gender-marked. The toys were matched intuitively for possibilities of use in active play, and duplicates were provided to reduce quarrels.

In the first study, analysis was based upon data from 60 pairs of children accustomed to playing together. They were blocked in four age groups: up to 2 years, 2½ years, 3 years, and 3½ years, and each age cohort was divided into five girl/girl pairs, five boy/boy pairs and five girl/boy pairs. In a replication and extension study 120 children of 3 to 4 years were recruited from the same community. These children, selected in triads, were also accustomed to playing together. All children were observed playing with their mothers, and one child, designated the target child, was also observed playing with a girl and a boy. Children were blocked for age; the replication group included children up to 3½ years old, the extension group children up to 4 years. In each group there were 10 target girls and 10 target boys.

Duration of toy use in action play

The duration of play with each toy was coded directly from the video record using a computer-assisted, video-linked keyboard which functioned as a multi-channel event recorder (Smith *et al.* 1982). Total time spent in action play was coded for each child in each of the 60 pairs in the first study. In the second study only the action play of target children was coded.

The analysis of duration of toy use in the first study is based upon pair data, i.e. the separately coded scores for each child in a pair were combined and used as a dependent variable in a three-way analysis of variance with four age groups, three pair types, and toys summed to yield totals for female and male toys. The main effects were not significant, although an overall preference for male toys almost achieved significance, $P = 0.053$ ($F = 3.95$; df 1, 48). The data (mean for play with male toys, 336.6 seconds and for female toys, 261.3 seconds) just fail to support the assertion that all the children spend more time playing with male toys.

There was a significant Pair type × Toy type interaction ($F = 13.09$; df 2, 48; $P < 0.001$), but the only paired comparisons of means which achieved significance indicate that boy/boy pairs used male toys more than female toys and that boy/boy pairs used male toys more than

Table 13.1 Duration of toy use in action play by pair type (in seconds)

Pair type	Female toys	Male toys
Girl/girl		
Mean	380.1	214.0
S.D.	152.5	130.1
Boy/boy		
Mean	155.2	463.6
S.D.	180.6	276.0
Girl/boy		
Mean	248.7	332.1
S.D.	130.9	175.3

girl/girl pairs. None of the comparisons relating to female toys reached significance (Table 13.1). These results show that when playing with a boy, boys assert a social gender identity through their greater use of male toys; girls playing together, however, do not show a preference for female-marked toys.

The three-way interaction including age was also significant ($F = 3.33$; df 6,48; $P < 0.01$). Comparisons of all pairs were assessed using Scheffe tests, but none of these were statistically significant. However, in the groups of children approaching 3 and 3½ years of age, the results were consistent with those already reported. In the two oldest groups boy/boy pairs tended to play more with male toys than with female toys and boy/boy pairs tended to play more with male toys than did girl/girl pairs. Boys' assertion of a differentiated social gender identity through toy use in play with other boys is a developmental phenomenon appearing in the two oldest groups of boy/boy pairs.

In the second study only the action play of target children was coded. Thus the analysis of duration of toy use appears in a different form. The results reported here are for play with first partner only, as these are directly comparable to the first study. The analysis of variance has four factors with two values on each: target child's gender, gender of partner, toy type, and age group. Both target child's gender and toy type were significant, indicating that boys spend more time in action play and that children in general play more with male toys (Table 13.2).

The gender of target child by toy type interaction was highly significant, and when the six possible pair comparisons were analysed

Table 13.2 Duration of toy use in action play by gender (in seconds)

Gender	Female toys	Male toys	Combined mean
Girls			
Mean	210.1	281.7	245.9
S.D.	144.1	180.9	
Boys			
Mean	46.5	534.7	290.6
S.D.	32.6	139.8	
Combined mean	128.3	408.2	

using the Scheffe test the only one which failed to achieve significance
was the comparison of girls' use of female toys and male toys. In other
words, boys assert a social gender identity by using male toys more
than female toys, using female toys less than girls do and by using male
toys more than girls do. There is a more limited differentiation of
female and male toys in the gender identity asserted by girls in action
play; girls use male toys less than boys do and female toys more than
boys do, but their use of female and male toys is not significantly
differentiated. Overall, girls do not differentiate their play with toys
according to gender markings, while boys show a strong tendency to
play with male-marked toys and to avoid female-marked toys.

Paradigmatic and syntagmatic toy choices

Analyses of duration of toy use in action play demonstrated that girls
and boys assert different social gender identities through the use of
toys in action play. Duration is a crude measure in the sense that the
hold toy code functions so that once children sit down on a sit-and-
ride or place a hat on their heads the count begins and only ceases
when the activity stops. A more sensitive measure was constructed in
order to assess the element of choice in toy use. For this analysis every
time a child made a toy choice it was classified as either paradigmatic
or syntagmatic. (A similar distinction was introduced by Catherine
Garvey [1977] in her analysis of the elements of ritual play in young
children.) The selection of toy marked for the child's own gender
constituted a paradigmatic choice, while selecting a toy marked for the

Table 13.3 Type of toy choice by gender

Gender	Paradigmatic choices	Syntagmatic choices	Combined mean
Girls			
Mean	8.5	8.8	8.7
S.D.	3.3	4.6	
Boys			
Mean	10.6	3.3	7.0
S.D.	3.5	1.9	
Combined mean	9.6	6.0	

Table 13.4 Boys' types of toy choices with each partner

Partner	Paradigmatic choices	Syntagmatic choices	Scheffe test
Mother			
Mean	10.2	3.2	$P < 0.01$
S.D.	4.3	3.1	
Girls			
Mean	10.5	4.7	$P < 0.01$
S.D.	4.0	3.8	
Boys			
Mean	11.2	1.9	$P < 0.01$
S.D.	5.0	1.8	

opposite gender constituted a syntagmatic choice. Thus for a girl, choosing a female-marked toy was paradigmatic and a male-marked toy syntagmatic, while for a boy a paradigmatic choice was a male-marked toy, and a syntagmatic choice a female-marked toy.

The toy choices of the 3- to 4-year-old children from the second study were analysed using these categories. The number of paradigmatic and syntagmatic choices made by the target child in each recorded session (with mother, with a girl peer, and with a boy peer) was used as a dependent variable in an analysis of variance with four factors: age, target child's gender, choice type, and partner, with repeated measures on the last two factors. The results showed that, overall, girls made more toy choices than boys (mean for girls 8.7; mean for boys 6.9; $F = 5.6$; df = 1,36; $0.05 > P > 0.01$), and that paradigmatic choices (mean = 9.6) were more frequent than syntagmatic choices (mean = 6.0; $F = 18.5$; df = 1,36; $P < 0.001$). A Gender by Toy Choice interaction ($F = 22.0$; df = 1,36; $P < 0.001$) showed that while girls made roughly equal numbers of paradigmatic and syntagmatic choices, boys made many more paradigmatic than syntagmatic choices (Table 13.3).

Further analyses by Scheffe test of all the possible pair comparisons among these means showed that the only significant ($P < 0.01$) difference occured between boys' scores for the two types of choices. The consistency of this response is shown by the detailed analysis of the significant three-way interaction Gender × Toy × Choice × Partner (Table 13.4; $F = 3.99$; df = 2,72; $0.05 > P > 0.01$).

Although boys' syntagmatic choices were highest when playing with girls and lowest when playing with boys this comparison was not significant. None of the complementary comparisons for girls were significant. Indeed, there were no significant variations as a function of partner for girls' or boys' use of either choice type. Comparisons between girls' and boys' use of paradigmatic choices also showed no differences as a function of partner. However, comparison of girls' with boys' scores did show one further significant difference in their use of syntagmatic choices. Girls (mean = 9.7) produced significantly more syntagmatic choices when playing with a boy than did boys (mean = 1.9; $P < 0.01$ for the Scheffe test). Girls do not discriminate between type of choice in any context, whereas boys always showed a marked preference for paradigmatic over syntagmatic choices in every context. Boys are likely to assert a differentiated social gender identity through their choice of gender-appropriate toys whether playing with another boy, a girl, or their mothers. Girls, however, do not assert a differentiated social gender identity in play either with girls or boys. Syntagmatic choice by girls cannot be ascribed to any lack of awareness of the stereotypical value of toys since they sorted photographs of the toys for gender more successfully than boys did (Lloyd 1987). Although toy use and toy choice are significant media through which boys express a differentiated social identity, they do not have the same significance for girls.

Pretend play

Pretend play was coded separately from action play using written transcriptions made from the video record of each child's speech and

Table 13.5 Units of pretend play by toy type

	Female toys	Male toys
Girls		
Mean	5.9	4.5
S.D.	6.8	4.0
Boys		
Mean	2.4	6.0
S.D.	3.0	5.4

action. A unit of pretend play was identified when children showed clearly that they were fantasizing by introducing elements that were not inherent in the toy as object, e.g. saying 'This is my baby' while hugging the doll. The child's speech identifies the unit as pretend play and places it in Nicolich's (1977) symbolic stage.

Pretend play was more common in the replication and extension groups and could be analysed using parametric statistics. In a four-way analysis of variance with the number of units of pretend play as the dependent variable there were two values on each of the factors: target child's gender, partner's gender, age group, and type of toy. Only two terms were significant at a level between $P = 0.05$ and $P = 0.01$; they were the interaction of age and gender of target child, and toy type and gender of target child (Table 13.5).

Pair comparisons failed to achieve significance in either of the Scheffe test analyses. The only comparisons to approach significance were the comparisons of girls' and boys' use of female toys and boys' use of female and male toys. In action play duration and toy choice boys displayed a social gender identity through the choice of male toys. In pretend play it appeared only as a trend. Although weaker, the pattern in these pretend play data repeats that found in duration and toy choice measures in action play. Boys use male toys more than female toys; they also use female toys less than do girls. On none of these measures have we observed any differences in girls' use of female and male toys.

Scripted play

In the previous section children's pretend play creations were examined in a simple quantitative manner. Each unit was also analysed in detail for evidence of children's discursive skills and the incorporation of social representations of gender into pretend play. To assess their grammatical competence, mean length of utterance (MLU) was computed for the 30 oldest children in the first study and for all target children in the second (cf. Brown 1973). In addition, the dialogic characteristics of pretend speech were analysed followed Nelson's work (Nelson and Seidman 1984); discontinous, continuous, and scripted discourse were identified. Analysis of the content of scripts allowed the assessment of gender knowledge.

Analysis of MLU in the first study yielded an expected result in that the MLU of the 15 oldest girls was significantly longer ($P < 0.05$) than that of the 15 oldest boys on a one-tailed t test. In the analysis based on the speech of target children in the second study there were no effects due to the child's own gender, though both girls and boys had longer MLUs when speaking with a girl than when speaking with a boy. It thus appears that the social gender identities of these older children take account of the gender marking of their partners. There is here an echo, at the level of representation, of the difference noted by Lieberman at the level of action.

The three discourse measures – discontinuous, continuous, and scripted dialogue – were each correlated significantly with MLU suggesting their inter-related nature as measures of linguistic development. However, scripts were still relatively rare in the fourth year. Only 14 of the 40 target children produced at least one script while playing with a girl and only 12 while playing with a boy. Although the gender marking of their partner was not related simply to the target children's script production, there is a different relationship between MLU and script production in the two gender contexts (Table 13.6). The MLUs of the 14 children who produced a script when playing with a girl were, on average, half a morpheme longer than those of the 26 who failed to produce a script, though this difference was not statistically significant. When playing with boys, however, the 28 children who failed to produce a script had a significantly lower MLU than the 12 children who produced at least one script ($t = 2.67$; df = 38; $P < 0.05$), the difference amounting to approximately one morpheme. Once again the gender context of play influences the expression of social gender identities.

Structural and content analyses were also undertaken on the scripts produced in the two gender contexts. When the structures of the scripts produced by children in the oldest group in the first study and the two groups of the second study are compared, it can be seen that differentiation between actors, roles, locations, properties, and goals

Table 13.6 Averaged mean lengths of utterance (MLU)

Children	With girls	With boys
Producing scripts	5.6 ($n = 14$)	5.5 ($n = 12$)
Not producing scripts	5.0 ($n = 26$)	4.6 ($n = 28$)

only becomes clear in the oldest group. This differentiation allows the coding of content as masculine and feminine. In the content analysis of the scripts of younger children between 70 and 85 per cent could not be marked for gender. This proportion falls to 40 per cent in the scripts of the 20 target children approaching 4 years of age. The gender marking of their scripts was skewed with 19 involving feminine role enactment and only three of them masculine roles.

The content analysis of scripts showed that over half of those produced by the older group of children (those approaching 4 years) were concerned with traditionally feminine roles, while very few related to traditionally masculine roles. Many of the scripts were located in domestic settings (ironing, cooking, shopping, etc.) which usually featured women. This difference suggests that feminine roles are more accessible to young children for re-creation in scripted pretend play. There was a sense in which feminine scripts were children's reconstructions of their own experience and observation of family life. When men were represented in scripts they figured in roles which were available to the children through the media of public representations (television, books, etc.) rather than through participant observation. Thus while children were able to give quite intricate performances of domestic routines, their enactments of occupational roles were impoverished.

GENDER AND DEVELOPMENTAL SOCIAL COGNITION

This review of data provides evidence for two complementary systems through which knowledge of the gender system is expressed – the linguistic and the ludic systems.

At birth, new parents employ gender-marked descriptions in speaking about their infants. By 6 months mothers address different instructions to infants according to their social gender identities. In the second half of the first year, the sounds infants make are modulated to suit the pitch of the parents' voices. Two-year-old children begin to use the formal linguistic system to express their understanding of gender categorization. Children approaching 4 years use language to re-create the routines of social life in scripted play.

The ludic or play system also begins with parental regulation. At 6 months, toy choice is regulated by mothers' gender marking, but duration measures reflect the absence of any gender marking by infants. At 13 months, infants express different social gender identities in their styles of play, and these differences are amplified in play with mothers. Our presentation of the 18-month to 4-year-old play data was deliberately structured in terms of an increasing developmental and conceptual complexity. Between 18 months and 4 years, duration measures express different social gender identities of girls and boys, with more differentiated gender marking by boys in duration, toy choice in action play, and in pretend play.

Pretend play only becomes frequent in the oldest groups when children employ the linguistic system to introduce new elements in their interaction with toys. At this point feminine concerns become salient and domestic: traditionally female routines are enacted by both girls and boys.

Our account of children's internalization of the gender system in their first four years can be encompassed by either a Vygotskian or a Piagetian account. There is evidence of gender regulation moving from the interpersonal to the intra-personal plane, but the evidence can also be marshalled to demonstrate the reconstruction of sensorimotor knowing into representational understanding. All of our results are based upon cross-sectional group comparisons. These data do not address the possibility of conflict between these two perspectives. To do so we require a more detailed appreciation of the processes of internalization. Perhaps the time has come for students of social cognition to follow their colleagues in child language in undertaking detailed longitudinal studies of individual children. Piaget's three books on infancy are testimony to the fruitfulness of this approach for wider developmental issues.

REFERENCES

Brown, R. (1973) *A First Language: The Early Stages*, Cambridge, Harvard University Press.

Bruner, J. S. (1975) 'From communication to language – a psychological perspective', *Cognition* 3: 255–87.

Coates, J. (1986) *Women, Men and Language*, London: Longman.

Duveen, G. and Lloyd, B. (1986) 'The significance of social identities', *British Journal of Social Psychology* 25: 219–30.

Duveen, G. and Lloyd, B. (1988) 'Gender as an influence on the development of scripted pretend play', *British Journal of Developmental Psychology* 6: 89–95.

Garvey, C. (1977) *Play*, London: Fontana.

Goldberg, S. and Lewis, M. (1969) 'Play behavior in the year-old infant: early sex differences', *Child Development* 40: 21–31.

Lieberman, P. (1967) *Intonation, Perception and Language*, Cambridge Mass.: MIT Press.

Lloyd, B. (1987) 'Social representation of gender', in J. Bruner and H. Haste (eds) *Making Sense: The Child's Construction of the World*, London: Methuen.

Lloyd, B. and Smith, C. (1985) 'The social representation of gender and young children's play', *British Journal of Developmental Psychology* 3: 65–73.

Lloyd, B., Duveen, G. and Smith, C. (1988) 'Social representations of gender and young children's play: a replication', *British Journal of Developmental Psychology* 6: 83–8.

Maccoby, E. E. and Jacklin, C. N. (1974) *The Psychology of Sex Differences*, Stanford, C.A.: Stanford University Press.

Money, J. and Ehrhardt, A. A. (1972) *Man and Womann, Boy and Girl*, Baltimore: Johns Hopkins University Press.

Nelson, K. and Seidman, S. (1984) 'Playing with scripts', in I. Bretherton (ed.) *Representing the Symbolic World in Play: Reality and Fantasy*, New York: Academic Press.

Nicolich, L. M. (1977) 'Beyond sensorimotor intelligence: assessment of symbolic maturity through analysis of pretend play', *Merrill-Palmer Quarterly* 23: 89–99.

Rheingold, H. and Cook, K. (1975) 'The contents of boys' and girls' rooms as an index of parents' behavior', *Child Development* 46: 459–63.

Rubin, J. Z., Provenzano, F. J. and Luria, Z. (1974) 'The eye of the beholder: parents' views on the sex of new borns', *American Journal of Orthopsychiatry* 44: 512–19.

Siegler, R. (ed.) (1978) *Children's Thinking: What Develops?*, Hillsdale, N.J.: Erlbaum.

Smith, C. (1982) 'Mothers' attitudes and behaviour with babies and the development of sex-typed play', unpublished D.Phil.thesis, University of Sussex.

Smith, C. and Lloyd, B. B. (1978) 'Maternal behavior and perceived sex of infant: revisited', *Child Development* 49: 1263–5.

Smith, C., Lloyd, B. and Crook, C. (1982) 'Instrumentation and software report: computer-assisted coding of videotape material', *Current Psychological Reports* 2: 289–92.

Vandell, D. L. and Wilson, K. S. (1987), 'Infants' interactions with mother, sibling and peer; contrasts and relations between interaction systems', *Child Development* 58: 176–86.

Winnicott, D. W. (1945/1958) 'Primitive emotional development', in *Through Paediatrics to Psycho-Analysis*, London: Hogarth Press.

14 Children caring for babies: age and sex differences in response to infant signals and to the social context

Phyllis W. Berman

Source: Eisenberg, N. (ed.) (1987) *Contemporary Topics in Developmental Psychology*, New York: Wiley.

This chapter focuses on the developmental roots of caregiving and the origins of the familiar differences between men and women in the quality and quantity of their interactions with babies and young children. Considering what is known about the early development of behaviors in other domains, it is surprising that so little is known about the early antecedents of adults' responsiveness and caregiving to the young. Fortunately, during the last 10 years the topic has enjoyed new attention from researchers.

It is obvious that there are practical reasons for scientific knowledge about the existing sex differences in responsiveness to children. There are additional factors that give impetus to this field of inquiry. In our society child care is typically considered a feminine task, and the development of child-rearing behaviors seems to be a prototypic aspect of gender role development. Furthermore, it is evident that biological, social, and experiential variables all contribute in an important way to these behaviors. Biological and environmental theories are relevant, and our increasing knowledge of the functioning and interaction of these variables should enrich both types of theories.

The research program described in this chapter addresses several questions: Are the sex differences in adults' assumption of responsibility for caregiving to be found during childhood, and if so, at what age do these differences arise? Are some features of infant stimuli – for example, physical appearance or cries – compelling for very young children, and are they so for both males and females? What do young children learn during the many years before parenthood that may be relevant to the demands of future parenting? Finally, how do sex differences arise in children's orientation toward and styles of interactions with younger children, toddlers, and infants?

It is particularly interesting to study the development of these sex differences in our children because children in our culture [USA] have so little responsibility for the care of younger siblings. There have been many societies in which young children played a major role in the care of infants and toddlers (Weisner and Gallimore 1977; Whiting and Whiting 1975). These children were usually assigned responsibility for caregiving very early, often as early as age 5 or before. Boys served as caregivers as well as girls, particularly when girls were unavailable. Clearly, young children are capable of many behaviors that are necessary to care for younger children and infants, but in modern America they are rarely asked to assume responsibility for this task. Several questions arise concerning the many children who have such minimal responsibility, and often, in fact, very little contact with younger children and babies.

The research has been guided by several assumptions. First, young children do learn patterns of interactions with babies, even when caregiving responsibilities are nonexistent. When children are given an opportunity to interact with babies, the nature of these interactions should vary with children's age as a result of this learning as well as cognitive maturation. It is also assumed that sex differences in responses to babies are embedded in larger, more general social role differences between men and women. Sex differences in responses to babies should, therefore, not be found among very young children, but they should arise with age as children learn the gender roles common to our culture.

Moreover, sex differences do not seem to be equally salient to all types of adult involvement with children. For example, a common finding is that fathers spend a greater proportion of their time in play with their babies than mothers do (cf. Parke 1981). Sex differences emerge predominantly in responsibility for child care, degree of investment of time and energy, and style of interactions with children (Berman 1980). It is also assumed that sex differences in children's behavior with babies should be differentially manifest in various contexts.

A helpful way to conceptualize children's interactions is that they develop 'scripts' that guide their responses to babies. These scripts should be well differentiated for specific social situations, and the likelihood that a specific script will be used should vary from one situation to another. In this chapter illustrative data are presented on children's responses to babies in several situations, and the utility of two conceptual approaches is explored. One highlights the role of infant stimuli, and the other emphasizes the role of children's understanding of the social situation and the formation of social scripts. It is proposed that these two approaches are not mutually exclusive, but that both are necessary to learn more about the variables that determine the development of children's interactions with infants. Questions will be raised about when each approach is most appropriate and useful.

THEORETICAL APPROACHES TO THE DEVELOPMENT OF RESPONSIVENESS TO BABIES

Our lack of knowledge about the early antecedents of adults' responsiveness to the young is partly due to the fact that over many years human caregiving interactions with the young have been widely considered to be 'natural'. By the same token, sex differences in these behaviors have also been considered 'natural' (Shields 1975, 1984). Researchers are affected no less than lay-people by a heritage from folklore and early philosophers. Parents' interactions with babies simply appear 'natural' to most of us.

During prescientific times the prevailing view of the development of caregiving was that these behaviors appear in full-blown form with little or no input from learning and experience (Shields 1975, 1984). Although human parent–infant interactions later became a popular research topic, several factors in the evolution of the psychology of parenting may have operated so that comparatively little attention was paid to the developmental aspects of learning caregiving or to the impact of social contexts, except when cross-cultural settings or abnormal clinical conditions were studied.

In 1943 Lorenz formulated the first well-articulated theory of human caregiving, attributing attraction to babies to an innate mechanism. According to the theory, a unique emotional response and motor response (i.e., pressing the baby against the heart) are released by the sight of the distinctive physical characteristics that are typical of infants. These characteristics include a head that is large in proportion to body size; a forehead large in proportion to facial size; large eyes; short, heavy, large-footed limbs; round, protruding cheeks; and soft, elastic skin. Lorenz was not explicit about possible age or sex differences in the response to these physical characteristics. However, he described his own daughters' responses when they were less than 2 years old and compared their responses to dolls, and in one case a soft round ball of woolen thread, to mature women's responses to babies. Thus in Lorenz's formulation adultlike responsiveness to the young also appears in very young children in a manner that is independent of experience and learning.

Historically the roots of ethological theory have been in animal research. This work has moved far beyond simple concepts of fixed action patterns. At its best, animal research in the ethological tradition is designed so that an organism's behavior can be studied as a product of biological biases, individual developmental history, and the demands and potential of the immediate situation. Experimental animal studies have shown major effects on parental behavior of systematically rearranged elements of the immediate situation interacting with hormones (cf. Lehrman 1961). It is quite possible to conduct comparable research with humans, studying the effects of small, ethically permissible but socially meaningful manipulations of the social context in which child care is given. Unfortunately, there have been few systematic research efforts of this sort. Similarly, Harlow's well-known work (cf. Arling and Harlow 1967) showing the effects of rhesus monkeys' early experience on later maternal behavior to offspring is believed to be relevant to human parenting behavior. Yet except for information gleaned from clinical and anthropological studies, little is known about the contributions of humans' early experiences to the development of adult caregiving behaviors.

Ethological theory has made major contributions to the study of caregiving. However, it has tended to concentrate on the role of infant signals and the adequacy of the adult's response to ensure survival. The starting point for such research has very often been to ask what needs of the offspring caregiver behaviors serve, what infant signals the caregiver responds to, and what the functions of the infant's signals and the caregiver's behavior are. There have been many productive investigations into adults' responses to infant stimuli such as cries, vocalizations, looks and smiles, and also physical features. Despite the considerable advances resulting from this research, ethological work needs to be complemented by research on the contribution of the caregiver's history and the social situation to the caregiver's responsiveness to the baby.

Social learning theory, particularly in its extension to gender role learning theory, approaches the development of caregiving behavior in ways that contrast rather sharply with prescientific notions about the 'natural' bases for caregiving. In contrast with ethological theorists, social learning theorists put less emphasis on the role of infant characteristics and signals in determining the nature of caregiving behaviors. Instead, reinforcement, cognitive approaches, and modeling have all been used to explain not only the course of acquisition of caregiving responses for males and females, but also the existence of sex, age, and stage of life differences in style and sheer amount of caregiving behavior (see, e.g., Berman 1980; Berman and Goodman 1984; Feldman and Nash 1978, 1979a, 1979b; Feldman, Nash and Cutrona 1977; Melson and Fogel 1982; Whiting 1983).

The most intriguing questions concern how we learn what behaviors are appropriate when; that is, for whom to perform, and in which situations. Since males and females are expected eventually to assume different caregiving roles, young boys and girls may very well be learning to make find discriminations about socially 'appropriate'. responses to a variety of somewhat different situations involving babies. These situations are at times distinctive in only very subtle ways (cf. Berman 1986; Weinstock 1979). That is, some of the most interesting but also most difficult questions are those that involve social discriminations, and those that involve performance rather than competence.

EARLY DEVELOPMENT OF CAREGIVING SCRIPTS

How then can we best conceptualize the operation of the many variables that determine the nature of human beings' interactions with their young? It is obvious that the physical and behavioral features of babies are important stimuli that may elicit caretaking responses from children and adults, although they do not do so reliably. The contributions of social and experiential variables are more difficult to understand. Elsewhere, the concept of *social scripting* has been used (Berman 1980) to characterize children's and adults' acquisition and performance of behaviors in the caregiving role. This term is not used to refer to prescriptions for overlearned rotely performed mundane behaviors. Rather, scripts for caregiving activities denote socially learned guides for highly motivated behaviors directed towards the young. These behaviors are often accompanied by emotional overtones that contribute to a sense of spontaneity, adding to the impression that the overt behaviors are 'natural', that is, unlearned.

In the sphere of sexual behavior, William Simon and John Gagnon (Gagnon 1973; Gagnon and Simon 1973; Simon and Gagnon 1969) have used the term *scripting* to refer to social processes by which meanings are assigned to body sensations and by means of which loosely organized plans, fantasies, and cognitions give direction to interpersonal events. The concept seems equally appropriate when applied to social processes that give meaning and direction to human beings' interactions with the young. Caregiving and playful interactions with babies and young children are similar to sexual interactions in that both types of interactions often seem to be spontaneous and biologically programmed.

Sex differences in caregiving, as well as sex differences in sexual behavior, may appear to be attributable to anatomical and hormonal differences between males and females. Nonetheless, men and women come to parental caregiving, as they come to sexuality, with vastly differing social and experiential histories. Even naive adults with very little experience with children have had a history of learning the elements of culturally approved scenarios that include relationships with babies and young children. This is particularly true of females. That is, although many children in our society have relatively little direct experience with babies, there is a well-defined ideology concerning mothers' roles and behaviors with children. In contrast, there is considerable ambiguity at this time about fathers' roles with children. Children's experiences with their own parents as well as cognitions gleaned from other social models and the media may all contribute to a sense of what adult males and females can and should do in various situations.

It is likely that parenting or caregiving scripts are assembled in a gradual but discontinuous manner throughout childhood, and it is reasonable to believe that early scripts may be precursors of and contributors to scripts generated in adulthood. Childhood scripts can function as flexible guidelines for behaviors with babies. Moreover, they depend not only upon child variables (such as age, sex, and experience) and infant variables (such as temperament, appearance, and behavior), but also on the child's understanding and perception of the social situation. Observations of children's interactions with toddlers and babies in varied semi-structured situations offer valuable evidence about the functioning of these variables.

In this chapter three early studies are described. In the first two, which will be described briefly, the effects of children's age and sex were studied in various social situations in which children were about to interact with babies. A third study that involved many babies is described in greater detail, and attention is given to the role of infant stimuli, as well as the social situation and the older children's age and sex. Taken together these studies serve to illustrate the complex interactions to be expected between all of these variables. Children's behaviors may be predicted from our understanding of both gender role development and the effects of infant characteristics and signals.

TWO EARLY OBSERVATIONAL STUDIES

Our theoretical position leads to several testable predictions: children of both sexes should be attracted to babies and should respond to infant signals. The extent and quality of such responses should depend, in large part, on the age and sex of the children and the demand qualities of the social situation, as well as the babies' behavior. Because children acquire caregiving scripts gradually, and in accord with their growing awareness of socially acceptable gender roles, we would expect little difference between very young boys' and girls' interactions with toddlers and babies. In contrast, sex differences should be found among older children. Older girls should have the highest and older boys the lowest levels of interaction with babies. Because in our society women have greater responsibility than men for care of the young, sex differences should be particularly pronounced in situations where there are heightened demands for children to take responsibility for caregiving.

The first study involved 86 boys and girls 32–63 months old in their regular day-care group situation (Berman, Monda and Myerscough 1977). Children were observed on 7 successive days during their daily free-play period. In a minimal alteration of the usual routine a visitors' area was marked off in a very large room that had areas for competing activities, such as art and nature study. During the observations the visitors' area contained a playpen with one side against the wall and an observer on each of the other three sides. Children wore identifying numbers. They were free to come and go as they pleased and individual children's presence in the area and behaviors were recorded. For the first 3 days of the study children were adapted to the procedures. Following this, a 13-month-old baby girl was placed in the playpen on 'baby days' (days 5 and 6). A fish tank with a goldfish was placed in front of the empty playpen as a control for novelty on 'fish days' (days 4 and 7).

As hypothesized, girls spent significantly more time in the area than boys did when the baby was present, but not on others days. Older boys in the group spent significantly less time in the area than younger boys did on the baby days, but not on other days, a finding that might be expected if the older boys had acquired gender role attitudes that were incongruent with attraction to infants.

There were many limitations to this first study. Among the most obvious limitation was the fact that it was a group study of attraction and, as such, it was not possible to study individual children's behaviors in detail. The playpen severely restricted the baby's mobility and potential behavior, and because of the size of the group children were prohibited from touching the baby, a prohibition that was not always effective. Above all, children's behavior was very much affected by the presence of their peers. It was not at all unusual for a child to call to a friend or physically lead a friend into or out of the visitors' area. Indeed, effects of the presence and character of a peer group is a subject that deserves intensive and systematic attention.

A second study was planned in order to observe the behavior of individual children who were segregated with a baby within a small space through no choice of their own. The rather narrow age range of participants in the first study was expanded because it was thought that there might be a trend for older girls to be more responsive than younger girls to the baby. Most important, the second study was planned to test whether children's responses to babies could be manipulated by varying the social circumstances in which children are given the opportunity to interact with babies.

In the second observational study (cf. Berman 1986; Berman, Smith and Goodman 1983), 38 children were enlisted from a different cohort of students at the same day-care center. On the basis of the previous study boys were expected to decrease in responsiveness to babies after approximately age $4\frac{1}{2}$. Therefore, the available children were divided into a group of 10 boys and 10 girls $3\frac{1}{2}$–$4\frac{1}{2}$ years old, and 9 boys and 9 girls $4\frac{1}{2}$–$5\frac{1}{2}$ years old. Each child was brought individually to a room at the day-care center with a partitioned-off area occupied by a boy or girl baby 13–16 months old and many toys. For the first 6 minutes subjects were told that they could play as they wished. After this time each child was told that the 'teachers' (observers) were busy, and was asked to help by 'taking care of' the baby. Children were then observed for an additional 3 minutes.

The most frequent activity was solitary play (recorded on 82 per cent of all 10-second intervals). Children played with, touched, or vocalized to the baby during only 17 percent of the intervals. The amount of baby-directed activity during the period of spontaneous play was not significantly related to the children's age or sex, or to an Age × Sex interaction. However, as predicted, after an adult made a caretaking request there were large, significant differences between groups in the amount of interaction with the baby. Older girls interacted with the baby the most (on 43 percent of all intervals), older boys the least (on 2 percent of all intervals), and the younger boys and girls were at intermediate levels (26 and 13 percent, respectively).

Our major hypotheses about the expected Age × Sex interaction

308 *The construction of identity*

were supported. Not only were older boys *less* responsive to babies, as in the previous study, but also older girls were *more* responsive to babies than were the younger children. Older girls were the only group of children who initiated interactions with the baby more often than they engaged in mutually initiated interactions. As predicted, the demand for caretaking was also effective in increasing the differences between the age–sex groups. In fact, it was only when children were asked to take responsibility for caregiving that the differences between groups were significant. The age–sex difference in children's behaviors appeared to be in response not only to the baby, but also to children's assignment to the role of caregiver.

CHILDREN'S RESPONSES TO VARIED BABIES AND SITUATIONS

Although our hypotheses about age and sex differences and the effects of demands for caretaking were verified, a third study was planned for several reasons. In order to determine the conditions that are associated with various types of responses to babies, it is necessary to vary the infant stimuli. That is, infant characteristics, as well as the social situations in which children meet, need to be explored. Children's interactions with toddlers are greatly affected by toddler's temperament and maturity, and we therefore enlisted a large number of toddlers in the study to eliminate sources of bias due to the idiosyncratic behavior of a particular baby. It was thus possible to analyze more accurately than in the previous studies several stimulus sources associated with babies' behaviors that were important determinants of children's caregiving.

We also hoped to be able to analyse in fine detail the stimulus conditions associated with children's baby-directed responses. To do this it was necessary to structure situations that might elicit fairly high rates of interactions with babies. In the previous study children engaged in solitary play during an average of 83 per cent of all intervals, but they interacted with the baby, on the average, during only 17 per cent of the intervals. In the third study (Berman and Goodman 1984) a few simple toys were substituted for the many attractive toys available in the earlier experiments. It was hoped that with fewer attractive toys children would spend less time playing alone, and more time interacting with the baby.

Because young children in our culture rarely interact with babies without adult supervision and direction, we designed a study to replicate age and sex differences in children's interactions with a baby.

Children were first observed after assignment to a caretaker role and then after an adult gave direct instructions concerning how the child could interact with the toddler. Four short scripts were developed, one for each of the sets of toys in the area. A male or female demonstrator showed the child how to use the toy to attract the toddler's attention and to entice the toddler to reach for the toy and join the child in mutual play.

Adults' instructions always followed a period of time when children were asked to assume the caretaker role without further instructions. In order to distinguish between the effects of the instructions, and the effects of simply spending time with the baby, a double baseline design was used. Half of the 12 children in each of the 4 age–sex groups were asked to 'take care of the baby' while the adults were 'busy' for 6 minutes, and the remaining children were asked to do so for only 3 minutes before the adult demonstrator entered the area and showed the child how to 'take care of' the baby. The length of the pre-demonstration period was not related to children's behavior before or after the demonstration and, therefore, data from both baseline conditions were combined for all subsequent analyses.

The setting for the study was a day-care center with a population of children similar to those in the previously described studies, but with a wider age range. In the younger group there were 12 boys and 12 girls between 2 years and 6 months old and 5 years and 3 months old, and in the older group there were 12 boys and 12 girls between 5 years and 9 months old and 7 years and 8 months old. These children and the 11 babies who were in the study were all regular attendees at the center.

Six male and 5 female babies 8–19 months old met the criteria to serve in the study; that is, they were mature enough to walk and approach children, but had not mastered more than a few words and were unlikely to be mature enough to be considered a peer, even by the youngest subjects. The baby for any particular session was chosen on a random basis from those of the group who were awake and available, with the restriction that close to half of the 12 subjects (5–7) in each of the 4 age–sex groups would be paired with girl babies, and the remaining subjects would be paired with boy babies.

A small area (approximately 100 sq. ft) in the corner of a large, unoccupied playroom at the day-care center served as the research location. The area was blocked off from the rest of the room by low bookcase dividers, with the observers outside. Four sets of simple toys were provided: balls, a set of blocks, toy trucks and cars, and a beanbag toss game. After the baby began playing, the older child was brought to the area and told, 'We really need someone to help us while we do some work. We're going to a room with some toys in it and a baby, and we'd like you to take care of the baby while we do some work. This is the baby we'd like you to take care of. We'll be doing some work right over here, and it's important that no one bothers or interrupts us while we do our work, so we'd like you to stay right in this area with the baby. You take care of the baby now.'

Half of the children in each of the 4 age–sex groups were randomly chosen to be in the baseline (uninstructed) caretaking condition for 6 minutes and the other half for 3 minutes before an adult entered the area for the demonstration. Toy interactions were chosen for the demonstration because our previous research had shown this to be the most likely type of interaction with the baby to occur for both sexes and both age groups.

The demonstrators each used one of the four toys saying, 'I'd like to show you something. Watch me a minute.' The demonstrator then used the randomly selected toy in a scripted manner, picking up the toy, showing the toy to the baby, and trying to induce the baby to reach for the toy. After the demonstration the experimenter left the area. The observation was continued for another 3 minutes. The sex of the demonstrator was balanced over the 4 age–sex groups.

The occurrence of each of several behaviors was recorded within 10-second intervals; solitary play, toy interaction, accidental physical touch, all other physical touch, verbal or vocal interactions, verbalizations or vocalizations to the self, and any response to the observers. Separate observers recorded the child's behavior and the baby's behavior. The initiator and nature of each recorded behavior were noted. At the end of each session each observer also wrote a narrative account of activities and behaviors observed (see Berman and Goodman 1984, for a detailed description of procedures).

Table 14.1 shows the mean percentage of all intervals before and after the demonstration when the children in each group engaged in particular activities. Total interaction scores were determined for each subject in order to assess the extent of his or her overall interactions with the baby. These scores were the sum of three percentage scores: toy interaction plus verbal or vocal interaction plus non-accidental physical interaction. Two total interaction scores were determined for each subject, one for the period before and another for the period after the caretaking demonstration.

The data presented in Table 14.1 show that efforts to reduce the extent of solitary play were successful (from 82 percent of all intervals in the previous study to 54 percent in this study). Almost all of the children engaged in some interactions with the babies. However,

Table 14.1 Mean percentage of all intervals before and after the demonstration when subjects in each group engaged in particular activities (n per group = 12)

Group	Older girls		Younger girls		Older boys		Younger boys	
Before or after demonstration	Before	After	Before	After	Before	After	Before	After
Interaction with toys	22.7	58.3	15.7	20.8	9.3	15.3	18.8	20.4
Verbal/vocal interaction	27.8	38.9	2.8	0.9	1.4	0.9	8.3	9.7
Physical interaction	25.2	15.7	8.6	7.4	0.0	0.0	0.0	0.0
Solitary play with toys	25.9	27.3	57.6	59.7	58.6	67.6	66.0	71.3
Vocalization to self	3.5	3.2	6.9	12.0	2.1	0.9	14.8	9.0
Accidental touch	1.4	0.5	0.7	0.5	0.0	0.0	0.0	0.0
Responses to observers	0.0	0.5	0.7	1.4	0.2	0.0	0.7	1.9

Source: Berman and Goodman (1984). Copyright 1984 by the Society for Research in Child Development, Inc.

solitary play was still the most common activity for all groups but the older girls. The most striking feature of the data is the contrast between the older girls' interactions with the toddlers and those of the other groups. In fact, the older girls' total interaction scores for the pre-demonstration period were almost three times higher than the younger boys' and girls', and more than seven times higher than the older boys'. The contrast between older girls' postdemonstration scores and the scores of other groups was even more striking.

Analyses (cf. Berman and Goodman 1984) showed that children's sex and age were significantly associated with the extent of their interactions with the baby, but that the high scores of the older girls were responsible for these effects. There was a highly significant statistical interaction between age and sex. As predicted, there was little difference between the extent of younger boys' and girls' interactions with the baby, but there was a large significant difference between older boys' and girls'. Older boys interacted *less* with the baby than the younger boys did, but this effect was not significant. However, older girls interacted with the baby significantly *more* than younger girls did.

The demonstration was an effective way of stimulating interactions with toddlers, and male and female adults were equally effective as demonstrators. However, the demonstration was reliably effective only for the older groups. It should be noted, though, that not only was the demonstration a very brief and modest intervention, but also its effects were tested for only a very short period of time immediately following the demonstration. Its lack of effect for the younger children and the lack of differences due to demonstrators' sex need to be tested with a longer-term intervention.

Qualitative aspects of children's interactions with babies

In order to examine more closely the nature of children's interactions with babies, a system was devised to classify the observers' descriptions of the behaviors that were recorded (cf. Berman and Goodman 1984). The classified behaviors are presented in Table 14.2. The numbers of children in each group who initiated specific types of interactions are listed. All activities initiated by at least 3 of the 48 subjects are included in the table. Baby-initiated interactions of the types listed were quite rare and were, therefore, excluded.

It can be seen from Table 14.2 that the older girls interacted with the baby not only more often than other children did, but also in many more different ways. For example, although most of the children in each group spent some time with the baby in interactions involving toys, these episodes were often brief and similar to young children's play with agemates. Occasionally toy play with the baby included showing, offering, or giving toys to the baby, but more often it involved only mutual play with the same toys. The older girls were the only group in which there were more children who offered, gave, or showed toys to the baby than those who merely engaged in mutual toy play with the baby.

Similarly, verbal interactions occurred among all groups but were common only for the older girls. Older girls often greeted or called to the babies, instructed them, and talked to them at some length. These verbal interactions were common before as well as after the demonstration. However, the extent and quality of older girls' physical interactions were most impressive, particularly when compared with the paucity of these behaviors in the other groups. Although none of the boys touched any of the babies, more than half of the older girls interacted physically with the baby in a variety of ways: lifting the baby, carrying or holding the baby, or taking the baby by the hand. A few of the younger girls also engaged in physical interactions with the baby, and these physical interactions resembled those of the older girls.

Children's behavior as a response to baby stimuli

The classification of children's behaviors reported in Table 14.2 was completed without the judges' awareness of the babies' behaviors that preceded them. Therefore, it is all the more interesting to speculate about how these behaviors might be related to the stimulus characteristics of the infants. Because many babies were enlisted in the third observational study, a wide range of infant characteristics and behaviors served as infant stimuli. We found no differences in any of the 4 age-sex groups' general responsiveness to babies based on babies' sex. That is, in no group were subjects' total interaction scores significantly different depending on whether the baby was a boy or a girl.

It might be that children's responsiveness to individual babies was influenced by the extent to which each baby possessed the type of infant features to which Lorenz has drawn our attention (1943), or by the baby's general physical attractiveness. Unfortunately, the babies' physical characteristics were not evaluated. Subjectively, all of the babies appeared to be at least moderately attractive and 'cute'. However, in future research it might be valuable to have ratings on the babies' physical appearance.

Table 14.2 Number of children in each group who initiated specific types of interactions with the baby before and after the demonstration (n per group = 12)

Group	Older girls		Younger girls		Older Boys		Younger boys		All ages	
Before (B) or after (A) the demonstration	B	A	B	A	B	A	B	A	B	A
Interactions:										
Mutual play	6	12	5	7	4	6	7	5	22	30
Offer, give, show	8	8	2	3	4	4	4	3	18	18
Any toy interaction	10	12	7	10	5	8	8	8	30	38
Greet, call	7	0	0	2	1	2	2	1	10	5
Instruct, command	6	6	1	0	1	1	1	0	9	7
Reassure, reinforce	3	1	1	0	1	0	1	1	6	2
Other talk	8	8	1	0	0	0	2	2	11	10
Any verbal interaction	9	10	3	2	1	3	3	4	16	19
Pick up, hold	5	3	0	2	0	0	0	0	5	5
Touch, carry, lead	7	4	3	3	0	0	0	0	10	7
Any physical interaction	7	5	3	4	0	0	0	0	10	9

Source: Berman and Goodman (1984). Copyright 1984 by the Society for Research in Child Development, Inc.

Babies did vary in their behavior, and these differences were documented by our data. Not only were there differences between babies, but there were also differences in individual babies' behavior from session to session. The tendency to cry was probably the most influential behavioral characteristic of the babies in our study. Crying is usually considered to be among the most powerful and compelling of all infant stimuli for adult caregivers (cf. Murray 1979). It would be interesting to know whether a baby's cries are also compelling for young children who are placed in a position of responsibility for a baby. If so, what kind of responses might children be most likely to make to a baby's cries?

Although everything possible was done to avoid babies' crying, 7 of the 11 babies who served in Study 3 cried at some time during a session with an older child. In fact, the baby cried at least briefly during 11 of the 48 sessions. Data for these 11 sessions are presented in Table 14.3. In order to augment these data, additional data have been added to the table from C8, a pilot subject who also encountered a crying baby.

Conclusions that might be drawn from the data in Table 14.3 are obviously limited. Both the small number of sessions when babies cried and the variable timing and duration of baby cries across sessions precluded the possibility of comparing the responses of children in the 4 age–sex groups. For example, it can be seen that the 3 babies who were paired with older boys cried for only 20 seconds whereas most of the remaining subjects listed in Table 14.3 were faced with babies who cried for much longer periods. It is not possible to know whether 2 of the 3 older boys failed to respond to crying babies because these babies cried for only a very short time, or because older boys were generally less responsive to babies.

Despite these limitations it is possible to make some observations about those children listed in Table 14.3 as a group, and to compare their behaviors with children who were in sessions with babies who did not cry. The data, though not extensive, are particularly valuable because they are unique. We have not been able to find in the existing literature any other reports of modern western children's responses to crying babies for whom they have caregiving responsibility.

Seven of the 11 babies who served in the study cried during the experimental sessions. Four of the babies were boys and 3 were girls. Three of the babies cried during only 1 session. The remaining 4 babies cried during 2 or 3 different sessions – that is, when paired with different subjects. Most often the babies seemed to cry when startled by some change, particularly the entry of a new person into the

Table 14.3 Children's behavior following onset of baby cries

Pair	Age	Cry onset	Cry duration	Cry[a] (stops)	Offer, give toy	Verbal response	Touch response	Vocal to self	Vocal to observers
C1[b] (F)[c]	2-9	Interval 1	6 min.	67%	Gives toy		Touch hand[d]		
B1[b] (M)[c]	1-7			(9)	Starts game	'Shhh'[d]			
C2 (F)	3-8	Demonstration	50 sec.	7%					
B2 (F)	1-1			(2)	Offers toy[d]		Holds[d]	Yes	
C3 (F)	4-7	Interval 3	8 min. 40 sec.	93%					
B3 (F)	1-1			(2)			Touch, caress	Yes	
C4 (F)	6-10	Interval 15	40 sec.	11%	Offers toy[d]	'Shhh. Want this?'			
B4 (F)	1-5			(1)					
C5 (F)	7-1	Interval 2	1 min. 10 sec.	13%		'Come here'			
B5 (M)	1-0			(1)			Picks up, cuddles		
C6 (F)	7-14	Interval 2	4 min. 50 sec.	33%	Offers toy[d] Mutual play[d]	Quiet talk[d]			
B3 (F)	1-0			(6)			Touch[d]		
C7 (F)	7-5	Interval 53	20 sec.	4%		'It's okay'			
B5 (M)	1-0			(0)					
C8 (M)	4-3	Interval 5	7 min. 20 sec.	46%				Sings	
B6 (M)	0-7			(6)	Offers toy[d]				
C9 (M)	4-3	Interval 1	6 min.	100%		'Shhh'[d]			
B3 (F)	0-10			(0)					
C10 (M)	6-8	Interval 17	20 sec.	3%					
B7 (M)	0-10			(1)					
C11 (M)	6-9	Interval 1	20 sec.	3%	Gives toy	'Hi. It's okay. Want the ball?'			
B4 (F)	1-4			(1)					
C12 (M)	7-6	Interval 2	20 sec.	4%					
B7 (M)	0-10			(1)					Yes

Note: [a] Percentage of all intervals during which the baby cried. Number of stops during crying are given in parentheses. [b] C1 refers to the Child Number 1. B1 refers to Baby Number 1. C1 and B1 are paired together. [c] (M) = male, (F) = female.

research area. Although children were brought to the area only after the baby was playing there contentedly, babies often cried soon after the child entered the area. In 8 of the 12 sessions listed in Table 14.3, the baby began to cry within the first 50 seconds after the child's entry, usually during the first 20 seconds. In 1 of the sessions (Child 2 with Baby 2), the baby began to cry when the demonstrator entered the area, and in another, the baby (Baby 5) cried after a tower of blocks that the older child (Child 7) had built 'for the baby' crashed to the floor. In the 2 remaining sessions the babies may have been responding to some sudden movement made by the older child.

The data in Table 14.3 clearly show that most of the children who were faced with the task of caring for a crying baby met that assignment with constructive and often persistent attempts to placate and calm the baby. Nine of the 12 children did so. Seven of the children offered or gave the baby a toy when the baby began to cry. An equal number of children offered verbal assurance to the babies when they cried, saying 'Shhh', or 'It's okay', or talking quietly to the baby while sitting close to the baby. In fact, it can be seen from a comparison of Tables 14.2 and 14.3 that children's verbal assurance to crying babies accounts for almost all of the behaviors that had been classified in Table 14.2 as 'Reassure, reinforce'. It should again be noted that the children's behaviors listed in Table 14.2 were classified earlier without knowledge of the infants' behaviors that preceded them.

Five of the girls also touched the baby, or caressed or cuddled the baby in an apparent attempt to comfort the distressed infant. Although older girls frequently touched babies whether they cried or not, the younger girls did so far less frequently. It is interesting that, although many of the older girls needed no such provocation, most of the younger girls who touched the baby did so only after the baby cried (cf. Tables 14.2 and 14.3).

In this study children's age seemed to be unrelated to responsiveness to crying babies. Even some of the youngest subjects responded amply to the babies' distress. For example, Baby 1 began to cry as Child 1 (a girl, 2 years and 9 months old) entered the research area. The baby continued to cry or whine intermittently throughout much of the session, stopping nine times for intervals of 10 seconds or more. Although Child 1 was only 14 months older than the baby, Child 1 offered him toys and touched his hand several times, repeatedly saying 'Shhhshhh' when he cried. She was finally able to engage the baby in a game, rolling a ball back and forth. This successful toy interaction with the baby occurred after an adult demonstrated the use of a toy other than the ball. Although the demonstration may have contributed to the child's ability to do so, considerable ingenuity was required for this young child to calm the baby and to initiate and sustain joint play activity.

Child 9 (a boy 4 years and 3 months old) was confronted by a 10-month-old baby who cried continuously, and often vigorously, throughout the session. Although his efforts met with no success, the 4-year old kept offering toys to the baby, moving close to her and saying 'Shhhshhh' over and over. This pattern was typical of many children 2–7 years old. Their responses to the babies' cries were almost immediate, and were repeated often when babies continued to cry.

Most of the babies began to cry very early in the session before the children had witnessed an adult's demonstration of how one might 'take care of' a baby. Therefore, it appeared as though these typical responses to crying babies were not dependent on formal instruction or modeling within the research situation. They may have been learned very early, perhaps from children's experiences with adults' attempts to relieve their own distress.

Not all of the children responded directly to the crying baby, although most of them did. Three of the children, all boys, made no effort to distract or comfort the distressed baby. Instead, some of the children may have directed their efforts toward self-distraction. For example, Child 12 was paired with a baby who cried briefly soon after the child entered the area. Although he had just been asked to take care of the baby, the child called to the observers, asking whether he could play with the toys. Child 8 was faced with a 7-month-old who cried during almost half of the intervals in the session. The 4-year-old boy did not respond directly to the crying baby. Instead, he vocalized to himself and sang the baby's name over and over. Behavior such as this might be considered peculiar unless it were interpreted as indicating that he was aware of the baby but sought to interfere with perception of the baby's cries.

To summarize, 9 of the 12 children who were with crying babies responded to the babies promptly, and often repeatedly. Although it was not possible to compare the responses of the 4 age–sex groups, even the youngest children responded appropriately and amply to the babies' distress. Boys and girls offered toys to the baby and offered verbal reassurance. Girls also touched, held, cuddled, or caressed the baby. Almost all the responses that previously had been classified as 'Reassure, reinforce' were made to babies who were crying. Although older girls were likely to touch the baby whether or not the baby was

Table 14.4 Latency of older girls' initial interactions with babies and of babies' cries (latency is in seconds; *n* = 12)

Subject (age)	With toy	Vocal	Physical	Onset of baby cry
1 (6–2)	AD[e]	10	20	No cry
2 (6–3)	140			No cry
3 (6–3)	10		10	No cry
4 (6–5)	60	AD[e]		No cry
5[a] (6–10)	90	100		140
6 (6–10)	20	10	50	No cry
7 (7–0)	110	50	10	No cry
8 (7–0)	40	20	130	No cry
9[b] (7–1)	160	10	60	10
10[c] (7–4)	30			10
11[d] (7–5)	40	110		520
12 (7–5)	110	10	20	No cry

Note: [e]Subject C4, Table 14.3.
[b]Subject C5, Table 14.3.
[c]Subject C6, Table 14.3.
[d]Subject C7, Table 14.3.
[e]After the demonstration.

crying, almost all of the younger girls' touch responses were to crying babies.

Older girls' responses to crying and noncrying babies

Baby cries seemed to be potent elicitors of heightened responsiveness to babies for many of the children. However, except for the fact that they verbally reassured crying babies, the older girls appeared, as a group, to behave similarly to babies who cried and those who did not cry during the research sessions. Older girls generally had very high rates of interaction with babies. To what stimuli were they responding? What might have motivated their baby-directed behavior?

Table 14.4 presents data for the 12 older girls in the study. Latency data are given for each girl's initial verbal, physical, and toy interactions with the baby. The time of onset of crying is also given if the baby cried during the session. In 8 of the 12 sessions the baby did not cry at all. In 3 of the 4 sessions with crying babies the crying began after the older girl had already interacted with the baby. Only one child, Subject 10, could possibly have been responding to cries in her initial interactions with the baby.

The most striking feature of these data is the very early onset of older girls' responses to the babies. Six girls, that is, fully half of the group, interacted with the baby in the first 10 seconds of the session. In fact, all but 2 of the older girls responded to the baby within the first minute. Not only did the older girls interact with the babies very early during the sessions, but many of the girls' behaviors seemed to follow a particular pattern. We might think of this behavioral pattern as an expression of a script, common to girls this age for use in caregiving situations. Two-thirds of the older girls talked to the baby, usually during the first minute, often greeting or calling to the toddler, then later showing a toy or instructing the baby about its use. More than half of the girls touched the baby during the first minute or two; five of them picked up, held, or carried the baby, led the baby by the hand, or assumed a position that maintained continuing physical contact with the baby.

These children gave the appearance of taking the babies physically in hand. Some of the older girls were successful in initiating and maintaining playful and often nurturant interactions with the babies. These girls combined close physical contact with much quiet talk to the babies, and the sharing of toys. The babies in these sessions were content to remain in physical contact. They exchanged toys, entered into joint play, and sometimes vocalized. For example, Subject 8, a 7-year old, talked quietly to the baby throughout the 6 minutes before an adult entered the situation to demonstrate how to 'take care of' a baby. She talked to the baby beginning in the first 10 seconds that she was with her, all the while offering several different types of toys. During the second minute the baby accepted a ball. The child and the baby then sat close together in continuous physical contact. After 3 minutes the child was able to engage the baby in a game wherein the children rolled the car to each other repeatedly, with the baby vocalizing to the child.

Subject 9 was confronted with a more difficult situation, a baby who began to cry after 10 seconds and persisted for more than 1 minute. She held and cuddled the baby, talked to him, and then offered toys that he accepted and later threw back to her. In the sixth minute (before the adult's demonstration) she 'sat him down' and showed him how to stack blocks, guiding his hand with her hand on his arm.

Not all the older girls' interactions were this successful. Occasionally a baby was startled by a child's overtures. For instance, the baby cried when Subject 5 gave her a ball after rolling the ball to her and unsuccessfully exhorting her, 'Get it'. Sometimes a baby appeared to find physical contact with an older girl too confining and moved away.

More frequently babies simply remained passive despite the older girls' ministrations. For example, Subject 7 picked up the baby during the first 10 seconds of the session, holding him in her lap for 1.5 minutes. She talked quietly to him, telling him, 'Look' and 'Give it to me'. Despite the fact that he followed her instructions, the baby did not initiate any activities.

Whether their interactions with the babies were successful or not, the older girls apparently believed that they knew how to 'take care of' babies and they went about doing so with very little hesitation soon after entering the experimental situation. They had obviously already acquired a 'script' that few of the younger girls had acquired. Even after an adult demonstrated how to 'take care of' a baby many of the older girls behaved in a manner that expressed elements of the original script. Although the adults' demonstrations did not include any physical contact with the baby, most of the older girls' scripts did. Despite the prestige and obvious expertise of the adults, and despite the fact that almost all of the older girls replicated the demonstrators' actions faithfully, five of them reverted to physical interactions after the demonstration. This usually happened after children's attempts to enlist the baby's cooperation by imitating the demonstrator failed.

As a group the older girls seemed to be quite different from the other children. Most of them responded promptly to the experimenters' requests for caregiving by talking to the baby and offering toys. Many of them also assumed physical control of the baby, a type of behavior not observed in the other children. Only a small proportion of their baby-directed behaviors seemed to be in direct response to the babies' cries. Instead they appeared to be responding with what they considered to be appropriate behavior to social cues denoting a general class of situations concerned with baby care.

SUMMARY AND FUTURE DIRECTIONS FOR RESEARCH

Despite the fact that parent–child interaction has been a thriving field of psychological research, relatively little is known about children's responses to babies or about the ways patterns of responsive, nurturant care develop in young girls or boys. In the modern western world the nature and extent of parental involvement with young children are obviously different for most men and women, but we know very little about the developmental course of sex differences in caregiving. Even less is known about how and why sex differences come about and the conditions that are necessary and sufficient for them to emerge.

Two different theoretical approaches have characterized research on development of caregiving in male and female children and adults. One has emphasized the importance of infant characteristics and signals, and the assumption is often made that there is a specieswide genetic bias to respond to infant stimuli. The other approach has emphasized the importance of experience, situational cues, changing roles during the life course, and the individual's cognitions and perceptions of appropriate gender roles. Both approaches are necessary to an understanding of the antecedents of various types of caregiving activities.

Much of what is known about the development of nurturance in young children comes from studies of traditional cultures where considerable childcare responsibility is allocated to older siblings (cf. Weisner and Gallimore 1977; Whiting and Whiting 1975). Whiting and Whiting have shown that infants elicited nurturant responses from children more than three times as often as their peers or elders did. It may even be the case that regular responsibility for infant care can influence children's behavioral repertoires, generally increasing the probability of habitual nurturant responses. Ember's (1973) observations of boys who were given responsibility for child care support this notion. Because children's tasks and responsibilities largely determine the social context within which they spend time, Whiting (1983) stresses the far-reaching consequences of the parents' role in task assignment. Boys as well as girls may respond with nurturance to infant signals when given an opportunity. However, cultural support is necessary for contact between children and infants to occur. Parents' cognitions, perceptions, and social attitudes, which usually differ for sons and daughters, determine the frequency of such contact.

Although much remains to be learned about the development of caregiving in traditional cultures, it is an even greater challenge to understand the origins of sex differences in societies such as ours, where boys and girls have little contact with infants, and even less responsibility for child care. Children in modern western societies presumably share with children in traditional societies any existing biases to respond nurturantly to infant signals. Our observations of the persistent and varied responses of even very young children to crying babies lend support to the theory that there may be specieswide biases to comfort distressed, crying infants (cf. Frodi and Lamb 1978). It is important to keep in mind that any such biases do not guarantee that behavior will be nurturant. A few of our subjects either were unresponsive or appeared to be attempting to interfere with the focal perception of aversive baby cries. It is also possible that there are age or sex differences in responsiveness to infant cries, but our data are not adequate to test for group differences.

Though there has been an upsurge of research on responses to baby cries, most of the research has been with adults, not children, and has relied heavily on self-reports. Unfortunately, we cannot make assumptions about the way subjects might behave based on their ratings of cries and reports of how they might act in real-life situations. An even greater problem is that self-reports tend to be biased so that traditional sex differences are exaggerated (cf. Berman 1980). In one study (Zahn-Waxler, Friedman and Cummings 1983), when children had an opportunity to 'help a mother find a lost bottle' for a baby who had presumably been crying, there were no significant sex differences in the amount of help offered but, during an interview, girls verbalized significantly more empathy for the crying baby than boys did.

It is certainly time-consuming to observe children's direct responses to crying babies in ecologically valid situations. It is also difficult to deal with responses to naturally occurring cries, which are neither uniform nor under the experimenters' control. However, data such as these are essential for both theoretical and practical purposes. In addition, similar information is needed about children's responses to other naturally occurring baby behaviors such as smiles and vocalizations. It may also be profitable to compare children's behaviors toward infants who vary in the degree to which they possess 'Lorenz-type' babyish physical characteristics.

Though children from both traditional and modern western societies share the tendency to respond to infant signals, western children must draw on different experiences to develop cognitions and expectations about appropriate baby-directed behaviors, and to create scripts for various social situations in which babies are encountered. Direct experience with babies may be minimal, but families, peers, the media, and many cultural institutions provide ample information to be used as guidelines for developing role behavior. Even preschool children seem to be aware of the various behavior patterns that are culturally approved in situations involving babies. Moreover, there is evidence (Weeks and Thornburg 1977) that young children articulate acceptance of future family roles that are even more traditional than their parents'.

Perhaps most important, young children make fine distinctions about the various behaviors that are 'appropriate' for males or for females in situations that seem on the surface to be only minimally different. For example, sex differences are most often found when there is a demand for caregiving responsibility, but there may be little difference between boys and girls in situations when a specific type of help is needed (Weinstock 1979), or when there is no demand for caregiving responsibility (Berman 1986; Berman *et al.* 1983). Young children not only appear to understand that women typically bear major responsibility for child rearing in our society (Melson, Fogel, and Toda 1985); they also know who usually assumes each role in a variety of situations.

A good example is the contrast between older boys' and girls' behavior in Experiment 3, following the experimenter's initial request that they 'take care of' the baby. Four of the 12 older boys spent at least 1 minute in the experimental situation without recordable behaviors. The observers noted that these children 'watched' or 'stared at' the baby. Berman and Goodman (1984: 1076) suggested that watching a baby may be a rather passive form of caregiving that is in accord with a young child's interpretation of the proper masculine role. They proposed that future research 'be directed toward understanding the developing differences between males and females in the way they construe their "proper" roles and responsibilities for child care' (Berman and Goodman 1984: 1076). These differences should be measured not only by interviews and children's self-reports but also by observations of children's behaviors in a variety of situations. Situations should be designed or selected because they vary with respect to the type of people present (i.e., age, sex, relationship with the child, and social status) and the explicit and implicit demands made on the child, as well as the babies' characteristics and behavior.

Observations of children's baby-directed behaviors are particularly valuable when behaviors can be related to infant variables and situational variables. However, there are also opportunities to explore subject variables beyond sex, age, life stage, and sibling status. The existing body of cross-cultural literature demonstrates that subject variables can also be a rich source of information about cultural variables that are important to the development of caregiving. The diversity of family forms and caregiving traditions provides contrasts that can be exploited in a selective fashion.

It has been suggested (Allen 1985; Brookins 1985) that black mothers' long tradition of employment in the United States has contributed to more egalitarian roles and more caregiving involvement for males in black families, compared with whites. Research is now under way comparing black boys' baby interactions with those of white boys (Reid 1985, personal communication). Furthermore, rapid changes in certain areas of the world afford unique opportunities for research. One example is modern urban China, where children from one-child families have no opportunities for experience with siblings. However, Chinese boys and girls are immersed in a family-oriented culture where young males and females are expected to be helpful and expressive toward their peers and younger children. These are only two of many populations with rich potential for research.

In summary, the early acquisition of ability to care for the young is a promising and important area for investigation. It is time to broaden our knowledge of not one but several classes of variables that interact to determine children's responsiveness to younger children and babies. Selective attention to particular situational variables, population variables, and variables associated with infant signals can greatly enhance our understanding of the processes that underlie the development of men's and women's emotional investment and competence to care for their young.

REFERENCES

Allen, W. R. (1985) 'Race, income and family dynamics: a study of adolescent male socialization processes and outcomes', in M. B. Spencer, G. K. Brookins and W. R. Allen (eds) *Beginnings: Social and Affective Development of Black Children*, Hillsdale, N.J.: Erlbaum.

Arling, G. L. and Harlow, H. F. (1967) 'Effects of social deprivation on maternal behavior of rhesus monkeys', *Journal of Comparative and Physiological Psychology* 64: 371–7.

Berman, P. W. (1980) 'Are women more responsive than men to the young? A review of developmental and situational variables', *Psychological Bulletin* 88: 668–95.

Berman, P. W. (1986) 'Young children's responses to babies: do they foreshadow differences between maternal and paternal styles?', in A. Fogel and G. F. Melson (eds) *Origins of Nurturance*, Hillsdale, N.J.: Erlbaum.

Berman, P. W. and Goodman, V. (1984) 'Age and sex differences in children's responses to babies: effects of adults' caretaking requests and instructions, *Child Development* 55: 1071–7.

Berman, P. W., Monda, L. D. and Myerscough, R. P. (1977) 'Sex differences in young children's responses to an infant: an observation within a day-care setting', *Child Development* 48: 711–15.

Berman, P. W., Smith, V. L. and Goodman, V. (1983) 'Development of sex differences in response to an infant and to the caretaker role', *Journal of Genetic Psychology* 143: 283–4.

Brookins, G. K. (1985) 'Black children's sex-role ideologies and occupational choices in families of employed mothers', in M. B. Spencer, G. K. Brookins and W. R. Allen (eds) *Beginnings: Social and Affective Development of Black Children*, Hillsdale, N.J.: Erlbaum.

Ember, C. (1973) 'Female task assignment and the social behavior of boys', *Ethos* 1: 424-39.

Feldman, S. S. and Nash, S. C. (1978) 'Interest in babies during young adulthood', *Child Development* 49: 617-22.

Feldman, S. S. and Nash, S. C. (1979a) 'Changes in responsiveness to babies during adolescence', *Child Development* 50: 942-9.

Feldman, S. S. and Nash, S. C. (1979b) 'Sex differences in responsiveness to babies among mature adults', *Developmental Psychology* 15: 430-6.

Feldman, S. S., Nash, S. C. and Cutrona, C. (1977) 'The influence of age and sex on responsiveness to babies', *Developmental Psychology* 13: 675-6.

Frodi, A. and Lamb, M. (1978) 'Sex differences in responsiveness to infants: a developmental study of psychophysiological and behavioral responses', *Child Development* 49: 1182-8.

Gagnon, J. H. (1973) 'Scripts and the coordination of sexual conduct', in J. K. Cole and R. Dienstbier (eds) *Nebraska Symposium on Motivation*, Lincoln, N.E.: University of Nebraska Press.

Gagnon, J. H. and Simon, W. (1973) *Sexual Conduct*, Chicago: Aldine.

Lehrman, D. S. (1961) 'Gonadal hormones and parental behavior in birds and infrahuman mammals', in W. C. Young and G. W. Corner (eds) *Sex and Internal Secretions* (vol. 2, 3rd ed.), Baltimore: Williams & Wilkins.

Lorenz, K. (1943) 'Die angebornen Formen moglicher Erfahrung', *Zeitschrift fur Tierpsychologie* 5: 235-582.

Melson, G. F. and Fogel, A. (1982) 'Young children's interest in unfamiliar infants', *Child Development* 53: 693-700.

Melson, G. F., Fogel, A. and Toda, S. (1985) *Children's Ideas about Infants and Their Care*, W. Lafayette, I.N.: Department of Family Studies, Purdue University.

Murray, A. D. (1979) 'Infant crying as an elicitor of parental behavior: an examination of two models', *Psychological Bulletin* 86: 191-215.

Parke, R. D. (1981) *Fathers*, Cambridge, Mass.: Harvard University Press.

Shields, S. A. (1975) 'Functionalism, Darwinism, and the psychology of women', *American Psychologist* 30: 739-54.

Shields, S. A. (1984) 'To pet, coddle and "do for": caretaking and the concept of maternal instinct', in M. Lewin (ed.) *In the Shadow of the Past: Psychology Examines the Sexes, 1800-1900*, New York: Columbia University Press.

Simon, W. and Gagnon, J. H. (1969) 'On psychosexual development', in D. A. Goslin (ed.) *Handbook of Socialization Theory and Research*, Chicago: Rand-McNally.

Weeks, M. O. and Thornburg, K. R. (1977) 'Marriage role expectations of five-year-old children and their parents' *Sex Roles* 3: 189-91.

Weinstock, S. C. (1979) *Preschool Children's Sex Differences in Prosocial Behaviors Directed Toward a Younger Child*, unpublished honors thesis, Florida State University, Tallahassee, Florida.

Weisner, T. S. and Gallimore, R. (1977) 'Child and sibling caretaking', *Current Anthropology* 18: 169-80.

Whiting, B. B. (1983) 'The genesis of prosocial behavior', in D. Bridgeman (ed.) *The Nature of Prosocial Development: Interdisciplinary Theories of Strategy*, New York: Academic.

Whiting B. B. and Whiting J. W. (1975) *Children in Six Cultures*, Cambridge, Mass.: Harvard University Press.

Zahn-Waxler, C., Friedman, S. L. and Cummings, E. M. (1983) 'Children's emotions and behaviors in response to infants' cries' *Child Development* 54: 1522–8.

15 The self-building potential of pretend play, or 'I got a fish, all by myself'

Greta G. Fein

Source: Yawkey, T. D. and Pellegrini, A. D. (eds) (1984) *Child's Play: Developmental and Applied*, Hillsdale, N.J.: Erlbaum.

Pretend play has offered much grist for the mills of developmental theories. One is hard pressed to find a major theoretical framework – especially of the grand genre – that has not offered an account of where pretense fits within its larger perspective. And so, from the perspective of Piagetian theory, we become oriented to the cognitive (or, more exactly, the counter-cognitive) aspects of pretense and, from the psychoanalytic theory, we become oriented to the affective-emotional aspects of this behavior. Vygotsky brings us to words or gestures in relation to meaning and Bateson calls our attention to the paradoxical nature of communications about communications. (See Fein [1979, 1981b] and Sutton-Smith [1982] for additional discussion of these theoretical variations.)

Pretense has provided so rich an arena for theorists interested in diverse issues that often it has seemed deprived of a theoretical framework uniquely its own. However, recent research suggests that this concern may be premature (Fein 1981a,b). Actually, the grand theories often provide little more than a beginning way of framing an interesting question. For example, in the work of Vygotsky (1967) and Piaget (1962) the notion of object transformation was rather general, illustrated either in anecdote or observational record. In pursuing this interesting question, investigators have gone considerably beyond this beginning by formulating specific statements about the behavioral forms and features of objects that support transformational activity at different ages (Elder and Pederson 1978; Fein 1975; Jackowitz and Watson 1980; Ungerer, Zelazo, Kearsley and O'Leary 1981; Watson and Fischer 1977). Bateson's notion (1956) of 'metacommunication' has also fostered research aimed at illuminating how children use language to convey the idea that in play the playful nip connotes the bite without connoting what a bite connotes. In these examples, grand theories give rise to 'mini theories' that, with carefully operationalized constructs, are able to generate testable hypotheses.

However, the work of one grand theorist – George Herbert Mead – who speculated about the significance of pretense has been largely neglected (Rubin and Pepler 1979; Fein and Kohlberg 1987). Mead's theory is important generally because it draws attention to the elusive question of the development of self during the early years. It is important particularly because Mead views the 'play stage' as concerned primarily with the child's organization of particular attitudes of others toward himself and toward one another in the specific social acts in which he participates or observes. In Mead's (1934) words,

> When a child does assume a role, he has in himself the stimuli which call out that particular response . . . (when playing Indian), the responses that they would call out in others, and which answer to an Indian. In the play period, the child utilizes his own responses to these stimuli which he makes use of in building a self. The responses which he has a tendency to make to these stimuli organise them.
>
> (Mead 1934: 213)

According to Mead, role playing constitutes a form of 'being another to one's self':

> The child says something in one character and responds in another character, and then his responding in another character is a stimulus to himself in the first character, and so the conversation goes on. A certain organized structure arises in him and in his other which replies to it, and these carry on the conversation of gestures between themselves.
>
> (Mead 1934: 213)

ROLE PLAYING AND ROLE TAKING

Two processes contribute to the self-building potential of play. One is overt role *playing* (i.e., the behavioral responses and the stimuli they provide to the player). In a sense, the child observes himself in the role of another. The other process is the covert role *taking* that accompanies the overt behavior. Psychologically, the role-playing child is organizing the attitudes and perspectives of the others whose role responses are being produced. However, the self is always at the center of the encounters, interpreting the social meaning of the relationships being enacted.

For all the potential importance of Mead's ideas, they have yet to be cast in a form amenable to systematic empirical study. Mead himself make no effort to investigate the development of role playing.

Therefore, the scheme outlined later in Figure 15.1 goes beyond what Mead actually proposed but attempts, nonetheless, to be faithful to what he meant.

In this scheme, role playing and its concomitant role taking develop through four levels. At each level, role playing acquires a new refinement and each new refinement implies an added complication in the child's perspective taking. In level 1 the child pretends to do something as himself/herself with no evidence that a generic role (i.e., of fisherman, mother, father) is intended. The perspective is simply that of the self doing something difficult, exciting, or even painful. In level 2, the child plays a generic role (e.g., a mother, but not necessarily a particular mother) by pretending to carry out an activity typical of the role, in a manner characteristic of persons who perform this activity. A generic role with complementarity marks level 3. Now the child as 'other' interacts with a complementary other (e.g., as mother comforting her hurt baby). In level 2 the child takes the other's perspective in relation to role-appropriate actions minus those actions that involve personal relationships. When these personal relations are added, the child must feel and think as the 'other' feels and thinks when feeling and thinking about the complementary other in the relationship. The pretending child therefore takes the attitude of the mother consoling a baby and acknowledging the baby's hurt. Level 4 represents the role reversal that so intrigued Mead. Here the child first plays the role of consoling mother and then switches to the role of crying baby. Again, for Mead, the important point is that the 'self' is producing these responses and thus the stimuli that feed back to the self. The solid lines in the figure indicate the *external* response – stimulus configuration, whereas the dotted lines indicate the *internal*, imaginal response–stimulus configuration. As these imagined encounters continue, the child's grasp of 'others' becomes organized internally (as well as externally), and as these others become orga- nized, they come differentiated from he 'self' while the 'self' organizes its relation to these others. This progressive organizational effort represents the construction of a social self – distinct from, but deeply tied to, persons in the child's social world. Taken as a whole, Mead's model implies something like decentration in Piaget's theory – but only insofar as the 'self' becomes progressively more fluent in moving through different perspectives.

Because the content of role play is drawn from the real world of people, role playing–role taking is inherently social, even though the child might be playing alone. However, role play with a partner adds measurably to the complexity of the play. Figure 15.2 indicates what

Figure 15.1 Basic structures in Mead's model of role playing and role taking

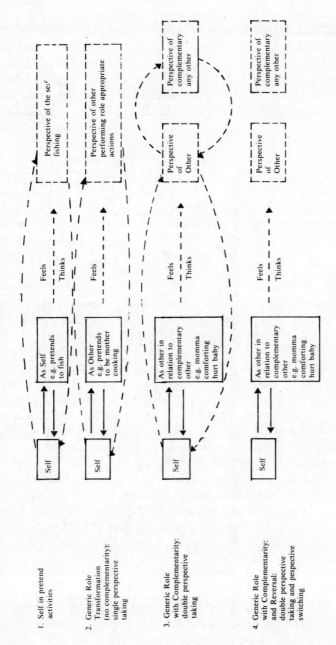

Figure 15.2 Social pretence: role complementarity and the perspective of others

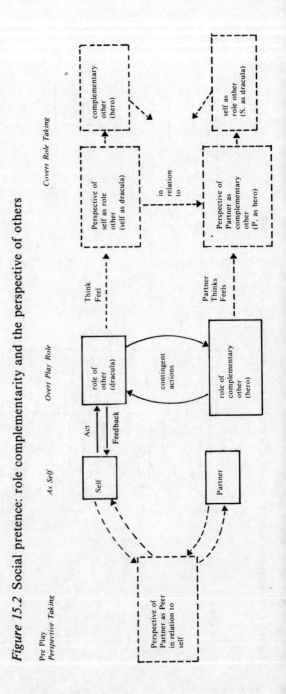

happens in level 3 when a partner plays the role of complementary other. When the levels of role playing – taking in a social mode are added to those in a solitary mode, the result is an eight-level developmental progression.

ILLUSTRATIONS OF THE MODEL

When actual play sequences are examined with respect to the model, it becomes clear that a major milestone occurs when children are able to play roles with a partner as a complementary other. The following episodes are taken from a study in which children were videotaped in four 15-minute play sessions with four different partners.

Consider the first transcript in which Alan, a 2½-year-old child, pretends to fish. Note that Richard, a peer, though present during the entire session, neither enters the play nor interacts with Alan aside from a few stray glances.

Transcript 1

Alan and Richard: 2½ years

Alan is sitting on a chair near the caregiver, swinging a mop in the air. Richard is sitting on the floor, looking at a book.

A: 'I'm gonna get a fish.' (Dips end of mop onto floor, brings it up, turns to caregiver)

R: (Looks at A, then resumes looking at book)

A: 'He got a fish, he got a fish, all by myself.' (Turns toward R) 'I got me wet . . . move . . . in the hair.'

A: 'That's nice sea water.' (Leaves with mop) 'I want to row.'

A: (Crosses mop and broom over head) 'I got my boat, over here.'

A: (Moves back to chair, extends mop and broom onto floor)

A: 'Eee, ooh! I'm in my boat . . .'

A: 'I'm gonna get two fish, fish.' (Extends mop and broom over corner of table) 'A fish!'

R: (Closes book, looks up at A)

A: (Turns towards caregiver) 'This . . . this is your fishing pole.' (Gives broom to caregiver)

Caregiver:
    'Okay, set it down here.' (Leans broom against table)

A: 'I don't want . . . it.' (Throws broom so it leans against buggy) 'You have it, you can take mine.'

R: (Puts book down, grunts, picks up rake, slides it along rug, glances at A)

A: (Dips mop over table onto rug, brings it back up, turns to caregiver) 'Give you a fish.'

A: (Turns back around, fiddles with end of mop) 'One here.' (Fiddles with end of mop) 'I don't want your fishing pole.' (Hits end of mop against buggy, turns mop around) 'I don't want your fishing pole.'

Except for a brief moment, when 'He got a fish', Alan's perspective is pretty consistently 'all by myself'. His play is rich in object and substance transformations in a material mode (e.g., mop and broom for fishing pole and oars) and in an ideational mode (e.g., fish, sea water, row boat). However, his effort to engage the caregiver in the play is poorly formed, and the caregiver misunderstands the overture.

The next transcript comes from Barb and Sandy, also 2½-year-olds. Barb is far more sophisticated than Alan in her orientation to her partner. However, Sandy has little grasp of what is being asked of him. Even though Barb turns didactic when instructing Sandy how to bed down a baby, Sandy seems not to comprehend.

Transcript 2

Barb and Sandy 2½ years

Barb is sitting in chair with doll and blanket on her lap. Sandy is raking floor near Barb.

B: 'You brushing?'

S: (Glances at B, continues to rake)

B: (Watches S, turns in chair, whispers) 'He's, he's brushing. Yeah.'

B: 'There's dad, working.'

B: (Places doll on floor, whispers to it, stands)

S: (Picks up truck, puts it in buggy, looks at B)

B: 'Cover you up.' (Covers doll with blanket)

B: 'Night-night, night-night. Don't cry . . . will you children go to sleep.' (Walks to toy shelf)

S: (Takes truck from buggy, places another truck in buggy)

B: 'Dad, do you want to stay with . . .'

S: (Looks at B)

B: 'Cover her up, all right Dad?'

S: (Pokes at truck in buggy)

B: (Gets broom and rake, drops rake, carries broom) 'I have my brush.' (Sweeps floor briefly, drops broom, picks up rake)

B: 'Get that one, that one.' (Rakes floor) 'I'm brushing.' (Rakes rug)

S: (Watches B, follows B as she rakes)

B: '. . . your brush, Sandy. Will you watch my baby?' (Falls next to doll) 'Uuh! Will you watch my baby so she's not gonna cry?'

S: (Sits next to doll, looks at it)

B: (Stands, rakes rug) 'All right, Dad? I'm brushing.'

S: (Feeds doll, with bottle)

B: (Rakes floor, puts rake back, approaches S) 'Thank you Dad, thank you, get up now.'

S: (Looks at B, continues to sit and feed doll)

B: (Stoops near doll as if listening) 'Let me see . . . I hear what you're saying.'

B: (Stands, gets blanket) 'The ba-by, da, ah, the ba-by.' (Approaches S and doll)

S: (Stops feeding doll, looks at B)

B: (Places doll and blanket in front of S) 'Wrap her up, right there.' (Spreads blanket onto floor)

B: 'Sheet on, put her right there, 'kay?'

S: (Fiddles with bottle, looks at B)

B: (Gets doll, puts it on sheet) 'Right there.' (Covers with blanket)

B: 'Good-night, baby.' (Turns to caregiver) 'You stay with her, Jane. Stay with her . . . she'll . . . so she'll f. . . she'll.'

B: (Complaining to caregiver) 'Sandy won't sit on the baby, but over here's a baby' (Picks up doll from corner, walks with it, singing) 'Rock, rock my baby.'

S: (Feeds doll with bottle)

B: (Approaches S) 'Give me my blank-ey. Get up, give it, Sandy.'

S: (Stops feeding doll, B lifts blanket from under his leg. Resumes feeding doll)

B: (Takes blanket and doll across room)

B: (Covers doll with blanket on floor, whispers to it)

B: 'See Sandy?'

S: (Looks at B, stops feeding doll)

B: 'She want her bottle. Go get the bottle, Sandy, you get my bottle.' (Takes truck from buggy)

Barb easily reaches level 3 on the scale shown in Fig. 15.1. She whispers to the baby and even listens to the response. Actually, Barb is a bit more advanced. As 'mother' she relates to the doll as 'baby', but she also tries to relate to Sandy as 'dad' and, in her conversations with her daughter, refers to this fatherly 'other'. Barb is able to project more than one complementary other, but her vision of the second is much thinner than her vision of the first.

The third transcript describes Alan with Harry, a more sophisticated 2½-year-old partner. Even though the boys interact with one another, the play is essentially parallel play, with Harry taking the lead as innovator.

Transcript 3

Harry and Alan 2½ years

Harry is feeding doll with bottle. Alan is feeding self with bottle, watching Harry.

H: 'Oh, don't cry.' (Watches A, walks with doll cradled in arms)

A: 'Gonna get my baby . . . baby.' (Gets baby from buggy) 'Baby, don't cry.' (Watches H, cradles doll)

H: 'Your arm is broken . . . Momma sees it.' (Walks toward A) 'Hey teacher . . .'
   (Sits down, feeds doll at table)

A: (Sits down, feeds doll at table)

H: (Gets up from table, feeds doll in his arms, looks at A)

A: (Watches H)

H: 'Uh, oh . . . it's . . . it's.'

H: (Kneels on floor) 'I got baby bottles.' (Drops doll, picks up bottle)

A: 'I got, I got my bottle.'

H: 'I got . . . I'm gonna drink it all up' (Drinks, steps on doll, picks doll up, feeds it with bottle) 'Come on baby, don't cry.'

A: (Watches H, holds doll and bottle)

H: 'Don't cry baby, don't cry, don't cry.'

A: 'Don't cry, don't, don't cry.'

H: 'Don't cry . . . come on Alan. You won't get a cough.'

A: 'All right.' (Approaches shelf) 'Get cough?'

H: (Gets spoon and feeds doll) 'Won't get cough.'

A: (Approaches H, feeds doll with bottle) 'I want to put some on there.'

H: (Leaves) 'No, no. Here's your spoon.'

A: (Gets spoon from shelf)

H: (Still holding doll) 'All finished.'

H: 'The doll is broken, we tell the doctor.'

A: (Watches H)

H: (Approaches door, moves to center of room, faces wall)

A: (Feeds doll with spoon)

H: 'Doctor, he got hurt . . . yep, he got hurt.'

H: (Approaches A) 'Will you go tell the doctor?'

A: 'Yeah.' (Moves to center of room, feeds doll as he approaches wall)

H: 'He got hurt?'

A: 'Mine got hurt . . . doctor? . . . tell that doctor.'

H: (Approaches wall) 'Doctor, he . . . whacked.'

A: (Watches H) 'Doctor . . . whack.'

H: 'He got a cough, got a cough, here.' (Gestures with spoon, holds doll out to wall, then hugs doll) 'Oh, you . . . doctor.'

H: (Knocks on wall with spoon)

H: 'He's not home, he's not home.' (Steps back from wall)

A: 'Let's see.' (Taps wall with spoon, looks at H)

H: (Steps forward, taps wall with spoon) 'Doctor.' (Continues to tap)

A: 'Doctor, he's not home.' (Looks at H)

H: 'He's not home, he's on vacation.'

H: (Turns with back to wall, then turns around again, bangs wall with spoon) 'Doctor.' (Looks at A)

A: 'Doctor.' (Bangs spoon on wall)

H: 'He's gonna go on vacation. He's not home.' (Walks away)

A: (Bangs on wall) 'Doctor, he's not home.'

H: (Approaches wall, bangs wall with spoon) 'Hey, Doctor!'

A: 'Doctor.' (Bangs, looks at H)

H: 'He's not home. Let's go.' (Leaves wall)

A: (Follows H) 'He's not home.'

H: 'Here he is, he's on vacation.' (Faces corner) 'Are you on vacation?'

H: (Turns, moves to wall) 'You gonna go home? . . . He go home.'

A: (Watches H, then approaches him) 'Doctor's home.'

H: (Throws doll against wall)

H: 'Doctor's home. He got hurt.'

H: (Picks up doll, cuddles it)

A: (Watches H)

H: 'Oh, baby.'

A: 'Who hurt her? . . . Who hurt her?' (Drops doll near wall) 'Here doctor, here, doctor, here it is.' (Looks down at doll)

H: 'Hey doctor.' (Bangs on wall with spoon)

A: (Bangs on wall)

H: 'Hey doctor . . . He's not home, he's on vacation.' (Leaves wall)

A: (Follows Harry) 'He's on vacation.'

In this episode Harry plays the role of 'momma' comforting the hurt baby, but he also switches to the role of 'parent–patient' interacting with an imaginary doctor. In this exchange, we receive additional glimpses of Mead's 'conversation of gestures between themselves'. Harry talks to someone at the doctor's house, and listens to what he is told, making sure that Alan also gets the message that 'He's not at home. He's on vacation.' Harry then invents the doctor himself, 'Are you on vacation? . . . You gonna go home?'

Harry's play involves at least three complementary others, along with recognition of Alan's need to follow the plot. Yet, Harry never suggests that Alan play the role of doctor, as if he had not yet thought of the possibility that a play companion might become a constituent part of the play.

In the next scene, Harry and Sarah (2½) produce the first example of social reciprocity in our series. Note, however, that the 'roles' are as 'giver' and 'taker' of medicine, not the generic complementary roles of parent–child or doctor–patient, even though we know that Harry can conceptualize these roles.

Transcript 4

Harry and Sarah: 2½ years

Harry is placing objects in buggy, changing nonsense syllables in process. Sarah is combing stuffed animal's hair, talking to it.

H: 'Did-ja-ja-ya-ya-ja.' (Gets spoon and bottle from table, stoops on floor with it) 'Get some medicine, okay?'

S: (Continues to talk to animal)

H: (Shakes bottle) 'Take this, okay? . . . okay?' (Feeds self with bottle, then stands, feeds doll on table with bottle) 'Hello, baby.' (Kneels with doll, throws it down)

S: (Looks at H, resumes animal play)

H: (Picks up comb from table, combs hair, then combs hair with bottle, puts comb down)

S: (Screams, stoops, picks up comb) 'That was my comb, my comb.'

H: (Gets up) 'It's my comb.'

S: 'Here.' (Hands comb to H, screams)

H: (Giggles, combs S's hair)

S: 'I'm gonna comb mine.' (Pushes H's hand away)

H: (Attempts to comb S's hair)

S: 'I will comb mine.' (Combs hair)

H: (Leaves, gets spoon and bottle) 'Take this for medicine in, okay?'

S: 'Okay, put my spoon.'

H: (Approaches S, tips bottle into spoon, feeds her with spoon)

S: 'You don't have that in.'

H: 'It's goop. It's for your nose. Take more?'

S: 'Yea, put it in my mouth.' (Stops combing hair as H feeds her)

H: (Feeds S, leaves) 'This is for your mouth, okay?'

S: 'Okay.' (Combs hair)

H: 'Broke . . .' (Approaches S) 'Drink, drink some lemonade.' (Puts object up to S's face)

S: 'Thanks, I'm not hungry.'

H: (Feeds S with spoon, puts bottle and spoon on table) 'Give me it, okay?'

S: 'Okay.' (Picks up bottle and spoon, feeds H with spoon) 'It's medicine, it's medicine, look.'

H: (Attempts to take spoon and bottle)

S: (Resists) 'I'll!' (Feeds H)

H: (Attempts to take spoon and bottle) 'It's mine!'

S: 'It's medicine! Okay.' (Gives H spoon, not bottle) 'Where's my bottle?'

H: (Points to floor, reaches for S's bottle) 'You, your bottle is down there.'

S: (Gives up bottle) 'Okay, thank you.'

H: (Takes objects from S's buggy)

S: 'Don't!'

H: 'Let me, let me show you.' (Shakes bottle)

S: 'Give me my doll back.' (Gets doll from floor)

H: (Takes toys out of S's buggy) 'I'll show you, okay, okay? Here it is, here it is . . . your spoon, here's your spoon.' (Drops spoon on table)

S: 'No! Put 'em back.' (Puts spoon back in buggy, leaves)

H: 'This is for your nose, okay?' (Approaches S, dips bottle onto spoon)

S: (Places toys from floor into buggy) 'Put 'em back, in there.'

H: 'This is for your nose, okay?' (Dips bottle onto spoon)

S: (Sits) 'Thanks.'

H: 'You gonna be all right.'

S: (Leaves)

H: (Puts bottle in mouth, places spoon on table, leaves)

S: 'I will? I will be alright?' (Puts toy in buggy)

H: 'Uhhuh. Come.'

S: 'Thanks.' (Puts toys in buggy)

H: 'You're welcome. I'm going for a . . . okay?'

S: 'Come here and give me your medicine. I will feed you, okay? Want me to feed you?'

H: (Picks up spoon) 'Want me to feed you?'

S: 'No, I will feed you.'

H: 'Uh'uh!'

S: 'Uh'uh!'

H: (Puts spoon on table) 'You want to drink it this way?'

S: 'No, I got, I got my bottle.' (Reaches into buggy for bottle)

H: (Attempts to take S's bottle) 'Ahh! . . . Uh'uh!' (Leaves)

S: (Dips bottle onto spoon) 'It's medicine . . . You won't be okay. Come here.'

H: 'Uh'uh.' (Holds bottle, looks at S)

S: (Holds out spoon) 'You will be okay . . . I'll drink from it.' (Drinks from bottle) 'It's Kool-aid, it's Kool-aid.'

H: (Approaches S)

S: 'Want some Kool-aid?'

H: (Nods head 'yes')

S: 'Okay, here, Kool-aid.' (Feeds H with spoon) 'Oh, it's good?'

H: (Puts bottle in mouth, leaves)

For a brief moment, Sarah almost plays a seducing adult as she drinks from the bottle and announces: 'It's Kool-aid, it's Kool-aid. Want some Kool-aid?' But for the most part, the children pretend to give and take medicines as they are (i.e., level 1 in the model). However, at the level of sensorimotor action roles, there is role reversal and social pretense in the sense of collective symbols. In this episode there is progress in the social interactive aspects of play, but regression in the conceptual social aspects of play (see Fein *et al.* [1982]) for a discussion of microdevelopmental progressions accompanied by apparent regressions to lower levels of functioning).

The last transcript leaps ahead to two 3½-year-olds pretending to be the 'dracula monster' and the monster-vanquishing hero. Here at last we have social pretense with generic roles, complementarity, and role reversals.

Transcript 5

Peter and Michael: 3½ years

M: (Points block at center of room) 'Pow!'

P: 'Pow!' (Points block at center of room)

M: 'Pow!' (Falls down)

P: (Swings hat in air, approaches M) 'You be dracula.'

M: 'Okay' (Gets up, extends arms in front of him) 'Grrow!'

P: (Points block at M) 'Pow!'

M: (Falls down)

P: (Approaches, points block at M) 'Pow!'

M: (Stirs slightly while lying down)

P: (Starts to put block in pocket)

M: (Starts to get up)

P: (Points block at M) 'Pow!'

M: (Falls down)
P: (Puts block in pocket)
M: (Gets up) 'Now you be dracula.'
P: 'Wait . . . I gotta put my cowboy hat on first.' (Puts hat on, approaches M)
M: (Points block at P) 'Pow!'
P: (Falls down)
M: (Points block at P) 'Pow, pow, pow, pow!' (Puts block in pocket) 'You're dead.' (leaves)
P: 'Hey, aahh!' (Gets up) 'Ahh, ahh!'
M: (Points block at P)
P: (Approaches M)
M: 'Prsh, prsh, prsh, prsh, prsh!'
M: (Pushes P down, places block in pocket)
P: (Falls down) (Gets up) 'Now you be dracula.'
M: (Gets toy from shelf) 'No, I . . . pow, pow, pow!' (Points toy at P)
P: 'You be dracula.'
M: (Pushes P)
P: 'Be you like you?'
M: 'No, you be dracula, and you say wow, and I push you down and I shoot you.' (Approaches P with block extended in front of him)
P: 'The hell you shoot me. No' (Pushes M's arm) 'You . . .'
M: 'All right' (lies down)
P: (Points block at M) 'Pow!'
M: (Stirs slightly)
P: (Puts block in pocket, puts hat on head)
M: (Gets up, points block at P) 'Pow, pow, pow!'
P: (Points block at M) 'Pow!' (Pushes M with block and arms extended in front of him)
M: (Pushes P with arms and block extended in front of him)
P: 'Pow, pow!'
M: (Falls down)
P: (Puts block in pocket)

This episode was diagramed in Figure 15.2 in a attempt to represent fully its psychological implications from Mead's perspective. Peter and Michael are enormously conscious of one another and of the obligations and destiny attendant upon their play roles in relation to their real selves. At one point, Michael becomes rambunctious, ignoring Peter's signal 'You be dracula.' Peter then queries, 'Be you like you?', checking to determine whether Michael's push was in play or for real. The role play of these children thus involves perspective taking at different levels – that is, with respect to their real selves becoming play selves and then with respect to the perspectives of the complementary roles that are enacted and reversed.

Peter and Michael have acquired a firm command of communications about play (i.e., the metacommunicative structures of Bateson's theory [1956]). For Mead, these structures indicate that a new layer of perspective taking (see Figure 15.2) has been added to those of earlier phases. Now the child acknowledges the perspective of his partner, whose intentions and understanding are so crucial to the collective symbols of sociodramatic play. Egocentric metacommunicative gestures seem present in Alan's fishing episode as he announces to no one in particular what is happening in the play. Barb tries unsuccessfully to talk to Sandy about his role as dad, whereas Harry does much better in keeping Alan informed about the unfolding doctor scenario. For a moment, Harry and Sarah step out of the medicine-giving pretense to negotiate who will give and who will take. But it is only Peter and Michael who mark their communications about play with at least three synchronized elements: (1) a standard linguistic form (e.g., 'You be - - -'); (2) communication directed to the partner with insistence on a response; and (3) termination of the pretend activity until satisfactory terms have been negotiated.

FROM STRUCTURE TO CONTENT

Mead offers a structural analysis of the role-playing child who steps outside himself to view the self from another perspective. Play, by allowing the child to imagine himself as an other, clarifies or consolidates a vision of aspects of the self that are either similar or different from others in the child's social world. In the process, the self gains coherence and the child gains a sense of his own identity as a distinct and distinctive human being. The model described in the previous section was inspired by the Meadian viewpoint, adding to this viewpoint the idea that the child's progress can be monitored as changes in the play itself.

Missing in Mead and in the discussion thus far is an analysis of the content of play, even though this content most certainly has a bearing on the self-building process. Several major developmental issues are expressed in the first five transcripts. For Alan, the issue is mastery, for Harry it is bodily injury and physical health. For Barb, the theme is nurturance and separation, whereas for Paul and Michael it is dominance and aggression. These themes are of great interest to psychoanalytic theorists (Erikson 1963, 1977; Mahler 1975; Peller

1954). Importantly, these themes identify those affective aspects of being that become organised between 2 and 6 years of age: a view of one's body, its strength and fragility; a view of one's affectional ties to significant others; and, a view of one's anger and hostility toward others.

In conclusion, consider a final transcript of play between two 5-year-olds. Lil and Jim. Note first that structurally Lil can contemplate a set of alternative role structures – mother–father, sister–brother, and, within the play, herself as 'sister' in relation to brother; daughter in relation to parents, and 'sister-as-baby sitter' in relation to younger siblings. However, it is in the content of the play that we find clues to those attributes of self and others that constitute gripping issues at this age.

Transcript 6

Lil and Jim: 5 years

L: 'Are you the father or the son?'

J: 'I'm the big brother.'

L: 'Okay, then I'll be the big sister.'

J: ' 'Cause fathers don't even play with toys.'

L: 'Well, I'm the big girl, I'm the big sister. Anyway, Mom told me to take care of the two babies, our little brother and sister and you better not touch them or I'm gonna tell Mom on you.'

J: 'You're not gonna tell anybody on me.'

L: 'Huh! I'm gonna tell someone on you, don't you think I'm not. So brother, if you want to say something, keep it to your own self.'

J: 'You know I'm bigger than you.'

L: 'Huh, you're not bigger than anybody.'

J: 'Hey, I'm bigger than you – you're just nine. So you better watch it!'

L: 'You're the biggest 'cause you're just 12 years old. You're even bigger than me.'

J: 'You're just . . .'

L: 'If you want to fight just go fight yourself.'

J: 'You think I'm bigger than you 'cause I'm 12 years old. You, you're just nine. Hey, hey, you better watch it 'cause I'm babysitting for you all.'

L: 'You mean us three?'

J: 'Yeah.'

L: 'One, two three.'

J: 'There, just . . .'

L: 'One, two three, four, and your own self. You're a baby; your own self.'

J: 'Hey, I ain't no baby girl, what goes and tattles on you.' (Jim and Lil begin to whisper)

L: 'You better watch it 'cause they're waking, brother.'

J: 'Shut up.'

L: 'Well, make me.'

J: 'Shut up before you make me wake the babies up.'

L: 'Listen I'll really tell Mom on you.'

J: 'Hey you can't, you cannot tell Mom on me. I'll . . .'

L: 'Then I'll tell Dad on you. Let me tell you; you be the dad and . . .'

J: 'Uh'uh, I ain't playing no dad and I'm certain not no daddy.'

L: 'And I'm certain not no mommy.'

J: 'If you wanna find a daddy, if you wanna find a daddy, ask John' (the children's teacher).

Jim vigorously refuses to play father (' 'Cause fathers don't even play with toys'), and yet he must find a basis for holding his own in relation to a dominating, provocative pretend sister. Jim's solution – to be 12 years old – is a marvelous compromise. Jim thereby deals with the vulnerability of being a 5-year-old male without taking on the burdens of adulthood, the complications of fatherhood, and the dangers of marital involvement. One must applaud the psychological brilliance of Jim's symbolic solution to the threat inherent in the Oedipal triangle and the tensions of sibling rivalry. The 'self' Jim projects is safe, enjoyable, developmentally sensible, and in touch with social reality.

Lil, as a female, confronts strikingly different issues: she is eager to play mother–wife but the role of sister will do. Note that Lil sees herself consistently on the side of parental authority, as a properly delegated carrier of this authority in the parents' absence. However, note also her expectation that this delegated authority will be challenged and her preventive maneuvers designed to protect it. Wonderfully, she takes advantage of Jim's guilty discomfort, in response to which Jim finally protests: 'Shut up before you make me wake the babies up.'

In the play, both children practice responses adapted to the exigencies of family relationships. Mead's theory tells us that these responses are cast to permit the playing child to penetrate the multiple viewpoints of significant others in relation to the child's self concept as it is and as it might become. The content insights of psychoanalytic theory fit nicely with the structural insights of symbolic interactionist theory. Together these insights provide a preliminary framework for investigating the child's vision of a changing self in a world of comprehensible others.

REFERENCES

Bateson, G. (1956) 'The message "This is play" ', in B. Schaffner (ed.) *Group Processes: Transactions of the Second Conference*, New York: Josiah Macy Foundation.

Elder J. L. and Pederson, D. R. (1978) 'Preschool children's use of objects in symbolic play', *Child Development* 49: 500–4.

Erikson, E. H. (1963) *Childhood and Society*, New York: Norton.

Erikson, E. H. (1977) *Toys and Reasons*, New York: Norton.

Fein, G. G. (1975) 'A transformational analysis of pretending', *Developmental Psychology* 11: 291–6.

Fein, G. G. (1979) 'Echoes from the nursery: Piaget, Vygotsky and the relation between language and play', *New Directions in Child Development* 6: 1–14.

Fein, G. G. (1981a) 'The physical environment: stimulation or evocation', in R.M. Lerner and N.A. Busch-Rossnagel (eds) *Individuals as Producers of Their Development*, New York: Academic Press.

Fein, G. G. (1981b) 'Pretend play: an integrative review', *Child Development* 52: 1095–118.

Fein, G. G. and Kohlberg L. (1987) 'Play and constructive work as contributors to development', in L. Kohlberg and R. DeVries (eds) *Programs of Early Education: The Constructivist View*, New York: Longman.

Fein, G. G., Moorin, E. R. and Enslein, J. (1982) 'Pretense and peer behavior: an intersectoral analysis', *Human Development* 25: 392–406.

Jackowitz, E. R. and Watson, M. W. (1980) 'The development of object transformations in early pretend play', *Developmental Psychology* 16: 543–9.

Mahler, M. (1975) *The Psychological Birth of the Infant*, New York: Basic Books.

Mead, G. H. (1934) *Mind, Self, and Society*, Chicago: University of Chicago Press.

Peller, L. (1954) 'Libidinal phases, ego development, and play', *Psychoanalytic Study of the Child* 9: 178–98.

Piaget, J. (1962) *Play, Dreams and Imitation in Childhood*, New York: Norton (originally 1945, English translation 1951).

Rubin, K. H. and Pepler, D. J. (1979) 'The relationship of child's play to social-cognitive growth and development', in H. Foot, J. Smith, and T. Chapman (eds) *Friendship and Childhood Relationships*, New York: Wiley.

Sutton-Smith, B. (1982) 'Piaget, play and cognition revisited', in W. Overton (ed.) *The Relationship Between Social and Cognitive Development*, Hillsdale, N.J.: Erlbaum.

Ungerer, J. A., Zelazo, P. R., Kearsley, R. B. and O'Leary, K. (1981) 'Developmental changes in the representation of objects in symbolic play from 18 to 34 months of age', *Child Development* 52: 186-95.

Vygotsky, L. S. (1967) 'Play and its role in the mental development of the child', *Soviet Psychology* 5: 6-18.

Watson, M. W. and Fischer, K. W. (1977) 'A developmental sequence of agent use in late infancy', *Child Development* 48: 828-36.

Name index

Aarts, R. 160
Adams, J. L. 15
Adamson, L. R. 24
Ainsworth, M. D. S. 3, 20–1, 25, 30–54, 77, 131, 151, 196
Alegria, J. 149
Allen, W. R. 324
Altmann, M. 48
Ames, G. J. 99
Anastasi, A. 169
Andersen, E. S. 211
Arling, G. L. 303
Arsenian, J. M. 36

Bakeman, R. 24
Bandura, A. 112
Barocas, B. 180
Barrett, D. E. 182
Bateson, G. 328, 342
Bateson, M. C. 196–7
Bateson, P. P. 96
Beach, F. 252
Beail, N. 74, 76, 86
Beckwith, L. 199
Bee, H. L. 241
Beg, M. A. 36
Bell, R. Q. 170
Bell, S. M. 30–54, 196
Bellugi, U. 217
Belsky, J. 236
Benedict, R. 57
Bentham, J. 270
Berger, P. L. 178
Berlin, I. 262
Berman, P. W. 279, 300–25

Birch, H. 188
Birch, H. G. 170, 258–9
Birns, 8, 180
Bishop, N. 251, 253–4, 256–7
Blauw, A. de 213
Block, S. C. 265
Bloom, B. 250
Bloom, L. 219, 223
Blount, B. 211
Bohannan, P. 231
Bornstein, M. H. 156
Borton, R. W. 126
Bowen, S. L. 77, 79–81, 83–4, 92
Bower, T. G. R. 124, 126
Bowerman, M. 211
Bowlby, J. 3, 10, 18–20, 22, 31–4, 151, 268
Boyd, C. 83
Brackhill, Y. 140
Brazelton, T. B. 63, 150, 207, 234
Bremner, G. 5
Bretherton, I. 23
Bril, B. 232, 235
Broen, P. A. 204–5
Broman, S. H. 180
Bronfenbrenner, U. xi, 167, 172–3, 175
Bronson, G. 11
Brookins, G. K. 324
Brown, A. 86
Brown, I. 86
Brown, R. 204, 216–17, 287, 295
Bruner, J. S. 10, 16, 22, 24, 112, 124, 133, 193–4, 216, 232, 234, 239, 242, 247–71, 286

Subject index